pastor Joel,

Words cannot  how much I Love and Appreciate you. Thank you for all your love and Care you've given me these last Twelve years.

God Bless you
your daughter
Shirley Moore

MEN AND WOMEN

OF THE

OLD TESTAMENT

MEN AND WOMEN OF THE OLD TESTAMENT

Sermons by
C. H. Spurgeon

Selected and Edited by Rev. Dr. Chas. T. Cook

AMG
PUBLISHERS
Chattanooga, TN 37422

MEN AND WOMEN OF THE OLD TESTAMENT

Originally published by
Marshall, Morgan, & Scott in London, 1960.

ISBN 0-89957-204-9

Printed in the United States of America

Contents

BOOK II

Sermons on Women of the Old Testament

FOREWORD

Men and Women of the Old Testament is a superb collection of thirty-six classic C. H. Spurgeon sermons. In his typically captivating style, Spurgeon here presents inspirational and practical lessons gleaned from Old Testament characters—both heroic and infamous—whom the Lord used in the divine unfolding of history.

In combining what was previously two volumes into this single edition, we at AMG Publishers have made some minor changes to the original works to help make their content more clear to modern readers: We have updated spelling and some archaic terms in accordance with how our language has changed over the years; in some cases, unusual forms of punctuation have been simplified in order to eliminate confusion. Readers should also note that points of current history cited by Spurgeon are from the latter half of the nineteenth century.

It is our hope that these compelling, insightful sermons by C. H. Spurgeon, the "prince of preachers," will inspire in readers an ever-growing love and appreciation for the Word of God.

Book I

Sermons on Men of the Old Testament

1

ADAM

How God Comes to Man

"And they heard the voice of the Lord God walking in the garden in the cool of the day: and Adam and his wife hid themselves from the presence of the Lord God amongst the trees of the garden. And the Lord God called unto Adam, and said unto him, Where art thou?" (Gen. 3:8, 9).

"HOW will God come to us now that we have rebelled against him?" That is a question which must have greatly perplexed our first parents, and they may have said to one another, "Perhaps God will not come to us at all, and then we shall be orphans indeed. If spared to live on, we must continue to live without God and without hope in the world." It would have been the worst thing that could have happened to our race if God had left this planet to take its own course, and had said, concerning the people upon it, "I will leave them to their own way, for they are given over to idols."

But if he came to our first parents, in what way would he come? Surely, Adam and Eve must have feared that he would be accompanied by the angels of vengeance, to destroy them straight away, or, at any rate, to bind them in chains and fetters forever. Their hearts must have been sorely perplexed within them while they were waiting to see what God would do to them as a punishment for the great sin they had committed. I believe they thought that he would come to them. They knew so much of his graciousness, from their past experience that they felt sure that he would come; yet they also understood so much of his holy anger against sin that they must have been afraid of his coming; so they went and hid themselves amongst the trees of the garden, although every tree must have upbraided them for their disobedience, for every one of the trees would

3

seem to say, "Why come you here? You have eaten of the fruit of the tree whereof you were forbidden to partake. You have broken your Maker's command, and his sentence of death has already gone out against you. When he comes, he will certainly come to deal with you in judgment according to his faithful word; and when he does, what will become of you?"

Now, "in the cool of the day," or, as the Hebrew has it, "in the wind of the evening," when the evening breeze was blowing through the garden, God came. It is difficult for us even to imagine how he revealed himself to our first parents. I suppose he condescended to take upon himself some visible form. It was "the voice of the Lord God" that they heard in the garden, and you that it is the Word of God who has been pleased to make himself visible to us in human flesh.

They heard his voice speaking as he walked in the garden in the cool of the day; and when he called unto Adam, albeit that there was righteous anger in the tone of his voice, yet his words were very calm and dignified, and, as far as they should be, even tender; for while you may read the words thus, "Adam, where art thou?" you may also read them thus, "Where art thou, poor Adam, where art thou?" You may put a tone of pity into the words and yet not misread them. So the Lord comes thus in gentleness in the cool of the day, and calls them to account; patiently listens to their wicked excuses, and then pronounces upon them a sentence, which, heavy though it be towards the serpent, and heavy though it be towards all who are not saved by the woman's wondrous Seed, yet has much mercy mingled with it in the promise that the Seed of the woman shall bruise the head of the serpent—a promise which must have shone in their sad and sinful souls as some bright particular star shines in the darkness of the night.

I learn, from this incident, that God will come to sinful men, sooner or later, and we may also learn, from the way in which he came to our first parents, how he is likely to come to us. His coming will be different to different men; but we gather, from this incident, that God will certainly come to guilty men, even if he waits till the cool of the day; and we also understand a little about the way in which he will ultimately come to all men.

Remember this, sinner, however far you may get away from God, you will have to come close to him one of these days. God and you have to meet, as surely as you are now living here; at some time or other, each one of you must hear the voice of the Lord God saying to you, as he said to Adam, "Where art thou?"

Now, from this meeting between God and fallen man, I learn a few lessons, which I will pass on to you as the Holy Spirit shall enable me.

The first is this. When God did meet with fallen man, it was not until the cool of the day. This suggests to me God's great patience with the guilty.

It is probable that the Lord allowed an interval to intervene between the sin and the sentence. He was not in a hurry to come, because he could not come except in anger, to bring their sins home to them. You know how quick the tempers of some men are. If they are provoked, it is a word and a blow with them, for they have no patience. It is our littleness that makes us impatient. God is so great that he can endure far more than we can; and though our first parents' sin greatly provoked him—and it is his glory that he is so holy that he cannot look upon iniquity without indignation—yet he seemed to say to himself, "I must go and call these two creatures of mine to account for their sin; yet judgment is my strange work, it is mercy in which I delight." God will do nothing in the heat of passion; everything shall be deliberate and calm, majestic and divine.

The fact that God did not come to question his sinful creatures till the cool of the day ought to teach us the greatness of his patience, and it should also teach us to be ourselves patient with others. How wondrously patient God has been with some of you! You have lived many years, and enjoyed his mercies, yet you have scarcely thought about him. Certainly, you have not yielded your hearts to him; but he has not come to deal with you in judgment yet. He has waited twenty years for you young people; thirty years, forty years, for you middle-aged folk; fifty years, sixty years, for you who are getting past that period; seventy years, perhaps, or even eighty years he has been known to tarry, for "he delighteth in mercy," but he does not delight in judgment. Seventy years form a long life-day, yet many persons spend all that time in perpetrating fresh sin. Called to repentance over and over again, they only become the more impenitent through resisting the call of mercy. Favored with blessings as many as the sands of the seashore, they only prove themselves the more ungrateful by failing to appreciate all those blessings. It is wonderful that God is willing to wait till the cool of such a long, long day of life as seventy or eighty years make up. How patient, then we ought to be with one another! Yet are you, parents, always patient with your children, your young children who may not have willingly or consciously offended you? What patience you ought always to exercise towards them! And have you a like patience towards a friend or a brother who may use rough speech, and provoke you? Yet such your patience ought to be.

The second thing that I gather from the Lord's coming to Adam and Eve in the cool of the day is HIS DIVINE CARE FOR THE GUILTY.

Though he did not come till the cool of the day, thus manifesting his patience, he did come then, thus manifesting his care for those who had sinned against him. He might have left them all night long—all night long without their God—all night long without him after they had done just what he had forbidden them to do—all night long—a sleepless night, a fearful night, a night that would have been haunted with a thousand fears—all night long with this great battle trembling in the balance, with the great question of their punishment unsolved, and an indefinable dread of the future hanging over them. Many of you know that the trial of being kept in suspense is almost worse than any other trouble in the world. If a man knew that he had to be beheaded, it would be easier for him to die at once than to have to kneel with his neck on the block, and the gleaming ax uplifted above him, and not knowing when it might fall. Suspense is worse than death; we seem to feel a thousand deaths while we are kept in suspense of one. So God would not leave Adam and Eve in suspense through the whole night after they had sinned against him, but he came to them in the cool of the day.

There was this further reason why he came to them: notwithstanding the fact that they had disobeyed him, and that the would have to punish them, he remembered that they were still his creatures. He seemed to be saying within himself, "What shall I do unto them? I must not utterly destroy them, but how can I save them? I must carry out my threatening, for my word is true; yet I must also see how I can spare them, for I am gracious, and my glory is to be increased by the display of my grace towards them." The Lord looked upon them as the appointed progenitors of his elect; and regarded Adam and Eve themselves also, let us hope, as his elect, whom he loved notwithstanding their sin, so he seemed to say, "I will not leave them all night without the promise which will brighten their gloom." It was only one promise; and, perhaps, it was not clearly understood by them; still, it was a promise of God, even though it was spoken to the serpent, "I will put enmity between thee and the woman, and between thy seed and her seed; it shall bruise thy head, and thou shalt bruise his heel." So, not one night were God's poor fallen creatures left without at least one star to gleam in the darkness for them, and thus he showed his care for them. And still, though God is slow to anger, yet is he always ready to pardon, and very tender and compassionate even when he has to pass sentence upon the guilty. "He will not always chide; neither will he keep his anger forever." You can see his care and consideration even for the most unworthy of us, because he has not cut us off in our sins. We can see the marks of his goodness in the very garments on our backs and the food of which we partake by his bounty. Many of his gifts come, not merely to those who do not deserve them, but to those who deserve to be filled with the gall and wormwood of almighty wrath forever.

Now, thirdly, I want to show you that, WHEN THE LORD DID COME, HE AFFORDED US A PATTERN OF HOW THE SPIRIT OF GOD COMES TO AROUSE THE CONSCIENCES OF MEN.

First, *he comes seasonably*: "in the cool of the day." Adam's work was done, and Eve had no more to do until the next day. At that hour, they had been accustomed, in happier times, to sit down and rest. Now God comes to them, and the Spirit of God, when he comes to arouse men, generally visits them when they have a little time for quiet thought. You dropped in, and heard a sermon; the most of it slipped from your memory, but there were some few words that struck you so that you could not get rid of them. Perhaps, though, you thought no more about the message to which you had listened. Something else came in, and took off your attention. But, a little while after, you had to watch all night by the bedside of a sick friend; and then God came to you, and brought to your remembrance the words that you have forgotten. Or it may be that some texts of Scripture, which you learned when you were a child, began to speak to you throughout the watches of the night. Or, perhaps, you were going along a lone country road, or, it may be, that you were out at sea on a dark night, and the billows rolled heavily so that you could not sleep, and you even feared that you would be swallowed up by the raging sea. Then—then came the voice of the Lord God speaking personally to you.

Not only did the Lord come to Adam and Eve seasonably, but *he spoke to Adam personally*, and said, "Where art thou?" One of the great mistakes in connection with all preaching is that so many hearers will persist in lending other people their ears. They hear a faithful Gospel sermon, and then say, "That message would fit Neighbor So-and-so admirably. What a pity Mrs. So-and-so did not hear it! That would have been the very word for her." Yes; but when God comes to you, as he came to Adam and Eve—and if you are not converted, I pray that he may— the sermon he will deliver to you will be every word of it for yourself. He will say, "Adam," or "John," or "Mary," or whatever your name be, "Where art *thou?*" The question will be addressed to yourself alone; it will have no relation to any of your neighbors, but to yourself alone. The question may take some such form as this: "Where are you? What have you been doing? What is your condition now? Will you now repent, or will you still go on in your sins?" Have not you, young man, had some experience as this? You went to the theater; but when you came home, you said that you had not enjoyed it, and that you wished you had not gone. You went to bed, but could not sleep. It seemed as if God had come to wrestle with you, and to reason with you about your past life, bringing up one thing after another in which you have sinned against him. At all events, this is the way he deals with many; and if he deals thus with you, be thankful for it, and yield yourself to him, and do not struggle against him. I am always glad when men cannot be happy in the world; for, as long as they can be, they will be. It is a great blessing when the Lord puts before you, personally, a true view of your own condition in his sight, and makes you look at it so earnestly, concentrating your whole thought upon it, so that you cannot even begin to think about others because you are compelled to examine your own selves, to see what your real condition is in relation to God.

When the Lord thus comes to men, and speaks personally with them, *he makes them realize their lost condition.* Do you not see that this is implied in the question, "Where art thou?" Adam was lost—lost to God, lost to holiness, lost to happiness. God himself says, "Where art thou?" May God the Holy Spirit convince every unconverted person here that he or she is lost—not only lost to themselves, and to heaven, and to holiness, and to happiness, but lost to God. It was God's lost ones of whom Christ so often spoke. He was himself the good Shepherd, who called together his friends and neighbors, saying unto them, "Rejoice with me; for I have found my sheep which was lost"; and he represents his Father saying of his son when he has come back to him, " 'This my son was dead'—dead to me—'and is alive again; he was lost'—lost to me—

'and is found.' " The value of a soul to God, and God's sense of loss in the case of each individual soul, is something worth thinking over, and worth calculating, if it can be calculated.

You will observe, too, that the Lord not only came to Adam, and questioned him personally, but *he also made Adam answer him*; and if the Lord has, in this way, laid hold of any of you, talking with you in the cool of the day, and questioning you about your lost condition, he will make you confess your sin, and bring you to acknowledge that it was really your own. He will not leave you as Adam wanted to be left, namely, laying the blame for the disobedience upon Eve; and he will not leave you as Eve tried to be left, namely, passing the blame on to the devil. Before the Lord has done with you, he will bring you to this point, that you shall feel, and confess, and acknowledge that you are really guilty of your own sin, and that you must be punished for it. When he brings you down to that point, and you have nothing at all to say for yourself, then he will pardon you. I recollect well when the Lord brought me to my knees in this way, and emptied out all my self-righteousness and self-trust, until I felt that the hottest place in hell was my due desert, and that, if he saved everybody else, but did not save me, yet still he would be just and righteous, for I had not right to be saved. Then, when I was obliged to feel that it must be all of grace, or else there could be no salvation for me, then he spake tenderly and kindly unto me; but, at the first, there did not seem to be any tenderness or pity to my soul. There was the Lord coming to me, laying bare my sin, revealing to me my lost condition, and making me shiver and tremble, while I feared that the next thing he would say to me would be, "Depart from me, accursed one, into everlasting fire in hell"; instead of which, he said to me, in tones of wondrous love and graciousness, "I have put thee among my children; 'I have loved thee with an everlasting love, therefore with lovingkindness have I drawn thee.' " Blessed be the name of the Lord, forever and ever, for such amazing treatment as this meted out to the guilty and the lost.

Now, fourthly, and very solemnly, I want to show you that THIS COMING OF THE LORD TO ADAM AND EVE IS ALSO PROPHETICAL OF THE WAY IN WHICH HE WILL COME AS A JUDGING SPIRIT TO THOSE WHO REJECT HIM AS AN AROUSING SPIRIT.

I have already reminded you unconverted ones that, as surely as you live, you will have to come to close terms with God, like the rest of us. Sooner or later, you will have to know him, and to know that he knows you. There will be way of escaping from an interview which will be most serious and most terrible for you. It will happen "in the cool of the day." I do not know when that may be. On my way to this service, I have called to see a young lady, to whom "the cool of day" has come at five-and-twenty, or thirty years of age. Consumption has made her life-day a comparatively short one; but, blessed be God, his grace has made it a very happy one, and she is not afraid, "in the cool of the day," to hear the voice of the Lord God calling her home. It is well that she is not afraid; but you, who have not believed in Jesus, will have to hear that same divine voice in the cool of your life's day. You may be spared to grow old; the strength of youth and of manhood will have gone, and you will begin to lean on your staff, and to feel that you have not the vigor you used to have, and that you cannot do such a hard day's work as you used to do, and you must not attempt to run up the hills as you once did. That will be "the cool of the day" to you, and then the Lord God will come in to you and say, "Set thine house in order, for thou shalt die, and not live."

Sometimes that cool of the day comes to a man just when he would have liked it to be the heat of the day. He is making money, and his children are multiplying around him, so he wants to stop in this world a little longer. But that cannot be; he must go up to his bed, and he must lie there for so many days and nights, and then he must hear the voice of the Lord God as he begins to question him, and say, "Where art thou in relation to me? Hast thou loved me with all thine heart, and mind, and soul, and strength? Hast thou served me? Art thou reconciled to me through the death of my Son?" Such questions as these will come to us as surely as God made us, and we shall have to give an account of the deeds done in the body, whether they have been good or whether they have been evil. I pray you to think of these things, and not to say, "Ah! that will not happen just yet." That is more than any of us can tell; and let me remind you that life is very short even at the longest. But, short or long, your share of it will soon be over, and you will be called upon to gather up your feet in the bed, and meet your fathers' God.

When that solemn and decisive hour comes, your interview with God will have to be a personal one. Sponsors will be of no use to anyone upon a dying bed. It will be of no avail, then, to call upon Christian friends to take a share of your burden. They will not be able to give you of their oil, for they have not enough grace for themselves and you. If you live and die without accepting the aid of the one Mediator between God and man, all these questions will have to be settled between your soul and God without anyone else coming between yourself and your Maker; and all this may happen at any moment. This personal talk between God and your soul, at the end of your life, may be ordained to take place this very night; and I am sent, as a forerunner, just to give you this warning, so that you may not meet your God altogether by surprise, but may, at any rate, be invited and exhorted to be prepared for that great interview.

Whenever that interview takes place, God will deal with you in solemn earnestness—personally bringing home your sin to you. You will be unable to deny it, for there will be One present, at that interview, who has seen it all, and the inquiries which he will make about the state of your soul will be very searching ones. He will not merely ask about one sin, but about all your sins. He will not only ask about your public life, but also about your private life; nor yet merely inquire about your doings, but about your sayings, and your willings, and your thinkings, and about your whole position in relation to himself, even as he asked Adam, "Where art thou?"

In imagination—I pray that it may be only imagination—I see some of you die unsaved; and I see you as you pass into the next world unpardoned, and your soul realizes, for the first time, what was the experience of the rich man, of whom our Savior said, "In hell he lifted up his eyes"—as though he had been asleep before, and had only just awakened to his true condition. "He lifted up his eyes," and gazed all around, but he could see nothing except that which caused him dismay and horror; there was no trace of joy or hope, no trace of ease or peace. Then, through the awful gloom, there came the sound of such questions as these, "Where are you sinner? You were in a house of prayer a few weeks ago, and the preacher urged you to seek the Lord; but you procrastinated. Where are you now? You said that there was no such place as hell; but what do you say about it now? Where are you? You despised heaven, and refused Christ; where are you now?" The Lord in mercy preserve all of you from that!

One of the most dreadful things in connection with this meeting of God with Adam was that Adam had to answer the Lord's questions. The Lord said to him, "Hast thou eaten of the tree, whereof I commanded thee that thou shouldest not eat?" In our courts of law, we do not require men to answer questions which would incriminate them, but God does; and, at the last great day, the ungodly will be condemned on their own confession of guilt. While they are in this world, they put on a brazen face, and declare that they have done no wrong to anybody—not even to God—they pay their way, and they are as good as their neighbors; and better than the most of them; but all their brag and bravado will be gone at the day of judgment, and they will either stand speechless before God—and by their speechlessness acknowledge their guiltiness in his sight; or if they do speak, their vain excuses and apologies will but convict themselves. They will, out of their own mouths, condemn themselves, like that wicked and slothful servant, who was cast into the outer darkness where there was weeping and gnashing of teeth. God grant that we may never know, from sad personal experience, what that expression means!

Now, lastly, this meeting of God with Adam should lead us, who believe in Christ, to EXPECT TO MEET HIM ON THE MOST LOVING TERMS; for if, even when he came to question guilty Adam, and to pass sentence upon him, he did it so gently, and mingled with the thunder of his wrath the soft shower of his grace, when he gave the promise that "the Seed of the woman" should bruise the serpent's head, may we not expect him to meet us, by-and-by, on the most loving terms, if we are in that woman's Seed, and have been saved by Jesus Christ his Son?

He will come in the evening, brother and sister, when the day's work is done; so do not fret about the burden and heat of the day. The longest and hottest day will come to an end; you will not live here forever. You will not always have to wear your fingers to the bone in trying to earn a scanty livelihood. You will not always have to look around upon your children, and wonder where the bread will be found with which to feed them. No; the days on earth cannot last forever; and, with many of you, the sun has already climbed the hill, and begun to go down the other side, and "the cool of the day" will soon come. I can look upon a good many of you who have already reached that period. You have retired from active service, you have shaken off a good deal of business care, and now you are waiting for your Master to come to you. Rest assured that he will not forget you, for he has promised to come to you. You will hear his voice, before long, telling you that he is walking in the garden, and coming to you. Good old Rowland Hill, when he found himself getting very feeble, said, "I hope they have not forgotten poor old Rowley up there." But he knew that he was not forgotten, nor will you be, beloved.

You will hear your Lord's voice ere long; and the mercy is, that you will know it when you do hear it. Have you not often heard it before now? Many a time, in this house, you have heard his voice, and you have been glad. In the cool of many an evening, you have sat still, and communed with God. I like to see an old Christian woman, with her big Bible open, sitting by the hour together, and tracing with her finger the precious words of the Lord; eating them, digesting them, living on them, and finding them sweeter to her soul that honey or the droppings of the honeycomb to her taste. Well, then, as you have heard your Lord's voice, and knot its tones so well, as you have been so long accustomed to hear it, you will not be astonished when you hear it in those last moments of your life's day. You will not run to hide yourself, as Adam and Eve did. You are covered with the robe of Christ's righteousness, so you have no nakedness to fear; and you may respond, "Didst thou ask, my Lord, 'Where art thou?' I answer, 'Here am I, for thou didst call me.' Didst thou ask where I am? I am hidden in thy Son; I am 'accepted in the Beloved.' Didst thou say, 'Where art thou?' Here I stand, ready and waiting to be taken up by him, according to his promise that, where he is, there I shall be also, that I may behold his glory." Why, surely, beloved, as this is the case, you may even long for the evening to come when you shall hear his voice, and shall be up and away from this land of shadows and chilly night-dews, into that blest place where the glory burneth on forever and ever, and the Lamb is the light thereof, and the days of your mourning shall be ended forever.

2

ENOCH

Walking with God

"And Enoch lived sixty and five years, and begat Methuse-
lah; and Enoch walked with God after he begat Methuse-
lah three hundred years, and begat sons and daughters;
and all the days of Enoch were three hundred sixty and five
years; and Enoch walked with God; and he was not; for God
took him" (Gen. 5:21–24).

"By faith Enoch was translated that he should not see
death; and was not found, because God had translated
him; for before his translation he had this testimony, that
he pleased God. But without faith it is impossible to please
him: for he that cometh to God must believe that he is,
and that he is a rewarder of them that diligently seek him"
(Heb. 11:5, 6).

"And Enoch also, the seventh from Adam, prophesied of
these, saying, Behold, the Lord cometh with ten thousands
of his saints, to execute judgment upon all, and to con-
vince all that are ungodly among them for all their un-
godly deeds which they have ungodly committed, and of all
their hard speeches which ungodly sinners have spoken
against him" (Jude 1:14, 15).

THE three passages of Scripture which I have read are all the authentic information we have concerning Enoch, and it would be idle to sup-
plement it with the fictions of ancient commentators. Enoch is called
the seventh from Adam, to distinguish him from the other Enoch of the
line of Cain, who was the third from Adam. In the first patriarchs God

was pleased to manifest to men portions of the truth in reference to true religion. These men of the olden times were not only themselves taught of God, but they were also teachers of their age, and types in whom great truths were exhibited. Abel taught the need of approaching the Lord with sacrifice, the need of atonement by blood: he laid the lamb upon the altar, and sealed his testimony with his own blood.

Enoch set before men the great truth of communion with God; he displayed in his life the relation of the believer to the Most High, and showed how near the living God condescends to be to his own children.

Perhaps a meditation upon the holy patriarch's life may help us to imitate it; while considering what he was, and under what circumstances he came to be so, we may by the Holy Spirit be helped to reach the point to which he attained. This is the desire of every godly man, all the saints desire communion with the Father, and with his Son Jesus Christ. The constant cry of our soul is to our Lord, "Abide with me." I buried yesterday one of the excellent of the earth, who loved and feared and served his God far better than most of us; he was an eminently devout brother, and one of his last wishes of his heart he had committed to writing in a letter to a friend, when he little thought of dying. It was this: "I have longed to realize the life of Enoch, and to walk with God"; he did but write what you and I also feel.

First WHAT IS MEANT BY ENOCH'S WALKING WITH GOD? Paul helps us to our first observation upon this by his note in the Hebrews. His walk with God was a testimony that *Enoch was well pleasing to God*. "Before his translation he had this testimony, that he pleased God." This is evidently the Apostle's interpretation of his walking with God, and it is a most correct one, for the Lord will not walk with a man in whom he has no pleasure. Can two walk together, except they be agreed? If men walk contrary to God, he will not walk *with* them, but contrary to them. Walking together implies amity, friendship, intimacy, love, and these cannot exist between God and the soul unless the man is acceptable unto the Lord. Doubtless Enoch, like Elias, was a man of like passions with ourselves. He had fallen with the rest of mankind in the sin of Adam, there was sin about him as there is sin about us by nature, and he had gone astray in act and deed as all we, like sheep, have done: and therefore he needed pardon and cleansing, even as we do. Then to be pleasing with God it was needful that he should be forgiven and justified, even as we are; for no man can be pleasing to God till sin is pardoned and righteousness is imputed. To this end there must be faith, for there can be no justification except by faith, and as we have said already, there is no pleasing God except our persons are justified. Right well, then, does the Apostle say, "Without faith it is impossible to please God," and by faith Enoch was made pleasing to God, even as we are at this day.

This is worthy of earnest notice, brethren, because this way of faith is open to us. If Enoch had been pleasing to God by virtue of some extraordinary gifts and talents, or by reason of marvelous achievements and miraculous works, we might have been in despair; but if he was pleasing to God through faith, that same faith which saved the dying thief, that same faith which has been wrought in you and in me, then the wicket gate at the head of the way in which men walk with God is open to us also. If we have faith we may enter into fellowship with the Lord. How this ought to endear faith to us! If you want to walk with God as a man of God, you must begin by believing in the Lord Jesus Christ, simply, as a babe in grace. The highest saintship must commence by the confession of our sinnership, and our laying hold upon Christ crucified. Not otherwise does the strongest believer live than the weakest believer; and if you are to grow to be among the strongest of the Lord's warriors, it must be by faith which lays hold upon divine strength. Beginning in the Spirit you are not to be made perfect in the flesh; you are not to proceed a certain distance by faith in Christ, and then to commence a living by your own works; your walk is to continue as it begun. "As ye have received Christ Jesus the Lord so walk ye in him." Enoch was always pleasing to God, but it was because he always believed, and lived in the power of his faith.

Next, when we read that Enoch walked with God we are to understand that *he realized the divine presence*. You cannot consciously walk with a person whose existence is not known to you. When we walk with a man, we know that he is there, we hear his footfall if we cannot see his face; we have some very clear perception that there is such a person at our side. Now, if we look to the Hebrews again, Paul tells us "He that cometh to God must believe that he is, and that he is the rewarder of them that diligently seek him." Enoch's faith, then, was a realizing faith. He did not believe things as a matter of creed, and then put them up on the shelf out of the way, as too many do: he was not merely orthodox in head, but the truth had entered into his heart, and what he believed was true to him, practically true, true as a matter of fact in his daily life. He walked with God: it was not that he thought of God merely, that he speculated about God, that he argued about God, that he read about God, that he talked about God, but he *walked* with God, which is the practical and experimental part of true godliness. In his daily life he realized that God was with him, and he regarded him as a living friend, in whom he confided and by whom he was loved. Oh, beloved, do you not see that if you are to reach to the highest style of Christian life you must do it through the realization of those very things which by faith you have received? You must see him who is invisible, and possess that which cannot be as yet enjoyed. God realized as existing, observing, judging, and rewarding human deeds: a real God, really with us—this we must know, or there is no walking with God.

Then, as we read that Enoch walked with God, we have no doubt it signifies that *he had very familiar intercourse* with the Most High. I scarcely know an intercourse that is more free, pleasant, and cordial than that which arises out of constant walking with a friend. If I wished to find a man's most familiar friend it would surely be one with whom he daily walked. If you were to say, "I sometimes go into his house and sit a little while with him"; it would not amount to so much as when you can say, "I have from day to day walked the fields and climbed the hills with him." In walking, friends become communicative—one tells his troubles, and the other strives to console him under it, and then imparts to him his own secret in return. When persons are constantly in the habit of walking together from choice, you may be quite sure there are many communications between them with which no stranger may intermeddle. But will God in very deed thus walk with men? Yes, he did so with Enoch, and he has done so with many of his people since. He tells us his secret, the secret of the Lord, which he reveals only to them that fear him, and we tell to him alike our joys in praise, our sorrows in prayer, and our sins in confession. The heart unloads itself of all its cares into the heart of him that careth for us; and the Lord pours forth his floods of goodness as he imparts to the beloved ones a sense of his own everlasting love to them. This is the very flower and sweetness of Christian experience, its lily and its rose, its calamus and myrrh.

Next it is implied in the term "walked" that *his intercourse with God was continuous*. As an old divine has well remarked, he did not take a turn or two with God and then leave his company, but he walked with God for hundreds of years. It is implied in the text that this was the tenor of his life throughout the whole of its 365 years! One might desire a change of company if he walked with anybody else, but to walk with God for three centuries was so sweet that the patriarch kept on with his walk until he walked beyond time and space, and walked into paradise, where he is still marching on in the same divine society. He had heaven on earth, and it was therefore not so wonderful that he glided away from earth to heaven so easily. He did not commune with God by fits and starts, but he abode in the conscious love of God. He did not now and then climb to the heights of elevated piety and then descend into the marshy valley of lukewarmness; but he continued in the calm, happy, equable enjoyment of fellowship with God from day to day.

It is implied also in this phrase that *his life was progressive:* for if a man walks either by himself or with anybody else, he makes progress, he goes forward. At the end of 200 years he was not where he began, he was in the same company, but he had gone forward in the right way. At the end of the third hundred years Enoch enjoyed more, understood more, loved more, had received more, and could give out more, for he had gone forward in all respects. A man who walks with God will necessarily grow in grace, and in the knowledge of God, and in likeness to Christ. You cannot suppose a perpetual walk with God year after year, without the favored person being strengthened, sanctified, instructed, and rendered more able to glorify God.

Suffer a few more observations upon Enoch's walk. His life must also have been a *holy* life, because he walked with God, and God never walks out of the way of holiness. If we walk with God, we must walk according to truth, justice, and love. The Lord has no company with the unjust and rebellious, and therefore we know that he who walked with God must have been an upright and holy man.

Enoch's life must, moreover, have been a *happy* one. Who could be unhappy with such a companion! With God himself to be with us the way can never be dreary. "Yea, though I walk through the valley of the shadow of death I will fear no evil, for thou art with me." Granted that God is your companion, and your road must be a way of pleasantness and a path of peace.

Did Enoch walk with God, then his pilgrimage must have been *safe.* What a guard is the Great Jehovah! He is sun and shield, he giveth grace and glory. He that dwelleth in the secret place of the Most High, shall abide under the shadow of the Almighty. Nothing can harm the man who is walking with the Lord God at his right hand.

And oh, what an *honorable* thing it is to walk with the Eternal! Many a man would give thousands to walk with a king. Numbers of people are such worshipers of dignities that if a king did but smile at them they would be intoxicated with delight. What, then, is the honor of walking with the King of kings! What a patent of nobility it is to be permitted to walk with the blessed and only Potentate all one's life long! Who is he that is thus favored to be the King's companion, to walk alone with him, and to become his familiar friend? Jehovah ruleth earth and heaven, and hell, and is Lord of all who shall walk with *him!* If it were only for the honor of it. O Christians, how you ought to pant to walk with God. Enoch found it safe, happy, holy, honorable, and I know now how much more that is excellent, but certainly this was a golden life; where shall we find anything to equal it?

Secondly, let us consider WHAT CIRCUMSTANCES WERE CONNECTED WITH ENOCH'S WALKING WITH GOD. The first remark is that *the details of his life are very few*. We do not know much about Enoch, and this is to his advantage. Happy is the nation which has no history, for a nation which has a history has been vexed with wars and revolutions, and bloodshed; but a nation that is always happy, peaceful, and prosperous has no chronicle to attract the lover of sensations. Happy is Enoch that we cannot write a long biography of him; the few words, "Enoch walked with God," suffice to depict his whole career, until "he was not, for God took him." If you go and look at a farmer's field, and you can say of it when you come back, "I saw yellow flowers covering it till it seemed a cloth of gold, and then I spied out here and there white flowers like silver buttons set on the golden vesture, and blue cornflowers also looked up with their lovely eyes, and begemmed the whole," you will think that it is a very pretty field if you are a child; but the farmer shakes his head, for he knows that it is in bad condition and overrun with weeds; but if you come back and simply say, "It is as fine a piece of wheat as ever grew, and that is all," then your description, though brief, is very satisfactory. Many of those dazzling events and striking incidents and sensational adventures which go to make up an interesting biography may attract attention, but they do not minister to the real excellence of the life. No life can surpass that of a man who quietly continues to serve God in the place where providence has placed him. I believe that in the judgment of angels and all pure-minded beings that woman's life is most to be admired which consists simply of this: "She did what she could";

and that man's life shall be the most noteworthy of whom it can be said: "He followed the Lord fully." Enoch's life has no adventures; is it not adventure enough for a man to walk with God? What ambition can crave a nobler existence than abiding in fellowship with the Eternal?

But some will say, "Well, but Enoch must have been very peculiarly situated: he was no doubt placed in very advantageous circumstances for piety." Now, observe that this was not so, for first *he was a public man.* He is called the "seventh from Adam." He was a notable man, and looked up to as one of the fathers of his age. A patriarch in those days must have been a man of mark, loaded with responsibility as well as with honor. The ancient custom was that the head of the family was prophet, priest, and king in his household, and abroad if he was a man of station and substance he was counselor, magistrate and ruler. Enoch was a great man in his day, one of the most important of the period; hence we may be sure he had his trials, and bore the brunt of opposition from the powerful ungodly party which opposed the ways of godliness. He is mentioned among a noble list of men. Some have unwisely thought, "I could walk with God if I had a little cottage, if I lived in a quiet village, but you see I am a public man, I occupy a position of trust, and I have to mix with my fellow men. I do not see how I am to walk with God." Ah, my dear friend, but Enoch did; though he was undoubtedly a man distinguished in his time, and full of public cares, yet he lost not the thread of sacred converse with heaven, but held on in his holy course through a life of centuries.

Note again that *Enoch was a family man.* "Enoch walked with God and begat sons and daughters." Some have said, "Ah, you cannot live as you like if you have a lot of children about you. Do not tell me about keeping up your hours of prayer and quiet reading of the Scriptures if you have a large family of little ones; you will be disturbed, and there will be many domestic incidents which will be sure to try your temper and upset your equanimity. Get away into the woods, and find a hermit's cell, there with your brown jug of water and your loaf of bread, you may be able to walk with God, but with a wife, not always amiable, and a troop of children who are never quiet, neither by day nor night, how can a man be expected to walk with God?" The wife on the other hand exclaims, "I believe that had I remained a single woman I might have walked with God. When I was a young woman I was full of devotion, but now with my husband, who is not always in the best of tempers, and with my children, who seem to have an unlimited number of wants, and never to have them satisfied, how is it possible that I can walk with God?" We turn to Enoch again, and we are confident that it can be done. "Enoch walked with God after he begat Methuselah three hundred years, and begat sons and daughters, and all the days of Enoch were three hundred and sixty-five years." Thus, you see, he was a public man, and he was a family man, yet he walked with God for more than 300 years. There is no need to be a hermit, or to renounce the married life in order to live near to God.

In addition to this, *Enoch lived in a very evil age.* He was prominent at a time when sin was beginning to cover the earth, not very long before the earth was corrupt and God saw fit to sweep the whole population from off its surface on account of sin. Enoch lived in a day of mockers and despisers. You know that from his prophecy, as recorded by Jude. He prophesied, saying, "The Lord cometh with ten thousands of his saints, to execute judgment upon all, and to convince all that are ungodly among them of all their ungodly deeds which they have ungodly committed, and of all their hard speeches which ungodly sinners have spoken against him." He lived when few loved God and when those who professed to do so were being drawn aside by the blandishments of the daughters of men. Church and state were proposing an alliance, fashion and pleasure ruled the hour, and unhallowed compromise was the order of the day. He lived towards the close of those primitive times wherein long lives had produced great sinners, and great sinners had invented great provocations of God. Do not complain, therefore, of your times and of your neighbors and other surroundings, for amid them all you may still walk with God.

Enoch walked with God, and in consequence thereof *he bore his witness for God.* "Enoch the seventh from Adam prophesied." He could not be silent, the fire burned within his soul and could not be restrained. When he had delivered his testimony it is clear that he encountered opposition. I am certain that he did so from the context in Jude, because the passage in Jude has to do with murmurers and "complainers, walking after their own lusts; and their mouth speaketh great swelling words," and Enoch is brought in as having had to do with such persons. His sermon shows that he was a man who stood firm amidst a torrent of blasphemy and rebuke, carrying on the great controversy for the truth of God against the wicked lives and licentious tongues of the

is not found, it shows that somebody looked for him. When Elijah went to heaven, you remember fifty men of the sons of the prophets went and searched for him. I do not wonder that they did; they would not meet with an Elijah every day, and when he was gone away, body and all, they might well look for him. Enoch was not found, but they looked for him. A good man is missed. A true child of God in a church like this, working and serving his Master, is only one among 5,000; but if he has walked with God his decease is lamented. We do not want so to live and die that nobody will care whether we are on earth or not. Enoch was missed when he was gone, and so will they be who walk with God.

Last of all, *Enoch's departure was a testimony.* What did he say by the fact that "he was not, for God took him," but this: there is a future state? Men had begun to doubt it, but when they said, "Where is Enoch?" and those who had witnessed his departure said, "God took him," it was to them an evidence that there was a God, and that there was another world. And when they said, "But where is his body?" there was another lesson. Two men had died before him, I mean two whose deaths are recorded in Scripture—Abel was killed, and his witness was that the seed of the serpent hates the woman's seed; Adam, too, had died about fifty years before Enoch's translation, whose witness was that, however late the penalty may come, yet the soul that sinneth it shall die. Now comes Enoch, and his testimony is that the body is capable of immortality. He could not bear testimony to resurrection, for he did not die: for that we have testimony in Christ, who is the first fruits from among the dead; but the testimony of Enoch went a good way towards it, for it bore evidence that the body was capable of being immortal, and of living in a heavenly condition. "He was not, for God took him."

His departure also was a testimony to mankind that there is a reward for the righteous, that God does not sit with stony eyes regardless of the sins of the wicked, or of the virtues of his saints, but that he sees and is pleased with his people who walk with him, and that he can give them even now present rewards by delivering them from the pangs of death, and therefore he will certainly give rewards to all his people in some way or other. Thus you see, living and dying—nay, living and being translated—Enoch was still a witness to his generation, and I do pray that all of us, whether we live or whether we sleep, may be witnesses for God.

3

ABRAHAM

Prompt Obedience to the Call of God

"By faith Abraham, when he was called to go out into a place which he should after receive for an inheritance, obeyed; and he went out, not knowing whither he went" (Heb. 11:8).

ONE is struck with the practical character of this verse. Abraham was called, and he obeyed. There is no hint of hesitation, parleying, or delay; when he was called to go out, he went out. Would to God that such conduct were usual, yea, universal; for with many of our fellowmen, and I fear with some now present, the call alone is not enough to produce obedience. "Many are called, but few are chosen." The Lord's complaint is "I called and ye refused." Such calls come again and again to many, but they turn a deaf ear to them; they are hearers only, and not doers of the word; and, worse still, some are of the same generation as that which Zechariah spake of when he said, "They pulled away the shoulder, and stopped their ears that they should not hear." Even among the most attentive hearers how many there are to whom the word comes with small practical result in actual obedience. How foolish to go on adding sin to sin, increasing the hardness of the heart, increasing the distance between the soul and Christ, and all the while fondly dreaming of some enchanted hour in which it will be more easy to yield to the divine call, and part with sin. Is it always going to be so? Shall God's longsuffering mercy only afford you opportunities for multiplying transgressions? Will ye always resist his Spirit? Always put him off with promises to be redeemed tomorrow? Forever and forever shall the tenderness and mercy of God be thus despised?

The sad point about the refusals to obey the call of the Gospel is that men are losing a golden opportunity, an opportunity for being numbered amongst the choice spirits of the world, amongst those who shall be blessed among men and women. Abraham had an opportunity, and he had grace to grasp it, and at this day there is not on the beadroll of our race a nobler name than that of "the father of the faithful." He obtained a supreme grandeur of rank among the truly great and good; far higher is he in the esteem of the right-minded than the conqueror blood-red from battle, or the emperor robed in purple. He was an imperial man, head and shoulders above his fellows. His heart was in heaven, the light of God bathed his forehead, and his soul was filled with divine influences, so that he saw the day of the Lord Jesus and was glad. He was blessed of the Lord that made heaven and earth, and was made a blessing to all nations. Some of you will never gain such honor, you will live and die ignoble, because you trifle with supreme calls; and yet, did you believe in God, did you but live by faith, there would be before you also a course of immortal honor, which would lead you to eternal glory. Instead thereof, however, choosing the way of unbelief, and neglect, and delay, you will, I fear, one day awake to shame and to everlasting contempt, and know, to your eternal confusion, how bright a crown you have lost.

WHAT WAS ABRAHAM'S SPECIAL EXPERIENCE, which led to his becoming so remarkable a saint? The secret lies in three things: he had a call, he obeyed it, and he obeyed it because he had faith.

First, then, *he had a call*. How that call came we are not told; whether it reached him through a dream, or by an audible voice from heaven, or by some unmentioned prophet, we cannot tell. Most probably he heard a voice from heaven speaking audibly to him and saying, "Get thee out from thy kindred and from thy father's house." We, too, have had many calls, but perhaps we have said, "If I heard a voice speaking from the sky I would obey it," but the form in which your call has come has been better than that, for Peter in his second epistle tells us that he himself heard a voice out of the excellent glory when he was with our Lord in the holy mount, but he adds, "We have also a more sure word of prophecy"; as if the testimony which is written, the light that shineth in a dark place, which beams forth from the word of God, was more sure than even the voice which he heard from heaven. I will show you that it is so; for, if I should hear a voice, how am I to know that it is divine?

Might it not, even if it were divine, be suggested to me for many reasons that I was mistaken, that it was most unlikely that God should speak to a man at all, and more unlikely still that he should speak to me? Might not a hundred difficulties and doubts be suggested to lead me to question whether God had spoken to me at all?

But the most of you believe the Bible to be inspired by the Spirit of God, and to be the voice of God. Now, in this book you have the call—"Come ye out from among them, be ye separate, touch not the unclean thing; and I will be a Father unto you, and ye shall be my sons and daughters." Do not say that you would accept that call if it were spoken with a voice rather than written; you know that it is not so in daily life. If a man receives a written letter from his father or a friend, does he attach less importance to it than he would have done to a spoken communication? By no means. I reckon that many of you in business are quite content to get written orders for goods, and when you get them you do not require a purchaser to ask you in person, you would just as soon that he should not; in fact, you commonly say that you like to have it in black and white. Is it not so? Well, then, you have your wish, here is the call in black and white; and I do but speak according to common sense when I say that if the Lord's call to you be written in the Bible, and it certainly is, you do not speak truth when you say, "I would listen to it if it were spoken, but I cannot listen to it because it is written." The call as given by the book of inspiration ought to have over your minds a masterly power, and if your hearts were right before God the word spoken in the Scriptures by the Holy Ghost would be at once obeyed.

Moreover, my undecided hearers, you have had other calls beside those from the Book. There have been calls through the living ministry, when the minister has spoken as pointedly to you as if he were a prophet, and you have known that the Lord spake by him, for he has depicted your circumstances, described your condition, and the word has come to you, and you have with astonishment owned that it found you out. The message has also been spoken to you by a mother's tender love and by a father's earnest advice. You have had the call too in the form of sickness and sore trouble. In the silence of the night, when you could not sleep, your conscience has demanded to be heard, the inward strivings of the Holy Ghost have been with you, and loud have been the knocks at your door. Who among us has not known the like? But, alas, the Lord has called and has been refused, he has stretched out his hands and has not been regarded. Is it not so with many of you? You have not been like Samuel who said, "Here am I, for thou didst call me," but like the adder which shutteth her ear to the voice of the charmer.

Abraham had a call, so have we, but here was the difference. *Abraham obeyed.* Well doth Paul say, "They have not all obeyed the Gospel": for to many the call comes as a common call, and the common call falls on a sealed ear, but to Abraham and to those who by grace have become the children of faithful Abraham, to whom are the blessings of grace, and with whom God has entered into league and covenant, to these it comes as a special call, a call attended with a scared power which subdues their wills and secures their obedience. Abraham was prepared for instant obedience to any command from God; his journey was appointed, and he went; he was bidden to leave his country, and he left it; to leave his friends, and he left them all. Gathering together such substance as he had he exiled himself that he might be a sojourner with his God, and took a journey in an age when traveling was infinitely more laborious than now. He knew not the road that he had to take, nor the place to which his journey would conduct him: it was enough for him that the Lord had given him the summons. Like a good soldier, he obeyed his marching orders, asking no questions. Towards God a blind obedience is the truest wisdom, and Abraham felt so, and therefore followed the path that God marked out for him from day to day, feeling that sufficient for the day would be guidance thereof. Thus Abraham obeyed!

Alas, there are some here present, some too, to whom we have preached now for years, who have not obeyed. O sirs, some of you do not require more knowledge, you need far more to put in practice what you know. Would you wonder if I should grow weary of telling some of you the way of salvation any longer? Again, and again, and again have I explained the demands of the Gospel, and described the blessings of it, and yet I see its demands neglected and its blessings refused. Ah sirs, there will be an end to this ere long, one way or the other, which shall it be? O that you were wise and would yield obedience to the truth! The Gospel has about it a divine authority, and is not to be trifled with. Notwithstanding that grace is its main characteristic it has all the authority of a command. It is awful work when through disobedience to the command of the Gospel it becomes a savor of death unto death instead of life unto life, and instead of a cornerstone it becomes a stone of stumbling and a rock of offense.

But I reminded you that the main point concerning Abraham was this, *he obeyed the call because he believed God.* Faith was the secret reason of his conduct. We read of certain persons that "the word preached did not profit them, not being mixed with faith in them that heard it," and again we read that "some when they had heard did provoke." But in Abraham's case there was neither unbelief nor provocation, he believed God with a childlike faith. His faith, I suppose, lay in the following items: When the Lord spoke he believed that it was the living God who addressed him. Believing that God spoke, he judged him worthy of his earnest heed; and he felt that it was imperative upon him to do as he was bidden. This settled, he desired nothing more to influence his course: he felt that the will of God must be right, and that his highest wisdom was to yield to it. Though he did not know where he was to go, he was certain that his God knew, and though he could hardly comprehend the reward promised to him, he was sure that the bounteous God never mocked his servants with deceitful gifts. He did not know the land of Canaan, but he was sure if it was a country chosen by God as a peculiar gift to his called servant, it must be no ordinary land. He left all such matters with his heavenly Friend, being fully persuaded that what he had promised he was able also to perform.

What a mighty sway faith has over a man, and how greatly it strengthens him. Faith was to the patriarch his authority for starting upon his strange journey, an authority which enabled him to defy alike the worldly wisdom which advises, and the worldly folly which scoffs. Perhaps they said to him, "Why wilt thou leave thy kinsfolk, Abraham?" but he replied, "God bids me." That was for him a sufficient warrant; he wanted no further argument. This also became to him the guide of his steps. If any said, "But, strange old man, how canst thou journey when thou knowest not the way?" He replied, "I go whither the Lord bids me." Faith found in God, chart, compass, and pole star, all in one. The word of the Lord also became the nourishment for his journey. If any said, "How wilt thou be supplied, Abraham, in those wild lands, where wilt thou find thy daily bread?" he replied, "God bids me go: it is not possible that he should desert me. He can spread a table in the wilderness, or make me live upon the word which cometh out of his mouth, if bread should fail."

This brings me to the second part of our subject, WHAT WAS THERE PECULIAR IN ABRAHAM'S CONDUCT? For whatever there was essential in his conduct there must be the same in us, if we are to be true children of the father of the faithful. The points of peculiarity in Abraham's case seem to me to have been five.

The first was this, that *he was willing to be separated from his kindred.* It is a hard task to a man of loving soul to put long leagues of distance between himself and those he loves, and to become a banished man. Yet in order to have salvation, brethren, we must be separated from this untoward generation. Not that we have to take our journey into a far country, or to forsake our kindred—perhaps it would be an easier task to walk with God if we could do so—but our calling is to be separate from sinners, and yet to live among them: to be a stranger and a pilgrim in their cities and homes. We must be separate in character from those with whom we may be called to grind at the same mill, or sleep in the same bed; and this I warrant you is by no means an easier task than that which fell to the patriarch's lot. If believers could form a secluded settlement where no tempters could intrude, they would perhaps find the separated life far more easy, though I am not very sure about it, for all experiments in that direction have broken down. There is, however, for us no "garden walled around," no "island of saints," no Utopia; we sojourn among those whose ungodly lives cause us frequent grief, and the Lord Jesus meant it to be so, for he said, "Behold I send you forth as sheep among wolves."

Come, now, my hearer, are you willing to be one of the separated? I mean this—Dare you begin to think for yourself? You have let your grandmother's religion come to you with the old arm chair and the antique china, as heirlooms of the family, and you go to a certain place of worship because your family have always attended there. You have a sort of hereditary religion in the same way as you have a display of family plate. Now, young man, dare you think for yourself? Or do you put out your thinking to be done for you, like your washing? I believe it to be one of the essentials of a Christian man, that he should have the courage to use his own mental faculties, and search the Bible for himself, for God has not committed our religious life to the guidance of the brain in our neighbor's head, but he has bestowed on each of us a conscience, and an understanding which he expects us to use. Do your own thinking, my friend, on such business as this. Now, if the grace of God helps you rightly to think for yourself, you will judge very differently from your ungodly friends; your views and theirs will differ, your motives will differ, the objects of your pursuit will differ. There are some things which are quite customary with them which you will not endure. You will soon become a speckled bird among them. We are not resident traders in this Vanity Fair, we pass through it because it lies in our way home, but we are ill at ease in it. In no tent of all the fair can we rest. O traders in this hubbub of trifles, we have small esteem for your great bargains and tempting cheats; we are not buyers in the Roman row nor in the French row, we would give all that we have to leave your polluted streets, and be no more annoyed by Beelzebub, the lord of the fair. Our journey is towards the celestial city, and when the sons of earth cry to us, "What do ye buy?" we answer, "We buy the truth." O young man, can you take up in the warehouse the position of being a Christian though there is no other believer in the house? Come, good woman, dare you serve the Lord, though husband and children ridicule you? Man of business, dare you do the right thing in business, and play the Christian, though around you the various methods of trading render it hard for you to be unflinchingly honest? This singularity is demanded of every believer in Jesus.

A second peculiarity of Abraham's conduct is seen in the fact that *he was ready for all the losses and risks that might be involved in obedience to the call of God.* He was to leave his native country, as we have already said: to some of us that would be a hard task, and I doubt not it was such to him. The smoke out of my own chimney is better than the fire on another man's hearth. There is no place like home, wherever we may wander. The home feeling was probably so strong in Abraham as in us, but he was never to have a home on earth any more, except that he was to realize what Moses afterwards sung, "Lord, thou hast been our dwelling place in all generations." For him there was no rooftree and paternal estate, he owned no portion of the land in which he sojourned, and his sole abode was a frail tent, which he removed from day to day as his flocks required fresh pasturage. He could say to his God, "I am a stranger and a sojourner with thee." He had to leave those whom he loved, for, though they accompanied him part of the way, they would not go further; if he followed the Lord fully he must go alone. The patriarch knew nothing of half measures, he went through with his obedience, and left all his kindred to go to Canaan, to which he had been summoned.

No doubt he had many risks to encounter on his journey and when he entered the country. The Canaanite was still in the land, and the Canaanites were a fierce and cruel set of heathen, who would have utterly destroyed the wanderer if the Lord had not put a spell upon them, and said, "Touch not mine anointed, and do my prophets no harm." It was a country swarming with little tribes, who were at war continually. Abraham himself was, for Lot's sake, to gird on his sword, and go forth to fight, peace-lover as he was. Of all discomforts and dangers, loss of property, and parting with friends, Abraham made small account. God commanded, and Abraham went.

Now, brethren, can you and I do the same? Oh, you who desire to be saved, I say, can you do this? Have you counted the cost and determined to pay it? You must not expect that you will wear silver slippers and walk on green rolled turf all the way to heaven: the road was rough which your Lord traversed, and if you walk with him yours will be rough too. Can ye bear for Jesus' sake all earthly loss? Can ye bear the scoff, the cold shoulder, the cutting jest, the innuendo, the sarcasm, the sneer? Could you go further, and bear loss of property and suffering in purse? Do not say that it may not occur, for many believers lose all by having to leave the ill pursuits by which they once earned their bread. You must in your intention give all up *for* Jesus, and in act you must give up all *to* Jesus. Except ye take up your cross, ye cannot be his disciples. Except you can give up everything for him do not pretend to follow him.

> Jesus, I my cross have taken,
> All to leave and follow thee,
> Destitute, despised, forsaken,
> Thou, from hence, my all shalt be.

If that be said in truth, it is well, my brother; you bid fair to be in all things a partaker with faithful Abraham: you also shall find much blessing in the separated life.

Thirdly, one great peculiarity in Abraham was that *he waived the present for the future.* He went out to go into a place which he should *after* receive for an inheritance. He left the inheritance he then had to receive one which was yet to come. This is not the way of the world. The proverb saith, "A bird in the hand is worth two in the bush," and especially in such a bush as Abraham saw before him. It did not seem very likely he would ever obtain that land; but still he let his bird in the hand go, and took to the bird in the bush, being fully persuaded that he should have it in God's good time. John Bunyan sets this forth in his picture of two children, Passion and Patience. Passion would have all his good things now, and he sat among his toys and joys, and laughed and rejoiced. Patience had to bear to see his brother, Passion, full of mirth, and to hear his scoffing; but then, as John Bunyan beautifully says, "Patience came in last for his portion, and it lasted forever, for there is nothing after the last." So, then if we are to have our heaven last it will last, and no cloud shall mar it, no calamity bring it to an end. God grant us grace to live more for the future than we have been accustomed to do.

O ye ungodly ones, you do not care about the future, for you have never realized death and judgment. You are afraid to look over the edge of this narrow life. As to death, nothing frightens you so much. As for hell, if you are warned to escape from it, instead of thanking the preacher for being honest enough to warn you of it, you straightway call him a "hell-fire" preacher, or give him some other ugly name. Alas, you little know how pained he is to speak to you on so terrible a subject! You little dream how true a lover of your soul he is, or he would not warn you of the wrath to come. Do you want to have flatterers about you? Such are to be had in plenty if you desire them. As for heaven, you seem to have no regard for it; at any rate you are not making your title to it sure or clear by caring about divine things. If you would have the birthright you must let the present mess of pottage go. The eternal future must come far before the fleeting trifles of today; you must let the things which are seen sink, and bid the "things not seen as yet" rise in all their matchless grandeur and reality before your eyes.

Fourthly, and this is the main point, *Abraham committed himself to God by faith.* From that day forward Abraham had nothing but his God for a portion, nothing but his God for a protector. No squadron of soldiers accompanied the good man's march, his safeguard lay in him who had said, "Fear not, Abraham, I am thy shield and thy exceeding great reward." He had to trust the Lord for his daily bread and daily guidance, for he was to march one and not know half a mile before him. He was ignorant when to stop and when to journey on, except as the Lord God guided him hour by hour. I must not say that Abraham became a poor pensioner upon the daily provision of God, but I will use a better terms and describe him as "a gentleman commoner upon the royal bounty of his heavenly King." His lot was to have nothing, but to be heir of heaven and earth. Can you thus walk by faith? Has the grace of God brought you who have been hesitating to resolve henceforth to believe God and trust him? If you do you are saved, for faith is the deciding matter. To realize the existence of God and to trust in him, especially to trust in his mercy, through Jesus Christ, is the essential matter. As for the life and walk of faith, they are the most singular things in the world. I seem myself to have been climbing a series of mysterious staircases, light as air and yet as solid as granite. I cannot see a single step before me, and often there seems to the eye to be nothing whatsoever to form a foothold for the next step. I look down and wonder how I came where I am, but still I climb on, and he who has brought me so far supplies me with confidence for that which lies before me. High into things invisible the ethereal ladder has borne me, and onward and forward to glory its rounds will yet conduct me. What I have seen has often failed me, but what I have not seen, and yet have believed, has always held me securely. Have not you found it so, all ye children of God? Let us pray that the Lord may lead others to tread the same mystic ascent by beginning today the life of faith.

The last specialty in Abraham's procedure was, *what he did was done at once*. There were no "ifs", considerings, and delays. He needed no forcing and driving—

> God drew him and he followed on,
> Charmed to confess the voice divine.

At once, I say, he went. Promptness is one of the brightest excellencies in faith's actings. Delay spoils all. Someone asked Alexander to what he owed his conquests, and he said, "I have conquered because I never delayed." While the enemy were preparing, he had begun the battle, and they were routed before they knew where they were. After that fashion faith overcomes temptation. She runs in the way of obedience, or rather she mounts on the wings of eagles, and so speeds on her way. With regard to the things of God our first thoughts are best: considerations of difficulty entangle us. Whenever you feel a prompting to do a good thing do not ask anybody whether you should do it or not; no one ever repents of doing good. Ask your friends afterwards rather than beforehand, for it is ill consulting with flesh and blood when duty is plain. If the Lord has given you substance, and you are prompted to be generous to the cause of God, do not count every sixpence over, and calculate what others would give; count it after you have given it, if it must be counted at all, but it would be better still not to let your left hand know what your right hand doeth. It cannot be wrong to do the right thing at once; nay, in matters of duty, every moment of delay is a sin. Thus we have Abraham before us; may the Holy Spirit make us like him.

We have to close with two or three words about what was THE RESULT OF ABRAHAM'S ACTION. The question of many will be, *did it pay?* That is the inquiry of most people, and within proper bounds it is not a wrong question. Did it answer Abraham's purpose? Our reply is, it did so gloriously. True, it brought him into a world of trouble, and no wonder: such a noble course as his was not likely to be an easy one. What grand life ever was easy? Who wants to be a child and do easy things? Yet we read in Abraham's life, after a whole host of troubles, "And Abraham was old and well stricken in years, and the Lord had blessed Abraham in all things." That is a splendid conclusion—God had blessed Abraham in all things. Whatever happened, he had always been under the divine smile, and all things had worked for his good. He was parted from his friends, but then he had the sweet society of his God, and was treated as the friend of the Most High, and allowed to intercede for others, and clothed with great power on their behalf. I almost envy Abraham. I should do so altogether if I did not know that all the saints are permitted to enjoy the same privileges. What a glorious degree Abraham took when he was called "the friend of God"; was not his loss of earthly friendships abundantly made up to him? What honor, also, the patriarch had among his contemporaries; he was a great man, and held in high esteem. How splendidly he bore himself; no king ever behaved more royally. That pettifogging king of Sodom wanted to make a bargain with him, but the grand old man replied, "I will not take from a thread even to a shoelatchet, lest thou shouldest say, I have made Abraham rich." Those sons of Heth also were willing to make him a present of a piece of land around the cave of Machpelah; but he did not want a present from Canaanites, and so he said, "No, I will pay you every penny. I will weigh out the price to you, whatever you may demand." In noble independence no man could excel the father of the faithful; his contemporaries look small before him, and no man seems to be his equal, save Melchizedek. His image passes across the page of history rather like that of a spirit from the supernatural realms than that of a mere man; he is so thorough, so childlike, and therefore so heroic. He lived in God, and on God, and with God. Such a sublime life recompensed a thousandfold all the sacrifice he was led to make.

Was not his life a happy one? One might wisely say, "Let my life be like that of Abraham." As to temporal things the Lord enriched him, and in spirituals he was richer still. He was wealthier in heart than in substance, though great even in that respect. And now Abraham is the father of the faithful, patriarch of the whole family of believers, and to him alone of all mortal men God said, "In thee shall all the families of the earth be blessed." This very day, through his matchless seed, to whom be glory forever and ever, even Jesus Christ of the seed of Abraham, all tribes of men are blessed. His life was, both for time and for eternity, a great success; both for temporals and for spirituals the path of faith was the best that he could have followed.

And now may we all be led to imitate his example. If we never have done so, may we this morning be led to give God his due by trusting him, to give the blood of Christ its due by relying upon it, to give the Spirit of God his due by yielding ourselves to him. Will you do so, or not? I pause for your reply. The call is given again, will you obey it or not? Nobody here will actually declare that he will not, but many will reply that they hope they shall. Alas! my sermon is a failure to those who so speak: if that be your answer, I am foiled again. When Napoleon was attacking the Egyptians he had powerful artillery, but he could not reach the enemy, for they were ensconced in a mud fort, and it made Napoleon very angry, because, if they had been behind granite walls, he could have battered them down, but their earthworks could not be blown to pieces, every ball stuck in the mud, and made the wall stronger. Your hopes and delays are just such a mud wall. I had a good deal sooner people would say, "There, now, we do not believe in God nor in his Christ," and speak out straightforwardly, than go on forever behind this mud wall of "We will by-and-by," and "We hope it will be so one day." The fact is, you do not mean to obey the Lord at all. You are deceiving yourselves if you think so. If God be God tomorrow he is God today; if Christ be worth having next week, he is worth having today. If there is anything in religion at all, it demands a present surrender to its claims and a present obedience to its laws; but if you judge it to be a lie, say so, and we shall know where you are. If Baal be God, serve him; but if God be God, I charge you by Jesus Christ, fly to him as he is revealed, and come forth from the sin of the world and be separate, and walk by faith in God.

4

JACOB

Worshiping on His Staff

"By faith Jacob, when he was a dying, blessed both the sons of Joseph; and worshiped, leaning upon the top of his staff" (Heb. 11:21).

"WHEN he was dying." Death is a thorough test of faith. Beneath the touch of the skeleton finger shams dissolve into thin air, and only truth remains; unless indeed a strong delusion has been given, and then the spectacle of a presumptuous sinner passing away in his iniquities is one which might make angels weep. It is hard, very hard, to maintain a lie in the presence of the last solemnities; the end of life is usually the close of self-deception. There is a mimic faith, a false assurance, which lasts under all ordinary heats of trial, but this evaporates when the fires of death surround it. Certain men are at peace and quiet in their conscience, they stifle convictions, they refuse to allow such a thing as self-examination, they count an honest self-suspicion to be a temptation of the devil, and boast of their unbroken tranquillity of mind, and go on from day to day with perfect confidence; but we would not be of their order. Their eyes are closed, their ears are dull of hearing, and their heart has waxen gross. A siren song forever enchants them with delight, but also entices them to destruction. Terrible will be their awakening when they lie a dying: as a dream their false peace will vanish, and real terrors will come upon them.

That expression, "When he was a dying," reminds me of many deathbeds; but I shall not speak of them now, for I desire each one of you to rehearse the scene of his own departure, for son of every one a tale will be told commencing—"When he was a dying." I want each one to project his mind a little forward to the time when he must gather up his feet in the bed, pronounce his last farewell, and yield up the ghost.

39

Before your actual departure, probably, there may be allotted to you, unless you are carried away with a sudden stroke, a little time in which it shall be said, "He was a dying." Perhaps it is a desirable thing to occupy some weeks in departure, till the mind seems to have passed through the gate and to be already in the glory, while yet the body lingers here; but as we have had no experience we are scarcely able to form a judgment.

The text tells us that the patriarch's faith was firm while he was a dying, so that he poured forth no murmurs, but plentiful benedictions, as he blessed both the sons of Joseph. May your faith and mine also be such that whenever we shall be a dying our faith will perform some illustrious exploit that the grace of God may be admired in us. Paul does not say anything about Jacob's life, but selects the death scene. There were many instances of faith in Jacob's life story, but you recollect that in the epistle to the Hebrews, Paul is walking through the histories and plucking a flower here and a flower there, and he complains that time fails him even in doing that, so fertile is the garden of faith. I do not doubt, however, that he gathered the best out of each biography; and, perhaps, the finest thing in Jacob's life was the close of it. He was more royal between the curtains of his bed than at the door of his tent: greater in the hour of his weakness than in the day of his power.

The old man of 147 might have been willing to depart through infirmities of age, but yet he had much to keep him below, and make him wish to live as long as possible. After a very troublous life he had enjoyed seventeen years of remarkable comfort, so much so that, had it been ourselves, we should probably have begun to strike our roots into the soil of Goshen, and dread the bare thought of removal; yet there sits the venerable patriarch, with his hand on his staff, ready to go, seeking no delay, but rather waiting for the salvation of God. After all his tossings to and fro, when he had been so long a pilgrim, it must have been a pleasant thing for him to have settled down in a fat land with his sons, and his grandsons, and great-grandsons all around him, all comfortably provided for, with Joseph at the head of the whole country—prime minister of Egypt—reflecting honor upon his old father, and taking care that none of the family wanted anything. The last course of Jacob's feast of life was by far the sweetest, and the old man might have been loathe to retire from so dainty a table. The children of Israel were a sort of foreign aristocracy in the land, and against them would not a dog dare to move its tongue, lest the renowned Joseph should put forth his hand. That seventeen years must have been bright, and full of rest to the old man. But sense has not killed his faith, luxury has not destroyed his spirituality; his heart is still in the tents where he had dwelt as a sojourner with God. You can see that he has not even with one single rootlet of his soul taken hold upon Egypt. His first anxiety is to take care that not even his bones shall lie in Goshen, but that his body shall be taken out of the country as a protest to his family that they are not Egyptians, and cannot be made into subjects of Pharaoh, and that Canaan is their possession to which they must come. By his dying charge to bury him in Machpelah, he practically teaches his descendants that they must set loose by all the good land which they possessed in Goshen, for their inheritance did not lie on the banks of the Nile, but on the other side of the desert in Canaan, and they must be on tiptoe to journey thither. The blessing which he gave to the sons of Joseph was but an utterance of his firm faith in the covenant which gave the land to him and to his seed. It was suggested by that faith of his which let go the present and grasped the future, renounced the temporal and seized the eternal, refusing the treasures of Egypt and clinging to the covenant of God.

First, then, HIS BLESSING. He blessed the two sons of Joseph. Will you have patience with me while I try to show that his blessing the sons of Joseph was an act of faith? because, first, *only by faith could the old man really give a blessing to any one.* Look at him. He is too feeble to leave his bed. When he sits up supported by pillows, at what is called the bedhead, he calls for his trusty staff that he may lean upon it while he raises himself up a little, to be in a position to stretch out his hands and to use his voice. He has no strength, and his eyes are dim, so that he cannot see which is Ephraim and which is Manasseh. He is failing in most of his faculties: every way you can see that he is a worn-out old man, who can do nothing for the children whom he loves. If he is able to bestow a blessing, it cannot be by the power of nature; and yet he can and does bless them, and therefore we feel sure that there must be an inner man within that feeble old Jacob; there must be a spiritual Israel hidden away in him, an Israel who by prevailing with God as a prince has obtained a blessing, and is able to dispense it to others. And so there is; and at half a glance we see it. He rises to the dignity of a king, a prophet, and a priest when he begins to pronounce a blessing upon his two grandchildren. He believed that God spoke by him; and he believed that God would justify every word that he was uttering. He believed in the God that heareth prayer; his benediction was a prayer; and as he pronounced blessings upon his grandsons he felt that every word he was speaking was a petition which the Lord was answering. They were blessed, and they should be blessed, and he discerned it by faith. Thus, we see, he was manifesting his faith in offering believing prayer, and in uttering a confident benediction.

Whether we live, or whether we die, let us have faith in God: whenever we preach or teach the Gospel, let us have faith; for without faith we shall labor in vain. Whenever you distribute religious books or visit the sick, do so in faith, for faith is the lifeblood of all our service. If only by faith can a dying Jacob bless his descendants, so only by faith can we bless the sons of men. Have faith in God, and the instruction which you give shall really edify, the prayers you offer shall bring down showers of mercy, and your endeavors for your sons and daughters shall be prospered. God will bless what is done in faith; but if we believe not our work will not be established. Faith is the backbone and marrow of the Christian's power to do good: we are weak as water till we enter into union with God by faith, and then we are omnipotent. We can do nothing for our fellowmen by way of promoting their spiritual and eternal interests if we walk according to the sight of our eyes; but when we get into the power of God, and grasp his promise by a daring confidence, then it is that we obtain the power to bless.

You will notice, also, that *not only the power to bless came to him by faith, but the blessings which he allotted to his grandsons were his upon the same tenure.* His legacies were all blessings which he possessed by faith only. He gave to Ephraim and Manasseh a portion each: but where and what? Did he fetch out a bag from an iron safe and say, "Here, young men, I give you the same portion of ready money as I give my sons"? No, there does not seem to have been a solitary shekel in the case. Did he call for the map of the family estates and say, "I give over to you, my boys, my freehold lands in such a parish, and my copy hold farms under such a manor"? No, no, he gave them no portion in Goshen, but each had a lot in Canaan.

Did that belong to him? Yes, in one sense, but not in another. God had promised it to him, but he had not yet a foot of land in it. The Canaanites were swarming in the land; they were dwelling in cities walled up to heaven, and held the country by the right of possession, which is nine points of the law. But the good old man talks about Canaan as if it was all his own, and he foresees the tribes growing into nations as much as if they were already in actual possession of the country. He had, as a matter of fact, neither house nor ground in Palestine, and yet he counts it all his own, since a faithful God had promised it to his fathers. God had said to Abraham, "Lift up now thine eyes and behold to the east and to the west, to the north and to the south. All this will I give thee." And Jacob realizes that gift of God as being a charter and title-deed of possession, and he acts upon it while he says, "This is for Ephraim: this is for Manasseh," though the sneering infidel standing by would have said, "Hear how the old man dotes and maunders, giving away what he has not got!" Faith is the substance of things hoped for, and she deals seriously and in a business manner with that which she makes real to herself: blind reason may ridicule, but faith is justified of all her children.

Beloved, in this manner believers bless the sons of men, namely, by faith. We pray for them, and we tell them of good things yet to come, not to be seen of the eye, or to be perceived by the senses, but inconceivably good—things laid up by God for them that love him, which shall be the portion of our children and our friends if they believe in the living God. By faith we believe in things not seen as yet. We confess that, like Abraham, Isaac, and Jacob, we are strangers here, and we are journeying towards a place of which God has spoken to us: "A city which hath foundations, whose builder and maker is God." We have learned to talk about the crown which the Lord has laid up for us, and not for us only but for all them that love his appearing; and we delight to tell others how to win this crown. We point them to the narrow gate and to the narrow way, neither of which they can see, and to the end of that narrow road, even to the hilltops crowned with the celestial city where the pilgrims of the Lord shall dwell forever, and enjoy an eternal reward. Faith is wanted to enable us to point men to the invisible and eternal, and if we cannot do this how can we bless them? We must believe for those we love, and have hope for them; thus shall we have power with God for them, and shall bless them. Oh, you worldly fathers, you may give your sons what heritage you can, and divide among your daughters what wealth you please, but as for us, our longing is to see our children and our children's children dowried with the riches which come from above. If they win a share in the land on the other side of Jordan, as yet unseen, and have a portion now in Christ Jesus, we shall be glad—infinitely more glad than if they were the richest among mankind. Our legacies to our sons are the blessings of grace, and our dowries to our daughters are the promises of the Lord.

It is well worthy of our notice that *the venerable patriarch Jacob in his benediction particularly mentioned the covenant*. His faith, like the faith of most of God's people, made the covenant its pavilion of delightful abode, its tower of defense, and its armory for war. No sweeter word was on his tongue than the covenant, and no richer consolation sustained his heart. He said to Joseph, "God almighty appeared unto me at Luz in the land of Canaan, and blessed me, and said unto me, Behold I will make thee fruitful, and multiply thee." His confidence rested in the promise of the Lord, and in the divine fidelity: that was the fountain truth from which he drew the inspiration which led him to bless his grandchildren. And, also, you notice, how he dwells upon the name of his father Abraham, and of his father Isaac, with whom the covenant had aforetime been established: the memories of covenant love are precious, and every confirmatory token is treasured up and dwelt upon. Dying men do not talk nonsense. They get to something solid, and the everlasting covenant made with their fathers, and confirmed in their own persons, has been one of the grand things about which dying saints have been wont to deliver their souls. Recollect how David said, "Although my house be not so with God, yet hath he made with me an everlasting covenant, ordered in all things and sure." While we are sitting here we can talk about the matter coolly, but when the death dew lies cold upon the brow, and the pulse is failing, and the throat is gradually choking up, it will be blessed to fix the eye upon the faithful promiser and to feel a calm within the soul which even death pangs cannot disturb, because we can then exclaim, "I know whom I have believed, and I am persuaded that he is able to keep that which I have committed to him until that day."

I want to call your attention to one point which I think extraordinarily illustrates the faith of Jacob. In distributing to these two grandchildren his blessings as to the future, he takes them right away from Joseph, and says, "As Simeon and Reuben shall they be mine." Do you know who those two young gentlemen were? Think awhile, and you will see that they were very different in rank, station, parentage, and prospects from any of the sons of Jacob. Jacob's sons had been brought up as laboring men, without knowledge of polite society or learned arts. They were countrymen, mere Bedouins, wandering shepherds, and nothing else; but these two young gentlemen were descended from a princess, and had, no doubt, been liberally educated. Pharaoh had given to Joseph a daughter of Potipherah, priest of On, and the priests of Egypt were the highest class of all—the nobility of the land. Joseph himself was prime minister, and these were partakers of his lofty rank. The sons of Reuben and Simeon were nobodies in the polite circles of Egypt—very good, decent people, farmers and graziers, but not at all of the high class of the Right Honorable Lord Manasseh and the Honorable Ephraim. Indeed, every shepherd was an abomination to the Egyptians, and therefore inadmissible to Egypt's nobility; but Manasseh and Ephraim were of a superior caste, and gentlemen of position and fortune. But *Jacob showed his faith by ignoring worldly advantages for his grandsons.* He says to Joseph, "They are not to be yours. I do not know them as Egyptians, I forget all about their mother's rank and family. The boys have attractive prospects before them; they can be made priests of the idol temple, and rise to high dignities among the Egyptians; but all that glitter we reject for them, and in token thereof I adopt them as my own sons; they are mine; as Simeon and Reuben they shall be mine. For all the gold of Egypt you would not have one of them serve an idol, for I know that you are true to your father's God and your father's faith." And so he takes the boys right away, you see, from all their brilliant opportunities, and bestows upon them that which, to the carnal mind, appears to be an estate in dreamland, a chateau in Spain, something intangible and unmarketable. This was a deed of faith, and blessed are they who can imitate it, choosing rather the reproach of Christ for their sons than all the treasures of Egypt. The joy of it is that these lads accepted the exchange, and let the golden possessions of Egypt go like Moses after them. May our heirs and successors be of like mind, and may the Lord say of them, "Out of Egypt have I called my son"; and again, "When Ephraim was a child then I loved him, and called my son out of Egypt."

This is how faith leads believers to bless their children. We are of the same mind as Jacob in this matter. We would sooner bury our little ones than that they should live to become amongst the richest and most famous of men, and yet not know or serve their father's God; better that we laid them quietly in such ground as our Christian brethren permit us to use as a sepulcher for our unbaptized babes; better that they were safely housed at God's right hand, than that they should grow up to plunge into dissipation or to follow false doctrine and perish out of Christ.

We have not done yet, for we notice that *Jacob showed his faith by blessing Joseph's sons in God's order.* He placed Ephraim before Manasseh. It was not according to the rule of nature, but he felt the impulse upon him, and his faith would not resist the divine guidance: blind as he was he would not yield to the dictation of his son, but crossed his hands to obey the divine monition. Faith resolves to do the right thing in the right way. Some persons' faith leads them to do the right thing the wrong way upwards, but matured faith follows the order which God prescribes. If God will have Ephraim first, faith does not quarrel with his decree. We may wish to see a favorite child blessed more than another, but nature must forego her choice, for the Lord must do what seemeth him good. Faith prefers grace to talent, and piety to cleverness; she lays her right hand where God lays it, and not where beauty of person or quickness of intellect would suggest. Our best child is that which God calls best; faith corrects reason and accepts the divine verdict.

Notice that *he manifested his faith by his distinct reference to redemption.* He alone who has faith will pray for the redemption of his children, especially when they exhibit no signs of being in bondage, but are hopeful and amiable. The good old man prayed, "The Angel which redeemed me from all evil, bless the lads." Let your faith bring down upon your children a share in redemption's blessings, for they need to be redeemed even as others. If they are washed in the blood of Jesus, if they are reconciled to God by the blood of his Son, if they have access to God by the blood of atonement, you may die well satisfied; for what is to harm them when once the Angel that redeemed you has also redeemed them? From sin, from Satan, from death, from hell, from self—"from all evil" does our Redeemer set us free; and this is the greatest of all benedictions which we can pronounce upon our dearest children.

Jacob showed his faith by his assurance that God would be present with his seed. How cheering is the old man's dying expression, made not only to his boys, but concerning all his family. He said, "Now I die, but God will be with you." It is very different from the complaints of certain good old ministers when they are dying. They seem to say, "When I die, the light of Israel will be quenched. I shall die, and the people will desert the truth. When I am gone the standard-bearer will have fallen, and the watchman on the walls will be dead." Many in dying are afraid for the chariot of Israel and the horsemen thereof; and, sometimes, we who are in good health talk very much in the same fashion as though we were wonderfully essential to the progress of God's cause. I have known some of our church members speak in that manner, and inquire: "What should we do if Mr. So-and-so were dead! If our pastor were gone, what would the church do?" I will tell you what you will do without us: I will put the case as though I were myself to die—"Now I die, but God will be with you." Whoever passes away, the Lord will abide with his people, and the church will be secure. The grand old cause does not depend on one or two of us. God forbid! The truth was mighty in the land before the best man living was born, and the truth will not be buried with him, but in its own immortal youth will still be powerful; yes, and fresh advocates will arise more full of life and vigor than we are, and greater victories will be won. It is grand to say with Jacob, "Now I die, but God will be with you." Such language honors God and bespeaks a mind greatly trustful, and completely delivered from the self-conceit which dreams itself important, if not necessary, to the cause of God.

We are told, next, that the old man "worshiped"—WORSHIPED BY FAITH. Very briefly let me tell you what worship I think he rendered.

First, while he was dying he offered the worship of *gratitude*. How pleasing is the incident recorded in the tenth and eleventh verses, "Now the eyes of Israel were dim for age, so that he could not see. And Joseph brought his two sons near unto him; and he kissed them and embraced them. And Israel said unto Joseph, I had not thought to see thy face: and, lo, God hath showed me also thy seed." Ah, yes, we shall often have to say, "O Lord, I had not thought that thou wouldst do as much as this, but thou hast gone far beyond what I asked or even thought." I hope that this will be amongst our dying speeches and confessions, that the half was never told us, that our good Lord kept the best wine till the last, and that the end of the feast on earth, being but the beginning of the feast eternal in heaven, was the crown of all. Let us declare concerning our Lord that we found him better and better and better and better, even till we entered into his rest. He has been at first better than our fears, then better than our hopes, and finally better than our desires.

Did he not also offer the worship of *testimony*, when he acknowledged God's goodness to him all his life? He says, "The God that fed me all my life long," thus owning that he had been always dependent but always supplied. He had been a shepherd, and he uses a word here which means "The God that shepherdized me—who was a shepherd to me all my life long." It was a testimony to the care and tenderness of Jehovah. Yes, and I hope we also shall finish life by magnifying the goodness of the Lord. Be this our witness, "He fed me all my life long. I was in straits sometimes, and I wondered where the next bit of bread would come from; but if he did not send a raven, or if he did not find a widow woman to provide for me, yet somehow or other he did feed me all my life long.

He worked in his own wise way, so that I never lacked, for the Lord was my shepherd all my life long."

Notice, too, how reverently he worships the covenant messenger with the adoration of *reverent love.* He speaks of "the Angel who redeemed me from all evil." He thinks of the Angel that wrestled with him, and the Angel that appeared to him when he fell asleep at Bethel. This is *the* Angel, not an ordinary angel, but the true *arch*angel—Jesus Christ—the messenger of the covenant whom we delight in. It is he that has delivered us from all evil by his redeeming blood, for no other being could have accomplished a redemption so complete. Do you remember when he came to you personally, and wrestled with you and tore away your self-righteousness, and made you limp upon your thigh? This it may be was your first introduction to him. You saw him by night, and thought him at the first to be rather your enemy than your friend. Do you recollect when he took your strength away from you, and then at last saved you, because in utter weakness, you were about to fall to the ground, you laid hold of him and said, "I will not let thee go except thou bless me," and so you won a blessing from him? You had thought aforetime that you had strength in yourself, but now you learned that you were weakness itself, and that only as you became consciously weak would you become actually strong. You learned to look out of self to him, and do you not bless him for having taught you such a lesson? Will you not when you come to die bless him for what he did for you then, and all your life long? O my brethren, we owe all things to the redeeming Angel of the covenant. The evils which he has warded off from us are terrible beyond conception, and the blessings he has brought us are rich beyond imagination.

Thus you have had a picture of the old man blessing by faith, and worshiping by faith: faith was the mainspring of the two actions, their essence, their spirit, and their crown.

The last matter for us to speak upon is HIS ATTITUDE. He "worshiped leaning upon the top of his staff." The Romanists have made fine mischief out of this text, for they have read it, "He worshiped the top of his staff," and their notion has been, I suppose, that there was a pretty little god carved on the top—an image of a saint or a cross, or some other symbol, and that he held up that emblem, and so worshiped the top of his staff. We know that he did not such thing, for there is no trace in Abraham, Isaac, or Jacob of anything like the worship of images; though teraph worship lingered in their families, it was not with their consent.

They were not perfect men, but they were perfectly clear from idolatry, and never worshiped an image. Nay, nay, nay; they worshiped God alone. He worshiped on the top of his staff—leaning on it, supporting himself upon it. In Genesis you read that he "bowed himself upon the bed's head." It is a very curious thing that the word for bed and the word for staff in the Hebrew are so exceedingly like each other that unless the little points had been used, which I suppose were not used at all in the olden time, it would be difficult to tell whether the word is "bed" or "staff." I do not, however, think either Moses or Paul can be wrong. Jacob strengthened himself and sat upon the bed, and he leaned upon his staff, too. It is very easy to realize a position in which both descriptions would be equally true. He could sit upon the bed, and lean on the top of his staff at the same time.

But why did he lean on his staff? What was that for? I think besides the natural need which he had of it, because of his being old, he did it emblematically. Do you not remember his saying, "With my staff I cross this Jordan"? It believe he kept that staff throughout life as a memorial. It was a favorite staff of his which he took with him on his first journey, and he leaned upon it as he took his last remove. "With my staff I crossed this Jordan," he had said before, and now with that staff in hand he crosses the spiritual Jordan. That staff was his life companion, the witness with himself of the goodness of the Lord, even as some of us may have an old Bible, or a knife, or a chair which are connected with memorable events of our lives.

But what did that staff indicate? Let us hear what Jacob said at another time. When he stood before Pharaoh he exclaimed, "Few and evil have been the days *of my pilgrimage.*" What made him use that word "pilgrimage"? Why, because upon his mind there was always the idea of his being a pilgrim. He had been literally so during the dearly part of his life, wandering hither and thither; and now, though he has been seventeen years in Goshen, he keeps the old staff, and he leans on it to show that he had always been a pilgrim and a sojourner like his fathers, and that he was so still. While he leans on that staff he talks to Joseph, and he says, "Do not let my bones lie here. I have come hither in the providence of God, but I do not belong here. This staff indicates that I am only a sojourner here, and want to be gone. I am in Egypt, but I am not of it. Take my bones away. Do not let them lie here, for if they do, my sons and daughters will mingle with the Egyptians, and that must not be, for we are a distinct nation. God has chosen us for himself, and we must keep separate. To make my children see this, lo, here I die with my pilgrim staff in my hand."

Now, Christian brother, I want you to live in the same spirit, feeling that this is not your rest nor your native country. There is nothing here that is worthy of you. Your home is yonder, on the other side the desert, where God has mapped out your portion. Christ has gone to prepare your place, and it would ill become you to have no desires for it. The longer you live the more let this thought grow upon you: "Give me my staff. I must be gone. Poor world, thou art no rest for me; I am not of thy children, I am an alien and a stranger. My citizenship is in heaven, I take my share in Egypt's politics and Egypt's labor, aye, and in Egypt's griefs, but I am no Egyptian, I am a stranger bound for another land." Worship on the top of your staff, and sing—

> A scrip on my back, and a staff in my hand,
> I march on in haste through an enemy's land;
> There is nothing on earth which can tempt me to stay,
> My staff is the emblem of 'up and away'.

Singular enough is it that each descendant of Jacob came to worship on the top of his staff at last, for on the paschal supper night, when the blood was sprinkled on the lintel and the side posts, they each one ate the lamb with their loins girt and with a staff in his hand. The supper was a festival of worship, and they ate it each one leaning on his staff, as those that were in haste to leave home for a pilgrimage through the wilderness.

My dear hearers, this advice does not apply to all of you, for you are not all Jacobs, nor do you belong to the believing seed. I cannot bid you take your staff, for if you were to take your staff and start off, where would you go? You have no portion in the next world, no promised land, no Canaan flowing with milk and honey. Whither will you go? You must be banished from the presence of the Lord, and from the glory of his power. Alas for you! You cannot worship, for you know not God; you cannot bless others, for you have not been blessed yourselves. May the Lord bring you to his dear Son Jesus Christ, and lead you to put your trust in him, and then I shall hope that being saved you will by faith imitate Jacob, and both bless men, worship God, and wait with your staff in your hand, ready to journey to the eternal rest.

5

JOSEPH

A Miniature Portrait

"The Lord was with Joseph" (Gen. 39:2).

SCRIPTURE frequently sums up a man's life in a single sentence. Here is the biography of Joseph sketched by inspiration: "God was with him," so Stephen testified in his famous speech recorded in Acts 7:9. Holy Scripture excels in this kind of full-length miniature painting. As Michelangelo is said to have drawn a portrait with a single stroke of his crayon, so the Spirit of God sketches a man to the life in a single sentence. "The Lord was with Joseph."

Observe, however, that the portraits of Scripture give us not only the outer, but the inner life of the man. Man looketh at the outward appearance, but the Lord looketh upon the heart; and so the Scriptural descriptions of men are not of their visible life alone, but of their spiritual life. Here we have Joseph as God saw him, the real Joseph. Externally it did not always appear that God was with him, for he did not always seem to be a prosperous man; but when you come to look into the inmost soul of this servant of God, you see his true likeness—he lived in communion with the Most High, and God blessed him: "The Lord was with Joseph, and he was a prosperous man." It is often thought wise, in writing a man's life, to suppress certain matters: this may be prudent if the design be to guard a reputation, but it is scarcely truthful. The Spirit of God does not suppress the faults even of those whom we most admire, but writes them fully, like the Spirit of truth, as he is. So here, the Spirit is not looking so much at Joseph as a favorite child, or an Egyptian prime minister, as at the innermost and truest Joseph, and therefore he thus describes him, "the Lord was with Joseph."

This striking likeness of Joseph strongly reminds us of our Master and Lord, that greater Joseph, who is Lord over all the world for the sake of Israel. Peter, in his sermon to the household of Cornelius, said of our Lord that he "went about doing good, and healing all that were oppressed of the devil; for *God was with him*." Exactly what had been said of Joseph. It is wonderful that the same words should describe both Jesus and Joseph, the perfect Savior and the imperfect patriarch. When you and I are perfected in grace, we shall wear the image of Christ, and that which will describe Christ will also describe us. Those who live with Jesus will be transformed by his fellowship till they become like him. To my mind, it is very beautiful to see the resemblance between the first-born and the rest of the family, between the great typical man, the Second Adam, and all those men who are quickened into his life, and are one with him.

This having the Lord with us is the inheritance of all the saints; for what is the Apostolic benediction in the Epistles but a desire that the triune God may be with us? To the church in Rome Paul saith, "Now the God of peace be with you all." To the church in Corinth he writes, "The grace of the Lord Jesus Christ, and the love of God, and the communion of the Holy Ghost be with you all. Amen." To the Thessalonians he saith, "The Lord be with you all." Did not our glorious Lord say, "Lo, I am with you alway, even unto the end of the world"? How better could I salute you this morning than in the words of Boaz to the reapers, "The Lord be with you"? What kinder answer could you give me than "The Lord bless thee"?

First, we will run over Joseph's life, and note THE FACT: "The Lord was with Joseph." God was gracious to Joseph as *a child*. His father loved him because he was the son of his old age, and also because of the gracious qualities which he saw in him. Before he was seventeen years of age, God had spoken with him in dreams and visions of the night, of which we read that "his brethren envied him; but his father observed the saying." Dear young people, it may be that God will not appear to you in dreams, but he has other ways of speaking to his young Samuels. You remember he said, "Samuel, Samuel," and the beloved child answered, "Speak, Lord, for thy servant heareth." May you answer in the same manner to the call of God by his word. It was the happy privilege of some of us before we had left boyhood and girlhood to have received gracious communications from God: he led us to repentance, he led us to faith in Christ, and he revealed his love in our hearts before we had left the schoolroom and the playground. They begin well who begin early with Christ: he will be with us to the end if we are with him at the beginning. If Joseph had not been a godly boy he might never have been a gracious man: grace made him to differ from his brothers in youth, and he remained their superior all his days. If we are gracious while we are yet children we may be sure that the Lord will be gracious to us even should we live to an old age, and see our children's children. Early piety is likely to be eminent piety.

"The Lord was with Joseph" when Joseph was at home, and he did not desert him when he was sent away from his dear father and his beloved home and was sold for *a slave*. Bitter is the lot of a slave in any country, and it was worst of all in those early days. We are told by Stephen that the patriarchs, moved with envy, sold Joseph into Egypt, but the Lord was with him; even when he was being sold the Lord was with Joseph. It must have been a very dreadful journey for him across the desert, urged onward by those rough Ishmaelites, probably traveling in a gang. This delicate child of an indulgent father, who had been clothed with a princely garment of many colors, must now wear the garb of a slave, and march in the hot sun across the burning sand; but never was captive more submissive under cruel treatment, he endured as seeing him who is invisible; his heart was sustained by a deep confidence in the God of his father Jacob, for "Jehovah was with him." I think I see him in the slave market exposed for sale. We have heard with what trembling anxiety the slave peers into the faces of those who are about to buy. Will he get a good master? Will one purchase him who will treat him like a man, or one who will use him worse than a brute? "The Lord was with Joseph" as he stood there to be sold, and he fell into good hands. When he was taken away to his master's house, and the various duties of his service were allotted to him, "the Lord was with Joseph." The house of the Egyptian had never been so pure, so honest, so honored before. Beneath Joseph's charge it was secretly the temple of his devotions, and manifestly the abode of comfort and confidence. That Hebrew slave had a glory of character about him, which all perceived, and especially his master, for we read—"His master saw that the Lord was with him, and that the Lord made all that he did to prosper in his hand. And Joseph found grace in his sight, and he served him: and he made him overseer over his house, and all that he had he put into his hand. And it came to pass from the time that he had made him overseer in his house, and over all that he had, that the Lord blessed the Egyptian's house for Joseph's sake; and the blessing of the Lord was upon all that he had in the house and in the field." Joseph's diligence, integrity, and gentleness won upon his master, as well they might. O that all of you who are Christian servants would imitate Joseph in this, and so behave yourselves that all around you may see that the Lord is with you.

Then came a crisis in his history, the time of testing. We see Joseph *tried by a temptation* in which, alas, so many perish. He was attacked in a point at which youth is peculiarly vulnerable. His comely person made him the object of unholy solicitations from one upon whose goodwill his comfort greatly depended, and had it not been that the Lord was with him he must have fallen. The mass of mankind would scarcely have blamed him had he sinned: they would have cast the crime upon the tempter, and excused the frailty of youth. I say not so; God forbid I should; for in acts of uncleanness neither of the transgressors may be excused; but God was with Joseph, and he did not slide when set in slippery places. Thus he escaped that deep pit into which the abhorred of the Lord do fall. He was rescued from the snare of the strange woman, of whom Solomon has said, "She hath cast down many wounded; yea, many strong men have been slain by her. Her house is the way to hell, going down to the chambers of death." Slavery itself was a small calamity compared with that which would have happened to young Joseph had he been enslaved by wicked passions. Happily, the Lord was with him, and enabled him to overcome the tempter with the question, "How can I do this great wickedness, and sin against God?" He fled. That flight was the truest display of courage. It is the only way of victory in sins of the flesh. The Apostle says, "Flee youthful lusts which war against the soul."

The scene shifts again, and he who had been first a favored child at home, and then a slave, and then a tempted one, now becomes *a prisoner*. The prisons of Egypt were, doubtless, as horrible as all such places were in the olden times, and here is Joseph in the noisome dungeon. He evidently felt his imprisonment very much, for we are told in the Psalms that "the iron entered into his soul." He felt it a cruel thing to be under such a slander, and to suffer for his innocence. A young man so pure, so chaste, must have felt it to be sharper than a whip of scorpions to be accused as he was; yet as he sat down in the gloom of his cell, the Lord was with him. The degradation of a prison had not deprived him of his divine companion. Blessed be the name of the Lord, he does not forsake his people when they are in disgrace: nay, he is more pleasant with them when they are falsely accused than at any other time, and he cheers them in their low estate. God was with him, and very soon the kindly manners, the gentleness, the activity, the truthfulness, the industry of Joseph had won upon the keeper of the prison, so that Joseph rose again to the top, and was the overseer of the prison. Like a cork, which you may push down, but it is sure to come up again, so was Joseph: he must swim, he could not drown, the Lord was with him. In the little kingdom of the prison Joseph reigned, for "God was with him."

He will rise higher than that, however, when opportunity arises for a display of *prophetic power*. Two of those under his charge appeared to be despondent one morning, and with his usual gentleness he asked, "Wherefore look ye so sadly today?" He was always kindly and sympathetic, and so they told him their dreams, and he interpreted them as the events actually fell out. But why did he interpret dreams? It was because God was with him. He tells them there and then that "interpretations belong unto God." It was not that he had knowledge of an occult art, or was clever at guessing, but the Spirit of God rested upon him, and so he understood the secrets veiled beneath the dreams. This led to further steps, for after having been tried from seventeen to thirty, after having served thirteen years' apprenticeship to sorrow, he came to stand *before Pharaoh*, and God is with him there. You can see that he is inwardly upheld, for the Hebrew youth stands boldly forth and talks of God in an idolatrous court. Pharaoh believed in multitudes of gods: he worshiped the crocodile, the ibis, the bull, and all manner of things, even down to leeks and onions, so that one said of the Egyptians, "Happy people, whose gods grow in their own gardens"; but Joseph was not ashamed to speak of his God as the only living and true God. He said, "What God is about to do, he showeth unto Pharaoh." Calmly, and in a dignified manner, he unravels the dream, and explains it all to Pharaoh, disclaiming, however, all credit for wisdom. He says, "It is not in me: God shall give Pharaoh an answer of peace." God was with him indeed.

Joseph was made *ruler* over all Egypt, and God was with him. Well did the king say, "Can we find such a man as this is in whom the Spirit of God is?" His policy in storing up corn in the plenteous years succeeded admirably, for God was evidently working by him to preserve the human race from extinction by famine. His whole system, if looked at as executed in the interest of Pharaoh, his master, was beyond measure sensible and successful. He was not the servant of the Egyptians: Pharaoh had promoted him, and Pharaoh he enriched, and at the same time saved a nation from hunger.

God was with him in bringing down his father and the family into Egypt, and locating them in Goshen, and with him till he himself came to die, when he "took an oath of the children of Israel, saying God will surely visit you, and ye shall carry up my bones from hence." The Lord was with him, and kept him faithful to the covenant, and the covenanted race, even to the close of a long life of 110 years. He died faithful to the close to the God of his fathers, for he would not be numbered with Egypt, with all its learning, and all its wealth; he chose to be accounted an Israelite, and to share with the chosen race, whatever their fortunes might be. He, like the rest of the patriarchs, died in faith, looking for the promised inheritance, and for its sake renouncing the riches and glories of the world, for the Lord was with him.

We shall next review THE EVIDENCE OF THE FACT that God was with him. What is the evidence that the Lord was with Joseph? The first evidence of it is this: *he was always under the influence of the divine presence*, and lived in the enjoyment of it. I shall not need to quote the instances—all of them, at any rate—for everywhere, whenever Joseph's heart speaks, he lets you know that he is conscious that God is with him. Take him under temptation especially. Oh, what a mercy it was for him that he was a God-fearing man! "How can I do this great wickedness and sin against *Potiphar?*" No. Yet he would have sinned against Potiphar, who had been a kindly master to him. Does he say, "How shall I do this great wickedness, and sin against *this woman?*" for it would have been a sin against her. No; but just as David said, "Against thee, thee only, have I sinned, and done this evil in thy sight," making the main point and consideration to be sin against God, so did Joseph, as he fled from the seducer, argue thus—"How can I do this great wickedness, and sin *against God?*" Oh, if you and I always felt that God was near, looking steadily upon us, we should not dare to sin. The presence of a superior often checks a man from doing what else he might have ventured on, and the presence of God, if it were realized, would be a perpetual barrier against temptation, and would keep us steadfast in holiness. When

Joseph afterwards at any time spoke of God, when God helped him not only to stand against temptation but to do any service, you will notice how he always ascribes it to God. He will not interpret Pharaoh's dream without first telling him, "It is not in me: God hath showed Pharaoh what he is about to do." He was conscious of the presence of God when he stood before the great monarch as when he refused that sinful woman. It was the same in his domestic life. Let me read out of his family register. "And unto Joseph were born two sons before the years of famine came, which Asenath the daughter of Poti-pherah priest of On bare unto him. And Joseph called the name of the firstborn Manasseh: For God, said he, hath made me forget all my toil, and all my father's house. And the name of the second called he Ephraim: For God hath caused me to be fruitful in the land of my affliction." When his aged father said to him, "Who are these?" he replied very beautifully, "They are my sons, whom God hath given me in this place."

I am afraid that we do not habitually talk in this fashion, but Joseph did. Without the slightest affectation he spoke out of his heart, under a sense of the divine presence and working. How like he is in this to our divine Lord! I cannot help speaking of it. If there is any good thing more marked about our Lord Jesus than another it is his sense of the divine presence. You see it when he is a child: "Knew ye not that I must be about my Father's business?" You hear it in the words, "I am not alone, because the Father is with me"; and again, "I know that thou hearest me always." You perceive it forcibly in the last moment of his earthly life, when the sharpest pang that tortures him is that which makes him cry, "My God, my God, why has thou forsaken me?" The presence of God was everything to Christ as it was to Joseph. Now, if you and I set the Lord always before us, if our soul dwells in God, depend upon it, God is with us. There is no mistake about it.

The next evidence is this: God was certainly with Joseph because *he was pure in heart.* "Blessed are the pure in heart, for they shall see God"; no other can do so. God will not manifest himself to those whose hearts are unclean. What fellowship hath light with darkness, or what concord hath Christ with Belial? The intense purity of Joseph was a proof that the thrice holy God was ever with him. His presence sheds an atmosphere of holiness around the heart in which he dwells.

The next evidence in Joseph's case was *the diligence with which he exercised himself wherever he was.* God was with Joseph, and therefore the man of God hardly cared as to the outward circumstances of his position, but began at once to work that which is good. He was in the pit: yes, but the Lord was with Joseph, and the pit was not horrible to him: he pleaded with his brothers, and although they would not hear, he did his duty in warning them of their crime. He was carried captive of the Ishmaelites; but in the caravan he was safe, for God was with him. When he came to be a slave in Potiphar's house, the Lord was with him, and he was a prosperous man; the change of scene was not a change of his dearest company. He did not strike an attitude, and make a display of his grand intentions, but he went to work where he was, and performed ordinary duties with great heartiness, for the Lord was with him. Many would have said, "I have been unrighteously sold for a slave. I ought not to be here, and I am not bound to perform any duties to Potiphar: rightfully I am a free man, as free as Potiphar, and I shall not work for him for nothing." No, the Lord was with him, and therefore he applied himself to that which lay next to hand, and went to work with a will.

The Lord was with Joseph none-the-less when he was cast into the prison. He knew God was with him in prison, and therefore he did not sit down sullenly in his sorrow, but he bestirred himself to make the best of his afflicted condition. He did not mourn and moan, and spend his time in writing petitions to Potiphar, or making appeals to Potiphar. He set himself to be of service to his fellow prisoners and the warders, and very soon he was to the front again, for "The Lord was with him." When he came to be exalted, and Pharaoh made him to be ruler over Egypt, notice what he did. He did not strut about, or take his ease at court; he did not stop to enjoy his honors in peace, and leave others to do the business, but he set to his work personally and at once. Read chapter 41:45: "And Joseph went out over all the land of Egypt." Then read the next verse: "And Joseph went out from the presence of Pharaoh, and went throughout all the land of Egypt." No sooner did he get the office than he gave himself to the execution of it, personally inspecting the whole country. Many are so worn out by their toils in getting a place that they have no strength left for performing its duties. They do as little as they can for the money, upon the theory that if you are too energetic, your labors will be too cheap. Joseph, however, was not of that sort, for no sooner was he made commissioner general of Egypt, than he was up to his eyes in the task of building storehouses, and gathering up grain to fill them. By his wonderful economic policy he supplied the people in the time of famine, and in the process the power of Pharaoh was greatly strengthened. The Lord was with him, therefore, he did not think of the honor to which he had been promoted, but of the responsibility which had been laid upon him, and he gave himself wholly to his great work.

But notice again, God was with Joseph, and *that made him tender and sympathetic*. Some men who are prompt enough in business are rough, coarse, hard; but no so Joseph. His tenderness distinguishes him; he is full of loving consideration. When he had prisoners in his charge he did not treat them roughly, but with much consideration. He watched their countenances, inquired into their troubles, and was willing to do all in his power for them. This was one secret of his success in life; he was everybody's friend. He who is willing to be the servant of all, the same shall be the chief of all.

Perhaps you will object to this, that Joseph seemed for a while to afflict and tantalize his brothers. By no means. He was seeking their good. The love he bore to them was wise and prudent. God, who is far more loving than Joseph, frequently afflicts us to bring us to repentance, and to heal us of many evils. Joseph wished to bring his brethren into a right state of heart, and he succeeded in it, though the process was more painful to him than to them. At last he could not restrain himself, but burst into weeping before them all, for there was a big loving heart under the Egyptian garb of Joseph. He loved with all his soul, and so will every man who has God with him, for "God is love." If you do not love, God is not with you. If you go through the world selfish and morose, bitter, suspicious, bigoted, hard, the devil is with you, God is not; for where God is he expands the spirit, he causes us to love all mankind with the love of benevolence, and he makes us take a sweet complacency in the chosen brotherhood of Israel, so that we especially delight to do good to all those who are of the household of faith.

Another mark of God's presence with Joseph is *his great wisdom*. He did everything as it ought to be done. You can scarcely alter anything in Joseph's life to improve it, and I think if I admire his wisdom in one thing more than another it is in his wonderful silence. It is easy to talk, comparatively easy to talk well, but to be quiet is the difficulty. He never said a word, that I can learn, about Potiphar's wife. It seemed necessary to his own defense, but the would not accuse the woman; he let judgment go by default, and left her to her own conscience and her husband's cooler consideration. This showed great power; it is hard for a man to compress his lips, saying nothing when his character is at stake. So eloquent was Joseph in his silence that there is not a word of complaint throughout the whole record of his life. We cannot say that of all the Bible saints, for many of them complained bitterly, indeed we have whole books of lamentations. We do not condemn those who did complain, but we greatly admire those who, like sheep before the shearers, were dumb. The iron entered into his soul, but *he* does not tell us so; we look to the Psalms for that information; he bore in calm resignation all the great Father's will. When his brothers stood before him, the cruel men who sold him, he did not upbraid them, but he comforted them, saying, "Now therefore be not grieved, nor angry with your selves, that ye sold me hither: for God did send me before you to preserve life." Making sweet excuse for them, he said, "And God sent me before you to preserve you a posterity in the earth, and to save yourselves by a great deliverance. So now it was not you that sent me hither, but God."

How different from the spirit of those people who pry about, seeking to discover faults, and when an imperfection is marked, they cry, "Look! Do you see that? I told you so. These good men are no better than they should be." Yes, it may be true that there are spots in the sun, but there are greater spots in your eyes or you would see more of the light. Those who see faults so readily have plenty of their own. May God make us blind to the faults of his people, sooner than allow us to have a lynx eye for their flaws and an inventive faculty to ascribe ill motives to them. I wish we were as wisely silent as Joseph was. We may often repent of speech, but I think very seldom of silence. You may complain, and be justified in the complaint, but you will have far more glory if you do not complain.

"God was with him," and this is the last evidence I give of it, that *he was kept faithful to the covenant*, faithful to Israel and to Israel's God right through. Pharaoh gave him in marriage the daughter of a priest; and the priests were the highest class throughout Egypt, and Joseph was thus promoted to be of the nobility by marriage, as well as to be at the head of all the nobility by office. They cried before him, "Bow the knee," and everyone honored him throughout all the land of Egypt. Yet he would not be an Egyptian: he was an Israelite still, and his good old father, when he came down into Egypt, found him one of the family in heart and soul. His father's blessing was greatly prized by him, and he obtained it for himself and for his sons.

I notice with much pain that many professors who prosper in this world have not God with them, for they turn into Egyptians: they do not now care for the simple worship of God's people, but they sigh for something more showy and more respectable. They want society, and so they seek out a fashionable church, and swallow their principles. They lay it all upon their children, for who can expect young ladies and gentlemen to attend an ordinary meeting-house, where such low people go? For the sake of the young people they are bound to mix with society, and so they leave their principles, their people, and their God. Off they go to Egypt, shoals of them, I have seen it, and shall see it again. If some of you get rich I dare say you will do the same; it seems to be the way of men. As soon as a professor prospers in the world he is ashamed of the truth he once loved. Verily, I say unto you, instead of their being ashamed of us, we have good reason to be ashamed of them, for it is to their disgrace that they cannot be content to associate with God's chosen because they happen to be poor, and perhaps illiterate. Joseph stuck to his people and to their God: though he must live in Egypt, he will not be an Egyptian; he will not even leave his dead body to lie in an Egyptian pyramid. The Egyptians built a costly tomb for Joseph: it stands to this day, but his body is not there. "I charge you," says he, "take my bones with you; for I do not belong to Egypt, my place is in the land of promise." "He gave commandment concerning his bones." Let others do as they will; as for me, my lot is cast with those who follow the Lord fully.

Thirdly, let us observe, THE RESULT OF GOD'S BEING WITH JOSEPH. The result was that "he was a prosperous man"; but notice that, although the Lord was with Joseph, *it did not screen him from hatred.* The Lord was with him, but his brethren hated him. Aye, and if the Lord loves a man, the world will spite him. We know that we are God's children, because the adversaries of God are our adversaries. Furthermore, "The Lord was with Joseph," but it did not screen him from *temptation* of the worst kind: it did not prevent his mistress casting her wicked eyes upon him. The best of men may be tempted to the worst of crimes. The presence of God did not screen him from *slander:* the base woman accused him of outrageous wickedness, and God permitted Potiphar to believe her. You and I would have said, "If the Lord be with us how can this evil happen to us?" Ah, but the Lord was with him, and yet he was a slandered man. Nay, the divine presence did not screen him from *pain:*

he sat in prison wearing fetters till the iron entered into his soul, and yet "The Lord was with him." That presence did not save him from *disappointment*. He said to the butler, "Think of me when it is well with thee"; but the butler altogether forgot him. Everything may seem to go against you, and yet God may be with you. The Lord does not promise you that you shall have what looks like prosperity, but you shall have what is real prosperity in the best sense.

Now, what did God's being with Joseph do for him? First, *it saved him from gross sin*. He flees, he shuts his ears: he flees and conquers; for God is with him. O young friend, if God is with you in the hour of temptation, you will want no better, no grander result than to remain perfectly pure, with garments unspotted by the flesh.

God was with him, and the next result was *it enabled him to act grandly*. Wherever he is he does the right thing, does it splendidly. If he is a slave his master finds that he never had such a servant before; if he is in prison, those dungeons were never charmed by the presence of such a ministering angel before; if he is exalted to be with Pharaoh, Pharaoh never had such a Chancellor of the Exchequer in Egypt before, never was Egyptian finance so prosperous.

In such a manner did God help Joseph that he was enabled *to fulfill a glorious destiny*. The human race had died of famine if Joseph's foresight had not laid by in store the produce of the seven plenteous years, for there was a famine over all lands. It was no mean position for the young Hebrew to occupy, to be manager of the commissariat of the whole known world. If God be with us we shall fulfill a noble destiny too. It may not be so widely known, so visible to human eye, but life is always ennobled by the presence of God.

Also *it gave him a very happy life*, for taking the life of Joseph all through, it is an enviable one. Nobody would think of putting him down among the miserable. If we had to make a selection of unhappy men, we certainly should not think of Joseph. No, it was a great life and a happy life; and such will yours be if God be with you.

And, to finish, God gave Joseph and his family *a double portion in Israel*, which never happened to any other of the twelve sons of Jacob. Jacob said, "And now thy two sons, Ephraim and Manasseh, which were born unto thee in the land of Egypt before I came unto thee in Egypt are mine; as Reuben and Simeon they shall be mine," thus making them into a tribe each. Ephraim and Manasseh each stood at the head of a tribe as if they had been actually sons of Jacob. Levi is taken out of the twelve, and provision is made for the Levites as servants of God, and then Ephraim and Manasseh are put in, so that Joseph's house figures twice among the twelve. Those who begin early with God, and stand fast to the end, and hold to God both in trouble and prosperity, shall see their children brought to the Lord, and in their children they shall possess the double, yea, the Lord shall render unto them double for all they may lose in honor for his name's sake. Who is willing to suffer with them that he may reign with them? Who is willing to cast the riches of Egypt behind his back that he may have a double portion in the promised land, the land flowing with milk and honey? I think I hear some of you say, "Here I am, sir. I shall be glad enough to share with God's people, be it what it may." Carry Christ's cross and you shall wear Christ's crown.

6

MOSES

His Noble Decision

"By faith Moses, when he was come to years, refused to be called the son of Pharaoh's daughter; choosing rather to suffer affliction with the people of God, than to enjoy the pleasures of sin for a season; esteeming the reproach of Christ greater riches than the treasures in Egypt: for he had respect unto the recompense of the reward" (Heb. 11:24, 25, 26).

MOSES belonged to the noblest order of men, but he was saved by faith alone, even by the same faith which saved Rahab. This faith moved him to the faithful service of God and to a self-denial unparalleled. My earnest prayer is that you who are moral, amiable, and educated, may see in the action of Moses an example for yourselves. No longer despise a life of faith in God. It is the one thing which you lack, the one thing above all others needful. Are ye young men of high position? Such was Moses. Are ye men of spotless character? Such also was he. Are ye now in a position where to follow out conscience will cost you dear? Moses endured as seeing him who is invisible, and though for a while a loser he is now an eternal gainer by the loss. May the Spirit of God incline you to follow in the path of faith, virtue, and honor, where you see such a man as Moses leading the way.

And first let us observe THE DECIDED ACTION OF MOSES. "When he had come to years he refused to be called the son of Pharaoh's daughter." We need not narrate the stories which are told by Josephus and other ancient writers with regard to the early days of Moses, such as, for instance, his taking the crown of Pharaoh and trampling upon it. These things may be true; it is equally possible that they are pure fiction.

The Spirit of God has certainly taken no notice of them in Holy Scripture, and what he does not think worth recording we need not think worth considering. Nor shall I more than hint at answers to the question why it was that Moses remained no less than forty years in the court of Pharaoh, and doubtless during that time was called "the son of Pharaoh's daughter," and, if he did not enjoy the pleasures of sin, at any rate had his share in the treasures of Egypt. It is just possible that he was not a converted man up to the age of forty. Probably during his early days he was to all intents and purposes and Egyptian, any eager student, a great proficient in Egyptian wisdom, and also, as Stephen tells us in the Acts, "a man mighty in words and in deeds." During those early days he was familiar with philosophers and warriors, and perhaps in his engrossing pursuits he forgot his nationality. We see the hand of God in his being forty years in the court of Pharaoh; whatever of evil or indecision in him may have kept him there we see the good result which God brought out of it, for he became by his experience and observation the better able to rule a nation, and a fitter instrument in the hand of God for fashioning the Israelitish state into its appointed form.

Perhaps during the forty years he had been trying to do what a great many are aiming at just now, he was trying whether he could not serve God and remain the son of Pharaoh's daughter too. Perhaps he thought he could share the treasures of Egypt and yet bear testimony with Israel. He would be known as a companion of the priests of Isis and Osiris, and yet at the same time would bear honest witness for Jehovah. If he did not attempt this impossibility others in all ages have done so. It may be he quieted himself by saying that he had such remarkable opportunities for usefulness that he did not like to throw them up by becoming identified with the Israelitish dissenters of the period. An open avowal of his private sentiments would shut him out from good society, and especially from the court, where it was very evident that his influence was great and beneficial. It is just possible that the very feeling which still keeps so many good people in a wrong place may have operated upon Moses till he was forty years of age; but then, having reached the prime of his manhood, and having come under the influence of faith, he broke away from the ensnaring temptation, as I trust many of our worthy brethren will ere long be able to do. If when Moses was a child he spoke as a child, and thought as a child, when he became a man he put away his childish ideas of compromise; if, when he was a young man, he thought he might conceal a part of the truth, and so might hold his position, when he came to ripe years enough to know what the truth fully was he scorned all compromise and came out boldly as the servant of the living God.

The Spirit of God directs our eye to the time when Moses came to years; that is to say, when his first forty years of life were over; then, without any hesitation he refused to be called the son of Pharaoh's daughter, and took his part with the despised people of God.

I beg you to consider first, *who he was that did this.* He was a man of education, for he was learned in all the wisdom of the Egyptians. Somebody says he does not suppose the wisdom of the Egyptians was anything very great. No, and the wisdom of the English is not much greater. Future ages will laugh as much at the wisdom of the English as we now laugh at the wisdom of the Egyptians. The human wisdom of one age is the folly of the next. Philosophy, so called, what is it but the concealment of ignorance under hard names, and the arrangement of mere guesses into elaborate theories? In comparison with the eternal light of God's word all the knowledge of men is "not light but darkness visible." Men of education, as a rule, are not ready to acknowledge the living God. Philosophy in its self-conceit despises the infallible revelation of the Infinite, and will not come to the light lest it be reproved. In all ages, when a man has considered himself to be wise, he has almost invariably contemned the Infinite wisdom. Had he been truly wise, he would have humbly bowed before the Lord of all, but being only nominally so he said, "Who is the Lord?" Not many great men after the flesh, not many mighty are chosen. Did not our Lord himself say it, and his word is for all time, "I thank thee, O Father, Lord of heaven and earth, that thou hast hid these things from the wise and prudent, and hast revealed them unto babes"? But yet, sometimes a man of education like Moses, is led by the blessing of heaven to take the side of truth, and of the right, and when it is so, let the Lord be magnified!

Beside being a man of education, he was *a person of high rank.* He had been adopted by Thermuthis, the daughter of Pharaoh, and it is possible, though we cannot be sure of it, that he was the next heir by adoption to the Egyptian crown. It is said that the King of Egypt had no other child, and that his daughter had no son, and that Moses would, therefore, have become the King of Egypt. Yet, great as he was, and mighty at court, he joined with the oppressed people of God. May God grant that we may see many eminent men bravely standing up for God and for his truth, and repudiating the religion of men; but if they do, it will be a miracle of mercy indeed, for few of the great ones have ever done so. Here and there in heaven may be found a king, and here and there in the church may be found one who wears a coronet and prays; but how hardly shall they that have riches enter into the kingdom of heaven? When they do so God be thanked for it.

In addition to this, remember that Moses was *a man of great ability*. We have evidence of that in the administrative skill with which he managed the affairs of Israel in the wilderness; for though he was inspired of God, yet his own natural ability was not superseded but directed. He was a poet: "Then sung Moses and the children of Israel this song unto the Lord." That memorable poem at the Red Sea is a masterly ode, and proves the incomparable ability of the writer. The ninetieth Psalm also shows the range of his poetic powers. He was both prophet, priest, and king in the midst of Israel, and a man second to no man save that Man who was more than man. No other man I know of comes so near in the glory of his character to Christ as Moses does, so that we find the two names linked together in the praise of heaven, "They sung the song of Moses the servant of God, and of the Lamb." Thus you see he was a truly eminent man, yet he cast in his lot with God's people. It is not many that will do this, for the Lord has usually chosen the weak things to confound the mighty, and the things that are not to bring to naught the things that are, that no flesh should glory in his presence. Yet here he, who will have mercy on whom he will have mercy, took this great man, this wise man, and gave him grace to be decided in the service of his God. Should I address such a one I would anxiously pray that a voice from the excellent glory may call him forth to the same clear line of action.

Next, consider *what sort of society Moses felt compelled to leave*. In coming forth from Pharaoh's court he must separate from all the courtiers and men of high degree, some of whom may have been very estimable people. There is always a charm about the society of the great, but every bond was severed by the resolute spirit of Moses. I do not doubt that being learned in all the wisdom of Egypt, such a man as Moses would be always welcome in the various circles of science; but he relinquished all his honors among the *élite* of learning to bear the reproach of Christ. Neither great men or learned men could hold him when his conscience had once pointed out the path. Be sure, also, that he had to tear himself away from many a friend. In the course of forty years one would suppose he had formed associations that were very dear and tender, but to the regret of many he associated himself with the unpopular party, whom the king sought to crush, and therefore no courtier could henceforth acknowledge him. For forty years he lived in the solitude of the desert, and he only returned to smite the land of Egypt with plague, so that his separation from all his former friendships must have been complete. But, O true-hearted spirit, should it break every fond connection, should it tear thy soul away from all thou lovest, if thy God requires it, let the sacrifice be made at once. If thy faith hath shown thee that to occupy thy present position involves complicity with error or sin, then break away, by God's help, without further parley. Jesus left the angels of heaven for your sake; can you not leave the best of company for his sake?

But I marvel most at Moses when I consider not only who he was and the company he had to forego, but *the persons with whom he must associate,* for in truth the followers of the true God were not, in their own persons, a lovable people at that time. Moses was willing to take upon himself the reproach of Christ and to bear the affliction of God's people when, I venture to observe again, there was nothing very attractive in the people themselves. They were wretchedly poor, they were scattered throughout all the land as mere drudges, engaged in brickmaking, and this brickmaking, which was imposed upon them for the very purpose of breaking down their spirit, had done its work all too well. They were utterly spiritless, they possessed no leaders, and were not prepared to have followed them if they had arisen. When Moses, having espoused their cause, informed them that God had sent him they received him at first, but when the prophet's first action prompted Pharaoh to double their toil by an enactment that they should not be supplied with straw, they upbraided Moses at once; even as forty years before, when he interfered in their quarrels, one of them said, "Wilt thou slay me as thou didst the Egyptian yesterday?" They were literally a herd of slaves, broken down, crushed and depressed. It is one of the worst things about slavery that it unmans men and unfits them even for generations for the full enjoyment of liberty. Even when slaves receive liberty we cannot expect them to act as those would do who were free born, for in slavery the iron enters into the very soul and binds the spirit. Thus it is clear that the Israelites were not very select company for the highly educated Moses to unite with: though a prince he must make common cause with the poor; though a free man he must mingle with slaves; though a man of education he must mix with ignorant people; though a man of spirit he must associate with spiritless serfs. How many would have said, "No, I cannot do that; I know what church I ought to unite with if I follow the Scriptures fully, and obey in all things my Lord's will; but then they are so poor, so illiterate, and their place of worship so far from being architecturally beautiful. Their preacher is a plain, blunt man, and they themselves are not refined. Scarce a dozen of the whole sect can keep a carriage; I should be shut out of society if I joined with them." Have we not heard this base reasoning till we are sick of it, and yet it operates widely upon this brainless, heartless generation. Are there none left who love truth even when she wears no trappings? Are there none who love the Gospel better than pomp and show? Where God raises up a Moses what cares he how poor his brethren may be? "They are God's people," says he, "and if they are very poor I must help them the more liberally. If they be oppressed and depressed, so much the more reason why I should come to their aid. If they loved God and his truth I am their fellow-soldier and will be at their side in the battle." I have no doubt Moses thought all this over, but his mind was made up, and he took his place promptly.

In addition to other matters, one mournful thing must be said of Israel, which must have cost Moses much pain. He found that among God's people there were some who brought no glory to God, and were very weak in their principles. He did not judge the whole body by the faults of some, but by their standards and their institutions: and he saw that the Israelites, with all their faults, were the people of God, while the Egyptians, with all their virtues, were not so. Now, it is for each one of us to try the spirits by the word of God, and then fearlessly to follow out our convictions. Where is Christ recognized as the head of the church? Where are the Scriptures really received as the rule of faith? Where are the doctrines of grace clearly believed? Where are the ordinances practiced as the Lord delivered them? For with that people will I go, their cause shall be my cause, their God shall be my God.

Consider now *what Moses left by siding with Israel.* He left honor—he "refused to be called the son of Pharaoh's daughter"; he left pleasure—for he refused to "enjoy the pleasures of sin for a season"; and, according to our Apostle, he left wealth as well, for in taking up the reproach of Christ he renounced "the treasures of Egypt." Very well, then, if it comes to this, if to follow God and to be obedient to him I have to lose my position in society and become a pariah; if I must abjure a thousand pleasures, and if I am deprived of emoluments and income, yet the demands of duty must be complied with. Martyrs gave their lives of old, are there none left who will give their livings? If there be true faith in a man's heart he will not deliberate which of the two to choose, beggary or compromise with error. He will esteem the reproach of Christ to be greater riches than the treasures of Egypt.

Consider yet once more *what Moses espoused* when he left the court. He espoused abounding trial, "choosing rather to suffer affliction with the people of God"; and he espoused reproach, for he "esteemed the reproach of Christ greater riches than the treasures of Egypt." O Moses, if you must needs join with Israel there is no present reward for you; you have nothing to gain but all to lose; you must do it out of pure principle, out of love to God, out of a full persuasion of the truth, for the tribes have no honors or wealth to bestow. You will receive affliction, and that is all. You will be called a fool, and people will think they have good reason for so doing. It is just the same today. If any man today will go without the camp to seek the Lord, if he go forth unto Christ without the gate, he must do it out of love to God and to his Christ, and for no other motive. When a fervent convert said to our Lord, "Lord, I will follow thee whithersoever thou goest," he received for answer, "Foxes have holes and birds of the air have nests, but I, the Son of Man, have not where to lay my head." To this hour truth offers no dowry but herself to those who will espouse her. Abuse, contempt, hard fare, ridicule, misrepresentation—these are the wages of consistency; and if better comes it is not to be reckoned on. If any man be of a noble enough spirit to love the truth for truth's sake, and God for God's sake, and Christ for Christ's sake, let him enlist with those of like mind; but if he seek anything over and above that, if he desire to be made famous, or to gain power, or to be well beneficed, he had better keep his place among the cowardly dirt-eaters who swarm around us. The church of God bribes no man. She has no mercenary rewards to proffer and would scorn to use them if she had. If to serve the Lord be not enough reward, let those who look for more go their selfish way: if heaven be not enough, let those who can despise it seek their heaven below.

Now, secondly, what was THE SOURCE OF MOSES' DECISION? Scripture says it was faith, otherwise some would insist upon it that it was the force of blood. "He was by birth an Israelite, and therefore," say they, "the instincts of nature prevailed." Our text assigns a very different reason. We know right well that the sons of godly parents are not led to adore the true God by reason of their birth. Grace does not run in the blood; sin may, but righteousness does not. It was faith, not blood, which impelled Moses in the way of truth. Neither was it eccentricity which led him to espouse the side which was oppressed. All his life through you cannot discover a trace of eccentricity in him: he was sober, steady, law-abiding; what if I say he was a *concentric* man, for his center was in the right place, and he moved according to the dictates of prudence. Not thus can his decision be accounted for. Neither was he hurried on by some sudden excitement when there burned within his soul fierce patriotic fires which made him more fervent than prudent. No, there may have been some haste in his slaying the Egyptian on the first occasion, but then he had forty more years to think it over, and yet he never repented his choice, but held on to the oppressed people of God, and still refused to think of himself as the son of Pharaoh's daughter.

What faith had he? First, he had *faith in Jehovah*. It is possible that Moses had seen the various gods of Egypt, even as we see them now in the drawings which have been copied from their temples and pyramids. We find there the sacred cat, the sacred ibis, the sacred crocodile, and all kinds of creatures which were reverenced as deities; and in addition there were hosts of strange idols, compounded of man, and beast, and bird, which stand in our museums to this day, and were once the objects of the idolatrous reverence of the Egyptians. Moses was weary of all this symbolism. He knew in his own heart that there was one God, one only God, and he would have nothing to do with Amun, Pithah, or Maut. Oh that God would give to men faith to know there is but one God, and that the one God is not to be worshiped with man-ordained rites and ceremonies, for he is "a Spirit, and they that worship him must worship him in spirit and in truth!"

The faith of Moses also *rested in Christ*. "Christ had not come," says one. Nay, but he was to come, and Moses looked to that coming one. He cast his eye through the ages that were to intervene, and he saw before him the Shiloh of whom dying Jacob sang. He knew the ancient promise which had been given to the fathers, that in the seed of Abraham, should all the nations of the earth be blessed; and he was willing, in order to share in the blessing, to take his part in the reproach. We shall never have a thorough faith in God unless we have also faith in Jesus Christ. Men have tried long, and tried hard, to worship the Father apart from the Son; but there stands it, and it always will be so: "No man cometh unto the Father but by me." You get away from the worship of the Father if you do not come through the mediation and atonement of the Son of God. Now, though Moses did not know concerning Christ all that is now revealed to us, yet he had faith in the coming Messiah, and that faith gave strength to his mind. Those are the men to suffer who have received Christ Jesus the Lord. If any man should ask me what made the Covenanters such heroes as they were; what made our Puritan forefathers fearless before their foes; what led the Reformers to protest and the martyrs to die; I would reply, it was faith in the Invisible God, coupled with faith in that dear Son of God who is God Incarnate. Believing in him they felt such love within their bosoms, that for love of him they could have died a thousand deaths.

But then, in addition to this, Moses had faith *in reference to God's people*. Upon that I have already touched. He knew that the Israelites were God's chosen, that Jehovah had made a covenant with them, that despite all their faults, God would not break his covenant with his own people, and he knew, therefore, that their cause was God's cause, and being God's cause it was the cause of right, the cause of truth. Oh, it is a grand thing when a man has such faith that he says, "It is nothing to me what other people do, or think, or believe; I shall act as God would have me. It is nothing to me what I am commanded to do by my fellow creatures, nothing to me what fashion says, nothing to me what my parents say, as far as religion is concerned; the truth is God's star, and I will follow wherever it may lead me. If it should make me a solitary man, if I should espouse opinions which no one else ever believed in, if I should have to go altogether outside the camp, and break away from every connection, all this shall be as immaterial to me as the small dust of the balance; but if a matter be true I will believe it, and I will propound it, and I will suffer for its promulgation; and if another doctrine be a lie I will not be friends with it, nay, not for a solitary moment; I will not enter into fellowship with falsehood, no, not for an hour. If a course be right and true, through floods and flames if Jesus leads me, I will pursue it." That seems to me to be the right spirit, but where do you find it nowadays? The modern spirit mutters, "We are all right, every one of us." He who says "yes" is right, and he who says "no" is also right.

You hear a man talk with mawkish sentimentality which he calls Christian charity. Such is the talk and cant of this present age, but I bear my witness that there is not truth in it, and I call upon every child of God to protest against it. There is truth somewhere, let us find it; the lie is not of the truth, let us abhor it. Surely truth is of some value to the sons of men, surely there must be something worth holding, something worth contending for, and something worth dying for; but it does not appear nowadays as if men thought so. May we have a respect for God's true church in the world which abides by the apostolic word and doctrine. Let us find it out, and join with it, and at its side fight for God and for his truth!

Once again, Moses had faith in the "recompense of the reward." He said thus within himself, "I must renounce much, and reckon to lose rank, position, and treasure; but I expect to be a gainer notwithstanding, for there will be a day when God shall judge the sons of men; I expect a judgment throne with its impartial balances, and I expect that those who serve God faithfully shall then turn out to have been the wise men and the right men, while those who truckled and bowed down to gain a present ease shall find that they missed eternity while they were snatching after time, and that they bartered heaven for a paltry mess of pottage." With this upon his mind, you could not persuade Moses that he ought to compromise, and must not be uncharitable, and ought not to judge other good people, but should be largeminded, and remember Pharaoh's daughter, and how kindly she had nurtured him, and consider what opportunities he had of doing good where he was; how he might befriend his poor brethren, what influence he might have over Pharaoh, how he might be the means of leading the princes and the people of Egypt in the right way, and perhaps God had raised him up on purpose to be there, who could tell, and so on, and so on, and so on—you know the Babylonian talk, for in these days you have all read or heard the plausible arguments of the deceivableness of unrighteousness, which in these last days teaches men to do evil that good may come. Moses cared for none of these things. He knew his duty, and did it, whatever might be the consequences. Every Christian man's duty is to believe the truth, and follow the truth, and leave results with God.

Thirdly, we are going to run over in our minds some of THE ARGUMENTS WHICH SUPPORTED MOSES in his decided course of following God.

The first argument would be, he saw clearly that God was God and therefore must keep his word, must bring his people up out of Egypt and give them a heritage. Now he said within himself, "I desire to be on the right side. God is almighty, God is all truthful, God is altogether just. I am on God's side, and being on God's side I will prove my truthfulness by leaving the other side altogether."

Then, secondly, we have it in the text that he perceived the pleasures of sin to be but for a season. He said to himself, "I may have but a short time to live, and even if I live to a good old age, life at the longest is still short; and where I come to the close of life what a miserable reflection it will be that I have had all my pleasure, it is all over, and now I have to appear before God as a traitorous Israelite who threw up his birthright for the sake of enjoying the pleasures of Egypt." Oh that men would measure everything in the scales of eternity! We shall be before the bar of God all of us in a few months or years, and then think you how shall we feel? One will say, "I never thought about religion at all," and another, "I thought about it, but I did not think enough to come to any decision upon it. I went the way the current went." Another will say, "I knew the truth well enough, but I could not bear the shame of it, they would have thought me fanatical if I had gone through with it." Another will say, "I halted between two opinions. I hardly thought I was justified in sacrificing my children's position for the sake of being out and out a follower of truth." What wretched reflections will come over men who have sold the Savior as Judas did! What wretched deathbeds must they who have been unfaithful to their consciences and untrue to their God!

But oh! with what composure will the believer look forward to another world! He will say, "By grace I am saved, and I bless God I could afford to be ridiculed, I could bear to be laughed at. I could lose that situation, I could be turned out of that farm, and could be called a fool, and yet it did not hurt me. I found solace in the society of Christ, I went to him about it all, and I found that to be reproached for Christ was a sweeter thing than to possess all the treasures of Egypt. Blessed be his name! I missed the pleasures of the world, but they were no miss to me. I was glad to miss them, for I found pleasure sweeter in the company of my Lord, and now there are pleasures to come which shall never end." O brethren, to be out and out for Christ, to go to the end with him, even though it involves the loss of all things, this will pay in the long run. It may bring upon you much disgrace for the present, but that will soon be over, and then comes the eternal reward.

And, then, again, he thought within himself that even the pleasures, which did last for a season, while they lasted were not equal to the pleasure of being reproached for Christ's sake. This ought also to strengthen us, that the worst of Christ is better than the best of the world, that even now we have more joy as Christians, if we are sincere, than we could possibly derive from the sins of the wicked.

We ought all of us to be ready to part with everything for Christ, and if we are not we are not his disciples. "Master, thou sayest a hard thing," says one. I say it yet again, for a greater Master has said it, "He that loveth son or daughter more than me is not worthy of me." "Unless a man forsake all that he has he cannot be my disciple." Jesus may not require you actually to leave anything, but you must be ready to leave everything if required.

We ought to abhor the very thought of obtaining honor in this world by concealing our sentiments or by making compromises. If there be a chance of your being highly esteemed by holding your tongue, speak at once and do not run the risk of winning such dishonorable honor.

We ought to take our place with those who truly follow God and the Scriptures, even if they are not altogether what we should like them to be. The place for an Israelite is with the Israelites, the place for a Christian man is with Christian men. The place for a thorough-going disciple of the Bible and of Christ is with others who are such, and even if they should happen to be the lowest in the land, and the poorest of the poor, and the most illiterate and uneducated persons of the period, what is all this if their God loves them and if they love God? Weighed in the scales of truth the least one among them is worth ten thousand of the greatest ungodly men.

> Must I be carried to the skies
> On flowery beds of ease,
> While others fought to win the prize,
> And sailed through bloody seas.
>
> Sure I must fight if I would reign,
> Increase my courage, Lord,
> I'd bear the toil, endure the pain,
> Supported by thy Word.

7

PHARAOH

The Question between the Plagues

"How long wilt thou refuse to humble thyself before me?"
(Ex. 10:3).

PHARAOH is the type and image of proud men. God permitted him to be left to the natural hardness of his heart, and he stood up against Jehovah in a very remarkable way. Those who are students of the ancient history of Egypt, those especially who have seen the remains of the colossal statues of the kings, and those tremendous pyramids which probably were the places of their sepulture, will know that man-worship was carried on to the very highest degree in connection with the ancient kingdom of Egypt. Our modern civilization has deprived kings of much of the dignity which once hedged them round, we have grown wonderfully familiar with our fellowmen in the very highest places of the earth; but in those olden monarchies, when the king was absolute and supreme, when his wish—even though he was little better than a maniac—was the law that governed the people—when not a dog dared move his tongue against the despot, then kings seemed to be like little gods, and they lorded it over their subjects with a vengeance. No doubt they grew intoxicated with the fumes of the incense which their subjects willingly offered to them, and so came to think themselves almost, if not quite, divine, and assumed the position and honors of God himself. It is not so very wonderful, therefore, that Pharaoh should have thought that, in the God of the Hebrews, he had merely met with just another one of the same stamp as himself, against whom he could carry on war, and whom he might even subdue. He said within himself, "Who are these Hebrews? Their fathers were a company of shepherds, who came and settled in Egypt; and as for these people, they are my slaves. I have built cities with their unpaid labor, and I mean still to hold them in captivity. They talk about their God, their 'Jehovah.' Who is Jehovah that I should obey his voice? Let it be a battle of Pharaoh against Jehovah, and let it be fought out to the bitter end. I will show these people that I care not for them, or their prophets, or their God."

That same pride which grew so strong in Pharaoh—growing upon that whereon it fed until it came to a colossal form—that same kind of pride is in the hearts of men even to this day. They do not take upon themselves the same high and mighty airs; but, as far as their circumstances will allow, it is still a duel between man and his Maker, between the sinner and his Judge. In the case of some here present, there is now going on a battle between yourselves and your God. Oh, that you would consider this matter in the right light, that you would look at it with calm, and steady, and reasonable consideration; for then, I think, you would at once throw down your weapons, and sue for peace on Gospel terms; and this would be the happiest hour that you have ever lived! God grant that it may be so! I am going to make a running application of my text all through my discourse, and I pray that the Holy Spirit himself may make a direct application of it to anyone whom it may concern.

To aid your memory, let me say, first of all, that THIS QUESTION HAS ABOUT IT AN AIR OF ASTONISHMENT: "How long wilt thou refuse to humble thyself before me?" I have no doubt that, as Moses and Aaron uttered this question, they put it in tones indicative of surprise: "How long is it to be that thou, proud Pharaoh, wilt refuse to humble thyself before the only living and true God?"

And, surely, that astonishment must have arisen partly *from the judgments which God had inflicted upon Pharaoh.* You know what Jehovah had already done. He had turned the water into blood, and destroyed the fish; he had made frogs to come even into the king's bedchamber; he had brought lice and flies innumerable throughout all the land; he had sent the murrain upon the cattle, boils and blains upon man and beast, storms of hail and rain, and mighty thunderings. With stroke after stroke, almost without a pause, Jehovah had smitten the proud king; yet still, after seven plagues, Pharaoh stood out as proud and obstinate as ever, and therefore the Lord sent to him the question of our text, "How long wilt thou refuse to humble thyself before me?"

I think I know some cases that are almost parallel with that of Pharaoh. Here is a man who has been very lofty and proud, but already he has been brought from wealth to poverty; at this moment, he scarcely knows where to lay his head, yet in his poverty he has not turned to God. He has been smitten with sickness, and that not merely once or twice, but many times. Turning over the pages of his dairy, he can note on such a day fever, on such a day some other deadly disease; and these strokes have followed one after another; yet, on being able to creep out again, and to come into the place of public worship, he is still found as hardened in heart as ever he was. How long will it be, my friend, ere thou dost humble thyself before God? The prophet Isaiah might well ask concerning you the question he put in his day, "Why should ye be stricken anymore?" The rod seems to be wasted upon you; you have been smitten till "the whole head is sick, and the whole heart faint," and you are covered with "wounds, and bruises, and putrefying sores"; yet you turn not unto the God who smites you, but you grow prouder and yet prouder still notwithstanding all his chastisements and judgments. What shall God do next with you? Where shall the next arrow be aimed? An eye, a hand, a foot—shall these be smitten? Or shall the Lord lay the cold hand of death upon your heart? Shall "the silver cord be loosed, or the golden bowl be broken, or the pitcher be broken at the fountain, or the wheel broken at the cistern"? I cannot tell how or when the summons may come for you; but I would very earnestly say to any of you who have been the subjects of many providential trials and divine judgments, "How long will it be ere ye humble yourselves before God?"

The question of our text may have been put in astonishment from another point of view, namely, *because of the many false pretenses of humility which Pharaoh had made.* When he was smitten, he sent for Moses and Aaron again and again, and he cried out to them, "I have sinned, pray for me. Forgive me just this once." Then, when his prayer had been heard, and the plague had been removed, Pharaoh went back again to his old natural hardness, and said, "I will not let the people go." Therefore the Lord sent to him the question, "How long wilt thou refuse to humble thyself before me?" Is it not much the same with some of you, my hearers? I want to speak right home to your hearts and consciences; have you ever, in the time of your sickness, promised God that, if you should get better, your life should be altogether different? Yet, though the Lord spared you, there has not been any true change in you. Did you not say, "Please God that I am delivered this time, I will be a better man in all respects?" Yet you are not any better than you used to be. Remember that those resolves of yours are all preserved upon God's file in heaven; you have the counterfoils of those resolutions in your memory; but the resolutions themselves are registered in the Court of King's Bench above; and one of these days you shall see those broken resolutions again, and as you hear them read, you shall have to answer for having acted falsely towards the Omniscient God, and for having lied unto him. God deliver you from the great sin of thus making a mock of him! Meanwhile, I press this question upon the heart and conscience of any to whom it applies, "How long will it be ere ye humble yourselves before the Lord? Will you go on all your lifetime with the mimicry of repentance, with the mere pretense of faith? Will you always be trying to play fast and loose with God? Will you never shake yourselves clear of this shameful play-acting, and come to downright earnest repentance before your God? Will you play yourselves into hell? Will you go on sporting with eternal realities, as if they were only a child's game?" Oh, let it not be so! Let this question of the Lord himself come rolling, like a peal of thunder, into your heart and conscience, "How long wilt thou refuse to humble thyself before me?"

Do you not think, too, that this question came from Moses with surprise as he recollected *the many mercies of God to Pharaoh?* God had heard the prayers of Moses on behalf of Pharaoh. The proud king might think it a little matter; but he who had prayed for him, and obtained the answer to his petitions, did not think it a small thing. When all the frogs were in all the land, by the prayer of Moses they were all slain; when the swarms of flies came, and defiled the whole country, it was the prayer of Moses that removed the plague, so that there remained not one. It might be a little matter to Pharaoh—for men who receive favors often think but little of them—but they who win favors from God by prayer always highly esteem them. So Moses seems to be astonished as he says to Pharaoh, "Has God done all this for thee? Hath he removed his rod from thee? Hath he said to the executioner, 'Put back the ax'? Has he fetched thee out of the prison house of his judgments, taken the chains from off thy wrists, and set thee free, and so thou still stand out against him? How long wilt thou refuse to humble thyself before him?"

Let me put this question to some who are here. God has been very gracious to you in delivering you from many accidents and diseases, and you are spared till your hair is turning gray. It would have been easy enough for your life to have come to an end long ago, yet here you are still spared by God's mercy. You are not a pauper, as you once thought you would be; you are still living in comfortable circumstances, and that great trial which, at one time, darkened your life like a heavy cloud, has passed away; and you can now look up with a cheerful countenance, and remember times of great despondency and threatened distress. Will you not then—won by this mercy, subdued by this great love—humble yourself before your God? What more can he do for you than he has already done? See how he has made you the special object of singular providential care. I refer you to your diary, and ask you to recollect how kindly and tenderly and graciously God has dealt with you these many years. O sirs, if terrors will not move you, let love subdue you! Oh! that the grace of God might find out the secret spring of your heart, and bring you now, at once, to humble yourselves before the Lord!

So I think I am right in saying, in the first place, that there is an air of surprise about this question to Pharoah, because of wasted judgments, forgotten promises, and neglected mercies: "How long wilt thou refuse to humble thyself before me?"

Now, in the second place, to change the strain a little, and but a little, let me add that THE QUESTION BREATHES A SPIRIT OF KINDNESS.

You know that, when a person does not intend another's good he strikes the fatal blow at once without a word of warning; but he who is a father, though he must use the rod, speaks many times, and pleads, and admonishes, and persuades before he gives a stroke. This is just what God did with Pharoah by his servants Moses and Aaron; he said, "How long wilt thou refuse to humble thyself before me?"

In Pharoah's case, *that which God required of him was right*. It was humbling to his pride, but it was right. What right had Pharoah to hold the Israelites as his slaves? They were not his people; they had been admitted into the kingdom as honored guests. One of that race had saved the nation in the time of famine; Joseph had preserved Egypt, and made the king strong in the midst of his people. Gratitude to Joseph ought to have caused the Israelites to be treated in a very different way; at any rate, if Pharoah did not wish to have them in Egypt, he ought at least to have permitted them to go in peace, and not to have held them in bondage. This was all that God asked of him: "Let my people go. They are none of yours, they are mine; let them go, that they may serve me."

And, brethren, that which God requires of a sinner is a right thing. He bids thee leave thy sin; is not that right? He bids thee break off thy sins by righteousness; is not that right? He has provided a way of salvation through the atonement of his Son, Jesus Christ, and he bids thee accept it; is not that right? All that he asks thee to do is to confess and forsake thy sin; is not that right? If you cannot undo your sin, the least you can do is to own it like a man; and that is what God asks of you. He bids you trust his dear Son. Is that a hard thing, an unreasonable thing? If he has appointed a Savior, and equipped him for the service of salvation, and has bidden you, who need salvation, to trust him to save you, and never think of self-salvation, but to take Jesus Christ to be the beginning and the end of salvation to you—is not that a right thing? Well, then, how long will it be that you will still refuse to humble yourself before him?

This question is put in a spirit of kindness, and I desire to put it very kindly to any one of you who has not yet yielded to the Lord: "How long wilt thou refuse to humble thyself before God?" You say that you do intend one day to humble yourself beneath the mighty hand of God; *do you think it will grow any easier while you delay?* Is it hard now to yield yourself to the Lord? It will be harder in a year's time, even if you are spared till then, for a man's habits harden every day that he lives. They spin new webs about him, they hold him fast, poor fly that he is, every hour that he lives. If it ever be an easy matter to bow before the Lord, it is easier at this moment than it will be tomorrow. Say not, therefore, "I am waiting for a more convenient season"; for the most convenient season that ever can come is now. There will be greater inconveniences tomorrow than there are tonight, and so will it be *ad infinitum.* If you would be free from your bondage, break loose at once. You have waited too long already, and you do not find it easier from day to day, neither will you if you still delay to submit to the Lord; therefore, yield to him at once.

Do you not know that, if God means to save you, *he will send heavier plagues upon you than any you have felt as yet?* If you will not come to him with one blow, you shall have two; and if two will not suffice, you shall have twenty, for he will have you. It would be better to yield at once; there is no greater wisdom than, the moment the Lord says, "Seek ye my face," to answer, "Thy face, Lord, will I seek." "Be ye not as the horse, or as the mule, which have no understanding," which must be driven to their work, and goaded on in their labor. There are some who come to Christ like vessels towed into port, all but wrecked, with rent sails, and broken timbers; it is better by far that thou be gently wafted into the haven by the soft south wind of love, or that thou spread thy canvas to a favoring gale, and fly before the breeze into the Fair Havens of salvation by Christ. I would put it to thee, dear friend—Why dost thou want to be beaten, and bruised, and cut, and wounded? Why not, as thou art, say—

> Just as I am—without one plea
> But that thy blood was shed for me,
> And that thou bidd'st me come to thee,
> O Lamb of God, I come.

At any rate, there is one other thing I will say to you, *a time for decision should be set.* I would like to press the question of the text, "How long wilt thou refuse to humble thyself before me?" I remember a man of God, who was talking with a young lady to whom he had spoken many times about her soul. At last he said to her, "Well, Hannah, you do intend to come to Christ one day?" "Yes, sir," she replied, "I do intend." "Well, now," he said "will you give me a date when you will come to Christ? You are twenty now, will you come to the Lord Jesus Christ when you are thirty? Will you put that down as a definite promise?" The young lady answered, "Well, sir, I should not like to promise that, because I might be dead before I was thirty. Ten years is a long time, and I might be dead and gone before that time; I hope I shall know the Lord before that." "Well, Hannah," the good man said, "we will say nine years, then; that is to be the time that you fix when you will yield to the mercy of God." "Well, sir," she said, "I hope it will be before then." "No," he said, "the bargain is made; you will have to run risks for nine years, you know. You make the bargain that you will come to Christ in nine years' time; let it stand so, and you must run the risk." "Oh, sir!" she exclaimed, "it would be an awful thing, a dreadful thing, for me to say that I would wait nine years, because I might be lost in that time." The friend then said, "Well, suppose we say that you will serve the Lord in twelve months' time; will you just take this year, and spend it in the service of Satan, and then, when you have enjoyed yourself that way, give your heart to Christ?" Somehow, the young woman felt that it was a long time, and a very dangerous time, so she answered, "I should not like to be hung over an awful chasm, and for somebody to say, 'I will pull you up at the end of a year, and set your feet on a rock.' " No, she could not bear that thought; and as her minister pressed her to set a time, and brought it down by little and little, at last she said, "Oh, sir, it had better be tonight; it had better be tonight! Pray to God that I may now give my heart to the Lord Jesus Christ, for it is such a dreadful thing to be without a Savior. I would have Christ as mine this very night." So I put it to you, yield to Christ at once, and do not keep on saying, "I hope it will not be long before I become a child of God."

The question of our text is asked, then, not only with an air of surprise, but also with a great measure of kindliness; and in that kindly spirit I wish you to suppose that I am walking round the front of this lower gallery, and shaking hands with every unconverted person, and saying, "How long will it be ere you trust in Jesus?" and then mounting the stairs to get to you who are in the upper gallery, that I may put to you the same question, and, after making the round of the whole building, threading my way as best I can through these crowded aisles, and taking each one by the had, giving a hearty grip, and saying, "How long is it to be? How long is it to be?" and "Had it not better be now?" God grant that it may be now that you humble yourself before the Lord, for Jesus' sake!

In the third place, I will deal with the text in rather a different style, yet still keeping to the same object though I change the line of argument. THIS QUESTION IS ASKED IN A TONE OF POWER.

If I could speak it as Jehovah would speak it by his servant Moses, I think it would run like this: "Thus saith Jehovah, God of the Hebrews, How long wilt thou refuse to humble thyself before me? Let my people go, that they may serve me." God as God says to Pharaoh, *"It is no use for you to stand out against me;* as well might a moth contend with the furnace. It is of no use for you to lift your puny hand against me. You know not how great my power is: I have given you a taste of it, but I have yet more terrible plagues in the rear which I will bring forward, and you will have to bow before me." And you know, brethren, how Pharaoh did at last have to bow before Jehovah. The firstborn of his strength was cut off in the dead of night, and there was wailing in the palace and in all the land; and then, what Pharaoh said, "I will pursue, I will overtake, I will divide the spoil; my lust shall be satisfied upon them; I will draw my sword, my hand shall destroy them"—he dashed forward to pursue the hosts of the Lord, and you know what followed: "For the horse of Pharaoh went in with his chariots and with his horsemen into the sea, and the Lord brought again the waters of the sea upon them." Then was heard the song of Miriam, "Sing ye to Jehovah, for he hath triumphed gloriously; the horse and his rider hath he thrown into the sea." As the rushing waters bore him away, proud Pharaoh learned when too late how great a fool he had been to contend against the infinite majesty of Almighty God.

And I say to you, sirs, who are fighting against God, *you must either bend or break.* As God lives, you must bow before him in repentance, or you shall be crushed beneath him in the day of his anger. Think now, when we talk to you of God's mercy, that we come to you as your equal might come, and reason with you as though God were afraid of you. Do you talk of your great strength? He is almighty! As for you, your breath is in your nostrils; and the Lord could cause you in a moment to fall dead in a fit, as many have done before you! If thou wilt not yield to him, he is infinitely glorious without you; and if you rebel against him, in what way can you affect the supremacy of his empire? As well might a drop of spray hope to shake the cliffs of Albion as for you to contend against the majesty of God. O sirs, fight not against your God! What profit can there be to you in this rebellion? Already you have found no profit in it; therefore, be not so mad as to continue warring against your God. "Come now, and let us reason together, saith the Lord: though yours sins be as scarlet, they shall be as white as snow; though they be red like crimson, they shall be as wool." He is a God ready to forgive; "He delighteth in mercy." He willeth not the death of any, but that they turn unto him and live. Still, if you will persist in contending against him, see what your end will be: "Everlasting destruction from the presence of the Lord, and from the glory of his power."

I conclude by trying to show that THE QUESTION OF OUR TEXT IS OF WIDE APPLICATION.

Let me try to put the case to you. Forget Pharaoh, and only think of yourself; let the Lord Jesus Christ himself, with the thorn-crowned head and the pierced hand, stand by your pew, and looking right down into your soul, say in his matchless tone of music—the music of the heart of love—"How long wilt thou refuse to humble thyself before me?"

What is your difficulty? What is the cause of your quarrel with your Lord? *Do you refuse even to think upon religion?* I know that many do;

they get up late on the Sunday morning, and loiter about the house all day, with no care to go to what they call these "preaching shops." They would rather go for a walk. The Bible is never read by them; they say that it is such a dreary book, which shows how unacquainted they are with its contents. Religion they regard as a mere makeup of priests, though they have never fairly examined its claims. Well, will you not at least give the Gospel a hearing before you condemn it? Will you not listen to God's message of salvation, that you may form a sober judgment concerning it? Will you not, at any rate, read that Book which you have hitherto despised, that you may find out whether it really is the Book of God? Oh, no! you know too much to read the Bible, you are far too cultured to listen to the common-place preaching of such poor folk as we are. That is how you talk, but are you not ashamed to speak so? Do you not yourself judge that, when a man thinks he knows everything, he really knows very little, and that, when he affects to be such a very superior person, he is not so high and mighty as he thinks himself to be? Humble yourself enough at least to be wise, humble yourself enough to listen to this question of Nicodemus, "Doth our law judge any man, before it hear him, and know what he doeth?" Hear the story of Christ, and examine and weigh the evidence of his Messiahship. Consider the claims of Christ, and confess that you have not met them; and then give your whole heart and soul to seek to know the way of salvation.

But, suppose you have thought of religion, what is your trouble? You say, "Well, I understand that *I cannot be saved except by confessing myself a sinner.*" You would not need salvation, would you, if you were not a sinner? Surely, there is no hardship in refusing to you what you profess you do not want. If I opened a doctor's shop, and posted in the window a notice stating that I would give away no pills or drafts to men who were perfectly well, nobody would accuse me of a want of humanity because I acted like that. Those who are well have no need of a physician. So, to qualify yourself for being saved, you must first confess that you need to be saved. Come, have you always been perfect? I should like to see you stand in the middle of the congregation, and let us all look you up and down; if you did not blush, I should know that you were not perfect, and if you did blush, it would be a confession that you were imperfect. We have all transgressed the law of our God; some in one way, and some in another, but "all have sinned, and come short of the glory of God," and we must confess that it is even so. When we have done this, then will be fulfilled to us the ancient promise, "Whoso confesseth and forsaketh his sins shall have mercy."

If you have made a confession of sin, what is further the matter with you? "Why," say you, "I am told that *I must be saved by grace.*" Yes, and how else would you like to be saved? Do you wish to be saved by your own merits? You have not any; you would like to set up some merit of your own, but why try to set up a lie? God is the God of truth, and he cannot endure that which is false. If ever anyone of us gets to heaven, it will be by the free and undeserved mercy of God; but why should you quarrel with such terms as these? When a thing is to be given away for nothing, I would be the last man to try to run it up in price; the richest man can have it for nothing, and that is a price which exactly suits the poorest. Blessed be God that salvation is all of grace from first to last! Humble yourself to accept it "without money and without price."

"But I understand," says one, "that *I am to be saved simply be believing in Christ,* and I do not like that way of salvation." Why do you not like it? Salvation by the atoning sacrifice of Christ, through the sinner simply trusting in Christ, will greatly glorify him. This makes the way of salvation possible to lame feet, and blind eyes, and deaf ears, and enables poor guilty souls to find perfect righteousness, which they could never find in any other way. Humble yourself, therefore, and submit to God's plan of salvation. Really, it seems to me that, if a man gives anything away, he has a right to give it in his own way; and if God gives salvation, surely he has the right to give it in his own style; and if he will give it to all who confess their need of it, and come and freely accept it because Christ has wrought it out, who shall quarrel with such terms as these?

I would very affectionately press home this passage upon all whom it concerns; listen to the Lord himself, as he puts to you this solemn question, "How long wilt thou refuse to humble thyself before me?" Here are many of us who, long ago, came to Jesus, and humbled ourselves before him, and we did not think it any degradation. I would sooner have some men to put their foot on my neck than I would have the best words of certain other men; one might be willing to sit still, and be abused of some men, and then say, "It is a pleasure even to be noticed by such persons"; while, if certain others were to praise you, you might ask as the philosopher did of old, "What have I been doing amiss that this wretch should speak well of me?" Ah, poor sinner! If you once get a view of the

Lord Jesus Christ, and know who he is, and what he is, if you can by faith perceive his beauties, you will say, "To fall at his feet, is a high privilege; to submit myself to such a one as Jesus Christ of Nazareth, is a higher honor than to receive a peerage from an earthly sovereign." Wherefore, let us go together—you who never went, and some of us who have often been—let us go together, and let us cry to Christ, "Lord, receive us! We are nothing but a mass of sin and misery; receive us, and save us, for thy mercy's sake; and unto thy name shall be the glory forever and ever!"

8

JOSHUA

Strengthening Medicine for God's Servants

"I will not fail thee, nor forsake thee" (Josh. 1:5).

NO DOUBT God had spoken to Joshua before. He had been a man of faith for many years, and his faith enabled him to distinguish himself by such simple truthfulness of character and thoroughly faithful obedience to the Lord's will, that he and another were the only two left of the whole generation that came up out of Egypt. "Faithful among the faithless found," he survived where all else died; standing erect in full vigor, he might have been compared to a lone tree which spreads its verdant branches untouched by the ax which has leveled its fellows with the ground. But now Joshua was about to enter upon a new work: he had become king in Jeshurun instead of Moses, from a servant he had risen to be a ruler, and it now fell to his lot to lead the people across the Jordan, and marshal their forces for the conquest of the promised land. On the threshold of this high enterprise the Lord appears to his servant and says, "As I was with Moses, so I will be with thee: I will not fail thee, nor forsake thee." When God's people come into fresh positions they shall have fresh revelations of his love. New dangers will bring new protections; new difficulties, new helps, new discouragements, new comforts; so that we may rejoice in tribulations also, because they are so many newly-opened doors of God's mercy to us. We will be glad of our extremities, because they are divine opportunities. What the Lord said to Joshua was particularly encouraging, and it came precisely when he needed it. Great was his peril, and great was the consolation of that word from the Lord of hosts, "Have not I commanded thee? Be strong and of a good courage; be not afraid, neither be thou dismayed: for the Lord thy God is with thee whithersoever thou goest."

Observe here, first, THE SUITABILITY OF THE CONSOLATION WHICH THESE WORDS GAVE TO JOSHUA. "I will not fail thee, nor forsake thee."

This must have been very cheering to him *in reference to himself.* He knew Moses, and he must have had a very high esteem for him. He was a great man, one of a thousand; scarcely among all that have been born of woman has there arisen a greater than Moses. Joshua had been his servant, and no doubt considered himself to be very far inferior to that great lawgiver. A sense of his own weakness comes over a man all the more from being associated with a grander mind. If you mingle with your inferiors you are apt to grow vain; but closely associated with superior minds there is a far greater probability that you will become depressed, and may think even less of yourself than humility might require; for humility is, after all, only a right estimate of our own powers. Joshua, therefore, may possibly have been somewhat despondent under a very pressing sense of his own deficiencies; and this cheering assurance would meet his case—"*I* will not fail thee: though thou be less wise, or meek or courageous than Moses, *I* will not fail thee, nor forsake thee." If God be with our weakness it waxes strong; if he be with our folly it rises into wisdom; if he be with our timidity it gathers courage. It matters not how conscious a man may be of being nothing at all in himself, when he is conscious of the divine presence he even rejoices in his infirmity because the power of God doth rest upon him. If the Lord say unto the weakest man or woman here, "I will not fail thee, nor forsake thee," no craven thought will cross that ennobled spirit; that word will nerve the trembler with a lion-like courage which no adversary will be able to daunt.

The consolation given to Joshua would be exceedingly suitable *in the presence of his enemies.* He had spied out the land, and he knew it to be inhabited by giant races, men famous both for stature and strength. The sons of Anak were there, and other tribes, described, as "great, and many, and tall." He knew that they were a warlike people, and expert in the use of destructive implements of war, such as brought terror upon men, for they had chariots of iron. He knew, too, that their cities were of colossal dimensions—fortresses whose stone at this very day surprise the traveler, so that he asks what wondrous skill could have lifted those masses of rock into their places. The other spies had said that these Canaanites dwelt in cities that were walled up to heaven; and, though Joshua did not endorse that exaggeration, he was very well aware that the cities to be captured were fortresses of great strength, and the people to be exterminated were men of ferocious courage and great physical energy. Therefore the Lord said, "I will not fail thee, nor forsake thee." What more was needed? Surely, in the presence of God, Anakim become dwarfs, strongholds become as a lodge in a garden of cucumbers, and chariots of iron are as thistledown upon the hillside driven before the blast. What is strong against the Most High? What is formidable in opposition to Jehovah? "If God be for us, who can be against us?" They that be with us are more than they that be against us, when once the Lord of hosts is seen in our ranks. "Therefore will we not fear, though the earth be removed, and the mountains be carried into the midst of the sea. Though a host should encamp against us, our heart shall not fear: though war should rise against us, in this will we be confident."

This consolation, too, was *sufficient for all supplies*. Perhaps Joshua knew that the manna was no longer to fall. In the wilderness the supply of heavenly bread was continuous, but when they crossed the Jordan they must quarter on the enemy; and with the myriads of people that were under Joshua's command, the matter of providing for them must have been no trifle. According to some computations nearly three million people came up out of Egypt: I scarcely credit the computation and am inclined to believe that the whole matter of the numbers of the Old Testament is not yet understood, and that a better knowledge of the Hebrew tongue will lead to the discovery that the figures have been frequently misunderstood; but still a very large number of people came with Joshua to the edge of the wilderness, and crossed the Jordan into the land of Canaan. Who was to provide for all these hungry bands? Joshua might have said, "Shall all the flocks and the herds be slain for this great multitude, and wilt the sea yield up her fish, when the manna ceases? How shall these people be fed?" "I will not fail thee, nor forsake thee" was a supply which would meet all demands of the commissariat. They might eat to the full, for God would find them food; their clothes might wax old upon them now that the miracle of the wilderness would cease, for new garments would be found for them in the wardrobes of their enemies. When the Lord opens all his granaries none shall lack for bread, and when he unlocks his wardrobes none shall go bare.

Surely this word must often have brought charming consolation to the heart of the son of Nun *when he saw the people failing him*. There was only the venerable Caleb left of all his comrades with whom he had shared the forty years' march through the great and terrible wilderness; Caleb and he were the last two sheaves of the great harvest, and they were both like shocks of corn fully ripe for the garner. Old men grow lonely, and a small wonder is it if they do. I have heard them say that they live in a world where they are not known, now that, one by one, all their old friends are gone home, and they are left alone—like the last swallow of autumn when all its fellows have sought a sunnier clime. Yet the Lord says, "I will not forsake thee: I shall not die: I am ever with thee. Thy Friend in heaven will live on as long as thou dost." As for the generation which had sprung up around Joshua, they were very little better than their fathers; they turned back in the day of battle, even the children of Ephraim, when they were armed and carried bows. They were very apt to go aside into the most provoking sin. Joshua had as hard a task with them as Moses had, and it was enough to break the heart of Moses to have to do with them. The Lord seems to bid him put no confidence in them, neither to be discomfited if they should be false and treacherous: "I will not fail thee: *they* may, but *I* will not. I will not forsake thee. They may prove cowards and traitors, but I will not desert thee." Oh, what a blessed thing it is in a false and fickle world, where he that eats bread with us lifts up his heel against us, where the favorite counselor becomes an Ahithophel, and turns his wisdom into crafty hate, to know that "there is a friend that sticketh closer than a brother," one who is faithful and gives us sure tokens of a love which many waters cannot quench.

Secondly, AT WHAT TIME MAY WE CONSIDER THIS PROMISE TO BE SPOKEN TO OURSELVES? It is all very well to listen to it, as spoken to Joshua, but, O God, if thou wouldst speak thus to us how consoled would we be! Dost thou ever do so? May *we* be so bold as to believe that thus thou comfortest *us*? Beloved, the whole run of Scripture speaks to the same effect to men of like mind with Joshua. No Scripture is of private interpretation: no text has spent itself upon the person who first received it. God's comforts are like wells, which no one man or set of men can drain dry, however mighty may be their thirst. The fountain of our text first gushed forth to refresh Joshua, but if we are in Joshua's position, and are of his character, we may bring our water pots and fill them to the brim.

Let me mention when I think we may safely feel that God says to us, "I will not fail thee, nor forsake thee." Surely it is when we are *called to do God's work.* Joshua's work was the Lord's work. It was God who had given the country to the people, and who had said, "I will drive out the Canaanite from before thee," and Joshua was God's executioner, the sword in the hand of the Lord for the driving out of the condemned races. He was not entering upon a quixotic engagement of his own choosing and devising; he had not elected himself, and selected his own work, but God had called him to it, put him in the office, and bidden him do it, and therefore he said to him, "I will not fail thee, nor forsake thee." Brother, are you serving God? Do you live to win souls? Is it your grand object to be the instrument in God's hand of accomplishing his purposes of grace to the fallen sons of men? Do you know that God has put you where you are, and called you to do the work to which your life is dedicated? Then go on in God's name, for, as surely as he called you to his work, you may be sure that to you also he says, as indeed to all his servants, "I will not fail thee, nor forsake thee."

But I hear some of you say, "We are not engaged in work of such a king that we could precisely call it 'work for God.' " Well, brethren, but are you *engaged in a work which you endeavor to perform to God's glory?* Is your ordinary and common trade one which is lawful—one concerning which you have no doubt as to its honest propriety; and in carrying it on do you follow right principles only? Do you endeavor to glorify God in the shop? Do you make the bells on the horses holiness to the Lord? It would not be possible for all of us to be preachers, for where would be the hearers? Many a man would be very much out of place if he were to leave his ordinary calling, and devote himself to what is so unscripturally called "the ministry." The fact is, the truest religious life is that in which a man follows the ordinary calling of life in the spirit of a Christian. Now, are you so doing? If so, you are as much ministering before God in measuring out yards of calico, or weighing pounds of tea, as Joshua was in slaying Hivites, and Jebusites, and Hittites. You are as much serving God in looking after your own children, and training them up in God's fear, and minding the house, and making your household a church for God, as you would be if you had been called to lead an army to battle for the Lord of hosts. And you may take this promise for yourself, for the path of duty is the path where this promise is to be enjoyed. "I will not fail thee, nor forsake thee."

Now, mark you, if you are living for yourself, if you are living for gain, if selfishness be the object of life, or if you are pursuing an unhallowed calling, if there is anything about your mode of business which is contrary to the mind and will of God and sound doctrine, you cannot expect God to aid you in sin, nor will he do it. Neither can you ask him to pander to your lusts, and to assist you in the gratification of your own selfishness.

But, mark you, there is another matter. *We must,* if we are to have this promise, *take God into our calculations.* A great many persons go about their supposed lifework without thinking about God. I have heard of one who said everybody had left him, and someone said, "But surely, as a Christian, God has not failed you? "Oh," said he, "I forgot God." I am afraid there are many who call themselves Christians and yet forget God in common life. Do you, brethren and sisters, habitually take God into your calculations? Do you calculate upon omniscient direction and omnipotent aid? I have heard of a certain captain who had led his troops into a very difficult position, and he knew that on the morrow he should want them all to be full of courage; and so, disguising himself, at nightfall he went round their tents, and listened to their conversations, until he heard one of them say, "Our captain is a very great warrior, and has won many victories, but he has this time made a mistake; for see, there are so many thousands of the enemy, and he has only so many infantry, so many cavalry, and so many guns." The soldier made out the account, and was about to sum up the scanty total when the captain, unable to bear it any longer, threw aside the curtain of the tent, and said, "And how many do you count *me* for, sir?"—as much as to say, "I have won so many battles that you ought to know that my skill can multiply battalions by handling them." And so the Lord hears his servants estimating how feeble they are, and how little they can do, and how few are their helpers; and I think I hear him rebukingly say, "But how many do you count your God for? Is he never to come into your estimate? You talk of providing, and forget the God of providence; you talk of working, but forget the God who worketh in you to will and to do of his own good pleasure."

How often in our enterprises have prudent people plucked us by the sleeve, and said we have gone too far. Could we reckon upon being able to carry out what we had undertaken? No, we could not reckon upon it, except that we believed in God, and with God all things are possible. If it be his work, we may venture far beyond the shallowness of prudence into the great deeps of divine confidence, for God who warrants our faith, will honor it ere long. Oh, Christian, if you can venture, and feel it to be no venture, then may you grasp the promise, "I will not fail thee, nor forsake thee."

Now, remember, that we may take this promise when we are engaged in God's work, or when we turn our ordinary business into God's work, and when we do really by faith take God into our calculations; but *we must also be careful that we walk in God's ways.* Observe that the next verse to the text runs thus, "Be strong, and of a good courage," and then the seventh verse is a singular one. "Only be thou strong and very courageous, that thou mayest observe to do according to all the law, which Moses my servant commanded thee: turn not from it to the right hand or to the left, that thou mayest prosper whithersoever thou goest."

"Be strong and very courageous." What for? To obey! Does it want courage and strength to obey? Why, nowadays, that man is thought to be courageous who will have no laws of God to bind him; and he is thought to be strong-minded who ridicules revelation. But let us rest assured that he is truly strong of mind and heart who is content to be thought a fool, and sticks to the good old truth, and keeps the good old way. I believe it wants more courage and strength of mind to keep to the old things, than to follow after novel and airy speculations.

Be careful how you live. To watch every putting down of our foot is a good thing. Be exact and precise as to the divine rule, careless about man's opinion, and even defying it wherein it is error; but dutiful to God's law, bowing before it, yielding your whole nature in cheerful subservience to every command of the Most High. He that walketh uprightly, walketh surely, and to him the promise is, "I will not fail thee, nor forsake thee."

But now, thirdly, let us consider WHAT THIS PROMISE DOES NOT PRECLUDE. "I will not fail thee, nor forsake thee." We must not misunderstand this gracious word, lest we be disappointed when things happen contrary to our expectations.

This promise does not exclude effort. A great many mistakes are made about the promises of God. Some think that if God is to be with them they will have nothing to do. Joshua did not find it so. He and his troops had to slay every Amorite, and Hittite, and Hivite that fell in battle. He had to fight, and use his sword-arm just as much as if there had been no God at all. The best and the wisest thing in the world is to work as if it all depended upon you, and then trust in God, knowing that it all depends upon him. He will not fail us, but we are not therefore to fold our arms and sit still. He will not forsake us; we are not, therefore, to go upstairs to bed and expect that our daily bread will drop into our mouths. I have known idle people who have said "Jehovah-Jireh," and sat with their feet over the fender, and their arms folded, and been lazy, and self-indulgent; and generally their presumption has ended in this—God has provided them rags and jags, and a place in the county jail before long; the very best provisions, methinks, that can be made for idle people, and the sooner they get it the better for society. God does not pander to our laziness, and any man who expects to get on in this world with anything that is good without work is a fool. Throw your whole soul into the service of God, and then you will get God's blessing if you are resting upon him. Oliver Cromwell had a common sense view of this truth, too. "Trust in God," said he, as they went to battle, "but keep your powder dry." And so must we.

Neither does this promise preclude occasional disaster. After Joshua had received this promise he went up to Ai, and suffered a terrible defeat there, because the regulations of the war had been violated. They had defrauded the Lord of a part of the spoil of Jericho, which was hidden in Achan's tent, and this troubled Israel. Yes, and without the violation of any law, the best man in the world must expect in the most successful enterprise that there will be some discouragements. Look at the sea: it is rolling in, it will rise to full tide before long, but every wave that comes up dies upon the shore; and after two or three great waves which seem to capture the shingle there comes a feebler one which sucks back. Very well, but the sea will win, and reach its fullness. So in every good work for God there is a back-drawing wave every now and then. In fact, God often makes his servants go back that they may have all the more room to run and take a longer leap than they could have taken from the place where they stood before. Defeats in the hand of faith are only preparations for victory. If we are beaten for a little, we grind our swords the sharper, and the next time we take more care that our enemies shall know how keen they are.

Nor, again, does this promise preclude frequent tribulations and testings of faith. In the autobiography of the famous Francké of Halle, who built, and, in the hand of God, provided for, the orphan-house of Halle, he says, "I thought when I committed myself and my work to God by faith, that I had only to pray when I had need, and that the supplies would come; but I found, that I had sometimes to wait and pray for a long time." The supplies did come, but not at once. The pinch never went so far as absolute want; but there were intervals of severe pressure. There was nothing to spare. Every spoonful of meal had to be scraped from the bottom of the barrel, and every drop of oil that oozed out seemed as if it must be the last; but still it never did come to the last drop, and there was always just a little meal left. Bread shall be given us, but not always in quartern loaves; our water shall be sure, but not always a brook full, it may only come in small cups. God has not promised to take any of you to heaven without trying your faith. He will not fail you, but he will bring you very low. He will not forsake you, but he will test you and prove you. You will frequently need all your faith to keep your spirits up; and unless God enables you to trust without staggering, you will find yourself sorely disquieted at times.

I would like to say, once more, about this, that *this promise does not preclude our suffering very greatly*, and our dying, and perhaps dying a very sad and terrible death, as men judge. God never left Paul, but I have seen the spot where Paul's head was smitten off by the headsman. The Lord never left Peter, but Peter, like his Master, had to die by crucifixion. The Lord never left the martyrs, but they had to ride to heaven in chariots of fire. The Lord has never left his church, but oftentimes his church has been trodden as straw is trodden for the dunghill; her blood has been scattered over the whole earth, and she has seemed to be utterly destroyed. Still, you know, the story of the church is only another illustration of my text; God has not failed her, nor forsaken her; in the deaths of her saints we read, not defeat, but victory; as they passed away one by one, stars ceasing to shine below, they shone with tenfold brilliance in the upper sky because of the clouds through which they passed before they reached their celestial spheres. Beloved, we may have to groan in a Gethsemane, but God will not fail us: we may have to die on a Golgotha, but he will nor forsake us. We shall rise again, and, as our Master was triumphant through death, even so shall we through the greatest suffering and the most terrible defeats rise to his throne.

I must occupy you for a few moments over a fourth point. WHAT, THEN, DOES THE TEXT MEAN, IF WE MAY HAVE ALL THIS TRIAL HAPPENING TO US? It means to those to whom it belongs, first, *no failure for your work*; secondly, *no desertion for yourself*.

"I will not fail thee." *Your labor shall not be in vain in the Lord.* What is it? Is it the great work of preaching the Gospel to thousands?

God will not fail you in that. I remember how twenty years ago I was preaching the Gospel in the simplicity of my heart, and some little stir was made, but the wise men made light of it and said it was all to end in six months' time. We went on, did we not? And by-and-by, when we had still greater crowds listening to us, it was "a temporary excitement, a sort of religious spasm"; it would all end like a mere flash in the pan. I wonder where those prophets are now. If there are any of them here, I hope they feel comfortable in the unfulfilled prophecy, which they can now study with some degree of satisfaction. Thousands on earth and hundreds in heaven can tell what God hath wrought. Is it another kind of work that you are engaged in? A very quiet, unobtrusive, unobserved effort? Well, I should not wonder that, little as it is, somebody or other sneers at it. There is scarcely a David in the world without an Eliab to sneer at him. Press on, brother! Stick to it, plod away, work hard, trust in your God, and your work will not fail. We have heard of a minister who added only one to his church through a long year of every earnest ministry— only one, a sad thing for him; but that one happened to be Robert Moffatt, and he was worth a thousand of most of us. Go on. If you bring but *one* to Christ, who shall estimate the value of the one? Your class is very small just now; God does not seem to be working. Pray about it, get more scholars into the class, and teach better, and even if you should not see immediate success do not believe that it is all a failure. Never was a true Gospel sermon preached yet, with faith and prayer, that was a failure. Since the day when Christ our Master first preached the Gospel, unto this day—I dare to say it—there was never a true prayer that failed, nor a true declaration of the Gospel made in a right spirit that fell to the ground without prospering according to the pleasure of the Lord.

And then there shall be *no desertion as to yourself*, for your heavenly Friend has said, "I will not *forsake thee*." You will not be left alone or without a helper. You are thinking of what you will do in old age. Do not think of that: think of what God will do for you in old age. Oh, but your great need and long illness will wear out your friends, you say. Perhaps you may wear out your friends, but you will not wear out your God, and he can raise up new helpers if the old ones fail. Oh, but your infirmities are many, and will soon crush you down: you cannot live long in such circumstances. Very well, then you will be in heaven; and that is far better. But you dread pining sickness. It may never come;

and, suppose it should come, remember what will come with it—"I will make all thy bed in thy sickness." "I will never leave thee, nor forsake thee"—so runs the promise.

And so this brings me to the last point, which is this: WHY MAY WE BE QUITE SURE THAT THIS PROMISE WILL BE FULFILLED TO US?

I answer, first, we may be quite sure because *it is God's promise.* Did ever any promise of God fall to the ground yet? There be those in the world who are challenging us continually, and saying, "Where is your God?" They deny the efficacy of prayer; they deny the interpositions of Providence. Well, I do not wonder that they do so deny, because the bulk of Christians do not realize either the answer of prayer or the interposition of Providence, for this reason, that they do not live in the light of God's countenance, or live by faith. But the man who walks by faith will tell you that he notices Providence, and never is deficient of a Providence to notice, that he notices answer to his prayer, and never is without an answer to his prayer. What is a wonder to others becomes a common fact of everyday life to the believer in Christ.

Rest ye well assured that if a man be called to do God's work, God will not fail him, because *it is not after the manner of the Lord to desert his servants.* David in the dark day of his sin bade Joab place Uriah, the Hittite, in the forefront of the battle, and leave him there to die by the hand of the children of Ammon. Was it not cruel? It was base and treacherous to the last degree. Can you suspect the Lord of anything so unworthy? God forbid. My soul has known what it is to plead with the Lord my God after this fashion, "Lord, thou hast placed me in a difficult position, and given me service to perform far beyond my capacity. I never coveted this prominent place, and if thou dost not help me now why has thou placed me in it?" I have always found such argument to be prevalent with God.

Besides, remember that *should God's servants fail,* if they are really God's servants, *the enemy would exult and boast against the Lord himself.* This was a great point with Joshua in after days. He said, "The Canaanites and all the inhabitants of the land shall hear of it, and shall environ us round, and cut off our name from the earth: and what wilt thou do unto thy great name?"

Besides, if God has raised you up, to accomplish a purpose by you, *do you think he will be defeated?* Were ever any of his designs frustrated? My God is one who, when he designs a thing, accomplishes it; he is a

God whose omnipotence none can resist, concerning whom it may be said, "Who shall stay his hand, or say unto him, What doest thou?" The mighty God of Jacob puts his hand to a design, and carries it through as surely as he begins; the weakness of the instrument in his hand does not hinder him, nor the opposition of his enemies deter him.

Besides, my brethren, if we trust God, and live for God, *he loves us much too well to leave us.* God sees his own self in all his servants. He sees in them the members of the body of his dear Son. The very least among them is dear to him as the apple of his eye, and beloved as his own soul. It is not to be imagined that he will ever put a load upon his own children's shoulders without giving them strength to bear the burden, or send them to labors for which he will not give them adequate resources. Oh, rest in the Lord, ye faithful.

As I have thus been bringing forth marrow and fatness, from the Word, I have been thinking of some of you, poor souls, who cannot eat thereof, and have no share in it. I am glad to see you here. You must have a hungering after these good things, or you would not be here in such numbers. I hope your mouths are watering after the good things of the covenant. I hope, as you see the promises of God on the table, and see how rich they are, you will say to yourself, "Would God I had a share in them." Well, poor soul, if God gives you an appetite, I can only say, the food is free to you. If thou wouldst have God to be thy helper—if thou wouldst indeed be saved by Christ—come and welcome, for thou art the soul that he desires to bless. If you have a half wish towards God, he has a longing towards you. If you desire him, you have not the start of him; depend upon it, he has long before desired you. Come you to him, rest in him, accept the atonement which his Son has presented, begin the life of faith in real earnest, and you shall find that what I have said is all true, only it falls short of the full truth, for you will say, like the Queen of Sheba when she had seen Solomon's glory, "The half hath not been told me."

9

GIDEON

One War Over and Another Begun

*"And when Gideon perceived that he was an angel of the
Lord, Gideon said, Alas, O Lord God! for because I have seen
an angel of the Lord face to face. And the Lord said unto
him, Peace be unto thee; fear not: thou shalt not die. Then
Gideon built an altar there unto the Lord, and called it
Jehovah-shalom"* (Judg. 6:4–22).

THESE Midianites were wandering Bedouins from Arabia, and from the
East country round about the Holy Land. They were masters of the art
of plundering, and knew no bowels of compassion. They generally
lived a hard life themselves, and when they had an opportunity to feast
on the spoils of others, they rioted without stint, and left a famine behind them. Most fitly does the Scripture compare them to grasshoppers,
for both in number and in destructive force they were like those terrible devourers. God had brought them upon Israel to scourge that nation because it had been so foolish and so ungrateful as to set up the gods
of the heathen, and to forget the one mighty God who was so specially
and graciously their patron and defender. They were impoverished
and ground down to the very last degree by these plunderers, who left
no food either for men or cattle. The poor Israelites, creeping forth from
their dens and caves, attempted to carry on the work of husbandry,
and sowed the land; but when the time came for reaping, the marauders came forth once more, took away their harvest, and despoiled
their pastures again. Then, as usual, Israel cried unto Jehovah, and
his ear was open to their groaning. Their afflictions made them weary
of their idols, and caused them to say, "We will return unto our first husband, for it was better with us then than now." God in his great mercy

raised up for them a deliverer, Gideon, a mighty man of valor, who distinguished himself in various skirmishes with the foe! His name was already a terror to Midian, for he who dreamed of the barley cake which smote the tent, and it lay along, said to his fellow—"This is none other than Gideon, the son of Joash."

His character has never been sufficiently admired: Scripture names much less bright than his have been preferred before him by the general ministry; yet he deserves far better treatment. He was a man gentle and yet strong, cautious and yet venturesome; a searching inquirer, and an intense believer. While he was a sort of foreshadowing of David, he had much of the afterglow of Joshua. He was a truly great man, though his latter days were overshadowed by a grievous religious error, and a sad moral fault. Despite his failings he was one of the greatest of the heroes of faith. He was not in a hurry to venture upon a pitched battle, but waited his time, and then by a sudden and unexpected attack he struck the whole host with panic, so that they fled at once, and Midian was smitten as one man. The leaders flee; two of the minor ones, Oreb and Zeeb, the raven and the wolf, are first captured, and by-and-by the greater generals, who had fled first of all, are taken by the victorious band. The leaders were ahead of all others in flight. In after days the destruction of their mighty ones became a proverbial curse, "Make their nobles like Oreb, and like Zeeb: yea, all their princes as Zebah, and as Zalmunna."

Let us think for a while of Gideon, in order that we may see that we ourselves are or may be somewhat parallels with him. We may not have to smite the Bedouin as he had, but unto a spiritual warfare God has called many of us: and though he intends to use us, and to get unto himself victory by us, yet it may be that at this moment we are in fear. We are now passing through the same mental processes as those which educated Gideon, and we are being prepared thereby for future conflict and conquest.

I shall begin by asking you to dwell for a minute upon GIDEON'S SIGH FOR PEACE; for he loved not war, but pined for quiet. He called the name of the altar "Jehovah-shalom," which the margin reads, "The Lord send peace." You see therefore that deeper down in his spirit than any desire for warlike honor there was a yearning after peace. He wanted not the spoils of princes; he only desired to plow, and sow, and reap in peace.

And do you wonder at it, when *the ills of war were all around?* He had for a long time seen in the cases of his friends and neighbors the desolating effects of war: their property was taken from them, their bread was stolen out of their mouths, their children were slain, and themselves made to hide away upon the tops of mountains or in caverns among the hills. Life became intolerable amid such privations and dangers. Gideon must have felt his heart swell with grief and indignation as he looked upon the remnant of Israel hunted like partridges upon the mountains, though once they had dwelt safely, every man under his vine and under his fig tree. The Bedouin styled the valley of Jezreel "the meadows of God": how grievous to see those fat pastures trodden down by the feet of the invaders! Ah, little can you and I imagine of the horrors of war. We read of it, and our sympathies are touched, but we know not the multiplied murders, the painful wounds, the desolating rapine, and the fierce crimes which attend the track of armies. If we saw battle with our own eyes, we should with burning fervor cry, "Send us peace in our days, good Lord."

Moreover, he had not only seen war, but he sighed for peace, because *he was himself feeling the mischief of it.* The dread of the conflict had come to his own mountain farm at Abiezer. There he was himself, threshing wheat by the wine press, in an unusual place, in an inconvenient place, that he might hide a little grain, for winter's food, from the Midianites who were eager to devour it. Aye, and when carnage smokes at your own door, and rapine is at your own gate, when you yourself are straitened and are hiding for fear, then comes from the deep recesses of the spirit the cry, "Oh, that God would send us peace, for this is a weary oppression; these ravens and wolves devour us utterly."

The way of peace was sufficiently well known to Gideon: the prophet of the Lord had indicated to the people that the only way of peace was for Israel to return unto Jehovah, her God. The great sin of departure from the glorious living God was set before them, and they could readily draw the inference that they would never have peace from their enemies till first of all they had made their peace with God. They must surrender to their sovereign, and renew their loyalty, and then he would drive out the foe from their land. They must confess their transgressions and renew their covenant, and then they would obtain deliverance. Then would the ancient promise be fulfilled, "One should chase a thousand, and two put ten thousand to flight." Gideon probably knew this before the prophet came; it was deeply imprinted on his thoughtful spirit, and as he was a man of faith in God, he did not doubt but that if Israel returned unto Jehovah then peace would follow.

While Gideon is meditating and working, an angel appears to him and *gives him the assurance that with him at least God was at peace.* The covenant angel said to him, "Jehovah is with thee, thou mighty man of valor." Methinks his spirit ought greatly to have rejoiced at that assurance, and perhaps it did; for what better thing can happen unto any man than to receive such a token for good? If God be for us, who can be against us? We know how sweet is the assurance that being justified by faith we have peace with God. It is well with us when we are assured that the Lord is with us, our helper, our shield, our portion forever and ever.

But *there arose in his mind a grave anxiety.* His was a very careful, thoughtful soul, for he was a man of prudence, large-hearted, far-seeing, and given to look at things coolly and steadily; and there arose in his heart a question serious and vital, "Is this the voice of God to me, or am I deluded? Is God at peace with me, or am I like the rest, plunged in a horrible warfare against the living God?" Therefore he puts a question, and he asks a sign that he might make sure of what he was about. Brethren, in spiritual matters you and I had need be sure. If we have peace within our spirit, let us make certain that it is the peace of God; for still are there voices that cry, "Peace, peace," where there is no peace. Still do siren songs charm men to ruin with their dulcet notes; still does the fatal river flow most smoothly as it approaches the dreadful cataract. Beware of that word of the Lord, "When they shall say, Peace and safety; then sudden destruction cometh upon them, as travail upon a woman with child; and they shall not escape." None are more quiet than the ungodly when they are given up to a strong delusion. The Psalmist says of them, "There are no bands in their death: but their strength is firm. They are not in trouble as other men; neither are they plagued like other men." It was no so with Gideon: his anxiety made itself visible. He was not the man to leap at a shadow: he sought for substance. If he was to have peace, he must have it from God: if he was to be delivered, he longed to have victory plain and permanent. The favor which he asked was requested because anxiety troubled him, and he wished to make assurance doubly sure. He desired to know from God himself that his mission was authentic and his success certain.

I believe that many of us have been, and perhaps are, in Gideon's position. Of course we have not his errand, but we have one of our own, and we are troubled because we are not personally sure of our peace. We are grieved by our past sins and their consequences. This is the lot of many men. "Conscience doth make cowards of us all," and when the mighty Spirit of God convinces us of sin then sin becomes a second sorrow; nay, worse than that, for if sorrow do chasten us with whips, sin doth scourge us with scorpions. We are consumed by God's anger, and by his wrath we are troubled. The mind is tossed to and fro and is confounded, but even in its confusion it seeks the true rest, and longs to gain peace in God. Like the needle in the compass, it is agitated and disturbed, yet still it knows its pole, and trembles towards it. It will never be still till it reaches the point of its rest. Have you ever been in that condition? I know you have if the Lord has loved you and ordained you to his work. Has God at such a time sent you a message of mercy? Have you searched the Scriptures and found a precious promise? Have you heard a faithful servant of God preach under his Master's anointing, and have you been comforted? Even then I should not wonder if the darkening thought has arisen like a cloud, "Is this the right comfort for me? May I really enjoy it? Will it be presumption or assurance?" There is often a fine line, thin as a razor's edge, between the two, and woe unto him who makes a mistake about it. O God, save us from carnal security. Prevent our crying "Peace, peace, where there is no peace." Better that we write bitter things against ourselves, if they be true, than that we say smooth things and flatter ourselves to destruction. Therefore, I should not wonder if you are asking the Lord to give you a token for good. You are praying to him and saying, "I will not be comforted except thou comfort me: thy dove shall find no rest for the sole of her foot except it be in the ark with the true Noah, in whom is rest." As for me, I will take no cup of consolation except that which Jesus proffers when he gives it me with his own pierced hands. If washed, it shall be in Jesus' blood: if clothed, it shall be in his righteousness.

From Gideon's longing, panting desire to obtain peace with God and then peace for his country we turn to look a little further into GIDEON'S FEAR WHICH HE MET WITH IN THE WAY OF PEACE. "An angel" appeared to him—so saith the text in the Authorized Version; but in truth it was *the* Angel of Jehovah, and this should have comforted him, even as it has comforted us. One would have thought that Gideon would have leaped for joy when he beheld his God veiled in angelic form, but instead therefore the shadow of death fell upon him. Here was a man panting for peace, and firmly following the way of peace, and yet afraid with a deadly fear. Peace cannot be had except by our drawing near to God and the Lord's drawing near to us; but as soon as this process commences poor humanity shrinks from the interview, and is melted with fear. "When Gideon perceived that he was an angel of the Lord, Gideon said, Alas, O Lord God! for because I have seen an angel of the Lord face to face." It usually happens that when God is bringing men into peace with himself, while the operation is going on thoroughly and soundly, there is a degree of trembling in the soul. I suspect that conversion which has no trembling in it: note the prodigal's cry, "I am not worthy to be called thy son." Note Peter's bitter weeping, and the three days' darkness of Saul of Tarsus. Even to believers the visitations of God are not without overwhelming awe: Jacob cries, "How dreadful is this place," Job abhors himself, Moses doth exceedingly fear and quake, and Isaiah cries, "Woe is me."

Why was Gideon afraid? *Not because he was a coward*—you will scarcely meet with a braver man in all Scripture than this son of Joash—but because even brave men are alarmed at the supernatural. He saw something which he had never seen before, an appearance celestial, mysterious, above what is usually seen of mortal men; therefore, as he feared God, Gideon was afraid. When the living God draws very near to a soul, even though it be in the person of Christ Jesus, that soul is struck with awe, and trembles before the Lord. It cannot well be otherwise. Recollect how it was with the beloved John. "When I saw him," says John—that was, his own dear Master, upon whose breast he had leaned his head—"when I," the disciple whom Jesus loved, "saw *him*, I fell at *his* feet as dead." You do not wonder, therefore, if a poor soul full of doubt and anxiety, vexed with a sense of sin, and greatly troubled by affliction, is full of fear when Jesus draws near. Though he comes with no feeling but of love, no thought but of mercy, no sentence but of free forgiveness, yet the heart is awe-struck at the wondrous sight.

Alas, some of you know not what it is to have the Lord drawing near to your spirits. If you did you would not think it strange that certain awakened ones have acted in a singular way, and for a while have forgotten to eat bread. Daniel saith, "I was left alone, and saw this great vision, and there remained no strength in me: for my comeliness was turned in me into corruption, and I retained no strength." When this glorious God comes near to the soul it is a solemn visitation, and the mind is bowed under it.

Moreover, *Gideon had been ill-taught by tradition*. There was a rumor abroad which was derived from truth, and yet was false, namely, that no man could see a heavenly being and live. It is true that the Lord expressly told his servant Moses that he could not see his face and live; but he did not say, "Thou canst not see an angel and live"; nor had he said, "Thou canst not see my veiled presence and live." The tradition was an accretion to the truth and a corruption of it. We may not see the face of God, but we may see Jesus; in fact, we live because we see him. Beware of the moss which grows upon a truth. Many a heart bleeds because it is wounded by its own imperfect ideas of God; and so when God does draw near, when the great Almighty overshadows it, there is a slavish dread for which there is no need. "I shall die," saith he, "I shall die." He sees his sin, and therefore he thinks that God has come in anger to punish him: he feels his weakness, and fainting under it he groans, "I shall die." No, soul, if God had meant to slay you he would have let you alone. Whom God destroys he first leaves to the madness of his own conceit. He does not take the trouble to show a man his sin, and reveal to him his transgression unless he means to pardon and save him. If the Lord has taken to strip you, he will clothe you, if he makes your righteousness to fade like the leaves of autumn, it is because he has a glorious robe with which to array you: therefore be not afraid.

Besides, *Gideon was in a state of mind in which he could be easily cast down*. He was a brave man, but long affliction had cast a tinge of sadness over him. His usual conduct in life is well pictured by the two signs which God gave him. When all the people around him were, with excitement, like the threshing floor, heated and dry, he, like the fleece, was cool and composed: and then, again, when all around him like the wet floor, were dampened with discouragement, he alone remained in his ordinary condition, with not a drop of cowardice within him. That was the kind of man: calm, quiet, determined, brave. But at the moment recorded in our text he was smarting under a cruel oppression, conscious of God's anger for Israel's sin, and overshadowed by God's own presence, and therefore his mind was ready to rush from one fear to another. Only, see the beauty of it, that he always tells his fear to God, always goes to him for comfort, and therefore always obtains succor. The brave man is not he who sees no fear, but he who, seeing the danger, rises superior to it. Such was this man, tossed to and fro from one fear to another, but never tossed off from his God, and so always sure to right himself.

One thing is noteworthy, namely, that *Gideon's greatest fear arose out of a sign which he had himself asked for.* He said, "Show me a sign," and when he had that sign, namely, God's coming to him, then it was that he was afraid. Be very chary how you ask for signs; for they may work your discouragement rather than your comfort. I have known some say, "I shall not believe I am a child of God unless I feel a deep sense of sin," and when they have entered into that feeling they have exclaimed, "I will never again ask for this." I have heard of others who thought they could come to Christ if they were gently drawn; and the Lord has been gently drawing them, and then they have wished that they had been more troubled and distressed. They imagine that they could have believed more readily had their despair been greater—a strange notion certainly. We are every busy in manufacturing fresh doubts, and for raw material we use the very tokens for which we so earnestly besought the Lord. We cry aloud, "Show me a token for good," and when the token is given we are amazed at being heard, and fall to fearing more sadly than before. Therefore pray for such boons with bated breath, and say twice over concerning such things, "Nevertheless, not as I will, but as thou wilt."

All this while *Gideon had one truth before him which ought to have prevented all his fears:* for the Lord had spoken to him, and said, "Go in this thy might, and thou shalt save Israel from the hand of the Midianites: have not I sent thee?" See, he goes home fearing that he will die, and yet that could not be. How could he die if he was to deliver Israel? He must be a live man to do that, and yet, you see, he forgets to reason for his own comfort, but takes care to argue for his fears. Have I never seen my hearers doing this? I have often caught myself at it—refusing to use my logic for the strengthening of my faith, but perverting reason in order to assist my unbelief. Is not this foolish and wicked? Too often we are industrious in the fabrication of discomfort, and utterly idle in the search for joy. This is folly, and yet better men than we are have fallen into this fault. The Lord save us from it. In drawing near to God is our peace, and if in that process a sense of the presence of God casts us down and creates a more poignant sorrow than we left at the first, let us not therefore shrink from the process, but push on with all our might. As our safety lies in coming to God, to him we must approach at all hazards. If he seem to stand before us with a drawn sword in his hand let us run upon the point of it. If even our God be a consuming fire let us still draw near to him, for this is indeed the high privilege of saints. "Our God," that is our God in Christ Jesus, "is a consuming fire." Who, then, shall dwell with the devouring fire?

Now let us spend a few minutes in considering GOD'S COMFORT OF HIS SERVANT. "The Lord said unto him, *Shalom*—peace be unto thee; fear not: thou shalt not die." The Lord would not have his Gideons disturbed in mind. If we are to trouble the enemy we must not be troubled ourselves. Notice, brethren, *the great power of God in speaking home the truth.* Suppose I salute you with, "Brethren, peace be to you." That would be a sweet word; but when the Lord says it, you feel the peace itself. Suppose Peter had stood up in that bark which was tossed upon the Galilean lake, and had said to the waves, "Be still": the waves would not have taken much notice of him, and the whistling blast would have defied him; but when Jesus said, "Peace, be still," the rampant lions of the sea crouched at his feet, and there was a great calm.

"Peace!" the word is *shalom*, the word which Gideon borrowed and applied to the altar which he raised in obedience to the Lord's bidding. It signifies not only quiet, but prosperity, success, "good fortune," as the multitude say. When God spoke that word home to his dear servant's heart a great joy was born within him to prepare him for his great warfare. The Lord also cheered him with, "Fear not." Oh, that charming word; as full as it is short—"Fear not." What is there to fear? If God is with you, of whom can you be afraid? Gideon feared himself, dreaded his own unfitness and unworthiness, feared in the awful presence of God; but the Lord said, "Fear not," and Gideon's heart grew calm.

Then the Lord added, "Thou shalt not die," thus meeting the special form of his dread. This is what the Lord says to every poor trembler who is holding to him by the desperate grip of faith—"Thou shalt not die. Thou shalt not die the second death: thou hast no sin to die for, for I have laid thy transgressions on my only-begotten Son. Thou shalt not die, for Jesus died. Thy spiritual life cannot expire, for thy 'life is hid with Christ in God,' and because Jesus lives thou shalt live also."

Let us now look at GIDEON'S MEMORIAL. His fears being banished, and being at perfect peace, *Gideon now goes to work*. Are any of you questioning whether you are saved or not? Do not go out preaching yet, for you may, perhaps, put others into bondage. Are any of you half afraid that you are not at peace with God? Be careful what you do! Strive after peace, lest you weaken your testimony. I recollect the lesson which I learned from my Sunday-school class: I was taught, if the other boys were not. Though yet a youth, I was teaching the Gospel to boys, and I said, "He that believeth and is baptized shall be saved." One of them asked somewhat earnestly, "Teacher, are you saved?" I answered, "I hope so." The boy replied, "Teacher, don't you know?" As if he had been sent to push the matter home to me, he further inquired, "Teacher, have you believed?" I said, "Yes," "Have you been baptized?" I said, "Yes." "Well, then," he argued, "you are saved." I was happy to answer, "Yes, I am"; but I had hardly dared to say that before. I found that if I had to teach other people the truth I must know and believe its sweet result upon myself. I believe that you will seldom comfort others except it be by the comfort with which you yourself are comforted of God. God would have his people be at peace with him, and know that they are so, for if they are fretted within, and worried in reference to their God, how can they fight the battles of life?

When Gideon is fully at peace, what does he begin to do for God? If God loves you he will use you either for suffering or service; and if he has given you peace you must now prepare for war. Will you think me odd if I say that our Lord came to give us peace that he might send us out to war? Gideon's first work was to go and *cut down his father's sacred grove*, which stood on the top of the hill, and enclosed an altar to Baal. He could not effect this business by day, because the foolish worshipers would have rallied to the defense of their dumb idol, and have overpowered the reformer; therefore with his ten men he performed the work by night. I think I see him and his people in the dim darkness, with their axes and saws, doing the work as quietly as they can, felling all those trees. A splendid clearance was made that night. "Now," cries he, "over with that detestable altar to Baal." Some people would have said, "Spare it as a fine piece of antiquity." Yes, and leave it to be used again! I say, down with it, for the older it is the more sin it has caused, and the more likely is it that it will be venerated again. I often wish the Reformers had been more thorough in their destruction of idolatrous images and Popish trumpery. In many a parish church of this land everything is ready for the restoration of the Roman idolatry.

But see, by the Lord's bidding, *he piles a new altar of earth*, or unhewn stone; and when that is done, he fetches his father's bullock and slays it for a sacrifice. How steadily they went about this re-establishment of the pure faith! See, they use the wood of the grove for burning the sacrifice, and the heavens are red with the blaze. I think I hear the gallant leader say, "Let them wake now; they cannot prevent our worshiping the Most High, nor can they cause the grove to grow again. By yon beacon-fire, Israel shall gather together to fight against Midian, and victory shall be ours." Beloved, if God has given you peace, go home and begin your reform. I would preach up the overthrow of every sin. Down with every idol. Have you one left? Over with it, and present a sacrifice to God.

But to pull down is not enough. Plenty of people can do that. Gideon, as we have seen, builds an altar to Jehovah. When you are at perfect peace with God, think what you can do for him: think of a new plan of work, or consider how to do the old work better: advance any part of divine truth that has been forgotten, any ordinance that has been neglected, any virtue that has been despised. Especially make prominent Christ Jesus, the altar and sacrifice so dear to God.

When he had built his altar *he called it "Jehovah-shalom,"* which was done by way of thanksgiving for peace received. The inscription declares that "Jehovah is our peace." Blessed be his name this day. We have entered on the battles of peace, for the Lord God is with us, and with his people we will go forth to win the peace which he has promised. It was a psalm in two words; it was a song of one verse, infinitely sweet. "Jehovah-shalom": the Lord our peace.

Moreover, it was a prayer, as the margin puts it—"Jehovah, send peace." If you have peace with God, let your next prayer be, "Lord, give peace to all thy people." "Pray for the peace of Jerusalem." Work it, O holy Spirit of peace! Then ask for peace by conquest of an ungodly world for Jesus till the first Christmas carol shall be sung again, "Glory to God in the highest, peace on earth, goodwill toward men."

See, brethren, and with that I finish, there may sit here this morning a young man who does not know what God is going to make of him. The capacities of service that God can infuse into a single individual are marvelous. At present you are disturbed in mind, afflicted in heart, ill at ease; you need perfect peace, but you have not found it yet. Rest not ill you have it. At God's own altar, where Jesus died, you will find it, and only there. When Jesus' blood makes peace with God there is your peace. Rest not till you are assuredly at peace with the Lord of all, so that your soul lies down in green pastures, and is led by the still waters.

10

SAMUEL

An Example of Intercession

"Moreover as for me, God forbid that I should sin against the Lord in ceasing to pray for you: but I will teach you the good and the right way" (1 Sam. 12:23).

IT IS a very great privilege to be permitted to pray for our fellowmen. Prayer in each man's case must necessarily begin with person petition, for until the man is himself accepted with God he cannot act as an intercessor for others; and herein lies part of the excellence of intercessory prayer, for it is to the man who exercises it aright a mark of inward grace, and a token for good from the Lord. Thou mayest be sure that thy King loves thee when he will permit thee to speak a word to him on behalf of thy friend. When the heart is enlarged in believing supplication for others, all doubts about personal acceptance with God may cease; he who prompts us to love has certainly given us that love, and what better proof of his favor do we desire? It is a great advance upon anxiety for our own salvation when we have risen out of the narrowness of dread about ourselves into the broader region of care for a brother's soul. He who in answer to his intercession has seen others blessed and saved may take it as a pledge of divine love, and rejoice in the condescending grace of God. Such prayer rises higher than any petition for ourselves, for only he who is in favor with the Lord can venture upon pleading for others.

Intercessory prayer is an act of communion with Christ, for Jesus pleads for the sons of men. It is a part of his priestly office to make intercession for his people. He hath ascended up on high to this end, and exercises this office continually within the veil. When we pray for our fellow sinners we are in sympathy with our divine Savior, who made intercession for the transgressors.

Such prayers are often of unspeakable value to those for whom they are offered. Many of us trace our conversion, if we go to the root of it, to the prayers of certain godly persons. In innumerable instances the prayers of parents have availed to bring young people to Christ. Many more will have to bless God for praying teachers, praying friends, praying pastors. Obscure persons confined to their beds are often the means of saving hundreds by their continual pleadings with God. The book of remembrance will reveal the value of these hidden ones, of whom so little is thought by the mass of Christians. As the body is knit together by bands and sinews, and interlacing nerves and veins, so is the whole body of Christ converted into a living unity by mutual prayers; we were prayed for, and now in turn we pray for others. Not only the conversion of sinners, but the welfare, preservation, growth, comfort and usefulness of saints are abundantly promoted by the prayers of their brethren; hence apostolic men cried, "Brethren, pray for us"; he who was the personification of love said, "Pray one for another that ye may be healed," and our great Lord and Head ended his earthly career by a matchless prayer for those whom the Father had given him.

Intercessory prayer is a benefit to the man who exercises it, and is often a better channel of comfort than any other means of grace. The Lord turned again the captivity of Job when he prayed for his friends. Even where such prayer does not avail for its precise object, it has its results. David tells us that he prayed for his enemies: he says, In Psalm 35:13, "As for me, when they were sick, my clothing was sackcloth: I humbled my soul with fasting." And he adds, "my prayer returned into mine own bosom." He sent forth his intercession, like Noah's dove, but as it found no rest for the sole of its foot, and no blessing came of it, it returned to him who sent it, and brought back with it an olive leaf plucked off, a sense of peace to his own spirit; for nothing is more restful to the heart than to have prayed for those who despitefully use us and persecute us. Prayers for others are pleasing to God and profitable to ourselves; they are no waste of breath, but have a result guaranteed by the faithful Promiser.

Let us first dwell upon HIS HABIT OF INTERCESSION, for it was most manifest in Samuel. We gather this from the text. He says, "God forbid that I should sin against the Lord in *ceasing* to pray for you." It is clear, therefore, that he had been in the continual habit and practice of praying for Israel; he could not peak of ceasing to pray if he had not hitherto continued in prayer. Samuel had become so rooted in the habit of prayer for the people that he seems to start at the very thought of bringing his intercession to an end. The people, measuring the prophet by themselves, half suspected that he would be irritated with them, and would, therefore, deny them his prayers; therefore in the nineteenth verse we read, "All the people said unto Samuel, Pray for thy servants unto the Lord thy God, that we die not." They greatly valued his prayers, and felt as if their national life, and perhaps their personal lives, depended upon his pleadings: therefore they urged him as men who plead for their lives that he would not cease to pray for them, and he replied, "God forbid that I should." The denial of his prayers does not seem to have entered his thoughts. To my mind the words represent him as astonished at the idea, horrified and half indignant at the suggestion—"What I, Samuel, I who have been your servant from my childhood, since the day when I put on the little ephod, and waited for you in the house of the Lord; I that have lived for you and have loved you, and was willing to have died in your service, shall I ever cease to pray for you?" He says, "God forbid." It is the strongest expression that one can well imagine, and this, together with his evident surprise, shows that the prophet's habit of intercession was rooted, constant, fixed, abiding, a part and parcel of himself.

If you will read his life you will see how truly this was the case. Samuel was born of prayer. A woman of a sorrowful spirit received him from God, and joyfully exclaimed, "For this child I prayed." He was named in prayer, for his name Samuel signifies, *"asked of God."* Well did he carry out his name and prove its prophetic accuracy, for having commenced life by being himself asked of God, he continued asking of God, and all his knowledge, wisdom, justice, and power to rule were things which came to him because "asked of God." He was nurtured by a woman of prayer at the first, and when he left her it was to dwell in the house of prayer all the days of his life. His earliest days were honored by a divine visitation, and he showed even then that waiting, watchful spirit which is the very knee of prayer. "Speak, Lord, for thy servant heareth" is the cry of a simple, sincere heart, such as the Lord ever accepts.

We all think of Samuel under that little figure so often painted and sculptured, in which a sweet child is seen in the attitude of prayer. We all seem to know little Samuel, the praying child: our boys and girls know him as a familiar friend, but it is as kneeling with clasped hands. He was born, named, nurtured, housed, and trained in prayer, and he never departed from the way of supplication. In his case the text was fulfilled, "Out of the mouth of babes and sucklings thou hast perfected praise"; and he so persevered in prayer that he brought forth fruit in old age, and testified of God's power to those who came after him. So famous did Samuel become as an intercessor that, if you will turn to the ninety-ninth Psalm, at the sixth verse, you will read a short but very fragrant eulogy of him: "Moses and Aaron among his priests, and Samuel among them that call upon his name." If Moses and Aaron are selected as being consecrated men, leaders of God's Israel in service and sacrifice, Samuel is selected as the praying man, the man who calls upon God's name. All Israel knew Samuel was an intercessor as well as they knew Aaron as a priest. Perhaps even more notably you get the same inspired estimate of him in Jeremiah 15, at the first verse, where he is again classed with Moses: "Then said the Lord unto me, though Moses and Samuel stood before me, yet my mind could not be toward this people: cast them out of my sight, and let them go forth." Here there is no doubt an allusion to the prevalent prayer of Moses, when in the agony of his heart he cried, "If not, blot me, I pray thee, out of thy Book which thou hast written." This was a high form of pleading, but such is God's valuation of Samuel as an intercessor that he puts him side by side with Moses, and by way of threatening to sinful Israel he tells Jeremiah that he would not even listen to Moses and Samuel if they stood before him. It is well to learn the art of prayer in our earliest days, for then we grow up to be proficient in it. Early prayer grows into powerful prayer. Hear this, you young people, and may the Lord now make Samuels of you. What an honor to be called to intercede for others, to be the benefactor of our nation, or even the channel of blessing to our own households. Aspire to it, my dear young friends. Perhaps you will never preach, but you may pray. If you cannot climb the pulpit you may bow before the mercy seat, and be quite as great a blessing.

As to the success of Samuel's prayers, read his life, and you will find that wrought great deliverances for the people. In the seventh chapter of this book we find that the Philistines grievously oppressed Israel, and Samuel bravely called the people together, to consider their condition, and bade them turn from idolatry, and worship the only true God, and promised them his prayers as a boon which they greatly valued. These are his words: "Gather all Israel to Mizpeh, and I will pray for you unto the Lord." He then took a lamb, and offered it up for a burnt-offering wholly unto the lord, "and Samuel cried unto the Lord for Israel, and the Lord heard him." This is one of the grand events of his life, and yet it is fairly descriptive of his whole career. He cried, and the Lord heard. In this instance the Israelites marched to battle, but Jehovah went before them, in answer to the prophet's prayer. You could hear the rolling of the drums in the march of the God of armies, and see the glittering of his spear, for so is the history of the battle recorded: "And as Samuel was offering up the burnt offering, the Philistines drew near to battle against Israel: but the Lord thundered with a great thunder on that day upon the Philistines, and discomfited them; and they were smitten before Israel. And the men of Israel went out of Mizpeh, and pursued the Philistines, and smote them." The conclusion of the whole is, "So the Philistines were subdued"; that is to say, the prayer of Samuel was the conquering weapon, and Philistia crouched beneath its power. Oh ye who know the power of prayer, write this on your banners, "So the Philistines were subdued."

Samuel's prayers were so prevalent that the very elements were controlled by him. Oh, the power of prayer! It has been ridiculed: it has been represented as an unscientific and an unpractical thing, but we who daily try it know that its power cannot be exaggerated, and do not feel even a shadow of doubt concerning it. There is such power in prayer that it "moves the arm that moves the world." We have but to know how to pray, and the thunder shall lift up its voice in answer to our cry, and Jehovah's arrows shall be scattered abroad to the overthrowing of his adversaries. How should those be able to judge of prayer who never ask at all, or never ask in faith? Let those bear witness to whom prayer is a familiar exercise, and to whom answers from God are as common as the day. Over a father's heart no power has so great a control as his child's necessity, and in the case of our Father who is in heaven it is especially so. He must hear prayer, for he cannot dishonor his own name, or forget his own children.

When in his old age the people began to turn against Samuel, and to express dissatisfaction with his unworthy sons, it is beautiful to notice how Samuel at once resorted to prayer. Look at the eighth chapter, the fifth verse: the people "said unto him, Behold, thou art old, and thy sons walk not in thy ways: now make us a king to judge us." The old man was

sorely grieved; it was natural that he should be. But look at the next words.
Did Samuel scold the people? Did he send them home in a huff? No.
It is written, "And Samuel prayed unto the Lord." He told his Master
about them, and his Master said to him, "Hearken unto the voice of the
people in all that they say unto thee: for they have not rejected *thee*," —
do not lay it to heart as if it were a personal affront to thee — "but they
have rejected me, that I should not reign over them." This slight upon
God's servant was a rejection of God himself, and he would not have
Samuel lay to heart their ingratitude to him, but think of their wicked
conduct to the Lord their God.

Thus, you see, Samuel was a man of abundant prayer, and in the twenty-
first verse we read that, after he had entered his protest, and told the people of all that they would have to suffer from a king, how he would tax
them and oppress them, and take their sons to be soldiers and their daughters to wait in his palace, and take their fields and vineyards, though they
still persisted in saying, "Nay, but we will have a king," he made no angry
answer but returned to his God in secret communion, "Samuel heard
all the words of the people, and he rehearsed them in the ears of the Lord."
Oh, that we were wise enough to do the like! Instead of going about and
telling one and another of the opprobrious things that have been said
about us, it were well to go straight away to our closet and rehearse them
in the ears of the Lord. Samuel was thus, you see, throughout his whole
official life, a man mighty in prayer, and when the people left him
and followed after their new-made king, our text shows that he did not
cease to intercede for them. He says, "God forbid that I should cease
to pray to God for you."

Nor was this all, when Saul had turned aside and become a traitor to
his divine Lord, Samuel made intercession for him. One whole night
he spent in earnest entreaty, though it was all in vain; and many a
time and oft did he sigh for the rejected prince. The old man had
been, from his youth up, an intercessor, and he never ceased from the
holy exercise till his lips were closed in death. Now, beloved, you are
not judges of the land, else would I plead with you to pray much for the
people whom you rule. You are not all pastors and teachers, else would
I say that if *we* do not abound in prayer the blood of souls will be upon
our skirts. Some of you, however, are teachers of the young: do not think
that you have done anything for your classes till you have prayed for them.
Be not satisfied with the hour or two of teaching in the week, be frequent

in your loving supplications. Many of you are parents. How can you discharge your duty towards your children except you bear their names upon your hearts in prayer? Those of you who are not found in these relationships have nevertheless some degree of ability, some measure of influence, some position in which you can do good to your fellows, and these demand your dependence upon God. You cannot discharge your responsibilities as relatives, as citizens, as neighbors, nay, as Christian men, unless you often make supplication for all ranks and conditions. To pray for others must become to you a habit from which you would not cease even if they provoked you to the utmost degree; for you would only cry out, God forbid that I should cease to pray for you, for it would be a great sin in the sight of the Most High.

Now, secondly, I call you to notice in Samuel's case HIS PROVOCATION TO CEASE FROM INTERCESSION, which provocation he patiently endured.

The first provocation was *the slight which they put upon himself.* The grand old man who had all the year round made his circuit from place to place to do justice had never looked at a bribe. He had done everything for them without fee or reward. Though he had a right to his stipend, yet he did not take it; in the generosity of his spirit he did everything gratuitously, like Nehemiah in after days who said, "The former governors that had been before me were chargeable unto the people, and had taken of them bread and wine, beside forty shekels of silver; yea, even their servants bare rule over the people: but so did not I, because of the fear of God." Samuel throughout a long life had kept the land in peace, and innumerable blessings had come to Israel through his leadership; but now he was getting old and somewhat infirm, though he was far from being worn out, and they seized on this excuse for setting up a king. The old man felt that there was life and work in him yet; but they clamored for a king, and therefore their aged friend must give up his office and come down from his high position. It displeases him when he first hears their demand, but after a little time spent in prayer he resigns his position very pleasantly, and all his anxiety is to find the right man for the throne. When the man is found he is full of care that the Lord's anointed shall be guided aright in the kingdom; and without a thought about himself he rejoices at the sight of one whose opening days promised so well. His deposition was a hard thing, mark you, an unkind, ungenerous thing; but he did not pray one atom the less for the people because or it; probably he prayed much more; for as his mother prayed most when the sorrow of her heart was greatest, so was it with him.

Beyond the provocation which came from slight upon himself he felt wounded by *their utter rejection of his solemn protest.* He stood before them and reasoned with them in the clearest possible manner: "What do you want a king for?" he seemed to say. "This will be the manner of the king that shall reign over you; he will take your sons and appoint them for himself, for his chariots, and to be his horsemen; and some shall run before his chariots. He will take your daughters to be confectionaries, and to be cooks, and to be bakers; and he will take your fields, and your vineyards, and your olive yards, even the best of them, and give them to his servants. He will take the tenth of your seed, and of your vineyards, and give to his officers, and to his servants; and he will take your menservants, and your maidservants, and your goodliest young men, and your asses, and put them to his work. He will take the tenth of your sheep; and ye shall be his servants; and ye shall cry out in that day because of your king which ye shall have chosen you; and the Lord will not hear you in that day." There was sound common sense in all these, and every word turned out to be true in fact before long, and yet they would not listen. They said, "Nay, but we will have a king over us; that we also may be like all the nations; and that our king may judge us, and fight our battles." Despite their rejection of his warning, the venerable man did not grow testy. It is sometimes the infirmity of wise men of years and weight, that when they have presented a clearer case, presented it earnestly in all simplicity of heart, and the thing looks as plain as that twice two make four, then if their hearers deliberately persist in defying their warning they grow peevish, or perhaps it is more fair to say they exhibit a justifiable indignation. Samuel is always hopeful, and if they will not do the best thing possible, he will try to lead them to do the second best. If they will not abide under the direct rule of the Lord, as their King, he hopes that they will do well under a human king who shall be a viceroy under God, and so he continues hopefully to pray for them, and to make the best he can of them.

At last it came to this, that the nation must have a king, and their king must be crowned. They must go to Gilgal to settle the kingdom, and then Samuel stood up and in the words which I read to you just now he declared how he had dealt with them, how he had never defrauded nor oppressed, nor taken anything from them, and he told them that their choice of a king was to some extent a rejection of God, that they were putting aside the best of rules and the most honorable of governments to go down to the level of the nations. Still, *they rejected his last appeal*, and it is beautiful to my mind to see how calmly he drops the question when he has given his last address, and made his most solemn appeal to heaven. Their obstinate adherence to their whim did not cause him to restrain prayer on their behalf.

The practical lesson of this is that when you are tempted to cease from pleading for certain persons you must not yield to the suggestion. They have ridiculed your prayers: they tell you that they do not want them: they have even made a taunt and a jest of your pious wishes on their behalf. Never mind. Retaliate by still greater love. Do not cease to wrestle with God for them. It may be you have been very much disappointed in them; your heart breaks to see how they have gone aside, yet go with your deep anxieties to the mercy seat, and cry out again for them. What will become of them if you leave them to themselves? Do not leave off interceding, though you are provoked to do so in ten thousand ways.

It may be that you think, partly in unbelief, and partly through trembling anxiety, that really their doom is sealed, and they will go on to perdition. Let this rather increase the intensity of your prayer than in the least degree diminish it. Till sinners are in hell cry to God for them. As long as there is breath in their bodies and your body cause the voice of our supplication to be heard. Your husband, good woman, what if he does grow more drunken and more profane, pray for him still; for God, who can draw out leviathan as with a hook, can yet take this great sinner and make a saint of him. What if your son does seem to be more profligate than ever, follow him with many entreaties, and weep before God about him still. Loving mother and gracious father, join your fervent cries day and night at the mercy seat and you shall yet obtain our desire.

I come, in the third place, briefly to notice Samuel in HIS PERSEVERING INTERCESSION. Though the people thus provoked him he did not cease from prayer for them; for, first, there and then, he offered fresh supplication for them, and that cry was heard, and Saul was dowried with a rich measure of favor to start with. Samuel did not cease his prayer for Saul when Saul had gone far astray, for we find this passage: "Then came the word of the Lord to Samuel, saying, It repenteth me that I have set up Saul to be king, for he has turned back from following me, and hath not performed my commandment; and it grieved Samuel, and he cried unto the Lord all night." *All night.* I think I see the old man in an agony for Saul, whom he loved. Old men need sleep, but the prophet forsook his bed, and in the night watches poured out his soul unto the Lord. Though he received no cheering answer, he still continued to cry; for we read, a little further on, that the Lord said to him, "How long wilt thou mourn for Saul?" He was pushing the case as far as ever he could push it, till the Lord gave him warning that there was no use in it. "How long wilt thou mourn for Saul?"

It is to be admired in Samuel, that, even though Saul may have committed the sin which is unto death, and Samuel had some fear that his fate was fixed, yet he prayed on in desperate hope. The Apostle John puts the case thus: "If any man see his brother sin a sin which is not unto death, he shall ask, and he shall give him life for them that sin not unto death. There is a sin unto death: I do not say that he shall pray for it." He does not in such a case forbid our prayers, neither does he encourage them, but I take it that he gives us a permit to pray on. We do not know for certain that the most guilty person has indeed passed the bound of mercy, and therefore we may intercede with hope. If we have a horrible dread upon us that possibly our erring relative is beyond hope, if we are not commanded to pray, we are certainly not forbidden, and it is always best to err on the safe side, if it be erring at all. We may still go to God, even with a forlorn hope, and cry to him in the extremity of our distress. We are not likely to hear the Lord say to us, "How long wilt thou mourn for Saul?" We are not likely to hear him say, "How long will you pray for your boy? How long will you mourn over your husband? I do not intend to save them."

When the prophet knew that Saul was hopelessly rejected he did not cease to pray for the nation, but went down to Bethlehem and anointed David, and when David was pursued by the malice of Saul we find him harboring David at Ramah, and exhibiting the power of prayer in his own house and in the holy place; for when Saul came down thinking to seize David, even in the seer's house, there was a prayer meeting being held, and Saul was so struck with it that he took to prophesying himself, and lay down all night among them disrobed and humbled. Men exclaimed, "Is Saul also among the prophets?" The malicious king could not venture to touch Samuel. The prophet was a gentle, mild, loving man; and yet the black-hearted Saul always had an awe of him, so that he took hold of his skirts for protection, and after he was dead wickedly sought to his supposed spirit for guidance. The man of God had evidently impressed the tall reprobate with the weight of his holy character. It is written that God was with him, and did let none of his words fall to the ground; and this was because he was a praying man. He who can prevail with God for man can always prevail with man for God. If you can overcome heaven by prayer, you can overcome earth by preaching: if you know the art of speaking to the Eternal, it will be a small thing to speak to mortal men. Rest assured that the very essence of all true power over men for their good must lie in power with God in secret: when we have waited upon the Lord, and prevailed, our work is well-nigh done.

I pray you, therefore, still persevere in supplication, and be supported in your perseverance by the knowledge that it would be a sin to cease to pray for those who have been the subjects of your petitions. Samuel confesses that it would have been sinful on his part to abstain from intercession. How so? Why, if he ceased to pray for that people, he would be neglecting his office, for God had made him a prophet to the nation, and he must intercede for them or neglect his duty. It would show a want of love to the Lord's chosen people if he did not pray for them. How could he teach them if he was not himself taught of God? How could he possibly hope to sway them if he had not enough affection for them to cry to God on their behalf? It would be in his case, too, a sin of anger. It would look as if he were in a pet with them and with God too, because he could not be all that he would wish to be. "God forbid," he said, "I should harbor such anger in my bosom as to cease to pray for you." It would have been a neglect of the divine glory; for whatever the people might be, God's name was wrapped up in them, and if they did not prosper the Lord would not be glorified in the eyes of the heathen. He could not give up praying for them, for their cause was the cause of God. It would have been a cruelty to souls if he who possessed such power in prayer had restrained it. Now, brethren and sisters, it will be sin on your part if you neglect the mercy seat. You will grieve the Holy Spirit, you will rob Christ of his glory, you will be cruel to souls dead in sin, and you will be false and traitorous to the Spirit of grace, and to your sacred calling.

Our last point is that Samuel showed HIS SINCERITY IN INTERCESSION by corresponding action, for he says in the words of the text, "God forbid that I should sin against the Lord in ceasing to pray for you: but I will teach you the good and the right way." So far from leaving off praying, he would be doubly diligent to each them: and he did so. He taught them by reminding them of God's promises, that he would not forsake his people: by directing them how to act—"Serve God in truth with all you heart": by urging motives upon them—"consider the great things he hath done for you": and by adding a solemn warning, "If you shall still do wickedly, ye shall be consumed, both ye and your king." After praying for your friends, do try as well as you can to answer your own prayer by using the means which God ordinarily blesses. Some persons make idle prayers, for they use no effort for obtaining their requests. If a husbandman asks for a harvest, he also plows and sows, for else his supplications would be hypocritical. If we wish to see our neighbors converted, we shall labor for it in all ways. We shall invite them to go with us where the Gospel is faithfully preached, or we shall place a good book in their way, or we shall speak with them personally about eternal things. If I knew where gold was to be had for the picking up, and I wanted my neighbor to be rich, I would tell him of the precious deposit, and ask him to come and gather some of the treasure with me. But many never think of inviting a neighbor or a friend who is a Sabbath-breaker to go with them to the house of God; and there are thousands in London who only want an invitation and they would be sure to come, once, at any rate, and who can tell but that once might lead to their conversion?

If I desire the salvation of anyone I ought to tell him as best as I can what his condition is, and what the way of salvation is, and how he may find rest. All men are approachable at some time or in some way. It is very imprudent to rush at everybody as soon as you see them, without thought or ordinary prudence, for you may disgust those whom you wish to win: but those who earnestly plead for others, and bestir themselves to seek them, are generally taught of God, and so they are made wise as to time, manner, and subject. A man who wishes to shoot birds will, after a while, become expert in the sport, because he will give his mind to it: he will after a little practice become a noted marksman and know all about guns and dogs. A man who wants to catch salmon has his heart set upon his angling, and becomes absorbed in the pursuit. He soon learns how to use his rod and how to manage his fish. So he who longs to win souls, and puts his heart into it, finds out the knack of it by some means, and the Lord gives him success. I could not teach it to you, you must practice in order to find out; but this I will say, no man is clear of his fellows' blood simply because he has prayed to be so. Supposed we had around this parish of Newington a number of people who were dying of hunger, and we were to have a prayer meeting that God would relive their wants: would it not be hypocrisy worthy to be ridiculed and help up to reprobation if, after having prayed for these people, we all went home and ate our own dinners and did not give them a farthing's worth of bread? The truly benevolent man puts his hand in his pocket and says, "What can I do that my prayer may be answered?" I have heard of one who prayed in New York for a certain number of very poor families that he had visited, and he asked the Lord that they might be fed and clothed. His little sons said, "Father, if I were God I should tell you to answer your own prayer, for you have plenty of money." Thus the Lord might well say to us when we have been interceding, "Go and answer your own prayer by telling your friends of my Son." Do you sing, "Fly abroad, thou mighty Gospel"? Then give it wings covered with silver. Do you sing, "Waft, waft, ye winds, his story"? Then spend your breath for it. There is a power in your gifts; there is a power in your speech; use these powers. If you cannot personally do much, you can do a great deal by helping another to preach Christ: but chief and first you ought to do somewhat by your own hand, heart, and tongue. Go and teach the good and right way, and then shall your prayers be heard.

11

DAVID

Encouraging Himself in God

*"And David was greatly distressed; for the people spake
of stoning him, because the soul of all the people was
grieved, every man for his sons and for his daughters: but
David encouraged himself in the Lord his God. . . . And David
inquired at the Lord, saying, Shall I pursue after this troop?
Shall I overtake them? And he answered him, Pursue: for thou
shalt surely overtake them, and without fail recover all"*
(1 Sam. 30:6, 8).

WE OUGHT to be deeply grateful to God for the inspired history of the
life of his servant David. It was a great life, a vigorous life, a life spent
in many positions and conditions. I almost rejoice that it was not a
faultless life, for its failings and errors are instructive. It is the life of a
man after God's own heart; but still, the life of one who went astray, like
a lost sheep, and was recovered by the great Shepherd's grace. By this
fact he comes all the near to us poor, faulty men and women. I would
venture to apply to David the description which has been applied to the
world's own poet—

> A man so various, that he seemed to be
> Not one, but all mankind's epitome.

Each one may find something like himself in the long, eventful, and
checkered life of the son of Jesse. Among other things we learn this, that
where there is faith there is sure to be trial; for David, though he trusted
God so heartily, had good need of all the faith he possessed. In his
early days he was hunted like a partridge upon the mountains by Saul,
and was constantly in jeopardy of his life. He had so choice a treasure

of faith about him, that Satan was forever trying to plunder him of it. Still, the worst trials that David suffered arose not out of his faith, but out of his want of it. That which he did to avoid trouble brought him into deeper distress than ordinary providences ever caused him. He left the country where he was so ill at ease, which was, nevertheless, thy land, O Emmanuel, and he went away into the land of the Philistines, expecting there to escape from further turmoil. In so doing he transgressed, and fresh trials came upon him, trials of a worse kind than those which had happened to him from the hand of Saul. If you have faith it must be tried, and should that faith fail you must be tried still more. There is no discharge from this war: difficulties must be faced. This is the day of battle, and you must fight if you would reign. You are like men thrown into the sea, you must swim or drown. It is useless to expect ease where your Lord had none. However rough the king's highway may be, the bypaths are far worse; therefore keep the way of the commandment, and bravely face its trials.

Another lesson is this: though we shall be tried, yet faith in God is an available resource at all times. Faith is a shield which you may use for warding off every kind of arrow, yea, even the fiery darts of the great enemy; for this shield cannot be penetrated even by javelins of fire. You cannot be cast into a condition in which faith shall not help you. There is a promise of God suitable for every state, and God has wisdom and skill and love and faithfulness to deliver you out of every possible jeopardy; and therefore you have only to confide in God, and deliverance is sure to come. Mainly note this, that *even when your trouble has been brought upon you by your own fault faith is still available.* When your affliction is evidently a chastisement for grievous transgression, still trust in the Lord. The Lord Jesus prayed for erring Peter that his faith might not fail him: his hope of recovery lay there. Faith under a sense of guilt is one of those noble kinds of faith at which some are staggered. To my mind the faith of a saint is comparatively easy; it is the faith of a sinner that is hard. When you know that you have walked uprightly before God, and have not stained your garments, then you can trust him without difficulty: but, oh, when you have stepped aside, and when at last the heavenly Father makes you smart under his rod—to cast yourself upon him then is faith indeed. If any of you at this time are in great distress, and are conscious that you richly deserve all your troubles because of your folly, still trust in the mercy of the Lord. Do not doubt the Lord your

Savior, for he invites his backsliding children to return unto him.

First, then, let us look at DAVID'S DISTRESS—"David was greatly distressed." His city was burnt, his wives were gone, the sons and daughters of his comrades, were all captive, and little Ziklag, where they had made a home, smoked before them in blackened ruins. The men of war, wounded in heart, mutinied against their leader, and were ready to stone him. David's fortunes were at their lowest ebb. To understand his position we must go a little further back in his history.

David was greatly distressed for *he had been acting without consulting his God*. It was his general habit to wait upon the Lord for direction, for even as a shepherd lad it was his joy to sing, "He leadeth me"; but for once David had gone without leading, and had chosen a bad road. Worn out by the persecution of Saul, in an evil moment his heart failed him, and he said, "I shall surely fall one day by the hand of Saul." This was a dangerous mood. Always be afraid of being afraid. Failing faith means failing strength. Do not regard despondency as merely a loss of joy, view it as draining away your spiritual life. Struggle against it, for it often happens that when faith ebbs sin comes to the flood. He who does not comfortably trust God will soon seek after comfort somewhere else, and David did so: without asking divine direction he fled to the court of the Philistine chieftain Achish, hoping to be quiet there. See what came of it! When he stood among the ashes of Ziklag he began to understand what an evil and bitter thing it is to lean to our own understanding, to forget God who guides us, and to become a law unto ourselves. Perhaps some of you are in distress in the same way; you have chosen your own path, and now you are caught in the tangled bushes which tear your flesh. David never made a heavier rod for himself than when he thought to avoid all further discomfort by leaving his true place.

Worse than this, if worse can be, *David had also followed policy instead of truth*. The Oriental mind was, and probably still is, given to lying. Easterns do not think it wrong to tell an untruth; many do it habitually. Just as an upright merchant in this country would not be suspected of a falsehood, so you would not in the olden time have suspected the average Oriental of ever speaking the truth if he could help it, because he felt that everybody else would deceive him and so he must practice great cunning. The golden rule in David's day was, "Do others, for others will certainly do you." David in his early days was not without the taint of his times. He became the commander of the bodyguard of Achish, king of Gath, and he lived in the royal city. As he found himself rather awkwardly situated in that idolatrous town, he said to the king, "If I have now found grace in thine eyes, let them give me a place in some town in the country, that I may dwell there: for why should thy servant dwell in the royal city with thee?" Achish appears to have been almost a convert to the worship of Jehovah, and certainly shines brilliantly in the narrative before us. At David's request he gave him the town of Ziklag. David and his men warred with the various tribes of Canaanites who dwelt in the south of Palestine, and took from them great spoil; but he greatly erred in making Achish believe that he was fighting against Judah. We read, "And Achish believed David, saying, He hath made his people Israel utterly to abhor him; therefore he shall be my servant forever." This was the result of David's acted and uttered lie, and lest the falsehood should be found out, David spared none of those whom he conquered, saying, "Lest they should tell on us, saying, So did David." So that beginning with policy he went on to falsehood, and from one falsehood he was driven to another, and his course became far other than that which man of God should have pursued. How different was such false conduct from the usual character of the man who said, "He that worketh deceit shall not dwell within my house: he that telleth lies shall not tarry in my sight."

See the fruit of his falsehood! Ziklag is burned with fire: his wives are captives; and his men speak of stoning him. If you and I ever get away from living by straightforward truth we shall wander into a maze from which it will be hard to extricate ourselves. We should each feel that we can die but we cannot lie, we can starve but we cannot cheat, we can be ground into the dust but we cannot do an unrighteous thing. If it be so, we may count upon the help of God, and may go bravely on under every difficulty. David had left the highway of righteousness, and was stumbling among the dark mountains of craft and deceit. He was plotting and scheming like the worst of worldlings, and he must be made to see his error, and taught to abhor the way of lying; hence in one moment the Lord launches at him bereavement, plunder, mutiny, danger of life, that he might be driven to his God, and made to hate the way of cunning. What wonder that David was greatly distressed?

Yet was his distress the more severe on another account, for *David had sided with the enemies of the Lord's people.* He had gone to the Philistines, and their prince had said to him, "I will make thee keeper of mine head forever." Think of David keeping the head of a Philistine! When Achish gathered the Philistine army to battle with Israel, we read with shame, "And the lords of the Philistines passed on by hundreds, and by thousands: but David and his men passed on in the reward with Achish." How dreadfully troubled David must have felt in this false position. Think of David, who was ordained to be king of Israel, marching his armed band to fight his own countrymen? How gracious was the Lord in bringing him out of that perilous position. The Philistine princes suspected him, as well they might, and said to Achish, "What do these Hebrews here?" They were jealous of the high office to which David had been promoted, and fearful of his turning against them during the fight. "And the princes of the Philistines were wroth with Achish; and the princes of the Philistines said unto him, Make this fellow return, that he may go again to his place which thou hast appointed him, and let him not go down with us to battle, lest in the battle he be an adversary to us: for wherewith should he reconcile himself unto his master? Should it not be with the heads of these men? Is not this David, of whom they sang one to another in dances, saying, Saul slew his thousands, and David his ten thousands?" Though the Philistine king, like the true man that he was, smoothed it down, he was forced to send David away. What a relief David must have felt! Well might he pen the words of the hundred and twenty-fourth Psalm, "Our soul is escaped as a bird out of the snare of the fowlers: the snare is broken, and we are escaped." What a horror would have been upon him if he had actually gone with the Philistines to the battle in which Saul and Jonathan were slain. It would have been a stain upon David all his life. The Lord delivered him, but he made him to feel his rod at the same time, for no sooner had David reached Ziklag, than he saw that the hand of the Lord was gone out against him, desolation smoked around him, and we do not marvel that David was greatly distressed.

Picture the position of David, in the center of his band. He has been *driven away by the Philistine lords with words of contempt;* his men have been sneered at—"What do these Hebrews here? Is not this David?" When he walked with God he was like a prince, and no man dared to sneer at him, but now he has been flouted by the uncircumcised Philistine, and has been glad to sneak back to his little city, ashamed of himself. It is terrible when a man of God falls into such a position that he gives the enemy opportunity to blaspheme God, and to despise his servant. It is terrible when even worldlings scout the inconsistency of the professed follower of Jesus. "What do these Hebrews here?" is the sarcastic question of the world. "How comes a professing Christian to be acting as we do? Look, he is trying to cultivate our acquaintance, and pass for one of ourselves, and yet he calls himself a servant of God!" They begin to point, as they did at Peter, "Thou also wast with Jesus of Nazareth, for thy speech betrayeth thee." "What doest thou here, Elijah?" is the voice which comes from God's mouth, and the lips of his adversaries repeat it. When the child of God feels that he is in that predicament, and in great trouble, too, it is not strange that he is greatly distressed.

At the back of this came *bereavement.* His wives were gone. He was a man of a large, affectionate, tender heart, and what grief it must have been to him! Nor was he a solitary mourner; but all those brave fellows who were joined with him were bereaved too. Hark to the common chorus of grief! They weep, until they have no more power to weep. It must have been a dread day for their leader to feel his own personal sorrow merged and drowned in the flood of grief which swept over his companions. As for his worldly possessions, he was now as *poor* as he possibly could be; for all that he had taken away, and his habitation was burnt with fire, and the rovers were gone he knew not whither. Worst of all, he was now *forsaken* by his followers. Those who had been with him in his worst fortunes now upbraided him with their calamity. Why did he leave the city to go off to help these enemies of the Lord, the uncircumcised Philistines? He might have known better; and they grew indignant, and one said, "Let us stone him"; to which others answered, "Let us do it at once." They were evidently in a great rage. He stands there faint with weeping, a friendless, forsaken man, with *his very life in danger* from furious mutineers. Do you wonder that it is written, "And David was greatly distressed"? He is surrounded with sorrow; but he has no need to gather ashes as the emblems of his woe; for ashes are everywhere about him, the whole place is smoking. He mourns greatly for his wives, and his soldiers mourn for their children, for they are as if they were slain with the sword. It is a case of deep distress, with this added sting—that he had brought it upon himself.

Secondly, let us consider DAVID'S ENCOURAGEMENT: *"And David encouraged himself."* That is well, David! He did not at first attempt to encourage anybody else; but he encouraged *himself.* He encouraged himself *"in the Lord his God,"* namely, in Jehovah. That is the surest way of encouraging yourself. David might have drawn, if he had pleased, a measure of encouragement from those valiant men who joined him just about this particular time; for it happened, according to 1 Chronicles 12:19, 20, that many united with his band at that hour. Let us read the passage. "And there fell some of Manasseh to David, when he came with the Philistines against Saul to battle, but they helped them not: for the lords of the Philistines upon advisement sent him away, saying, He will fall to his master Saul to the jeopardy of our heads. As he went to Ziklag, there fell to him of Manasseh, Adnah, and Jozabad, and Jediael, and Michael, and Jozabad, and Elihu, and Zilthai, captains of the thousands that were of Manasseh. And they helped David against the band of the rovers: for they were all mighty men of valor, and were captains in the host. For at that time day by day there came to David to help him until it was a great host, like the host of God." These newcomers had not lost their wives and children, for they had not been in Ziklag; but David did not look round to them and beg them to stand by him, and put down the mutiny. No, he had by this time become sick of men, and wary of trusting to himself. God was beginning to cure his servant by a bitter dose of distress, and the evidence of the cure was that he did not encourage himself by his new friends, or by the hope of others coming; but he encouraged himself in the Lord his God.

Do you not feel a wind from the hills? The air blows strong and fresh from the everlasting mountains, now that the man of God is looking to God alone. Before, David was down there in the valleys, with his policy and his craft, in the stagnant atmosphere of self-trust and worldliness; but now he stands in Ziklag, a friendless man, but free and true. How grand he is amid the ruins! He rises to his full height, while his fortunes fall! He reminds you of his youthful days when he said, "The Lord that delivered me out of the paw of the lion, and out of the paw of the bear, he will deliver me out of the hand of this Philistine." He is no longer in bondage to craft, but he is a man again, strong in the strength of God; for he casts himself away from all earthly trusts, and encourages himself in the Lord.

He did not sit down in sullen despair, nor did he think, as Saul did, of resorting to wrong means for help; but he went, sinner as he was, confessing all his wrong doing, straightway to his God, and asked for the priest to come that he might speak with him in the name of the Most High. Brothers and sisters, if you are in trouble, and your trouble is mixed with sin, if you have afflicted yourselves by your backslidings and perversities, nevertheless I pray you look nowhere else for help but to the God whom you have offended. When he lifts his arm, as it were, to execute vengeance, lay hold upon it and he will spare you. Does he not himself say, "Let him lay hold on my strength"? I remember old Master Quarles has a strange picture of one trying to strike another with a flail, and how does the other escape? Why, he runs in and keeps close, and so he is not struck. It is the very thing to do. Close in with God. Cling to him by faith; hold fast by him in hope. Say, "Though he slay me, yet will I trust in him." Resolve, "I will not let thee go."

Let us try to conceive of the way in which David would encourage himself in the Lord his God. Standing amidst those ruins he would say, "Yet the Lord does love me, and I love him. Though I have wandered, yet my heart cannot rest without him. Though I have had but little fellowship with him of late, yet he hath not forgotten to be gracious, nor hath he in anger shut up his bowels of compassion." He would look back upon those happy days when he kept sheep, and sang psalms unto the Lord his God amid the pastures of the wilderness. He would recollect those peaceful hours of happiest communion, and long to have them o'er again. His own psalms would tend to comfort him as he saw how his heart had once been glad. He would say to himself: "My experience of divine love is not a dream, I know it is not a myth or a delusion. I have known the Lord, and I have had near and dear intercourse with him, and I know that he changes not, and therefore he will help me. His mercy endureth forever. He will put away my transgression." Thus he encouraged himself in the Lord his God.

Then he went further, and argued, "Hath not the Lord chosen me? Has he not ordained me to be king in Israel? Did he not send his prophet Samuel, who poured oil upon my head, and said, 'This is he'? Surely the Lord will not change his appointment, or suffer his word to fail. I have been separated from my kinsfolk, and hunted by Saul, and driven from rock to cave and from cave to wilderness, and I have known no rest, and all because I was ordained to be king in Saul's place; surely the Lord will carry out his purpose, and will set me on the throne. He has not chosen, and ordained, and anointed me in mockery."

Do you need an interpretation of this parable? Can you not see its application to yourselves? Are you not saying, "The Lord called me by his grace, brought me out from my love of the world, and made me a priest and a king unto himself, and can he leave me? Is not the oil of his Spirit still upon me? Can he cast me off? He separated me to himself, and gave me to know that my destiny was not like that of the ungodly world, but that he had ordained me and chosen me to be his servant forever—will he leave me to perish? Shall his enemy rejoice over me?" Thus may you encourage yourself in God.

Then he would go over all the past deliverances which he had experienced. I see the pictures which passed like a panorama before David's eye. He saw himself when he slew the lion and the bear. Did God deliver him then, and will he not deliver him now? He pictured himself going out to meet the giant Goliath, with nothing but a sling and a stone, and coming back with the monster's head in his hand; and he argued, "Will he not rescue me now?" He saw himself in the courts of Saul, when the mad king sought to pin him to the wall with a javelin, and he barely escaped it. He saw himself let down by the kindnesses of Michal from the window, when her father sought to slay him in his bed. He saw himself in the cave of Engedi, and upon the tracks of the wild goats, pursued by his remorseless adversary, but always strangely guarded from his cruel hand. He cheers himself, as one had done, before him, with the inference, "If the Lord had meant to destroy me, he would not have showed me such things as these."

Come now, take down your diaries and refer to the days when the Lord helped you again and again. How many times has he blessed you? You could not count them, for God has been so gracious and tender that he has aided you ten thousand times already. Has he changed in love, in faithfulness, in power? God forbid that we should indulge such a wicked thought. He is still the same, and so let us encourage ourselves in him.

"Alas," say you, "I have done wrong." I know you have; but HE has not. If your confidence were in yourself, that wrong of yours might crush your hope; but since your confidence is in God, and he has not changed, why should you fear? "Oh, but I am so sinful." Yes; I know you are, and so you were when he first looked upon you in love. If his love had sought to come to you by the way of merit it never would have reached you; but it comes to you by way of free, rich, sovereign grace, and therefore it will come to you evermore. Do you not feel refreshed this morning as you think of what the Lord has done? And do you not feel that after doing so much it would be wrong now to distrust him? Will you not even now encourage yourself in your God?

Perhaps David at that moment perceived that this crushing blow was sent in infinite tenderness to clean him right out of the condition into which he had fallen. The Lord seems to say to David, "All that you have ever got of Achish is this village of Ziklag, and I have caused it to be burnt up, so that you have nothing left to be a tie between you and Philistia. The princes said, 'Send this fellow away,' and they have sent you away; and now the town that Achish gave you is utterly destroyed; there is no ink left between you and the Philistines, and you have come back to your natural standing." The hardest blow that our God ever strikes, if it puts us right and separates us from self and sin, and carnal policy, is a *coup de grâce*, a blow of love. If it ends our life of selfishness, and brings us back into the life of trust, it is a blessed blow. When God blesses his people most it is by terrible things in righteousness. He smote David to heal him. He fetched him out from the snare of the Philistine fowler, and delivered him from the noisome pestilence of heathen association, by a way that brought the tears into his eyes till he had no more power to weep. Now the servant of the Lord begins to see the wonderful hand of God, and he shall yet say, "Before I was afflicted I went astray, but now have I kept thy word."

I, the preacher of this hour, beg to bear my little witness that the worst days I have ever had have turned out to be my best days, and when God has seemed most cruel to me he has then been most kind. If there is anything in this world for which I would bless him more than for anything else it is for pain and affliction. I am sure that in these things the richest, tenderest love has been manifested towards me. I pray you, if you are at this time very low, and greatly distressed, encourage yourselves in the abundant faithfulness of the God who hides himself. Love letters from heaven are often sent in black-edged envelopes. The cloud that is black with horror is big with mercy. We may not ask for trouble, but if we were wise we should look upon it as the shadow of an unusually great blessing. Fear not the storm, it brings healing in its wings, and when Jesus is with you in the vessel the tempest only hastens the ship to its desired haven.

And now, thirdly, we have DAVID INQUIRING OF GOD. "And David inquired at the Lord, saying, Shall I pursue after this troop? Shall I overtake them?"

Note well that as soon as David had come to be right with God he longed to know the Lord's mind as to his next action. You and I would have said, "Let us hasten after these marauders; let us not stop an instant, we can pray as we march, or at some other time. Haste! haste! for the lives of our wives and children are at stake." It was a time for hurry if ever there was; but, as the good proverb says, "Prayer and provender hinder no man's journey." David wisely stops. "Bring hither the ephod," cries he, and he waits till the oracle answers his inquiries. He will not march till the Lord shall give the word of command. This is well. It is a sweet frame of mind to be in to be brought to feel that you must now wait the Lord's bidding, that your strength is to sit still till God bids you go forward. Oh that we could always keep up this submission of heart! Oh that we never leaned to our own understanding, but trusted solely in God!

Observe, that David takes it for granted that his God is going to help him. He only wants to know how it is to be done. "Shall I pursue? Shall I overtake?" When you are inquiring of the Lord, do not approach him as if he would not help you, or could hardly be expected to aid you. You would not like your children to ask a favor of you as if they were afraid of their lives to speak to you. I am sure you would not like a dear child, whatever wrong he had been doing, to feel a suspicion of your love, and doubt your willingness to help; for whatever he has done he is your child still. David has encouraged himself in his God, and he is sure that God is ready to save him; all that he wants to know is how he is himself to act in the business.

It is to be remarked, however, that David does not expect that God is going to help him without his doing his best. He inquires, "Shall I pursue? Shall I overtake?" He means to be up and doing. Sad as he is, and faint as he is, he is ready for action. Many who get into trouble seem to expect an angel to come and lift them up by the hair of their heads; but angels have other matters in hand. The Lord generally helps us by enabling us to help ourselves, and it is a way which does us double good. It was more for David's benefit that he should himself smite the Amalekites than that God should hurl hailstones out of heaven upon them, and destroy them. David will have their spoil for the wage of battle, and be rewarded for the forced march and the fight. Brother, you will have to work and labor to extricate yourself from debt and difficulty, and so the Lord will hear your prayer. The rule is to trust in God to smite the Amalekites, and then to march after them, as if it all depended upon yourself. There is a God-reliance which arouses all our self-reliance and yokes it to the chariot of providence, making the man ready for action because God is with him.

It is instructive to notice that, although David was thus ready for action, trusting in God, he greatly distrusted his own wisdom; for he asked, "Shall I pursue them?" That man is wise who counts his own wisdom to be folly; and he who lays his judgment down at Jesus' feet, is a man of soundest judgment. He who tarries till the divine wisdom shall guide him, he shall be expert and prudent in all things.

David also distrusted his own strength though quite ready to use what he had; for he said, "Shall I overtake?" Can my men march fast enough to overtake these robbers? And what a blessed state of heart that is when we have no strength of our own, but seek unto God! It is good to be insufficient, and to find God all-sufficient. I pause here a minute and pray God ever to keep you and me in just the condition into which he brought his servant David. I do not care so much about his overtaking the robbers, and all that: the glory was to have overtaken his God, and to be waiting at his feet. He could not be brought to this without his city being burnt, without his being bereaved, robbed, and ready to die by the hands of his own warriors; but it was worth all the cost to be brought to rest on the bare arm of God, and to wait in childlike dependence at the great Father's door.

We close with the fourth note, which is a note of jubilation and praise unto God, who helped his servant—DAVID'S ANSWER OF PEACE. The Lord heard his supplication. He says, "In my distress I cried unto the Lord and he heard me." But mark this, he was not delivered without further trial. David marched with his 600 men on foot after the foe, with all speed, and the band became so worn and weary that one-third of them could not ford the brook Besor, which, though usually dry, was probably at that time flowing with a strong stream. Many a leader would have given up the chase with one out of three of his troop in the hospital, but David pursued with his reduced force. When God means to bless us, he often takes away a part of the little strength we thought we had. We did not think our strength equal to the task, and the Lord takes away a portion even of the little power we had. Our God does not fill till he has emptied. Two hundred men must be rent away from David's side before God could give him victory, for he meant to have David's whole force to be exactly equal to the 400 Amalekites who fled, that he might make the victory the more memorable and renowned. Expect then, O troubled one, that you will be delivered, but know that your sorrow may yet deepen, that you may have all the greater joy by-and-by.

Leaving the 200 men behind, David dashes ahead, and by forced marches overtakes the enemy; finds them feasting; smites them hip and thigh, and destroys them, and takes the spoil, but in such a way that manifestly it was the gift of God. He speaks of the spoil as "That which the Lord hath given us, who hath preserved us, and delivered the company that came against us into our hand." God will help his servants who trust him, but he will have all the honor of the victory. He will deliver them in such a way that they shall lift their psalms and hymns unto God alone, and this shall be the strain: "Sing unto the Lord, for he hath triumphed gloriously. We were unworthy, we were faint, we were distressed, but God has made us more than conquerors through his great love."

David's victory was perfect. We are told over and over again that "David recovered all." Nothing was lost: not a piece of money nor a garment, not an ox nor a sheep, much less a child, or one of woman kind—"David recovered all." How well the Lord works when he once lays his hand to it. "He will perfect that which concerneth me." Salvation is of the Lord, and it is an everlastingly complete salvation. Trust ye in the Lord forever, for in the Lord Jehovah there is everlasting strength. He will work, and work perfectly, till he shall say, "It is finished." The battle is the Lord's and his saints shall be more than conquerors.

Not only did God give David complete rescue, but he awarded him great spoil. "And they said, This is David's spoil." David became rich and able to send presents to his friends; but he was also the better man, the holier man, the stronger man, the more fit to wear that crown which was so soon to adorn his brow. Oh, brothers and sisters, the deeper your trouble the louder will be your song, if you can but trust in God and walk in fellowship with Jesus. Little skiffs that keep near the land carry but small cargoes, and their masters see little save the shore; but they that go down to the sea in ships, that do business in great waters, these see the works of the Lord and his wonders in the deep. It is something to be out on the wide main in a terrific storm, when the ship is tossed to and fro like a ball, when the heavens are mixed up with the ocean, and all is uproar. Then great thunder contends with the roaring of the sea, and the lightning flames are quenched by the boiling of the mighty waves. When you reach the shore again, you know a gladness which the landsman cannot feel, and you have a tale to tell to your children, and your children's children, of what you have seen in the deep, such as lubberly landsmen scarce can understand.

Trust in the Lord your God. Believe also in his Son Jesus. Get rid of sham faith, and really believe. Get rid of a professional faith, and trust in the Lord at all times, about everything. "What, trust him about pounds, shillings, and pence?" Assuredly. I dread the faith that cannot trust God about bread and garments—it is a lying faith. Depend upon it, that is not the solid practical faith of Abraham, who trusted God about his tent and his cattle, and about a wife for his son. That faith which made David trust God about the sons and daughters and the spoil, that is the sort of faith for you and for me. If God cannot be trusted about loaves and fishes how shall he be trusted about the things of eternity and the glories which are yet to be revealed? Stay yourself on God with an everyday faith. Faith in God is the exercise of sanctified common sense. The purest reason approves reliance upon God. The end shall declare the wisdom of believing God. At the last, when we with all believers shall lift up the great hallelujah unto the Lord God of Israel who reigneth over all things for his people, it shall be known by all that faith is honorable and unbelief contemptible.

12

REHOBOAM

The Unready

"And he did evil, because he prepared not his heart to seek the Lord" (2 Chr. 12:14).

YOU have probably noticed that, as a general rule, the sacred historians, at the end of each king's reign, sum up the character of the monarch, and describe him as either doing evil in the sight of the Lord, or doing that which was right in the sight of the Lord. They give a summary of his whole life in one or other of these sentences; and there will come a day when there will be a summary of your life and mine; and when it is given, it will run on this wise, "He did evil in the sight of the Lord," or else on this blessed fashion, "he did that which was right in the sight of the Lord." There is no other course beside these two; these characters comprehend all of us, and the summary given in our case, as it was in the case of Rehoboam, will be given with great accuracy. It will be infallible, and it will be irreversible.

This man, Rehoboam, was not half as bad as some other kings; still, the inspired historian was compelled to say, "He did evil." He was not such an obstinate and outrageous sinner as some were. He was not an Ahab; he was not even a Manasseh, he did not live as that king did in his evil time; yet "he did evil." That is the summary of his whole career. There were some good points about him, as I shall try to show you presently; he did good sometimes: still, when it is all added up, this is the total of it, "He did evil"; and the reason why he did evil is given. One reason, I should think, was that he had a bad mother; observe how it is written, just before the summary of his life, "His mother's name was Naamah, an Ammonitess,"—one of Solomon's numerous wives— one whom he favored most of all; but she was an idolatrous woman, "an

Ammonitess." And there is little wonder that, when the father was no better than he should have been, and when the mother was exceedingly bad, the summary of the son's life should be, "He did evil." This makes marriage a most important step, though it is often taken without a single serious thought. See how a woman's life projects itself, and either casts a ray of brightness over her children's characters, or a cloud of shame over their entire being. What some of us owe to our mothers, we shall never be able to tell. If we had to write down the choicest mercies that God has bestowed upon us, we should have to mention first the mother who prayed for us, and taught us to trust in Jesus, by the Holy Spirit's blessing upon the sweet way in which she spoke to us about the Savior. But a mother, trained in the school of Satan, and who has become a mistress in the art of sin, is a terrible source of evil to her children. May God have mercy upon any of you mothers who have sons growing up to follow the evil example which you are setting them! Mothers, by the love you bear your children—and there is no stronger love, I think, on earth—if you will not think of your own soul's best interests, I do pray you, for your children's sake, consider your ways, and seek the Lord with the purpose in your heart that your children may, if possible, live in the presence of God.

But the Scripture does not give this as the reason why Rehoboam did evil. It does not say that he did evil because he had a bad mother, nor because his father had not walked with God as he ought to have done. No, the reason was, "because he prepared not his heart to seek the Lord." The Hebrew proverb was, "The fathers have eaten sour grapes, and the children's teeth are set on edge"; but the Lord said to his ancient people, through the prophet Ezekiel, "Ye shall not have occasion any more to use this proverb in Israel. . . . The soul that sinneth, it shall die." God will judge each one according to his own deeds; and if you should, unhappily, have been born of the most ungodly parents who ever lived, there is no reason why God's grace should not begin to work in your family with you. If all your training has been adverse to godliness, the sovereign grace, that takes one of a city, and two of a family, and brings them to Zion, may select you as its object. "He did evil, because he prepared not his heart to seek the Lord."

What does this expression mean? I am going to try to find out, because I feel sure that the same reason is operating upon a good many other people. It does not say that Rehoboam did evil because he was of a vicious temperament, or because he had strong passions, or because he was a downright thoroughly bad fellow. No, he was not quite that; but he did evil because of something which he did not do.

So I judge that this expression means, first, that HE DID NOT BEGIN LIFE WITH SEEKING THE LORD.

His father Solomon did; when he found himself lifted up to the throne of Israel while he was yet a young man, Solomon spread his case before the Lord, and asked for wisdom; and, in consequence, taking it as a whole, his reign was a grand one, and his kingdom attained to a high state of prosperity. He was faithful to the worship of Jehovah, in the main, though there was a sad turning aside to idols, and he acted wisely in most of his ways, so that the wisdom of Solomon became proverbial. That result was due to the fact that God gave to him "wisdom and understanding exceeding much, and largeness of heart, even as the sand that is on the seashore." He asked of God wisdom, and God gave it to him; but this foolish son of his asked not for wisdom. The scepter was there, so he grasped it; there was an empty throne, so he sat down upon it. I daresay he fancied it was a very fine thing to be king over Israel, and his thoughts did not go much beyond the mere external pomp and splendor of royalty. He did not intend any ill, and he was not very determined upon doing that which was right; and probably he never thought of commencing his career by asking the blessing of God upon it.

I hope no one, whom I am addressing, would really resolve to lead a bad life; but, mind you, it may happen to you, as it did to Rehoboam, that the summary of your life will be, "He did evil, because he prepared not his heart to seek the Lord." So much in life depends upon how we begin that I could wish that no boy ever left his home to go to school, that no boy ever left school to go to a clerkship, or to serve his apprenticeship to a business, without stopping a while, and praying the Lord to guide him in every step so that he might act wisely.

This young man Rehoboam felt that he needed some kind of guidance, yet he did not seek the Lord, but *he called together a number of counselors.* Now, it is quite right to seek counsel of men who are wiser than we ourselves are; but he who trusts to earthly counselors, instead of to God, is guilty of great provocation against him who is full of wisdom, and who ought to be the Guide of our youth and of our whole lives. Calling his father's wise counselors together, at the beginning of his reign, Rehoboam submitted the people's grievances to them; but, like the fool that he was, he rejected their counsel, and followed the foolish advice of the younger men like himself, the fops about the court, the swells, the gilded youths of the period, and so committed a gross act of folly.

It usually happens that, when men will not ask counsel of God, if they go to other sources for guidance, *they generally accept the very worst form of advice.* When men trust in men, it is strange how often they trust in the worst and not in the best of men. Yet I know not that it is strange, for that same infatuation, which leads a man to reject his God, almost necessarily leads him to despise those upon whom God has bestowed any measure of light and wisdom. So this young prince asked counsel of others, who were as foolish as he himself was, and the result of following their advice was that ten tribes out of the twelve were rent away from him, and formed into an independent kingdom. What a different life there might have been, not only for himself, but for those who were dependent upon him, if he had but humbly waited upon God for guidance, and had given the people a gentle reply to their very reasonable demands, and had ruled them, not with a rod of iron, but with gentleness and kindness! However, so it was, because he did not begin by seeking the Lord, he made a fool of himself, and a failure of his life.

Perhaps some of you young people say, "Well, we are not going to give our hearts to God, yet we shall not be fools." Ah, but you are fools already, or else you would not talk like that; and the probability is that, before long, in the plenitude of your self-sufficient wisdom, you will take a step, which seems plain enough to you, but which will lead you into a world of sorrow, and to no end of trouble. Blessed is that young man who says, "My Father, thou shalt be the Guide of my youth,"—who gets God on board the vessel of his life at the start, with his hand on the rudder, to steer the vessel through a safe and prosperous voyage till he reaches the Fair Heavens, and casts anchor in the Port of Peace.

But our text means more than that; it means, next, that REHOBOAM SHOWED NO HEART IN DOING WHAT WAS RIGHT.

He did what was right at the first, but he had no heart in doing it. The prophet came to him when he had mustered his forces, and forbade him to go to war with the followers of Jeroboam, and he disbanded all his troops. That was, truly, a most worthy thing to do; and you and I, looking on at the scene, would have said, "That is a noble young prince; if he obeys the voice of a prophet like that, surely he fears God." But he did not.

He did right because, *from the training his father had given him, he had a high esteem for prophets of God*. He had seen his father entertain prophets with great honor, and he did not like to despise them. There is many a young man, nowadays, who has great regard for God's ministers, though he is not himself a Christian. He recollects the times when they used to be at his father's house, when they slept in the prophet's chamber. He remembers many happy evenings he had, as a boy, when they were guests at his home, and he could not bring his mind to despise them, and to make a jest of what they say. Nay, to some extent, he gives heed to what they have to say, and he tries to shape his moral character according to their teaching, yet he does not yield himself to Christ, so nothing comes of it all.

If it had been a prophet of Baal who had come to him, I am afraid that Rehoboam would have done just what he told him to do, and there are many young men now, who appear to be excellent, simply because they are in good hands; but if they had been under the influence of evil men, they would have been as bad as could be, for they have no individuality, they have no heart in doing the right thing.

It is well to worship the Lord heartily, with a zest, with holy fervor, to do it because you like to do it, and take a delight in it. It is one thing to be right in appearance, and another thing to be right in your soul. "But," says one, "I thought it best to do right when you do not like to do it; I thought there was something very meritorious if a person was religious though he could not endure it." No; that is hypocrisy, and nothing else. When a person puts on the garb of religion, all the while feeling that he would gladly take it off if he could—pretending to be a Christina, when, if he could have his own way, he would have a Continental Sabbath, he is nothing but a hypocrite. When he does get his own way, he manages to have his Continental Sabbath, and he just amuses himself all that he possibly can on God's holy day. No matter what the foreigners do, he is among them in the very thick of it, and he thinks they have a very blessed kind of Sunday. When he is at home, he does not do such naughty things; oh no, certainly not! And this hypocrisy is what you think is virtue? Because you do not like true godliness, you think it must be good for you to pretend to imitate it; but that will never do.

It was soon evident that his heart was not right towards God, for *he imitated his father Solomon in his faults*. His father's great fault was the multiplication of wives, and into this evil Rehoboam fell. And, moreover, all the strength of Rehoboam's heart and soul went in what was a very proper direction in itself; namely, in the building of cities, and the storing of them with provisions, and fencing and garrisoning the towns; yet that direction was a very bad one because it took him away from God. I like to see a young man, whatever he does, throw his whole soul into it; but not so act that he throws his soul away from God by it. There is such a little real force in man, at his best, that he must put all of it into one thing if he is to have success in it. So this Rehoboam put his whole soul into one thing; and, therefore, "he did evil, because he prepared not his heart to seek the Lord"; but prepared his heart to seek after other things.

"But," someone asks, "may not a man be attentive to business?" He ought to be; he should be diligent in business, but ever with this higher motive outreaching everything else, that he may win Christ, and be found in him, that his life may bring glory to the God who made him, and to the Christ who redeemed him with his precious blood. But, oh, young man, if you do not prepare your heart to seek the Lord, if what you do, that is good, is done in a happy-go-lucky style, if you are good because you happen to be in a good connection, and you keep right because Christian people round about you keep you right, and you would not like to grieve your father, and vex your friend, then there is nothing in it at all. You will go to the bad, one of these days, when you get into other circumstances, and meet with new temptations. If you profess to be a Christian, throw your whole soul into it, and say, "Let others do as they will, as for me, I will serve the Lord, and not feel it a bondage, but take a delight in it, and I will serve him with all my heart."

There is a third point about Rehoboam, contained in the words of our text, "He did evil, because he prepared not his heart to seek the Lord"; that is HE WAS NOT FIXED AND PERSEVERING IN HIS RELIGION. The original bears that sense.

He began well, and in the first three years of his reign, the nation worshiped God. I do not suppose that he really did so himself; but, still, he was on that side. He was one of the Evangelical party; he was one of the God-fearing party, and therefore he prospered. His apparent reverence for God brought the Levites to live in his dominions, and brought others of the best people of Israel to come there, and to strengthen his hands. Thus he prospered; and you might have thought that, as his religion brought him prosperity, he would stick to it. Not he; there was no "stick to it" in him.

As soon as ever he prospered, *he began to grow proud.* He was a fine fellow, he had a splendid kingdom, a very attractive dominion; did not the good people all come there? So, growing proud, he began to forsake the Lord; and the people, following his evil example, worshiped in groves instead of coming to the temple at Jerusalem. Worse than that, they set up graven images and idolatrous pillars, and their heart went aside from God, and they practiced the most accursed sin that ever stained and defiled the face of the earth. You know the sin for which God sent the judgment of fire upon Sodom and Gomorrah; and there were some of these people who thus sinned, making an act of worship out of the most bestial crime. Yet Rehoboam did not trouble himself about that. When the people feared God, he was willing that they should do so; and now, if they followed Ashtaroth, they might do as they liked. He was, after all, but a young ruler, who thought that the principal business of a king was to enjoy himself; so he let things go just as they could. He was king; but still—well, if God was good, it was proper for good people to reverence him; but if other people did not, he did not trouble his head much about that matter, it sat very lightly upon him.

In consequence of this, *God brought up Shishak from Egypt,* with multitudes of chariots and horsemen, and an innumerable host of people. Then were the Jews in a state of great alarm; and Rehoboam, who went to be molded any way—for he had a sort of India-rubber heart— humbled himself, and the princes of Israel humbled themselves. God knew that these other people were sincere in humbling themselves, so he allowed their sincerity to season the whole bulk, and he therefore accepted the humiliation of king and people, and delivered them.

You see how readily Rehoboam went, first toward God, then towards idols, and then back again towards God; *he was always ready to shift and change.* He wrought no great reforms in the land; we do not read that he held a great Passover, as Hezekiah did, or that the high places were taken away; but, as soon as Shishak was gone, he felt perfectly content. There was not anything real and permanent in his religion; it did not hold him. He held it sometimes, but it never held him.

O dear friends, is not this Rehoboam a specimen of a great many people who are living now? They get into a warm-hearted meeting, and they feel the power of it; they meet a friend, and he takes them into different society altogether, where there are merry songs and plentiful jokes, and they feel the power of that. They hold with the hare, and they run with the hounds. They are "everything by starts, and nothing long"; and the result is that they do evil; for, when a man is not fixed in his resolve to do good—when he does not take his stand, in the name of God, with a life and death determination, it is not doubtful which way he will go.

The last point involved in this description of Rehoboam is this, HE HAD NO CARE ABOUT SERVING GOD.

He did not care whether he served the Lord or not; and as to serving him in a right spirit, that never entered into his head. He never "prepared his heart." If he went to a service—well, he was there, but that was all. Some people, who have come here tonight, never thought of breathing a prayer before they came, nor after they entered the building. They would even venture, if we allowed them, to partake of the communion at the Lord's table without self-examination and without prayer; they do everything without any preparation of the heart.

But look you, sirs, *if there is no care about making the heart go right, it must go wrong,* because the natural tendency of our mind is toward evil. If you leave your heart to follow its own natural impulse, it is impossible that it should seek the Lord. It is only when it is prepared to seek the Lord that it ever seeks him, and that preparation of the heart is from God; so that, if we do not ask the Lord to prepare our hearts to seek him, we shall never seek his face at all.

What is preparing the heart to seek the Lord? I should say that it is something like this. First, *to feel my need of God.* What can I, a creature, do without my Creator? What can I do without a Father in heaven? I have offended him, I have sinned against him, I have gone far away from him; but I want him to forgive me, and to save me. We must be conscious of this need; may the Spirit of God prepare us to seek the Lord by giving us a deep sense of our desperate need of God's mercy!

The next thing is, *to cry unto God for help:* "Lord, save me! God be merciful to me a sinner! Renew my heart, change my nature, subdue my stubborn will, and make me thy child!" Prayer prepares the heart to seek the Lord, and you will never seek him if you do not pray to him. In fact, prayer is an essential exercise in seeking the Lord.

Then, further, if we would be prepared to seek the Lord, there must be *a submission of ourselves to his guidance*—a coming to him, and saying, "Here I am, Lord; make me what I ought to be. I agree to thy commandments; I delight in them, help me to run in them. I yield my proud selfhood, and lay down at thy feet my prejudices and my willfulness, and ask thee now to guide me in the right way."

There must also be *the acceptance of God's plan of salvation.* He who would live the right kind of life must come to God, and say, "My God, thou savest them that believe; help me to believe. Thou givest eternal life to as many as believe in Jesus Christ, thy Son. Lord, I believe; help thou mine unbelief." This is the true way of preparing the heart to seek the Lord.

And even when that faith is given, the right preparation is *to serve God always with thoughtfulness and care* — not to go blundering on anyhow, hit or miss, as some do. It is a terribly sad thing to pretend to serve God without thought, without watchfulness, without care, for God is not such a one that we may rush into his presence whenever we like, without premeditation, solemnity, or reverence. Every holy duty ought to be thought over carefully. Every prayer, every almsgiving, every attempt to serve God, should be done with due consideration and with holy anxiety to do it in the right manner, at the right time, and in the right spirit.

Now, because Rehoboam did not act thus, and did not, indeed, care to trouble his brain about such things as this, "he did evil." And if any man here says, "Well, I do not trouble about religion; I believe I shall be all right. I cannot be always sitting down, and pulling a long face, and reading the Bible, and trying to find out how I am to live. I just take the first chance that comes, and do the best I can." If you talk like that, you will do evil as surely as you are a man, for he who devotes not his whole soul to fighting the battle of life will certainly lose it.

Now I want just two or three minutes more in order to make an application of my subject; and, first, is it not possible — I want to whisper this round among the members of this church — is it not quite possible that there may be some nominal professors who come under the description in the text? Their conduct appears to be admirable, and hitherto probably has been so; but they have never prepared their heart to seek the Lord. I fear that, in all our churches, there are people who are called Christians simply because they were brought up among Christians. They need to be brought down, to be converted, regenerated, born again, for they have only been born after the flesh.

There was an Ishmael in the household of Abraham, so we need not wonder if there are such people in all our churches. They have never prepared their hearts to seek the Lord; it has not been heart-work with them. It will be well for each of us to ask these questions, "Is my heart prepared to seek the Lord? Is my heart in my religion? Do I try to serve God with all my heart? Do I make it a matter of serious thought, or is my religion all upon the outside?" If it be so, the probability is that, one of these days, there will come a sudden temptation to you, and over you will go. I have known ministers, deacons, and elders—gray old men— fall into sins which one would have thought only silly boys would fall into; and we can only think, when we see such men apostatize, that they never prepared their heart to seek the Lord. Their religion was only skin deep; it was not that true Christianity which has its root in the soul by the effectual working of the Holy Spirit.

Now, another question. Are there any young men here, who are very hopeful and promising characters, who like religious gatherings, and attend to everything that is of good repute, and yet have not sought and found the Lord? Shall I tell you what troubled me before I gave my heart to Christ? It was something which had great influence upon me in bringing me to decision. There was a boy at school, who was some few years older than I was; and he was a very excellent lad. My father (you know that fathers speak thus sometimes) used to tell me he wished I was half as good as that boy was; he was a kind of pattern lad. Well, he grew up, and came to London to a drapery establishment. He wrote home most delightful letters to his mother, telling her that he was going to hear such-and-such a minister on Sunday morning, and such another one on Sunday evening; and I used to hear what a good lad he was. All of a sudden he came home; he could not be kept in the establishment, there was money missing, and he was suspected of stealing it. He had not been to those places of worship at all; he had spent his Sundays—well, Satan knew where; he had been as bad as bad could be all the while he was there. My father never mentioned him to me any more, but I distinctly recollect feeling just this, "Well, if So-and-so, whom I thought and believed, and who seemed to be such a good lad, to whom I used to look up, has turned out such a downright scamp, may not I do the same?" It seemed to me that, if I did not begin in a better way than he did, by really getting a new heart and a right spirit, I might come morally to the same sort of smash as he did. I earnestly entreat you not to commence life even with the best moral resolutions. Go straightway to the Lord Jesus, and ask him to grant you grace that you may give yourself up wholly to him. You cannot keep yourself, but he can keep you, and he will keep you even unto the end, for he hath said, "My sheep hear my voice, and I know them, and they follow me: and I give unto them eternal life; and they shall never perish, neither shall any man pluck them out of my hand."

Lastly, do I address anyone—old or young, it is no matter—who, like Rehoboam, has not sought the Lord, and like Rehoboam has got into a world of trouble through it? Have you lost the ten tribes? Has Shishak come against you? You did wrong, you know you did, for you forsook your God; and now, after that, do you still refuse to seek him? For, mark you, Rehoboam did not prepare his heart to seek the Lord even after he had been attacked by the king of Egypt. Chastisements are lost upon some people; there is someone of Rehoboam's sort here tonight; it is the first time he has been out since his serious illness. Blessed be God that you did not die then, my friend. You know what the angels heard you say when you were lying on your bed. "Please God, if I am ever raised up from this illness, I will seek the Lord." That is partly the reason why you are here, and I am very glad to see you; but you must not think that coming here will save you. It is no use seeking the Tabernacle; you must seek the Lord. Oh, do not, I pray you, let this warning be neglected, nor let the vow that was registered in heaven be forgotten; but do seek the Savior with all your heart!

But where was Rehoboam? He never sought the Lord; so, perhaps, when he had passed out of this world, where he had shilly-shallied and vacillated, where he had been pliable and plastic to every influence — when he passed into the next world, there was realized by him the terror of that dreadful curse, "Then shall they call upon me, but I will not answer; they shall seek me early, but they shall not find me." Then was fulfilled to him that other terrible prophecy, "Because I have called, and ye refused; I have stretched out my hand, and no man regarded; but ye have set at naught all my counsel, and would none of my reproof, I also will laugh at your calamity; I will mock when your fear cometh." Think of God's laughing and mocking at a soul that has passed into eternity without him; it is a most dreadful thing, whatever it may mean, and it will be fulfilled in you—you hopeful people, you plausible people, you undecided people, unless you prepare your heart to seek the Lord. It may be that some of you are standing, at this moment, on the very verge of everlasting life; and if the devil can keep you there he will be perfectly satisfied, for you will perish if you remain there. Do not satisfy him, I implore you. O mighty grace, come upon them now, and make them each one say, "I will stand here no longer; I will cross the line; I will give myself up once for all to Jesus."

13

JOB

The Turning of Captivity

"The Lord turned the captivity of Job, when he prayed for his friends: also the Lord gave Job twice as much as he had before" (Job 42:10).

SINCE God is immutable he acts always upon the same principles, and hence his course of action in the olden times to a man of a certain sort will be a guide as to what others may expect who are of like character. God does not act by caprice, nor by fits and starts. The Lord has ways as high above our ways as the heavens are above the earth, and these are not fickle and arbitrary. These ways, although very different if we view them superficially, are really always the same when you view them with understanding. The ways of the Lord are right, though transgressors fall therein by not discerning them; but the righteous understand the ways of the Lord, for to them he makes them known, and they perceive that grand general principles govern all the actions of God. If it were not so, the case of such a man as Job would be of no service to us. It could not be said that the things which happened aforetime happened unto us for an example, because if God did not act on fixed principles we could never tell how he would act in any fresh case, and that which happened to one man would be no rule whatever, and no encouragement whatever, to another. We are not all like Job, but we all have Job's God. Though we have neither risen to Job's wealth, nor will, probably, ever sink to Job's poverty, yet there is the same God above us if we be high, and the same God with his everlasting arms beneath us if we be brought low; and what the Lord did for Job he will do for us, not precisely in the same form, but in the same spirit, and with like design. If, therefore, we are brought low tonight, let us be encouraged with the thought that God will turn again our captivity; and let us entertain the hope that after the time of trial shall be over, we shall be richer, especially in spiritual things, than ever we were before.

First, then, the Lord can soon turn his people's captivity.

That is a very remarkable expression—"captivity." It does not say, "God turned his poverty," though Job was reduced to the extremity of penury, having lost all his property. We do not read that the Lord turned his sickness, though he was covered with sore boils. It does not say that he turned away the sting of bereavement, reproach, and calumny, although all those are included. But there is something more meant by the word *captivity*. A man may be very poor, and yet not in captivity, his soul may sing among the angels when his body is on a dunghill, and dogs are licking his sores. A man may be very sick, and yet not be in captivity; he may be roaming the broad fields of covenant mercy though he cannot rise from his bed; and his soul may never enjoy greater liberty than when his body is scarcely able to turn from side to side. Captivity is bondage of mind, the iron entering into the soul. I suspect that Job, under the severe mental trial which attended his bodily pains, was, as to his spirit, like a man bound hand and foot and fettered, and then taken away from his native country, banished from the place which he loved, deprived of the associations which had cheered him, and confined in darkness. I mean that, together with the trouble and trial to which he was subjected, he had lost somewhat the presence of God; much of his joy and comfort had departed; the peace of his mind had gone, and the associations which he had formed with other believers were now broken: he was in all these respects like a lone captive. His three friends had condemned him as a hypocrite, and would not have association with him except to censure him, and thus he felt like one who had been carried into a far country, and banished both from God and man. He could only follow the occupation of a captive, that is, to be oppressed, to weep, to claim compassion, and to pour out a dolorous complaint. He hung his harp on the willows, and felt that he could not sing the Lord's song in a strange land.

Poor Job! He is less to be pitied for his bereavements, poverty, and sickness than for his loss of that candle of the Lord which once shone about his head. That is the worst point of all when trouble penetrates to the heart. All the bullets in the battle, though they fly thick as hail, will not distress a soldier like one which finds a lodging in his flesh. "To take arms against a sea of troubles, and by opposing end them," is a grand and manly thing; but when that sea of trouble fills the cabin of the heart, puts out the fires of inward energy, washes the judgment from the wheel, and renders the pumps of resolution useless, the man becomes very nearly a wreck. "A wounded spirit, who can bear?" Touch a man in his bone, and in his flesh, and yet he may exult; but touch him in his mind—let the finger of God be laid upon his spirit—and then, indeed, he is in captivity. I think the term includes all the temporal distress into which Job came, but it chiefly denotes the bondage of spirit into which he was brought, as the combined result of his troubles, his sickness, the taunts of his friends, and the withdrawal of the divine smile. My point is that God can deliver us out of that captivity; he can both from the spiritual and the temporal captivity give us a joyful release.

The Lord can deliver us out of spiritual captivity, and that very speedily. I may be addressing some who feel everything except what they want to feel. They enjoy no sweetness in the means of grace, and yet for all the world they would not give them up. They used at one time to rejoice in the Lord; but now they cannot see his face, and the utmost they can say is, "Oh that I knew where I might find him!" It little matters that some live in perpetual joy, the triumphs of others cannot cheer a man who is himself defeated. It is idle to tell a distressed soul that it ought to rejoice as others do. What one ought to do and what one can do are sometimes very different, for how to perform that which we would we find not. In vain do you pour your glad notes into a troubled ear. Singing songs to a sad heart is like pouring vinegar upon niter, the elements are discordant, and cause a painful effervescence. There are true children of God who walk in darkness and see no light; yea, some who are the excellent of the earth, nevertheless are compelled to cry aloud, "My God, my God, why hast thou forsaken me?" Throughout all time some of these have been in the church, and there always will be such, let our perfect brethren condemn them as they please. The Lord will always have his mourners, his church shall always have an afflicted and poor people in her midst. Let us all take warning, for we also may be tried and cast down ere our day is over; it may be that the brightest eye among us may yet be dimmed, and the boldest heart may yet be faint, and he that dwells nearest to his God at this moment may yet have to cry out in bitterness of soul, "O God, return unto me, and lift up the light of thy countenance upon me."

Therefore mark well this cheering truth, God can turn your captivity, and turn it at once. Some of God's children seem to think that to recover their former joy must occupy a long period of time. It is true that if you had to work your passage back to where you came from it would be a weary voyage. There would have to be most earnest searchings of heart and purgings of spirit, strugglings with inbred lusts and outward temptations, and all that, if joy were always the result of inward condition. There must needs be a great deal of scrubbing and cleansing and furbishing up of the house, before you could invite your Lord to come, if he and you dwelt together on terms of law. But albeit, that all this cleansing and purifying will have to be done, it will be done far better when you have a sense of his love than it ever can be if you do it in order to make yourself fit for it. He came to you just as you were, and when he came he himself drove out the intruders which profaned the temple of your soul, and he dwelt with you, in order to perfect the cleansing. Now he will vouchsafe to you the conscious enjoyment of his presence on the same terms at first, that is, on terms of free and sovereign grace. Did you not at that time admit the Savior to your soul because you could not do without him? Was not that the reason? Is it not a good reason for receiving him again? Was there anything in you when you received him which could commend you to him? Say, were you not all over defilement, and full of sin and misery? And yet you opened the door, and said, "My Lord, come in, in thy free grace, come in, for I must have thee or I perish." Dare you invite him now on other terms? Having begun in the Spirit, wouldst thou be made perfect in the flesh? Having begun to live by grace, wouldst thou go on to live by works? When thou wast a stranger, didst thou trust in his love, and now that thou art his friend, wilt thou appeal to the law? God forbid. O brother, Jesus loves thee still, and in a moment he will restore thee. O sister, Jesus would fain come back to thy heart again and that in an instant. After all, you are not worse than you were when he first visited you; you are not in so sorry a plight after all, as your first natural state, for then you were dead in trespasses and sins altogether, and he quickened you, and now, though you say you feel dead, yet the very expression proves that there is some life lingering in you.

Why, those sighs and groans are sweet to the Lord, and they would not have been in thee if he had not put them there; they are sure tokens that his grace has not been altogether taken from thee. Knowest thou not, O child of God, that the grace of God is intended to meet all thy sins after conversion as well as before conversion? Dost thou not know that the Lord loved thee of old, despite thy sins, and he loves thee still? Understandest thou not that the ground of thy salvation is not thy standing or thy character, but the standing of Christ before God, and the character and work of Christ in the presence of God? Believe thou firmly that still he loves thee, for so indeed he does. Cast thine eyes upon those dear wounds of his, and read his love still written there. O unbelieving Thomas, do not put thy finger into thine own wounds, for that will not help thee, but place them in the wounds of Jesus. Come close to him, and thou shalt cry with ecstasy of spirit, "My Lord and my God." Well do I know what it is to feel this wondrous power of God to turn our captivity. When one is constantly engaged in ministry, it sometimes happens that the mind wanders, the spirit flags, and the energy is damped, yet, all in a minute, the Lord can quicken us into vigorous activity; the tow catches fire and blazes gloriously, when the Holy Spirit applies the fire. We have heard a hymn sung, and we have said, "I cannot join in that as I could wish," and yet, on a sudden, a mighty rushing wind has borne us away with the song right into heaven. The Lord does not take days, months, weeks, or even hours, to do his work of revival in our souls. He made the world in six days, but he lit it up in an instant with one single word. He said, "light be," and light was, and cannot he do the same for us, chase away our gloom before the clock ticks again? Do not despair, nay, do not even doubt your God. He can turn your captivity as the streams in the south.

Beloved, *he can do the same as to our temporal captivity*. We do not often say much about temporals when we are preaching; I fear we do not say enough about them, for it is wonderful how the Old Testament is taken up with the narration of God's dealings with his people as to temporal things. Many people imagine that God has a great deal to do with their prayer closet, but nothing to do with their store-closet; it would be a dreadful thing for us if it were so. Indeed, my brethren, we ought to see as much the hand of our Lord on the table in the kitchen when it is loaded as we do at the communion table, for the same love that spreads the table when we commemorate our Savior's dying love, spreads the table which enables us to maintain the bodily life without which we could not come to the other table at all. We must learn to see God in everything, and praise him for all that we have.

Now, it may be I address some friend who has been a great sufferer through pecuniary losses. Dear friend, the Lord can turn your captivity. When Job had lost everything, God readily gave him all back. "Yes," say you, "but that was a very remarkable case." I grant you that, but then we have to do with a remarkable God, who works wonders still. If you consider the matter you will see that it was quite as remarkable a thing that Job should lose all his property as it was that he should get it back again. If you had walked over Job's farm at first, and seen the camels and the cattle, if you had gone into his house and seen the furniture and the grandeur of his state — if you had seen how those who passed him in the street bowed to him, for he was a highly respected man, and if you had gone to his children's houses, and seen the comfort in which they lived, you would have said, "Why, this is one of the best established men in all the land of Uz." There was scarcely a man of such substance to be found in all that region, and if somebody had foretold that he would in one day lose all this property — all of it — and lose all his children, why, you would have said, "Impossible! I have heard of great fortunes collapsing, but then they were built on speculations. They were only paper riches, made up of bills and the like; but in the case of this man there are oxen, sheep, camels, and land, and these cannot melt into thin air. Job has a good substantial estate, I cannot believe that ever he will come to poverty." Why, when he went out into the gate where the magistrates sat to administer justice, they rose up and gave him the chief seat on the bench. He was a man whose flocks could not be counted, so great were his possessions — possessions of real property, not of merely nominal estate: and yet suddenly, marvelously, it all took to itself wings and disappeared. Surely, if God can scatter he can gather. If God could scatter such an estate as that, he could, with equal ease, bring it back again. But this is what we do not always see. We see the destructive power of God, but we are not very clear about the upbuilding power of God. Yet, my brethren, surely it is more consonant with the nature of God that he should give than take, and more like him that he should caress than chastise. Does he not always say that judgment is his strange work? I feel persuaded that it was strange work with God to take away all Job's property from him and bring him into that deep distress; but when the Lord went about to enrich his servant Job again, he went about that work, as we say, *con amore* — with heart and soul. He was doing then what he delights to do, for God's happiness is never more clearly seen than when he is distributing the largesses of his love. Why can you not look at your own circumstances in the same light? It is more likely that God will bless you and restore to you than it was ever likely that he would chasten you and take away from you. He can restore you all your wealth, and even more.

I pass on to our second remark which is this. THERE IS GENERALLY SOME POINT AT WHICH THE LORD INTERPOSES TO TURN THE CAPTIVITY OF HIS PEOPLE.

In Job's case, I have no doubt, the Lord turned his captivity, as far as the Lord was concerned, because *the grand experiment which had been tried on Job was now over.*

The suggestion of Satan was that Job was selfish in his piety—that he found honesty to be the best policy, and, therefore, he was honest—that godliness was gain, and therefore he was godly. "Hast thou not set a hedge about him and all that he hath?" said the old accuser of the brethren. The devil generally does one of two things. Sometimes he tells the righteous that there is no reward for their holiness, and then they say, "Surely, I have cleansed my heart in vain and washed my hands in innocency"; or else he tells them that they only obey the Lord because they have a selfish eye to the reward. Now, it would be a calamity if the devil could charge the Lord with paying his servants badly: it would have been an ill thing if the fiend had been able to say, "There is Job, a perfect and an upright man, but thou hast set no hedge about him. Thou hast given him no reward whatever." That would have been an accusation against the goodness and justice of God; but, as the devil cannot say that, he takes the other course, and says—"Thou hast set a hedge about him and all that he has; he serves thee for gain and honor; he has a selfish motive in his integrity."

By God's permission the matter was tested. The devil had said, "Put forth now thy hand and touch his bone and his flesh, and he will curse thee to thy face." But Job had done no such thing. In his extremity, he said, "The Lord gave and the Lord hath taken away, and blessed be the name of the Lord." God puts his servants sometimes into these experiments that he may test them, that Satan himself may know how true-hearted God's grace has made them, and that the world may see how they can play the man. Good engineers, if they build a bridge, are glad to have a train of enormous weight go over it. You remember when the first Great Exhibition was built they marched regiments of soldiers, with a steady tramp, over the girders, that they might be quite sure that they would be strong enough to bear any crowd of men; for the regular tramp of well disciplined soldiers is more trying to a building than anything else. So our wise and prudent Father sometimes marches the soldiery of trouble right over his people's supports, to let all men see that the grace of God can sustain every possible pressure and load. I am sure that if any of you had invented some implement requiring strength you would be glad to have it tested, and the account of the successful trial published abroad. The gunsmith does not object to a charge being fired from the barrel at the proof-house far greater than any strain which it ought ordinarily to bear; for he knows that it will endure the proof. "Do your worst or do your best; it is a good instrument; do what you like with it"; so the maker of a genuine article is accustomed to speak; and the Lord seems to say the same concerning his people. "My work of grace in them is mighty and thorough. Test it Satan; test it world; test it by bereavements, losses, and reproaches; it will endure every ordeal." And when it is tested, and bears it all, then the Lord turns the captivity of his people, for the experiment is complete.

Most probably there was, in Job's character, some fault from which his trial was meant to purge him. If he erred at all, probably it was in having a somewhat elevated idea of himself and a stern manner towards others. A little of the elder-brother spirit may, perhaps, have entered into him. A good deal that was sour came out of Job when his miserable comforters began to tease him—not a hundredth part as much as would come out of me, I warrant you, or, perhaps, out of you; but, still, it would not have come out if it had not been in. It must have been in him or otherwise all the provocation in the world would not have brought it out; and the Lord intended by his trials to let Job have a view of himself from another standpoint, and discover imperfections in his character which he would never have seen if he had not been brought into a trial condition. When through the light of trial, and the yet greater light of God's glorious presence, Job saw himself unveiled, he abhorred himself in dust and ashes. Probably Job had not humbled himself of late, but he did it then; and now, if any sort of selfishness lurked in him it was put away, for Job began to pray for his cruel friends. It would take a good deal of grace to bring some men to pray for such friends as they were. To pray for one's real friends, I hope, comes natural to us; but to pray for that Bildad and the other two, after the abominable things they had spoken and insinuated—well, it showed that there was a large amount of sweetness and light in Job's character, and abounding grace deep down in his soul, or he would scarcely have interceded for such ungenerous tramplers upon a fallen friend. Now, behold, Job has discovered his fault, and he has put it away, and the grand old man bows his knee to pray for men who called him hypocrite—to pray for men who cut him to the very soul. He pleads with God that he would look in mercy upon men who had no mercy upon him, but had pitilessly heaped all kinds of epithets upon him, and stung him in his tenderest places, just when they ought to have had pity upon him. His misery alone ought to have stopped their mouths, but it seems as if that misery egged them on to say the most cruel things that could possibly have been conceived—the more cruel because they were, all of them, so undeserved. But now Job prays for his friends. You see the trial had reached its point. It had evidently been blessed to Job, and it had proved Satan to be a liar, and so now the fire of the trial goes out, and like precious metal the patriarch comes forth from the furnace brighter than ever.

Beloved friends, the point at which God may turn your captivity may not be the same as that at which he turned Job's, for yours may be a different character. I will try and indicate, briefly, when I think God may turn your trial.

Sometimes he does so *when that trial has discovered to you your special sin.* You have been putting your finger upon diverse faults, but you have not yet touched *the* spot in which your greatest evil is concentrated. God will now help you to know yourself. When you are in the furnace you will begin to search yourself, and you will cry, "Show me wherefore thou contendest with me." You will find out three or four things, perhaps, in which you are faulty, and you will commit yourself to the Lord and say: "Give me grace, good Lord, to put away these evil things." Yes, but you have not come to the point yet, and only a greater trial will guide you to it. The anger of the Lord smokes against your house, not for this or that, but for another evil, and you have need to institute another search, for the images may be under the seat whereon a beloved Rachel sits. The evil in your soul may be just at the point where you think that you are best guarded against temptation. Search, therefore, and look, for when the sin has been found out, and the Achan has been stoned, then the valley of Achor shall be a door of hope, and you shall go up to victory, the Lord going with you.

Perhaps, too, your turning point will be *when your spirit is broken*. We are by nature a good deal like horses that want breaking in, or, to use a scriptural simile, we are as "bullocks unaccustomed to the yoke." Well, the horse has to go through certain processes in the *ménage* until at last it is declared to be "thoroughly broken in," and we need similar training. You and I are not yet quite broken in, I am afraid. We go very merrily along, and yield to the rein in certain forms of service; but if we were called to other sorts of work, or made to suffer, we should need the kicking strap put on, and require a sharper bit in our mouths. We should find that our spirit was not perfectly broken. It takes a long time of pain and sickness to bring some down to the dust of complete resignation to the divine will. There is something still in which they stick out against God, and many it is true, "Though thou shouldest bray a fool in a mortar among wheat with a pestle, yet will not his foolishness depart from him." We have been brayed in that mortar, and with that pestle day after day, and week after week, and yet we are still foolish. When our soul shall cheerfully say, "Not as I will, but as thou wilt," Then our captivity will be almost over, if not quite. While we cry, "It must not be so, I will not have it so," and we struggle and rebel, we shall only have to feel that we are kicking against the pricks, and wounding our foot every time we kick; but when we give up all that struggling, and say, "Lord, I leave it entirely with thee, thy will be done" — then will the trial cease, because there will be no necessity for it any longer.

Sometimes, again, trial may cease *when you have learned the lesson which it was intended to teach you, as to some point of Gospel truth*. I think I have sometimes said that many truths of the Gospel are like letters written with sympathetic ink. If you have ever had a letter written with that preparation, when you look at it you cannot see anything whatever; it is quite illegible. The proper thing to do is to hold the writing up to the fire. As it warms at the fire the acid writing becomes manifest, and the letters are before you. Many of God's promises need to be held before the scorching fires of adversity and personal trouble, and then we read the precious secret of the Spirit's consolation. You cannot see the stars in the day time upon the surface of the earth, but if you go down into a well you can, and when you go down the deep well of trouble it often happens that you see a beauty and luster in the promises which nobody else can see, and when the Lord has brought you into a certain position in which you can see the glory of his grace as you never could have seen it anywhere else, then he will say, "It is enough; I have taught my child the lesson, and I will let him go."

I think, too, it may be with some of us that God *gives us trouble until we obtain a sympathetic spirit*. I should not like to have lived forty years in this world without ever having suffered sickness. "Oh," you say, "that would have been very desirable." I grant you it appears so. When I met with a man that never had an ache or a pain, or a day's sickness in his life, I used to envy him; but I do not now, because I feel very confident that he is a loser by his unvarying experience. How can a man sympathize with trouble that he never knew? How can he be tender in heart if he has never been touched with infirmity himself? If one is to be a comforter to others, he must know the sorrows and the sicknesses of others in his measure. It was essential to our Lord, and, certainly, what was essential to him is necessary to those who are to be shepherds of others, as he was. Now, it may be that by nature some of us are not very sympathetic; I do not think Job was: it is possible that though he was kind, and generous to the poor, yet he was rather hard, but his trouble taught him sympathy. And, perhaps, the Lord may send you trouble till you become softer in heart, so that afterwards you will be one who can speak a word in season to the weary. As you sit down by the bedside of the invalid, you will be able to say, "I know all the ins and outs of a sick man's feelings, for I have been sore sick myself." When God has wrought that in you, it may be he will turn your captivity.

In Job's case, the Lord turned his captivity *when he prayed for his friends*. Prayer for ourselves is blessed work, but for the child of God it is a higher exercise to become an intercessor, and to pray for others. Prayer for ourselves, good as it is, has just a touch of selfishness about it: prayer for others is delivered from that ingredient. Herein is love, the love which God the Holy Spirit delights to foster in the heart, when a man's prayers go up for others. And what a Christlike form of prayer it is when you are praying for those who have ill-treated you and despitefully used you. Then are you like your Master. Praying for yourselves, you are like those for whom Jesus died; but praying for your enemies, you are like the dying Jesus himself. "Father, forgive them, for they know not what they do," has more of heaven in it than the songs of seraphs, and your prayer when offered for those who have tread you ill is somewhat akin to the expiring prayer of our Lord. Job was permitted to take a noble revenge, I am sure the only one he desired, when he became the means of bringing them back to God. God would not hear them, he said, for they had spoken so wrongly of his servant Job, and now Job is set to be a mediator, or intercessor on their behalf: thus was the contempt poured upon the patriarch turned into honor. If the Lord will only save the opposer's soul through your prayer, it will be a splendid way of returning bitter speeches. If many unkind insinuations have been thrown out, and wicked words said, if you can pray for those who used such words, and God hears you and brings them to Jesus, it will be such a triumph as an angel might envy you. Never use any other weapon of retaliation than the weapon of love. Avenge not thyself in anywise by uttering anything like a curse, or desiring any hurt or mischief to come to thy bitterest foe, but inasmuch as he curses, overwhelm him with blessings.

The third word I have to say is this, that BELIEVERS SHALL NOT BE LOSERS FOR THEIR GOD. God, in the experiment, took from Job all that he had, but at the end he gave him back twice as much as he had—twice as many camels and oxen, and twice as many of everything, even of children. I heard a very sweet remark about the children the other day, for somebody said, "Yes, God did give him twice as many children, because his first family were still his. They were not lost but gone before." So the Lord would have his people count their children that are gone to heaven, and reckon them as belonging to the family still, as the child did in Wordsworth's pretty poem, "Master, we are seven." And so Job could say of his sons and daughters, as well as of all the other items, that he had twice as many as before. True, the first family were all gone, but he had prayed for them in the days of their feasting, he had brought them together and offered sacrifice, and so he had a good hope about them, and he reckoned them as still his own. Tried brother, the Lord can restore to you the double in temporal things if he pleases. If he takes away he can as certainly give, and that right early. He certainly can do this in spiritual things; and if he takes away temporals and gives spirituals we are exceedingly great gainers. If a man should take away my silver and give me twice the weight in gold in return, should I not be thankful? And so, if the Lord takes away temporals and gives us spirituals, he thus gives us a hundred times more than he takes away.

Dear brethren, you shall never lose anything by what you suffer for God. If, for Christ's sake, you are persecuted, you shall receive in this life your reward; but if not, rejoice and be glad, for great is your reward in heaven. You shall not lose anything by God's afflicting you. You shall, for a time, be an apparent loser; but a real loser in the end you shall never be. When you get to heaven you will see that you were a priceless gainer by all the losses you endured. Shall you lose anything by what you give to God? Never. Depend on it, he will be no man's debtor. There dwells not in earth or heaven any man who shall be creditor to the Most High. The best investment a man makes is that which he gives to the Lord from a right motive. Nothing is lost which is offered to the cause of God. The breaking of the alabaster box of precious ointment was not a wasteful thing, and he who should give to the Lord all that he had would have made a prudent use of his goods. "He that giveth to the poor lendeth to the Lord," and he that giveth to the Lord's church and to the Lord himself lays up his treasure in heaven, where it shall be his forever.

I wish I could feel that this subject had something to do with you all, but it is not the case. Oh, no, there are some of you who have felt no captivity, but you have a dreadful captivity to come, and there is no hope of God's ever turning that captivity when once you get into it. Without God, without Christ, strangers from the commonwealth of Israel, you are in bondage until now, and there will ere long come upon you bondage that will never end. You cannot pray for your friends: you have never prayed for yourself. God would not hear you if you did pray for others, for, first of all, you must be yourself reconciled to him by the death of his Son. Oh, that you would mind these things and look to Jesus Christ alone for our salvation, for if you do he will accept you, for he has promised to cast out none who come to him. And then look at this: after all is right between God and your soul you need not fear what happens to you in the future, for, come sickness or health, come poverty or wealth, all is right, all is safe, all is well.

14

ISAIAH

Messengers Wanted

"Also I heard the voice of the Lord, saying, Whom shall I send, and who will go for us? Then said I, Here am I; send me" (Is. 6:8).

GOD'S great remedy for man's ruin of man is the sacrifice of his dear Son. He proclaims to the sons of men that only by the atonement of Jesus can they be reconciled unto himself. In order that this remedy should be of any avail to any man he must receive it by faith, for without faith men perish even under the Gospel dispensation. There is at the present moment great lack of men to tell out the story of the cross of Jesus Christ, and many considerations press that lack upon our hearts. Think how many voices all mingle into this one—"Who will go for us?" Listen to the wounds of Jesus, as they plaintively cry, "How shall we be rewarded? How shall the precious drops of blood be made available to redeem the souls of men, unless loving lips shall go for us to claim by right those who have been redeemed by blood?" The blood of Jesus cries like Abel's blood from the ground, "Whom shall I send?" and his wounds repeat the question, "who will go for us?" Does not the purpose of the Eternal Father also join with solemn voice in this demand? The Lord has decreed a multitude unto eternal life. He has purposed, with a purpose which cannot be changed or frustrated, that a multitude whom one man can number shall be the reward of the Savior's travail; but how can these decrees be fulfilled except by the sending forth of the Gospel, for it is through the Gospel, and through the Gospel alone, that salvation can come to the sons of men. Methinks I hear the awful voice of the purpose mingling with the piercing cry of the cross, appealing to us to declare the word of life. I see the handwriting of old Eternity bound in one volume with the crimson writing of Calvary, and both together write out most legibly the pressing question, who shall go for us to bring home the elect and redeemed ones?

The very sins of men, horrible as they are to think upon, may be made an argument for proclaiming the Gospel. Oh the cruel and ravenous sins which destroy the sons of men, and rend their choicest joy in pieces! When I see monstrous lusts defiling the temple of God, and gods many and lords many usurping the throne of the Almighty, I can hear aloud the cry, "Who will go for us?" Do not perishing souls suggest to us the question of the text? Men are going down to the grave, perishing for lack of knowledge, the tomb engulfs them, eternity swallows them up, and in the dark they die without a glimmer of hope. No candle of the Lord ever shines upon their faces. By these perishing souls we implore you this morning to feel that heralds of the cross are wanted, wanted lest these souls be ruined everlastingly; wanted that they may be lifted up from the dunghill of their corruption, and made to sit among princes redeemed by Christ Jesus. The cry wells into a wail of mighty pathetic pleading; all time echoes it, and all eternity prolongs it, while heaven, and earth, and hell give weight to the chorus.

Beloved, there are two forms of missionary enterprise, conducted by two classes of agents. I so divide them merely for the occasion, they are really not divided by any rigid boundary. The first is the agency of those specially dedicated to the ministry of the word, who give themselves wholly to it, who are able by the generous effort of the Christian church, or by their own means, to set their whole time apart for the great work of teaching the truth. As there are but few in this assembly who can do this, I shall not translate my text in its reference to ministers, although it has a loud voice to such, but I shall rather refer to another and equally useful form of agency, namely, the Christian church as a whole; the believers who, while following their secular avocations, are heralds for Christ and missionaries for the cross. Such are wanted here, such are needed in our colonies, such might find ample room in the great world of heathendom, men and women, who, if they did not stand up beneath the tree to address the assembled throng, would preach in the workshop; who, if they did not teach the hundreds, would at the fireside instruct the twos and threes. We want both sorts of laborers, but I may do more good on this present occasion by stirring up this second sort. You may all be teachers of Christ in another sense, you can all give yourself to the work of God in your own calling, and promote your Master's glory perseveringly in your daily avocations. I lift up an earnest cry in God's name for consecrated men and women, who, not needing to wait till the church's hands can support them, shall support themselves with their own hands, and yet minister for Christ Jesus wherever Providence may have cast their lot.

THE PERSON WANTED, as described in the questions, "Whom shall I send? Who will go for us?"

The person wanted is viewed from two points. He has a character bearing two aspects. The person wanted has a divine side; "Whom shall *I* send?" Then he has a human aspect; "Who will go *for us?*" But the two meet together—the human and divine unite in the last words, "*for us.*" Here is a man, nothing more than a man of human instincts, but clad through divine grace with superhuman, even with divine authority.

Let us look, then, at this two-sided person. He is *divinely chosen*— "Whom shall *I* send?" As if in the eternal counsels this had once been a question, "Who shall be the chosen man, who shall be the object of my eternal love, and in consequence thereof shall have this grace given him that he should tell to others the unsearchable riches of Christ?" Beloved, what a mercy it is to us who are believers that *to us* this is no more a question; for sovereignty has pitched upon us and eternal mercy, not for anything good in us, but simply because God would have it so, has selected us that we may bring forth fruit unto his name. As we hear the question, let us listen to the Savior's exposition of it. "Ye have not chosen me, but I have chosen you and ordained you that ye should go and bring forth fruit, and that your fruit should remain." The workers for the living God are a people chosen by the Most High. He sendeth whom he wills, he maketh choice of this man and not another, and in every case exercises his own sovereign will.

This question indicates a person *cheerfully willing*, and this is what I meant by the human side of the messenger. "Who will *go for us?*" The man sought for is one who will go with ready mind; there would be no need to ask, "who will go?" if a mere slave, or machine without a will could be sent. Beloved, the purpose of God does not violate the free agency, or even the free will of man. Man is saved by the will of God, but man is made willing to be so saved. The fault is not in the hyper-Calvinist that he insists upon sovereignty, nor in the Arminian that he is so violent for free agency; the fault is in both of them, because they cannot see more truths than one, and do not admit that truth is not the exclusive property of either, for God is a sovereign, and, at the same time, man is a responsible free agent. Many among us are perpetually seeking to reconcile truths which probably never can be reconciled except in the divine mind. I thank God that I believe many things which I do not even wish to understand. I am weary and sick of arguing, and understanding, and misunderstanding. I find it true rest and joy, like a little child, to believe what God has revealed, and to let others do the puzzling and the reasoning. If I could comprehend the whole of revelation I could scarcely believe it to be divine; but inasmuch as many of its doctrines are too deep for me, and the whole scheme is too vast to be reduced to a system, I thank and bless God that he has deigned to display before me a revelation far exceeding my poor limited abilities. I believe that every man who has Jesus, has him as a matter of his own choice; it is true it is caused by grace, but it is there—it is there. Ask any man whether he is a Christian against his will, and he will tell you certainly not, for he loves the Lord, and delights in his law after the inward man. Thy people are not led unwillingly to thee in chains, O Jesus, but thy people shall be *willing* in the day of thy power. We willingly choose Christ, because he has from of old chosen us.

In the matter of holy work, every man who becomes a worker for Jesus is so because he was chosen to work for him; but he would be a very poor worker if he himself had not chosen to work for Jesus. I can say that I believe God ordained me to preach the Gospel, and that I preach it by his will, but I am sure I preach it with my own; for it is to me the most delightful work in all the world, and if I could exchange with an emperor, I would not consent to be so lowered. To preach the Gospel of Jesus Christ is one of the sweetest and noblest employments, and even an angel might desire to be engaged in it. The true worker for God must be impelled by divine election, but yet he must make and will make, by divine grace, his own election of his work.

The two meet together in this—the man is sent by the Three One, who here asks, "Who will go for us?" Every faithful Christian laborer labors for God. Brethren, when we tell others the story of the cross, we speak of *God the Father*. It is through our lips that the prodigal son must be reminded that the hired servants have bread enough and to spare. It may be through us that he will be shown his rags and his disgrace; through us he will discover more clearly the disgrace of feeding swine.

The Spirit of God is the efficient agent, but it is by us that he may work. It is by us that the divine Father falls upon the neck of his prodigal child. *He* does it, but it is through the teaching of his Word in some form or other. The promises are spoken by our lips, the sweet invitations are delivered by our tongues. We, as though God did beseech them by us, are to pray them in Christ's stead to be reconciled to God. God the Father says to you who know and love him, "Will you go for me and be an ambassador for me?" Nor must we forget our tender *Redeemer*. He is not here, for he is risen. He will come again, but meanwhile he asks for someone to speak for him, someone to tell Jerusalem that her iniquity is forgiven; to tell his murderers that he prays for them, "Father, forgive them"; to assure the blood-bought that they are redeemed; to proclaim liberty to the captive, and the opening of the prison doors to them that are bound. Jesus from his throne of glory says, "Who will go for me and be a speaker for me?" Moreover, that blessed *Spirit*, under whose dispensatorial power we live at the present hour, has no voice to speak to the sons of men audibly except by his people; and though he works invisibly and mysteriously in the saints, yet he chooses loving hearts, and compassionate lips, and tearful eyes to be the means of benediction. The Spirit descends like the cloven tongue, but he sits *upon* disciples; there is no resting place for the Spirit of God nowadays within walls, and even the heaven of heavens contains him not, but he enthrones himself within his people. He makes us God-bearers, and he speaks through us as through a trumpet to the sons of men. So that the adorable Trinity cry to you, ye blood-bought, blood-redeemed sons of God, and say, "Are you seeking to promote our glory? Are you effecting our purposes? Are you winning those purchased by our eternal sacrifice?" Turning to the church here assembled, the Lord pronounces those ancient questions, "Whom shall I send? Who will go for us?"

By God's help, we would say a little upon THE PERSON OFFERING HIMSELF. "Here am I; send me."

The person offering himself is described in the chapter at very great length — he must be an Isaiah. Being an Isaiah, he must in the first place *have felt his own unworthiness.* My brother, my sister, if you are to be made useful by God in soul-winning you must pass through the experience which Esaias describes in the chapter before us. You must have cried in bitterness of spirit, "Woe is me, for I am a man of unclean lips!" God will never fill you with himself until he has emptied you of your own self. Till you feel that you are weak as water, you shall not see the splendor of the divine power. May I ask then those of you who feel desirous to serve God this experimental question, "Have you been made fully conscious of your own utter unfitness to be employed in any work for God, and your own complete unworthiness of so great an honor as to become a servant of the living God? If you have not been brought to this you must begin with yourself; you cannot do any good to others: you must be born again; and one of the best evidences of your being born again, will be a discovery of your own natural depravity and impurity in the sight of God.

Now, beloved, I want you to notice how it was that Isaiah was made to feel his unworthiness. It was first by *a sense of the presence of God.* "I saw the Lord sitting upon a throne, high and lifted up." Have you ever had a consciousness of the presence of God? The other day I was prostrated in soul, utterly prostrated, with this one word "I AM!" There is everything in that title, the I AM! God is the truest of all existences. With regard to all other things, they may or may not be, but I AM! It came with such power to me. I thought, Here am I sitting in my study, whether I am, or whether that which surrounds me really is, may be a question, but, God *is*—God *is here*. And when I speak God's word in his name, though I am nothing, God is everything, and as to whether or not his word shall be fulfilled there cannot be any question, because he still is called not "I was," but "I am," infinite, omnipotent, divine. Think of the reality of the divine presence, and the certainty of that divine presence, everywhere, close here, just now! "I am!" O God, if *we* be not, yet *thou art!* I scarcely think that any man is fitted to become a teacher of others till he has had a full sense of the glory of God crushing him right down into the dust, a full sense of that word, "I am." You know a man cannot pray without it, for we must believe that *he is*, and that he is the rewarder of them that diligently seek him; and if a man cannot pray for himself, much less can he rightly teach others. There must be the fullest conviction of the reality of God, an overwhelming sight and sense of his glory, or else you cannot benefit your fellows.

The source of Isaiah's sense of nothingness was this, that Isaiah *saw the glory of Christ.* Have you ever sat down and gazed upon the cross till, having read your own pardon there, you have seen that cross rising higher and higher till it touched the heavens and overshadowed the globe? Then you have seen and felt the glory of him who was lifted up, and have bowed before the regal splendor of divine love, incarnate in suffering humanity, and resplendent in agony and death. If you have ever beheld the vision of the Crucified, and felt the glory of his wounds, you will then be fit to preach to others. I have sometimes thought that certain brethren who preach the Gospel with such meager power and such lack of unction have no true knowledge of it. There is no need to talk of it with bated breath. It is sneered at as being such a very simple tale—"Believe and live"; but after all, no philosopher ever made such a disclosure; and if a senate of discoverers could sit through the ages they could not bring to light any fact equal to this, that God was in Christ reconciling the world unto himself. Well mayest thou open thy mouth boldly when thou hast such a subject as this to speak upon; but if thou hast never perceived its glory, thou art utterly incapable of fulfilling God's errand. Oh, to get the cross into one's heart, to bear it upon one's soul, and above all, to feel the glory of it in one's whole being, is the best education for a Christian missionary whether at home or abroad.

It will strike you too, dear friends, that the particular aspect in which this humiliation may come to us will probably be, *a sense of the divine holiness*, and the holiness of those who see his face. "Holy, holy, holy, Lord God of hosts!" was the song which overawed the prophet. What messengers are those who serve so holy a God? From earth and all its grossness free, like flames of fire they flash at his command. Who then am I, a poor creature, cribbed, cabined, and confined within this house of clay? Who am I, a sinful worm of the dust, that I should aspire to the service of so thrice holy a God? Oh let us serve the Lord with fear and rejoice with trembling; fearful lest we should do mischief while seeking to do good, and pollute the altar while attempting to offer sacrifice upon it.

The next preparation for Christian work is, we must possess *a sense of mercy*. Then flew one of the seraphims and took a live coal from off the altar. We explained in our reading that the altar is for sacrifice, and that the lip must be touched with a coal of that sacrifice; then, being so touched, it derives two effects therefrom. In the first place, *the lip is purged of iniquity*; and in the next place, *it feels the influence of fire*, enabling it to speak with vehemence and force. Beloved hearer, thou sayest perhaps in zeal, "I desire to serve Christ and to tell abroad the story of his cross." Hast thou proved that story to be true? Wert thou ever washed in the fountain? How canst thou bid others come if thou hast never come thyself? Have thy sins been put away? "I hope so." Doest thou know it? I question if thou canst preach with any power till thou hast a full assurance of thine own salvation. To teach the Gospel with "but" and "if" is a poor teaching. You Sunday School teachers cannot hope to do much good to others while you doubt your own acceptance in the Beloved. You must know that you are saved. Oh beloved, you must feel the touch of that live coal, you must feel that Christ gave himself for you. You Littlefaiths may get to heaven, but you must keep in the back rank while here, we cannot put you in the front of the battle. Though God may make you of service, we cannot expect you to be eminently of service. The man who would serve God must know himself to be saved.

The effect of that live coal will be to fire the lip with heavenly flame. "Oh," says one man, "a flaming coal will burn the lip so that the man cannot speak at all." That is just how God works with us; it is by consuming the fleshly power that he inspires the heavenly might. Oh let the lip be burnt, let the fleshly power of eloquence be destroyed, but oh for that live coal to make the tongue eloquent with heaven's flame; the true divine power which urged the Apostles forward, and made them conquerors of the whole world.

According to the text, *the man who will be acceptable must offer himself cheerfully.* "Here am I." Though how few of us have in very deed given ourselves to Christ. It is with most professors, "Here is my half guineas, here is my annual contribution"; but how few of us have said, "Here am I." No; we sing of consecration as we sing a great many other things which we have not realized, and when we have sung it we do not wish to be taken at our word. It is not, "Here am I." The man whom God will use must in sincerity be a consecrated man. I have explained that he may keep still to his daily work, but he must be consecrated to God in it; he must sanctify the tools of his labor to God, and there is no reason why they should not be quite as holy as the brazen altar or the golden candlestick.

You will observe that the person who thus volunteered for sacred service gave himself *unreservedly.* He did not say, "Here am I; use me where I am," but "send me." Where to? No condition as to place is so much as hinted at. Anywhere, anywhere, anywhere—send me. Some people are militia-Christians—they serve the King with a limitation and must not be sent out of England; but others are soldier-Christians, who give themselves wholly up to their Lord and Captain; they will go wherever he chooses to send them. Oh come, my Master, and be absolute Lord of my soul! Reign over me, and subdue my every passion to do and be, and feel all that thy will ordains. Blessed prayer! May we never be content till we get all that is to be got by way of joyful experience and holy power, nor until we yield all that is to be yielded by mortal man to the God whose sovereign right to us we claim.

Notice one more thought, that while the prophet gives himself unreservedly, he gives *obediently*, for he pauses to ask directions. It is not, "Here am I; away I will go," but "Here am I; *send* me." I like the spirit of that prayer. Some people get into their head a notion that they must do something uncommon and extraordinary, and though it may be most unreasonable and most irrational, it is for that very reason that the scheme commends itself to their want of judgment. Because it is absurd, they think it to be divine; if earthly wisdom does not justify it, then certainly heavenly wisdom must be called in to endorse it. Now, I conceive that you will find that whenever a thing is wise in God's sight it is really wise, and that a thing which is absurd is not more likely to be adopted by God than by man; for though the Lord does use plans which are called foolish, they are only foolish to fools, but not actually foolish; there is a real wisdom in their very foolishness, there is a wisdom of God in the things which are foolish to man. When a project is evidently absurd and ridiculous, it may be my own but it cannot be the Lord's, and I had better wait until I can yield up my whims, and subject myself to divine control, saying, "Here am I, send me."

In the last place, THE WORK WHICH SUCH PERSONS WILL BE CALLED TO UNDERTAKE. Isaiah's history is a picture of what many and many a true Christian laborer may expect. Isaiah was sent to preach very unpleasant truth, but like a true hero he was very bold in preaching it. "Isaiah is very bold," says the Apostle. Now if you are called of God either to preach or teach, or whatever it is, remember the things you have to preach or teach will not be agreeable to your hearers. Scorn on the man who ever desires to make truth palatable to unhallowed minds. If he modulates his utterances or suppresses the truth which God has given him even in the slightest possible degree to suit the tastes of men, he is a traitor and a coward: let him be drummed out of God's regiment, and driven from the army of God altogether. God's servants are to receive God's message, and whether men will hear or whether they will forbear, they are to deliver it to them in the spirit of old Micaiah, who vowed,

"As the Lord my God liveth, whatsoever the Lord saith to me, that will I speak.

But this is not the hardest task; the severest labor is this; we may have to deliver unpleasant truth to people who are resolved not to receive it, to people who will derive no profit from it, but rather will turn it to their own destruction. You see in the text that ancient Israel was to hear but not to receive; they were to be preached to, and the only result was to be that their heart was to be made fat, and their ears dull of hearing. What! Is that ever to be the effect of the Gospel? The Bible tells us so. Our preaching is a savor of death unto death, as well as of life unto life. "Oh," says one, "I should not like to preach at that rate." But remember, brother, that the preaching of the cross is a sweet savor of Christ either way. The highest object of all to a Christian laborer is not to win souls, that is *a* great object; but *the* great object is to glorify God; and many a man has been successful in this who did not succeed in the other. If Israel be not gathered, yet, if we bear our testimony for God, our work is done. No farmer thinks of paying his men in proportion to the harvest. He pays his workers for word done, and so will it be with us, by God's grace, and if I happen to be a very successful laborer here, I boast not, nor claim any large reward on that account. I believe that had I preached the Gospel with earnestness and waited upon God, if he had denied me conversions, my reward would be as great at the last, in some respects, because the Master would not lay to my door a non-success which could not be attributed to myself.

Now it would be a very pleasant thing for me to ask you whether you would go for God in your daily vocation and tell of Jesus to sinners who are willing to hear of him, you would all be glad to do that. If I were to ask which sister here would take a class of young women, all anxious to find Christ, why you would all hold up your hands. If I could say, "Who will take a class of boys who long to find the Savior?" you might all be glad of such an avocation; but I have to put it another way lest you should afterwards be dispirited. Who among you will try and teach truth to a drunken husband? Who among you will carry the Gospel to despisers and profligates, and into places where the Gospel will make you the object of rage and derision? Who among you will take a class of ragged roughs? Who among you will try and teach those who will throw your teaching back upon you with ridicule and scorn? You are not fit to serve God unless you are willing to serve him anywhere and everywhere. You must with the servant be willing to take the bitter with the sweet; you must be willing to serve God in the winter as in the summer. If you are willing to be God's servant at all, you are not to pick and choose your duty and say, "Here am I, send me where there is pleasant duty." Anybody will go then; but if you are willing to serve God you will say today, "Through floods and flames if Jesus leads, I will by the Holy Spirit's aid be true to my following."

Now, though I have said nothing particularly with regard to foreign missions, I have preached this sermon with the view that God will stir you all up to serve his cause, and particularly with the hope that the missionary feeling being begotten may show itself in a desire also to carry the Gospel into foreign parts. Pastor Harms has lately been taken to his rest, but those of you who know the story of his life must have been struck with it; how an obscure country village, on a wild heath in Germany, was made to be a fountain of living waters to South Africa. The poor people had little care for the name of Jesus till Harms went there; and, notwithstanding that, I have no sympathy with his Lutheran High-churchism and exclusiveness: I may say he went there to preach Christ with such fire that the whole parish became a missionary society, sending out its own men and women to preach Christ crucified. That ship, the *Candace*, purchased by the villagers of Hermansburgh with their own money, went to and from South Africa, taking the laborers to make settlements, and to undertake Christian enterprise in that dark continent. The whole village was saturated with a desire to serve God and preach the Gospel to the heathen, and Harms at the head of it acted with a simple faith worthy of apostolic times. I would that my God would give me what I should consider the greatest honor of my life, the privilege of seeing some of the brethren and sisters of this church devoted to the Lord, and going forth into foreign parts. One gave his farm for students to be educated, another gave all he had, until throughout Hermansburgh it became very much like apostolic days when they had all things in common, the grand object being that of sending the Gospel to the heathen. The day may come when we who have been able to do something for this heathen country of England may do something for other heathen countries in sending out our sons and daughters.

15

JONAH
Sleepers Aroused

"But Jonah was gone down into the sides of the ship; and he lay, and was fast asleep" (Jon. 1:5).

WE ARE told, before this fact is mentioned, that the Lord sent out a great wind into the sea to overtake the bark in which Jonah was sailing for Tarshish. The great wheels of providence are continually revolving in fulfillment of God's purposes concerning his own people. For them, winds blow, and tempests rise. It is a wonderful thing that the whole machinery of nature should be made subservient to the divine purpose of the salvation of his redeemed. I was in a diamond-cutting factory at Amsterdam, and I noticed that there were huge wheels revolving, and a great deal of power being developed and expended; but when I came to look at the little diamond—in some cases a very small one indeed—upon which that power was being brought to bear, it seemed very remarkable that all that power could be concentrated upon such a little yet very precious object. In a similar style, all the wheels of providence and nature, great as they are, are brought to bear, by divine skill and love, upon a thing which appears to many people to be of trifling value, but which is to Christ of priceless worth; namely, a human soul.

Here is this common-looking Jew—Jonah, named, according to the general rule that names go by contraries, "a dove", for, at any rate, on this occasion, he looked more like the raven that would not come back to the ark; and for this one man—this altogether unamiable prophet—the sea must be tossed in tempest, and a whole ship full of people must have their lives put in jeopardy. This truth is a very far-reaching one. You cannot well exaggerate it. The vast universe is but a platform for the display of God's grace, and all material things, that now exist, will be set

179

aside when the great drama of grace is completed. The material universe is but scaffolding for the Church of Christ. It is but the temporary structure upon which the wonderful mystery of redeeming love is being carried on to perfection. See, then, that, as the great wind was raised to follow Jonah, and to lead to his return to the path of duty, so all things work together for the good of God's people, and all things that exist are being bowed and bent towards God's one solemn eternal purpose—the salvation of his own.

But note also that, while God was awake, Jonah was asleep. While storms were blowing, Jonah was slumbering. It is a strange sight, O Christian, that you should be an important item in the universe, and yet that you should not know it, or care about it; that for you all things are keeping their proper place and time, and yet that you are the only one who does not seem to perceive it; and, therefore, you fall into a dull, lethargic, sleepy state. Everything around you is awake for your good, yet you yourself are slumbering even as the fugitive prophet was while the storm was raging.

First, then, I shall use the case of Jonah as A USEFUL LESSON TO THE PEOPLE OF GOD; and I may very fairly do so when we remember who Jonah was.

First, *Jonah was a believer in God.* He worshiped no false god; he worshiped only the living and true God. He was a professed and avowed believer in Jehovah. He was not ashamed to say—even when his conduct had laid him open to blame, and when there was nobody to support him— "I am a Hebrew; and I fear the Lord, the God of heaven, which hath made the sea and the dry land." Yet, though he was a believer in God, he was in the sides of the ship, fast asleep. O Christian man—a real Christian man, too—if you are in a similar condition, how is it that you can be slumbering under such circumstances? Should not the privileges and the honor, which your being a believer has brought to you by divine grace, forbid that you should be a slumberer, inactive, careless, indifferent? I may be addressing dozens of Jonahs, those who are really God's people, but who are not acting as if they were chosen of the Most High; but are forgetful of their election, their redemption, their sanctification, the life they have begun to live here below, and the eternal glory that awaits them hereafter.

Beside being a believer, or as a natural consequence of being a believer, *Jonah was a man of prayer.* Out of the whole company on board that ship, he was the only man who knew how to pray to the one living and true God. All the mariners "cried every man unto his god." But those were idle prayers because they were offered to idols; they could not pre-vail because they were presented to dumb, dead deities. But here was a man who could pray—and who could pray aright, too—yet he was asleep. Praying men and praying women—you who have the keys of the king-dom of heaven swinging at your girdle—you who can ask what you will, and it shall be done for you—you who have, many a time in the past, prevailed with God in wrestling prayer—you who have received count-less blessings in answer to your supplications—can you be, as Jonah was, sleeping in the time of storm? Can it be possible that he, who knows the power of prayer, is restraining it—that he, to whom God has given this choice privilege, is not availing himself of it? I fear that this may be the case with some of you; and looking at Jonah, a praying man sinfully asleep, I cannot help feeling that I may be speaking to many others who are in exactly the same condition.

More than this, Jonah was not merely a believing man, and a pray-ing man, but *he was also a prophet of the Lord.* He was one to whom God had spoken, and by whom God had spoken. He was a minister; that is to say, one of God's own sent servants, though he was not in his proper place when he was in the ship sailing towards Tarshish. But can God's ministers neglect their duty like this? If I had been asked at that time, "Where is the prophet of the Lord?"—perhaps the only prophet of his age—at any rate, a man who was the very foremost in his time—if I had been asked, "Where is he?" I should have said that he must be looked for amidst the masses of the dense population of Nineveh, car-rying out his Master's commission with unstaggering faith; or else that he might be looked for amidst the thousands of Israel, denouncing their idol gods and their wicked ways. But who would have thought of finding Jonah asleep on board such a ship as that? He is a seer, yet he sees not, for he is sound asleep. He is a watchman, but he is not watch-ing, for he is slumbering and sleeping. Everything is in confusion; yet this man, upon whom rests the divine anointing, and into whose mouth God has put a message to multitudes of his fellow creatures, is sleeping instead of witnessing. Come, Mr. Preacher, see to yourself while I am talking about Jonah, and I will take the message to myself while I am talking to you; for this is a matter which ought to come home to all of us upon whom such great responsibilities are laid, and to whom such high privileges are given. But all of you, who love the Lord, are witnesses for Christ in some capacity or other; and it would be a very sad thing if you, who are called to speak in the name of the Lord, though it should only be in your Sunday School class, or in a little cottage meeting, or to your own children, should be asleep when you ought to be wide awake and active. May the Lord awaken you; for you are the wrong person to be asleep! You, above all others, are bound to have both your eyes open, and to watch day and night to hear what God the Lord will speak to you, and what he would have you say to the ungodly or to his own chosen people in his name.

It is also worthy to notice that, at the very time when Jonah was asleep in the ship, he was not only a prophet, but he was *a prophet under a special commission*. He was not on furlough; he was, on the contrary, empowered by special warrant, under the King's seal and sign manual, to go at once to a certain place, and there to deliver the King's message; and yet there he is, asleep in this ship, and going in the very opposite direction to the one given him! When prophets sleep, it should be when their errand has been done, and their message has been delivered; but Jonah had not been on his Lord's errand, nor had he delivered his Lord's message; nay, he had refused to obey his Lord, and had run away from the path of duty, and here he lies, fast asleep, in the sides of the ship. O dear brothers and sisters, if we could truthfully say that our own work for the Lord was done, we might be somewhat excused if we took our rest. But is our life work done? Mine is not; that I feel certain; it seems to be scarcely begun. Is yours finished, my brother, my sister? Have you so lived that you can be perfectly content with what you have done? Would it not be a cause for grief to you if you were assured that you would have no more opportunities of glorifying God upon the earth? I think you would feel that very much. Well, then, how can you be willing to be indifferent, cold, and dead, when so much of God's work lies before you scarcely touched as yet? All that you and I have done, so far, has been like apprentice work; we have been just getting our hand in, we have not become journeymen in God's great workshop yet; certainly, we cannot claim to be wise master builders yet. Few of us, if any, have attained to that degree; so let us not go to sleep. O sir, shame on thee! Asleep in the early morning? A man may take his rest when he gets weary after a long day's toil; but not yet, with all that work to be done—with the King's commission pressing upon us. With the call of the myriads of Nineveh sounding in his ears, Jonah, God's appointed messenger, should not have been found asleep in the sides of the ship.

He was a believing man and a praying man, and a prophet, and a prophet under a special commission. But where was he? Where had he got to? Well, he had gone down into the sides of the ship; that is to say, *he had gone where he hoped he should not be observed or disturbed.* He had gone down into the sides of the ship—not among the cargo; the mariners threw that overboard, yet the noise did not wake the sleeping prophet. He was not upon the deck, ready to take a turn at keeping watch; but he had got as much out of the way as ever he could; and I have known Christian people try, as far as they could, to get out of the way. Possibly, they are not living inconsistently, or doing, as far as others can see, anything that is glaringly sinful; but they have just retired from their Master's business. They have got into a little quiet place where nobody notices them. I wonder whether there is a Christian man, who has gone to live in a country village, where he has not yet said anything for Christ, although, when he lived in London, he was a busy worker for God. He has, like Jonah, gone down into the sides of the ship, into a quiet place where nobody can see him. Around him there are very few Christian people—perhaps hardly any—and he does not want anybody to know that he is a Christian. He would like now to live in quite a private way. If he were asked about himself, he would answer, as Jonah did, "I fear God"; but he does not wish to be asked anything upon himself. He does not want people to fix their eyes upon him; he is afraid of being too conspicuous. He says that he always was of a retiring disposition, like the soldier, who ran away as soon as the first shot of the battle was fired, and so was shot as a deserter. He says that he is like Nicodemus, who came to Jesus by night, or like Joseph of Arimathea, a disciple, but secretly, for fear of the Jews. He was gone down into the sides of the ship, though, at one time, he was one of the foremost workers for Christ.

He has gone, too, *where he will not lend a hand in any service that needs to be done.* He was in the Sunday School once, but he says that he has had his turn at that, and does not intend to do anything more. He used to be, perhaps, a deacon of a church, but now he does not wish for such a position as that. He says there is a great deal of trouble and toil in connection with such offices, and he intends, for the future, to avoid everything that will give him trouble, or cause him the slightest toil. Once, he took delight in preaching the Word; and, in those days, if anybody had said that he would live to be silent, and not speak in Christ's name, he would have been very angry at the man who made such a statement; but it has come true now.

Observe, too, that *Jonah was stopping away from the prayer meeting.* Do you ask, "What prayer meeting?" Why, every other man on board that ship was crying unto his god, but Jonah was asleep in the sides of the ship. He was not praying; he was sleeping, and perhaps dreaming, but he was certainly not praying; and it is a very bad thing when a true servant of God, a praying man, and one by whom God has spoken aforetime, begins to get into such a spiritually sleepy state that he not only does nothing to help the church, but he does not even join in prayer in the time of danger.

This man, asleep in the sides of the ship, represents *one who was not even taking any notice of what was going on around him.* At first, he did not wish to be himself observed; but now, he does not care to observe others. What is the condition of the millions of heathen in foreign lands? That is a subject that he avoids; he is of opinion that they will be converted in the millennium, or that, even if they are not converted, their future lot may be a happy one. At any rate, it is a subject about which he does not concern himself. Jonah is asleep in the sides of the ship, and he appears quite content to let the millions of heathen perish. Then, with regard to the Church of Christ at home, sometimes he is told that everything is prospering, but from other quarters he is informed that we are all going to the bad. Well, he does not know which report is the true one, and he does not particularly care; and, as for the church of which he is a member, does he not care for that? Well, yes, in a certain fashion; but he does not care enough for the Sunday School, for instance, to lend a hand there, or for the preaching society to lend a hand there. He never encourages the minister's heart by saying that the love of Christ constraineth him to take his share of holy service. Jonah is asleep in the sides of the ship. He is not much noticed, if at all, for those around him have come to the conclusion that he is good for nothing; and he himself, as I have shown you, does not take much notice of what is going on, though all the while he is a man of God, a man of prayer, and one whom God has used in times past.

Now, further, what was Jonah doing at that time? *He was asleep—asleep amid all that confusion and noise.* What a hurly-burly there was outside that vessel—storms raging, billows roaring—and Jonah was not a sailor, but a landsman, yet he was asleep. Certainly he must have been in a remarkable state to be able to sleep through such a storm as that. Jonah was asleep amid all that confusion and noise; and, O Christian man, for you to be indifferent to all that is going on in such a world as this, for you to be negligent of God's work in such a time as this, is just as strange. The devil alone is making noise enough to wake all the Jonahs if they only want to awake. Then there are the rampant errors of the times, the sins of the times, the confusions of the times, the controversies of the times, all these things ought to wake us. And then, beyond the times, there is eternity, with all its terrors and its glories. There is the dread conflict that is going on between Christ and Belial—between the true and the false—between Jesus and antichrist. All around us there is tumult and storm, yet some professing Christians are able, like Jonah, to go to sleep in the sides of the ship.

Notice, also, that *Jonah was asleep when other people were awake.* All around us people seem to be wide awake, whether we are asleep or not. When I see what is being done by Romanists, and observe the zeal and self-denial of many persons who have dedicated themselves to the propagation of their fake faith, I am astonished that we are doing so little for the true faith. Is it really the case that God has the dullest set of servants in the whole world? It is certain that men are all alive in the service of Satan; then we should not be half alive in the service of our God. Are the worshipers of Baal crying aloud, "O Baal, hear us," and the devotees of Ashtaroth shouting, "Hear us, O mighty Ashtaroth"; and yet the prophet of Jehovah is lying asleep in the sides of the ship? Is it so? Does everything else seem to arouse all a man's energies, but does true religion paralyze them? I have really thought, when I have been reading some books written by very good men, that the best thing for sending a man to sleep was a book by an evangelical writer; but that, the moment a man becomes unsound in the faith, it seems as if he woke up, and had something to say which people were bound to hear. Yet I fear that it is still only too true that those who serve the living God are not half filled with the arousing fervor which ought to possess them for the honor of the Lord Most High.

Jonah was asleep, next, not only in a time of great confusion, and when others were wake, but also *in a time when he was in great danger,* for the ship was likely to sink. The storm was raging furiously, yet Jonah was asleep. And, believer, when you, and those about you, are in danger of falling into great sin through your careless living—when your family is in danger of being brought up without the fear of God—when our servants are in danger of concluding that religion is all a farce because you act as if it were—when those who watch you in business are apt to sneer at Christian profession because they say that your profession is of very little worth to you—when all this is taking place, and there is imminent danger to your own soul, and to the souls of others, can you still sleep in unconcern?

And Jonah was asleep when *he was wanted to be awake*. He, above all other men, was the one who ought to wake, and call upon his God. If anybody goes to sleep nowadays, it certainly ought not to be the believer in the Lord Jesus Christ. All things demand that Christians should be in real earnest. I know of no argument that I could gather from time or eternity, from heaven, or earth, or hell, to allow a Christian man to be supine and careless; but if I am asked for reasons why Christians are wanted to be in downright earnest and full of consecrated vigor in the service of God, those arguments are so plentiful that I have no time to mention them all. The world needs you; careless souls need to be awakened, inquiring souls need to be directed; mourning souls need to be comforted; rejoicing souls need to be established; the ignorant need to be taught; the desponding need to be cheered. On all sides, for every Christian man, there is an earnest cry; and, certainly, in these days. God has made a truly godly man to be more precious than the gold of Ophir; and that man, who keeps himself back from earnest service for God in such a time as this, surely cannot expect the Lord's blessing to rest upon him.

Jonah was asleep, with all the heathen around him, upbraiding him by their actions. They were praying while he was sleeping; and, at last, it came to this—that the shipmaster sternly addressed the prophet of God, and said, "What meanest thou, O sleeper?" It is sad indeed when things have come to such a pass that a heathen captain rebukes a servant of God; and yet I am afraid that the Church of God, if she does not mend her ways, will have a great many similar rebukes from heathen practices and heathen utterances. Look at the enormous sums that the heathen spend upon their idols and their idol temples and worship, and then think how little we spend upon the service of the living God. One is amazed to read of the lakhs of rupees that are given by Indian princes for the worship of their dead deities; and yet our missionary societies languish, and the work of God in a thousand ways is stopped, because God's stewards are not using what he has entrusted to them as they should. Think, too, of the flaming zeal with which the votaries of false faiths compass sea and land to make one proselyte, while we do so little to bring souls to

Jesus Christ. One of these days you will have Hindus and Brahmins talking to us in this fashion, "You profess that the love of Christ constrains you, but to what does it constrain you?" They quote our great national sins against us, and I do not wonder that they do. I only wish that they could be told that Christians reprobate those evils, and that they are not Christians who practice them.

But why was Jonah asleep? I suppose that it was partly the reaction after the excitement through which is mind had passed in rebelling against God. He had wearied himself with seeking his own evil way; so now, after the disobedience to God of which he had been guilty, his spirit sinks, and he sleeps. There is no opiate like the commission of an evil deed. Jonah's conscience had become hardened by his willful rejection of his Lord's commands, and therefore he could sleep when he ought to have been aroused and alarmed.

O sleepy Christian, there is something wrong about you, too! Conscience has been stupefied. There is some darling sin, I fear, that you are harboring. Search it out, and drive it out. Sin is the mother of this shameful indifference. God help thee to get rid of it!

Now, more briefly, I want to give A WARNING TO THE UNCONVERTED.

Jonah, asleep on board that ship, is a type of a great number of unconverted people who come to our various places of worship. Jonah was in imminent danger, for God had sent a great storm after him; and, my unconverted hearer, *your danger, at this present moment, is beyond description.* There is nothing but a breath between you and hell. One of our beloved elders was with us here last Sabbath day; he is now with the spirits of just men made perfect; but if it had been the lot of any unconverted person here to suffer and to expire in the same manner, alas, how sad it would have been for you, my hearer!

You are asleep, too, *when there are a great many things to awake you.* As I have already said, there was a great noise in the vessel where Jonah was, a great noise inside and outside the ship, yet he did not awake. I do believe that many of you, unconverted people, find it hard to remain as you are. You get hard blows, sometimes, from the preacher. At family prayer, often, your conscience is touched. When you hear a passage from the Bible read, or when you hear of a friend who has died, you get somewhat aroused. Why, the very conversion of others should surely awaken you. If nothing else had awoke Jonah, the prayers of the mariners ought to have awakened him; and the earnestness of your mother and father, the pleading of your sister, the cries of new converts, the earnest anxieties of inquiries, ought to have—and if you were not so deeply sunken in slumber, would have—some influence over you to arouse you.

You are asleep, brother, *while prayer would save you.* If your prayers could not be heard, I think I should say, "Let him sleep on." If there were no possibility of your salvation, I do not see why you should be aroused from your slumbers. Despair is an excellent excuse for sloth; but you have no reason to despair. "Arise, call upon thy God," said the shipmaster to Jonah; and we say to you, "Friend, how is it that you are so indifferent, and do not pray, when it is written, 'Ask, and it shall be given you; seek, and ye shall find'; and when the facts prove the truth of the words of Jesus, 'for he that asketh receiveth, and he that seeketh findeth'?" Heaven is within your reach, yet you will not stretch out your hand. Eternal life is so nigh to thee that Paul writes, "If thou shalt confess with thy mouth the Lord Jesus, and shalt believe in thine heart that God hath raised him from the dead, thou shalt be saved." You are sleeping while God's people are wondering at you, just as those mariners in the ship wondered at Jonah; and while they were weeping over you, and praying for you. There are some, in this place, who are the constant subjects of prayer. Some of you, who are seated here, do not perhaps know it; but there are those who love you, and who mention your name day and night before God; and yet, while they are concerned about you, you are not concerned about yourself. O God, if storms cannot awaken these sleeping Jonahs, awaken them by some other means, even though it be by one like themselves, or one even worse than themselves!

Oh, I pray you, if you are out of Christ, do not pretend to be happy! Do not accept any happiness till you find it in him. To some of you, I would speak very pointedly. Are you sick? Do you feel that your life is very precarious? O my dear friend, you are like Jonah when the ship was like to be broken. Do not delay. Are there the beginnings of consumption about you? Is it supposed to be so? Do not delay. Has some relative been taken away, and does there seem some likelihood that you may have the same disease? Oh, do not sleep, but awake! Are you getting old, friend? Are the gray hairs getting thick around your brow? Oh, do not delay!

May God's Holy Spirit bestir you to make your calling and election sure! Lay hold on Jesus Christ with the grip of an earnest, humble faith, and surrender yourself, henceforth, to the service of him who has bought you with his precious blood. God grant to all of us the grace to awake, and arise, that Christ may give us life and light, for his dear name's sake!

16

DANIEL

Undaunted Courage

"Now when Daniel knew that the writing was signed, he went into his house; and his windows being open in his chamber towards Jerusalem, he kneeled upon his knees three times a day, and prayed, and gave thanks before his God, as he did aforetime" (Dan. 6:10).

DANIEL had been exalted to very great worldly prosperity, but his soul had prospered too. Oftentimes outward advancement means inward decline. Tens of thousands have been intoxicated by success. Though they bade fair in starting in the race of life to win the prize, they were tempted to turn aside to gather the golden apples, and so they missed the crown. It was not so with Daniel—he was as perfect before God in his high estate as in his lowlier days; and this is to be accounted for by the fact that he sustained the energy of his outward profession by constant secret communion with God. He was, we are told, a man of an excellent spirit, and a man abundant in prayer; hence his head was not turned by his elevation, but the Lord fulfilled in him his promise to "make his servant's feet like hinds' feet, that they may stand upon their high places." Yet, although Daniel preserved his integrity, he did not find a position of greatness to be one of rest. As the birds peck at the ripest fruit, so his envious enemies assailed him; and as the most conspicuous warriors most attract the arrows of the foe, so the honors of Daniel brought upon him the enmities of many.

Seek not then, beloved, seek not then, with an excess of desire, or an unrest of ambition, to be great among the great ones of the earth. There are more precious things than honor and wealth. A Persian king, wising to give two of his courtiers a token of his regard, gave to one of them a golden cup and to the other a kiss: he who had obtained the golden cup considered that he was hardly done by, and envied the courtier who received the kiss from the monarch's own mouth. And let me say, let who will receive the wealth and honors of the world, which make up her golden cup, if you receive a kiss of favor from the lip of God, and feel the sweetness of it in your inmost soul, you have received more than they; you have no reason whatsoever to repine though that kiss should come to you in poverty and sickness, but rather to rejoice that God has counted you worthy, in his infinite grace, to receive the more of spirituals though you have the less of temporals.

Luther declared that all the greatness of the world was but a bone which God threw to a dog, "For," says he, "he gives more to the Pope and to the Turk than to all his saints put together," and so verily it is. To be great, distinguished, and wealthy, may be the lot of a Haman, who shall be hanged upon a gallows, while God's true servant may sit at the gate and bear contempt as did Mordecai. Better to pine with Lazarus than feast with Dives, for the love of God more than compensates for temporary disadvantages. Better an ounce of divine grace than a tone of worldly goods. Though the good things come not as the left-handed blessings of outward prosperity, be thou more than content if thou win the right-handed benediction of spiritual joy.

The example of Daniel I present you for your observation today, believing that these are times when we need to be as firm and resolute as he, and that at any rate, occasions will come to every one of us before we win our crown, when we shall need to put our foot down firmly, and be steadfast and unflinching for the Lord and his truth.

First, let me invite your attention to DANIEL'S HABITUAL DEVOTION: it is worthy of our study. We might never have known of it if he had not been so sorely tried, but fire reveals the hidden gold.

Daniel's habitual devotion. We are told that aforetime, before the trial, he had been in the constant habit of prayer. *He prayed much.* There are some forms of spiritual life which are not absolutely essential, but prayer is of the very essence of spirituality. He that hath no prayer lacks the very breath of the life of God in the soul. I will not say that every man who prays is a Christian, but I will say that every man who prays sincerely is so; for, recollect, men may pray after a fashion, and even practice private prayer too, and yet may be deceiving themselves; for as the frogs of Egypt came up into the bedchambers, so doth hypocrisy intrude itself even into the private places where men pretend to worship God; but I do say that a cheerful constancy in sincere private devotion is such a mark of grace, that he who hath it may fairly conclude himself to be one of the Lord's family.

Daniel always had subjects for prayer and reasons for prayer. He prayed for himself that in his eminent position he might not be uplifted with pride, might not be taken in the snares of those who envied him, might not be permitted to fall into the usual oppressions and dishonesties of Eastern rulers. He prayed for his people. He saw many of the house of Judah who were not in such prosperous circumstances as himself. He remembered those who were in bonds, as being bound with them. Those who were bone of his bone, and flesh of his flesh, he brought in the arms of faith before his God. He interceded for Jerusalem. It grieved him that the city was laid waste, that still the brand of the Chaldean destroyer was upon Mount Zion, so beautiful, and once the joy of the whole earth. He pleaded for the return from the captivity, which he knew was ordained of his God. He prayed for the glory of his God, that the day might come when the idols should be utterly abolished, and when the whole earth should know that Jehovah ruleth in heaven, and among the sons of men. It would have been a delightful thing to have listened at the keyhole of Daniel's closet, and to have heard the mighty intercessions which went up to the Lord God of Hosts.

We read next, that with all his prayers he mingled *thanksgiving*. Do observe it, for so many forget this, "He prayed and gave thanks to God." Surely, it is poor devotion which is always asking and never returning its gratitude! Am I to live upon the bounty of God, and never to thank him for what I receive? Surely, prayers in which there is no thanksgiving are selfish things: they rob God; and will a man rob God—rob God even in his prayers—and yet expect that his prayers should be successful? Have I not often said in this place that prayer and praise resemble the process by which we live? We breathe in the atmospheric air, and then breathe it out again: prayer takes in deep drafts of the love and grace of God, and then praise breathes it out again.

> Prayer and praise, with sins forgiven,
> Bring down to earth the bliss of heaven.

Good Daniel had learned to praise as well as to pray, and to offer to God that sweet incense which was made of diverse spices, of earnest desires and longings mingled with thanksgivings and adorations.

It is worthy of notice, that the text says, "Daniel prayed and gave thanks *before his God.*" This enters into the very soul of prayer—this getting before God. O brethren, do you not often catch yourselves praying to the wind, and in private uttering words as though you were only to be heard by the four walls which bound your little room? But prayer, when it is right, comes before God, in realizing the majesty of the throne of his grace, and seeing the blood of the eternal covenant sprinkled thereon; in discerning that God is gazing right through you, reading every thought and interpreting every desire; in feeling that you yourself are speaking into the ear of God, and are now, as it were,

> Plunged in the Godhead's deepest sea,
> And lost in his immensity.

This is praying, when we draw near to God. I shall not care if you do not use a single word, if you feel the majesty of God to be so overwhelming that words are out of place; and silence becomes far more expressive when you bow with sobs, and tears, and groanings that cannot be uttered. That is the prayer which wins its suit of God, and is dear to the majesty of heaven. Thus Daniel prayed and gave thanks, not before men to be seen of them, nor yet in private before himself to satisfy his conscience, but "before God," of whom he had an audience thrice each day.

That little word "*his*" I must not let slip, however. He prayed and gave thanks before *his* God. He spake not to God merely as God who might belong to any man and every man, but unto *his* God, whom he had espoused by a solemn determination that he would not turn aside from his service, that determination having resulted from God's having determined to select him and to make him his own man, peculiarly set apart unto his own praise. "*His* God." Why, it seems to me to bring up that word "covenant"—his "covenant God," as though he had entered into covenant with God according to the language of the Most High, "I will be their God, and they shall be my people." True son of Abraham, and Isaac, and Jacob, was this Daniel when he looked upon God as being his own, his property, could claim him, could say as we sometimes sing in that sweet psalm, "Yea, mine own God is he!" Oh, to feel that the Lord belongs wholly to me! *My* God, *my* God, if no other man can claim him; *my* Father, *my* Shepherd, *my* Friend, *my* Lord, and *my* God! Yes, here lies power in prayer, when a man can talk with God as his covenant God. That man cannot miss; every arrow sticks in the center of the target when he pleads "before his God." That man must conquer the angel at Jabbok's brook who grips him with both hands by a faith which knows its heaven-wrought claims. It is not winning mercies from another's God, nor pleading outside the covenant, but the believer feels that he is asking of his own God mercies already promised and made sure to him by oaths, and covenant, and blood.

Some other particulars in the text are not quite so important; nevertheless, observe that he prayed *three times a day*. That does not tell you how often he prayed, but how often he was in the posture of prayer. Doubtless he prayed 300 times a day if necessary—his heart was always having commerce with the skies; but thrice a day he prayed formally. It has been well said that we usually take three meals in the day, and that it is well to give the soul as many meals as the body. We want the morning's guidance, we need the eventide's forgiveness, do we not also require the noontide's refreshment? Might we not well say at noontide, "Tell me, O thou whom my soul loveth, where thou feedest, where thou makest thy flock to rest at noon." If you find from morn till eve too long an interval between prayer, put in another golden link at midday. There is no rule in Scripture as to how often you should pray, and there is no rule as to when you should pray; it is left to the man's own gracious spirit to suggest season. We need not come back to the bondage of the Mosaic covenant, to be under rule and rubric; we are left to that free Spirit who leads his saints aright. Yet, three times a day is a commendable number.

Notice, also, *the posture*. That, also, is of little consequence, since we read in Scripture of men who prayed on the bed, with their face to the wall. We read of David sitting before the Lord. How very common and acceptable a posture was that of *standing* before God in prayer! Yet there is a peculiar appropriateness, especially in private prayer, in the posture of kneeling. It seems to say, "I cannot stand upright before they majesty; I am a beggar, and I put myself in the position of a beggar; I sue of thee, great God, on bended knee, in the posture of one who owns that he deserves nothing, but humbles himself before thy gracious majesty." The reason why he kneeled on the particular occasion mentioned in the text was, no doubt, because he always had kneeled, and therefore always would kneel, and he would not be driven from the posture, little as that might be, at a tyrant's word. Nay, if all earth and hell should be against him, if he had found it more to God's honor to kneel, then kneel still he would, even though he should be cast into the lions' den for it.

One more observation. We are told that Daniel kneeled upon his knees *with his window open towards Jerusalem*. This was not done with any view to publicity. It may be that nobody could see him, even when his window was open, except the servants in the court. I suppose the house to have been erected as most Eastern houses were, with an open square in the center; and though he would be looking towards Jersualem, the windows would be looking into the court, where he could only be observed by those who might be residents in the house or visitors on business. Probably his fellow counselors knew the hour which he usually set apart for devotion, and therefore called in so as to find him in the act. Besides, you must recollect that, though it would be strange here for a man to pray with his windows open, where he could be heard, it was not at all strange among the Orientals, since you will find the Pharisees and others not at all slow to perform their devotions in any place, when the hour of prayer comes, and therefore it would not be regarded at all as being of a Pharisaic nature, that he should pray with his window open.

The window being open towards Jerusalem, may have been suggested by the prayer of Solomon, when he asked that if the Lord's people were banished at any time, when they sought the Lord with their faces towards that holy place, God would hear them. It may have helped him also to recollect that dear city towards which every Jew's heart turns with affection, even as the needle trembles towards its pole. The thought of its ruin assisted his earnestness, the recollection of its sin humbled him, and the promises concerning it comforted him. He turned towards Jerusalem. And what does this say to us? Men and brethrén, it tells us that we ought to take care when we pray, to have our window open towards Calvary. Neither turn you to the East, nor to the West, but let your spirits turn towards the cross of Christ. That is the great point towards which all the faces of the faithful must continually be turned, where Jesus died, where Jesus rose, where Jesus intercedes before the throne of mercy. There it is that the eyes of faith must look. With your windows open towards Calvary always pray; look upon the precious blood; gaze steadfastly upon the risen Lord; behold the authority of his plea, as before his Father he wins his suit for his people, and you will grow strong to wrestle until you prevail.

We must now turn to a second consideration, DANIEL'S ACTION UNDER TRIAL.

There is nothing that kings and queens are much fonder of than meddling with religion. Though the Prussian king tried to make a number of watches all tick together, and could not do it, yet notwithstanding the experiment and its failure, there are always evil counselors who would force men's consciences to keep stroke. Folly is in the throne when monarchs patronize or oppress religion. Caesar always muddles when he meddles with the things of God. In Daniel's day there was an act of uniformity passed in some respects similar to the famous act which was thrust upon this land. Darius ordained that no man should pray for thirty days: the other Act of Uniformity commanded that no man should pray at any time in public without his book. There is not very much to prefer between the two. When this act of uniformity was passed, several courses were open to Daniel. He might, for instance, have said, "This does not answer my purpose. I have a high position in society. I am chief president over all these dominions, and though I am willing to suffer something for my religion, yet gold may be bought too dear, and therefore I shall cease to pray." He might have found many precedents and many companions. What crowds, when it has come to a question between life and truth, between honor and Christ, have made the evil choice and perished infamously? Daniel does not seem to have raised that question. Yet he might have said, "Well, well, we must be prudent; God must be worshiped certainly, but there is no particular reason for my worshiping him in the usual room, nor even in the city where I live; I can retire in the evening, or find some more secret spot in my own house, and especially there is no occasion to open the window. I can pray with the window shut, and I shall be just as acceptable before God. I think, therefore, I shall keep my conscience clear, but not obtrude my religion in these evil days."

Daniel did not so reason; he was a lion-like man, and scorned to lower his standard in the presence of the foe; for see, in his position, if he had not prayed as before, it would have been a scandal to the weak and a scorn to the wicked; for the weak would have said, "See, Daniel is cowed by the decree." Then every poor Jew throughout the realm would have found excuse for forsaking his principles; and the wicked would have said, "Note, he serves his God when all goes well, but see where he drifts when trouble comes!" He would not seek the secrecy which prudence might have suggested. Still, it might have suggested to him that he could pray inwardly. Prayers without words are just as acceptable to God: could he not do this? He felt he could not, inasmuch as the decree was not inward, and the king's opposition to religion was not inward. He did not believe in opposing outward falsehood by an inward truth. He did, in the language of the hymn we were singing, "strength to strength oppose." He would give distinct outward avowal of his own convictions in opposition to the outward persecuting edict.

As Daniel did not happen to have one of those rotating, double-acting consciences, he did not try to import a new meaning into the terms of the decree, or invent a compromise between it and his own convictions, but he went straightforward in the plain path. He knew what the edict meant, and therefore down on his knees he went before his God in direct defiance of it. Whether the edict might be read in a milder sense or not, did not trouble him; he knew what Darius meant by it, and what the captains and the counselors meant by it, and he knew also what he himself intended to do, and therefore he did the right thing, and before his God he dared the lions, rather than soil his conscience with aught of ill.

Observe with care what Daniel did. He made up his mind to act as he had done aforetime. Note how *quietly* he acted. He did not say to any of his enemies, "I mean to carry out my convictions." Not at all; he knew that talk was lost upon them, so he resorted to actions instead of words. He quietly went home when he found the law was passed—though grieved that such a thing was done—without a single word of repining or caviling he sought his chamber. I do not find that he was at all distracted or disturbed. The words, "As he had done aforetime," seem to imply that he went upstairs as calmly as he had been accustomed to do. His servants would not have known from his behavior that any law had been made. He always had gone at that hour to pray, and they could hear him pray just as earnestly as he ever had done. He was stayed on God, therefore continued at perfect peace.

Note again, how he acted unhesitatingly—*immediately!* He did not pause; he did not ask for time to consider what he should do. In matters of perilous duty, our first thoughts are best. When there is anything to be lost by religion, follow out the first thought of conscience, namely, "Do the right." Who needs to question where duty points the way? Where God commands, there is no room for reason to raise cavils. Yet

I have no doubt, if the devil could have whispered into the prophet's ear, he would have said, "Now, Daniel, you had better consider a little while. You are in a position where you can materially help your friends. You are of very great authority in this court; you may be of assistance to the true religion. You do not know how many may be converted by your example. You ought not lightly to give up a position where you can do so much good." That argument I have heard hundreds of times when people have been urged to come out of false positions and do the right. But what have you and I to do with maintaining our influence and position at the expense of truth? It is never right to do a little wrong, to obtain the greatest possible good. Your duty is to do the right: consequences are with God; and after all it never can be, in the long run, a good thing either for you or for others to do wrong.

You will observe also, that Daniel did not act under excitement, but *with a full knowledge of the result.* The record expressly hath it—"When Daniel knew that the writing was signed." Many people will do right in a hurry, and under strong excitement will go further than they would have done in cold blood; but Daniel, probably shut out from the council by some crafty device of the counselors, no sooner heard that the statute stood good than, without parley, his resolution was formed and his mind made up. It was not for him to delay and to hesitate; he had all the data before him, and obedience made her determination known. Count the cost, young man, before you profess to be a Christian; do not espouse, upon a sudden, an enterprise for which you will be unequal. Devote yourselves to the Lord your God by his grace, but let it be according to the command of Christ, after having first made an estimate of that which will be required of you, and seek grace from on high that you may accomplish what otherwise will be impossible.

I like that word, and must go back to it again, *"as he had done aforetime."* Here he makes no alteration; he takes not the slightest possible notice of the king's decree. At the same place, at the same hour, in the same posture, and in the same spirit, the prophet is found. This indicates to us the Christian's duty under persecution—he should act under persecution as he would have done if none had arisen. If you have worshiped God under the smile of your Christian friends, worship him under the crown of the ungodly. If you have, as a tradesman, pursued a course of honest action in more prosperous times, do not for God's sake, for Christ's sake, tamper with that honest course because the times have changed. What has been right is right, and therefore abide by it. What you have done sincerely still do, and God will give you a blessing in it. Daniel could not have performed that act of praying, when the lions' den was to be the penalty, if he had not fallen into the habit of constant prayer beforehand. It was his secret communion with God which gave him strength and vigor to push on. Because he was right, he found it easier to keep right, whatever the penalty might be. I dare say I address some young man who has come from the country from a godly family where true religion has been daily set before him, and now he is placed in a workshop where he is startled to find that Jesus is ridiculed, and religion is a by-word. Now, friend, so as you used to do at home; make no difference to please vain men; take care that you begin as you mean to go on. I would not say merely, "Do not give up the spirit of religion," but "Do not even yield the form." The devil never gives up to us; do not give up to him. He takes care to fight us with all his might; let us do the same to him.

I believe hundreds of Christian men make a hard lot to themselves by little yieldings at first, for generally is it so in this world, that if a man is determined and makes up his mind, after a while the world will let him alone. In the barrack-room, when the soldier kneels to pray, how often has he been the subject of a thousand ribald jests, and so have given up all thought of bowing the knee! Yet we have heard of a real convert, who, when he came into the regiment, having been converted, knelt down to pray, and as he persisted in so doing, his comrades said, "Ah! he's one of the plucky ones; he's a genuine fellow"; and they left him alone afterwards; whereas, if he had once sneaked into his bed without prayer, he would never after that have dared to kneel. There is nothing like following Daniel's example, by never giving in, for thus you will win the respect of those who otherwise would have sneered at you. How soon the world will find out our real meaning! We may think we are playing our game so prettily that they cannot make us out, and that we shall be pleasing the world and pleasing God too, but it always comes to a dead failure, and then, while the world despises, we have not the comfort of our conscience to sustain us.

Oh, if our fathers, the Puritans, would but have yielded a little; if they could have made but a nick in their consciences, as some are now doing, then, instead of being cast out of house and home, and prevented from opening their mouths to preach Christ, their yielding and consenting would have kept them in ease and honor; but where, then, would have been that Gospel light which gladdens the nations? Where those pure and sacred institutions which they have handed down to us? Now, at this hour, through their intrepid resolution, they remain amongst the blessed, and men honor them. Let us not, the sons of brave fathers, let us not be craven. Recollect the days of Cromwell, and the times when the godless Cavaliers felt the edge of the Roundheads' sword, and though we take not carnal weapons, but eschew them utterly, let us show our foemen that the manhood of England is in us still, and we are of the same metal as our sires.

Let us turn to the third point, with which we conclude, THE SECRET SUPPORT OF DANIEL. There was something in the man which gave him this backbone; there was a secret something which made him so magnanimous. What was it? It resulted from several things. It sprang from the fact that *Daniel's religion was not the offspring of passion, but of deep-seated principle.*

There are some men whose religion is like the flower which lives upon the surface — they soon dry up when the sun of persecution burns; but there are others who, like the forest trees, send down their roots into the deep soil of principle, who know what they know, have learned thoroughly what they have learned, and hold fast what they have received, and these, in the time of trial, are sustained by springs of secret grace, and their leaf is not withered. Because the Holy Ghost had inwrought into Daniel's' spirit the principles of faith, he was sustained in the time of trial; but I doubt not that Daniel was also supported *by what he had read of the works of God* in the olden times. He was a great searcher of books, and he had found that in olden times Jehovah was always victorious. The prophet's eye gleamed as he thought of Pharaoh and the Red Sea, as he remembered Og, king of Basham, and the books of Arnon, and as his mind flew on to Sennacherib and the hook put into leviathan's jaws to turn him back by the way which he came. Recollecting the works of the Lord, for which his spirit made diligent search, he felt quite certain that the living God would prove himself true to his own.

Besides, the prophet's spirit was sustained *by what he had himself seen.* He had been brought in close contact with the three holy children who were brought before Nebuchadnezzar. Where Daniel was at that time we do not precisely know, but he must have been well aware of that heroic deed. He had seen king Nebuchadnezzar defied, had beheld the Son of God walking in the furnace with the three heroes, and had seen them come forth with not so much as the smell of fire passed upon them: here was grand encouragement. Besides, *Daniel had personal* experience of his God. He stood before Nebuchadnezzar to tell him the dream, and the interpretation thereof; yea, on a yet more dread occasion, without fear and trembling, he had faced the king Belshazzar, when the thousands of his guests were shouting to their gods, and the king and his wives and concubines in gorgeous state were drinking wine out of the bowls consecrated to Jehovah. That lone man stood erect amid the ribald crew, and pointing to the mysterious letters, read the terrible sentence, "Mene, Mene, Tekel, Upharsin," a monarch's doom proclaimed in his presence by a man unarmed! Was such a one likely now to be afraid! He that trembled not before tens of thousands of fierce soldiery, shall he fear now, when nothing but lions are in his way? Not he. He had looked into the face of his God, and would not fear the face of a lion; Jehovah had overshadowed him, and the den into which he would be cast had nothing in it terrible to him. His own experience helped to strengthen him. He had this conviction, that God could deliver him, and that if God did not deliver him, yet still such was *his love to the God of Israel* that he would be content to give himself to die.

It is blessed to have such a confidence as this. You good people who are tried, and who may expect to be tried yet more, you will never stand unless you come to this: "God can deliver me; but if he does not deliver me, still I am well content to be a sacrifice for Jesus' sake." Ah! some of you would fain be Christians, but in the time of trial you give it up; like the freshwater sailor, who, seeing the ship decked with all her colors, and her fair white sails bellying to the wind, thinks it must be a fine thing to be a mariner, but he is not far out to sea before qualms have come upon him; he dreads the storm, and vows, "IF I can but once get safe to shore, I had done with sailoring forever." Many have said, "We will follow the Lord with Daniel." Yes, and well-content they are to be with Daniel at Shushan, in the king's palace, but when it comes to the lions' den, then, "Daniel, good-bye." Take heed to yourselves that ye be not deceived with a fair profession which shall afterwards fail you. Daniel failed not, because his love to his God rested deep in his inmost heart: it had become part and parcel of himself, and sustained by the two hands of love and faith, he was graciously upborne over the rough and thorny places.

Remember that Daniel is a type of our Lord Jesus Christ. Jesus had enemies who sought to destroy him; they could find nothing against him except, "touching his God." They accused him of blasphemy, and then afterwards, as they did Daniel, they brought a charge of sedition. He was cast into the den, into the grave: his soul was among the lions. They sealed his tomb with their signet, lest any should steal him by night, but he arose as Daniel did, alive and unhurt, and his enemies were destroyed. Now, if Daniel is a type of Christ, and the Lord Jesus is the great representative Man for all who are in him, you, believer, must expect that there will be those who will attack you, who will assail you especially in your religion. You must expect, too, that they will prevail against you for a time, so that you may be cast into the den, that they will seek to fasten you in as though you were destroyed forever; but there will be a resurrection not only of bodies but of reputations, and you shall arise. When the trumpet shall sound, not merely the corporeal particles, which make the man, but the man's memory shall rise; his good name, which has been buried beneath the clods of slander, shall rise to life, while as to his enemies, they and their reputations shall find devouring destruction from the presence of the Lord. Oh, to be a follower of Jesus, the great Daniel! To tread in his footsteps wherever he goes! To be much with him, whether in private or public! This is a thing to be desired, and though I exhort you to it, I do not expect you to attain to it in your own strength, but I point you to the Holy Ghost, who can work this in you, and make you to be greatly beloved as was this prophet of old.

17

NEHEMIAH

Ejaculatory Prayer

"So I prayed to the God of heaven" (Neh. 2:4).

NEHEMIAH had made inquiry as to the state of the city of Jerusalem, and the tidings he heard caused him bitter grief. "Why should not my countenance be sad," he said, "when the city, the place of my fathers' sepulchers, lieth waste, and the gates thereof are consumed with fire?" He could not endure that it should be a mere ruinous heap—that city which was once beautiful for situation and the joy of the whole earth. Laying the matter to heart, he did not begin to speak to other people about what they would do, nor did he draw up a wonderful scheme about what might be done if so many thousand people joined in the enterprise; but it occurred to him that he would do something himself. This is just the way that practical men start a matter. The unpractical will plan, arrange, and speculate about what may be done, but the genuine, thorough-going lover of Zion puts this question to himself—"What can you do? Nehemiah, what can you do yourself? Come, it has to be done, and you are the man that is to do it—at least, to do your share. What can you do?" Coming so far, he resolved to set apart a time for prayer. He never had it off his mind for nearly four months. Day and night Jerusalem seemed written on his heart, as if the name were painted on his eyeballs. He could only see Jerusalem. When he slept he dreamed about Jerusalem. When he woke, the first thought was "Poor Jerusalem!" and before he fell asleep again his evening prayer was for the ruined walls of Jerusalem. The man of one thing, you know, is a terrible man; and when one single passion has absorbed the whole of his manhood something will be sure to come of it. Depend upon that. The desire of his heart will develop into some open demonstration, especially if he talks the matter over before God in prayer. Something did come of this. Before long Nehemiah had an opportunity. Men of God, if you want to serve God and cannot find the propitious occasion, wait awhile in prayer and your opportunity will break on your path like a sunbeam. There was never a true and valiant heart that failed to find a fitting sphere somewhere or other in his service. Every diligent laborer is needed in some part of his vineyard. You may have to linger, you may seem as if you stood in the market idle, because the Master would not engage you, but wait there in prayer, and with your heart boiling over with a warm purpose, and your chance will come. The hour will need its man, and if you are ready, you, as a man, shall not be without your hour.

God sent Nehemiah an opportunity. That opportunity came, 'tis true, in a way which he could not have expected. It came through his own sadness of heart. This matter preyed upon his mind till he began to look exceedingly unhappy. I cannot tell whether others remarked it, but the king whom he served, when he went into court with the royal goblet, noticed the distress on the cupbearer's countenance, and he said to him, "Why is thy countenance sad, seeing thou art not sick? This is nothing else but sorrow of heart." Nehemiah little knew that his prayer was making the occasion for him. The prayer was registering itself upon his face. His fasting was making its marks upon his visage; and, though he did not know it, he was, in that way, preparing the opportunity for himself when he went in before the king.

But you see when the opportunity did come there was trouble with it, for he says, "I was very sore afraid." You want to serve God, young man: you want to be at work. Perhaps you do not know what that work involves. It is not all pleasure. You are longing for the battle, young soldier: you have not smelt powder yet, but when you have been in a battle, and have had a few cuts, or a bullet or two have pierced you, you may not feel quite so eager for the fray. Yet the courageous man sets those things aside, and is ready to serve his country or his sovereign, and so the courageous Christian puts all difficulty aside, and he is ready to serve his comrades and his God, cost what it may. What if I should be sore afraid? Yet so let it be, my God, if thus there shall be an opportunity to seek and to secure the welfare of Jerusalem for they servant, who longs to promote it with all his heart.

Thus have we traced Nehemiah up to the particular point where our text concerns him. The king, Artaxerxes, having asked him why he was sad, he had an opportunity of telling him that the city of his fathers was a ruin. Thereupon the king asks him what he really wishes; by the manner of the question he would seem to imply an assurance that he means to help him. And here we are somewhat surprised to find that, instead of promptly answering the king—the answer is not given immediately—an incident occurs, a fact is related. Though he was a man who had lately given himself up to prayer and fasting, this little parenthesis occurs—"So I prayed to the God of heaven." My preamble leads up to this parenthesis. Upon this prayer I propose to preach.

THE FACT THAT NEHEMIAH PRAYED CHALLENGES ATTENTION. He had been asked a question by his sovereign. The proper thing you would suppose was to answer it. Not so. Before he answered he prayed to the God of heaven. I do not suppose the king noticed the pause. Probably the interval was not long enough to be noticed, but it was long enough for God to notice it—long enough for Nehemiah to have sought and have obtained guidance from God as to how to frame his answer to the king. Are you not surprised to find a man of God having time to pray to God between a question and an answer? Yet Nehemiah found that time. We are the more astonished at his praying, because he was so evidently perturbed in mind, for, according to the second verse, he was very sore afraid. When you are fluttered and put out you may forget to pray. Do you not, some of you, account it a valid excuse for omitting your ordinary devotion? At least, if anyone had said to you, "You did not pray when you were about that business," you would have replied, "How could I? There was a question that I was obliged to answer. I dared not hesitate. It was a king that asked it. I was in a state of confusion. I really was so distressed and terrified that I was not master of my own emotions. I hardly knew what I did. If I did not pray, surely the omission may be overlooked. I was in a state of wild alarm." Nehemiah, however, felt that if he was alarmed it was a reason for praying, not for forgetting to pray. So habitually was he in communion with God that as soon as he found himself in a dilemma he flew away to God, just as the dove would fly to hide herself in the clefts of the rock.

His prayer was the more remarkable on this occasion, because *he must have felt very eager about his object.* The king asks him what it is he wants, and his whole heart is set upon building up Jerusalem. Are you not surprised that he did not at once say, "O king, live forever. I long to build up Jerusalem's walls. Give me all the help thou canst"? But no, eager as he was to pounce upon the desired object, he withdraws his hand until it is said, "So I prayed to the God of heaven." I confess I admire him. I desire also to imitate him. I would that every Christian's heart might have just that holy caution that did not permit him to make such haste as to find ill-speed. "Prayer and provender hinder no man's journey." Certainly, when the desire of our heart is close before us, we are anxious to seize it; but we shall be all the surer of getting the bird we spy in the bush to be a bird we grasp in the hand if we quietly pause, lift up our heart and pray unto the God of heaven.

It is all the more surprising that he should have deliberately prayed just then, because *he had been already praying for the past three or four months* concerning the selfsame matter. Some of us would have said, "That is the thing I have been praying for; now all I have got to do is to take it and use it. Why pray any more? After all my midnight tears and daily cries, after setting myself apart by fasting to cry unto the God of heaven, after such an anxious conference, surely at last the answer has come. What is to be done but to take the good that God provides me with and rejoice in it?" But no, you will always find that the man who has prayed much is the man who prays more. "For unto every one that hath shall be given, and he shall have abundance." If you do but know the sweet art of prayer, you are the man that will be often engaged in it. If you are familiar with the mercy seat you will constantly visit it.

> For who that knows the power of prayer
> But wishes to be often there?

Although Nehemiah had been praying all this while, he nevertheless must offer another petition. "So I prayed to the God of heaven."

One thing more is worth recollecting, namely that *he was in a king's palace,* and in the palace of a heathen king too; and he was in the very act of handing up to the king the goblet of wine. He was fulfilling his part in the state festival, I doubt not, amongst the glare of lamps and the glitter of gold and silver, in the midst of princes and peers of the realm. Or even if it were a private festival with the king and queen only, yet still men generally feel so impressed on such occasions with the responsibility of their high position that they are apt to forget prayer. But this devout Israelite, at such a time and in such a place, when he stands at the king's foot to hold up to him the golden goblet, refrains from answering the king's question until first he has prayed to the God of heaven.

There is the fact, and I think it seems to prompt further inquiry. So we pass on to observe—THE MANNER OF THIS PRAYER.

Well, very briefly, it was what we call *ejaculatory prayer*—prayer which, as it were, hurls a dart and then it is done. It was not the prayer which stands knocking at mercy's door—knock, knock, knock; but it was the concentration of many knocks into one. It was begun and completed, as it were, with one stroke. This ejaculatory prayer I desire to commend to you as among the very best forms of prayer.

Notice, how very *short* it must have been. It was introduced—slipped in—sandwiched in—between the king's question and Nehemiah's answer; and, as I have already said, I do not suppose it took up any time at all that was appreciable—scarcely a second. Most likely the king never observed any kind of pause or hesitation, for Nehemiah was in such a state of alarm at the question that I am persuaded he did not allow any demur or vacillation to appear, but the prayer must have been offered like an electric flash, very rapidly indeed. In certain states of strong excitement it is wonderful how much the mind gets through in a short time. You may, perhaps, have dreamed, and your dream occupied, to your idea, an hour or two at the very least, yet it is probably—nay, I think certain—that all dreaming is done at the moment you wake. You never dreamed at all when you were asleep: it was just in that instant when you woke that the whole of it went through your mind. As drowning men when rescued and recovered have been heard to say that while they were sinking they say the whole panorama of their lives pass before them in a few seconds, so the mind must be capable of accomplishing much in a brief space of time. Thus the prayer was presented like the winking of an eye; it was done intuitively; yet done it was, and it proved to be a prayer that prevailed with God.

We know, also, that it must have been *a silent prayer*; and not merely silent as to sounds but silent as to any outward signs—perfectly secret. Artaxerxes never knew that Nehemiah prayed, though he stood probably within a yard of him. He did not even move his lips as Hannah did, nor did he deem it right even to close his eyes, but the prayer was strictly within himself offered unto God. In the innermost shrine of the temple—in the holy of holies of his own secret soul—there did he pray. Short and silent was the prayer. It was a prayer on the spot. He did not go to his chamber as Daniel did, and open the window. Daniel was right, but this was a different occasion. Nehemiah could not have been permitted to retire from the palace just then. He did not even turn his face to the wall or seek a corner of the apartment. No, but there and then, with the cup in his hand, he prayed unto the God of heaven, and then answered the question of the king.

I have no doubt from the very wording of the text that it was *a very intense and direct prayer*. He says, "So I prayed to the God of heaven." That was Nehemiah's favorite name of God—the God of heaven. He knew whom he was praying to. He did not draw a bow at a venture and shoot his prayers anyhow, but he prayed to the God of heaven—a right straight prayer to God for the thing he wanted; and his prayer sped, though it occupied less, perhaps, than a second of time.

It was a prayer of *a remarkable kind*. I know it was so, because Nehemiah never forgot that he did pray it. I have prayed hundreds of times, and thousands of times, and not recollected any minute particular afterwards either as to the occasion that prompted or the emotions that excited me; but there are one or two prayers in my life that I never can forget. I have not jotted them down in a diary, but I remember when I prayed, because the time was so special and the prayer was so intense, and the answer to it was so remarkable. Now, Nehemiah's prayer was never, never erased from his memory; and when these words of history were written down he wrote that down. "So I prayed to the God of heaven"—a little bit of a prayer pushed in edgeways between a question and an answer—a mere fragment of devotion, as it seemed, and yet so important that it is put down in a historical document as a part of the history of the restitution and rebuilding of the city of Jerusalem, and a link in the circumstances which led up to that event of the most important character. Nehemiah felt it to be so, and therefore he makes the record—"So I prayed to the God of heaven."

Now, beloved friends, I come, in the third place, to recommend to you THIS EXCELLENT STYLE OF PRAYING.

I shall speak to the children of God mainly, to you that have faith in God. I beg you often, nay, I would ask you always to use this method of ejaculatory prayer. And I would to God, also, that some here who have never prayed before would offer an ejaculation to the God of heaven before they leave this house—that a short but fervent petition, something like that of the publican in the temple, might go up from you—"God be merciful to me a sinner."

To deal with this matter practically, then, *it is the duty and privilege of every Christian to have set times of prayer*. I cannot understand a man's keeping up the vitality of godliness unless he regularly retires for prayer, morning and evening at the very least. Daniel prayed three times a day, and David says, "Seven times a day will I praise thee." It is good for your hearts, good for your memory, good for your moral consistency that you should hedge about certain portions of time and say, "These belong to God. I shall do business with God at such-and-such a time, and try to be as punctual to my hours with him as I should be if I made an engagement to meet a friend." When Sir Thomas Abney was Lord Mayor of London the banquet somewhat troubled him, for Sir Thomas always had prayer with his family at a certain time. The difficulty was how to quit the banquet to keep up family devotion; but so important did he consider it that he vacated the chair, saying to a person near that he had a special engagement with a dear friend which he must keep. And he did keep it, and he returned again to his place, none of the company being the wiser, but he himself being all the better for observing his wonted habit of worship.

But now, having urged the importance of such habitual piety, I want to impress on you the value of another sort of prayer; namely, *the short, brief, quick, frequent ejaculations* of which Nehemiah gives us a specimen. And I recommend this, because it hinders no engagement and occupies no time. You may be measuring off your calicoes, or weighing your groceries, or you may be casting up an account, and between the items you may say, "Lord, help me." You may breathe a prayer to heaven and say, "Lord, keep me." It will take no time. It is one great advantage to persons who are hard pressed in business that such prayers as those will not, in the slightest degree, incapacitate them from attending to the business they may have in hand. It requires you to go to no particular place. You can stand where you are, ride in a cab, walk along the streets, be the bottom sawyer in a saw pit, or the top one either, and yet pray just as well such prayers as these. No altar, no church, no so-called sacred place is needed, but wherever you are, just a little prayer as that will reach the ear of God, and win a blessing. Such a prayer as that can be offered anywhere, under any circumstances. I do not know in what condition a man could be in which he might not offer some such prayer as that. On the land, or on the sea, in sickness or in health, amidst losses or gains, great reverses or good returns, still might he breathe his soul in short, quick sentences to God. The advantage of such a way of praying is that you can pray often and pray always. If you must prolong your prayer for a quarter of an hour you might possibly be unable to spare the time, but if it only wants the quarter of a minute, why, then, it may come again and again and again and again—a hundred times a day. The habit of prayer is blessed, but the sprit of prayer is better; and the spirit of prayer it is which is the mother of these ejaculations; and therefore do I like them, because she is a plentiful mother. Many times in a day may we speak with the Lord our God.

Such prayer may be suggested by all sorts of surroundings. I recollect a poor man once paying me a compliment which I highly valued at the time. He was lying in a hospital, and when I called to see him he said, "I heard you for some years, and now whatever I look at seems to remind me of something or other that you said, and it comes back to me as fresh as when I first heard it." Well, now, he that knows how to pray ejaculatory prayers will find everything about him helping him to the sacred habit. Is it a beautiful landscape? Say, "Blessed be God who has strewn these treasures of form and color through the world, to cheer the sight and gladden the heart." Are you in doleful darkness, and is it a foggy day? Say, "Lighten my darkness, O Lord." Are you in the midst of company? You will be reminded to pray, "Lord, keep the door of my lips." Are you quite alone? Then can you say, "Let me not be alone, but be thou with me, Father." The putting on of your clothes, the sitting at the breakfast table, the getting into the conveyance, the walking the streets, the opening of your ledger, the putting up of your shutters—everything may suggest such prayer as that which I am trying to describe if you be but in the right frame of mind for offering it.

These prayers are commendable, *because they are truly spiritual.* Wordy prayers may also be windy prayers. There is much of praying by book that has nothing whatever to recommend it. Pray with your heart, not with your hands. Or, if you would lift hands in prayer, let them be your own hands, not another man's. The prayers that come leaping out of the soul—the gust of strong emotion, fervent desire, lively faith—these are the truly spiritual; and no prayers but spiritual prayers will God accept.

This kind of prayer is free from any suspicion that it is prompted by the corrupt motive of being offered to please men. They cannot say that the secret ejaculations of our soul are presented with any view to our own praise, for no man knows that we are praying at all; therefore do I commend such prayers to you, and hope that you may abound therein. There have been hypocrites that have prayed by the hour. I doubt not there are hypocrites as regular at their devotions as the angels are before the throne of God, and yet is there no life, no spirit, no acceptance in their pretentious homage; but he that ejaculates—whose heart talks with God—he is no hypocrite. There is a reality, and force, and life about it.

Short, ejaculatory prayers are of great use to us. Oftentimes they check us. Bad-tempered people, if you were always to pray just a little before you let angry expressions fly from your lips, why many times you would not say those naughty words at all. They advised a good woman to take a glass of water and hold some of it in her mouth five minutes before she scolded her husband. I dare say it was not a bad recipe, but if, instead of practicing that little eccentricity, she would just breathe a short prayer to God, it would certainly be more effectual, and far more scriptural. I can recommend it as a valuable prescription for the hasty and the peevish; for all who are quick to take offense and slow to forgive insult or injury. When in business you are about to close in with an offer about the propriety of which you have a little doubt, or a positive scruple, such a prayer as "Guide me, good Lord" would often keep you back from doing what you will afterwards regret.

The habit of offering these brief prayers would also check your confidence in yourself. It would show your dependence upon God. It would keep you from getting worldly. It would be like sweet perfume burnt in the chamber of your soul to keep away the fever of the world from your heart.

Besides, they *actually bring us blessing from heaven*. Ejaculatory prayers, as in the case of Eliezer, the servant of Abraham, as in the case of Jacob when he said even in dying, "I have waited for thy salvation, O God,"—prayers such as Moses offered when we do not read that he prayed at all, and yet God said to him, "Why cryest thou unto me"; ejaculation such as David frequently presented, these were all successful with the Most High. Therefore abound in them, for God loves to encourage and to answer them.

I might thus keep on recommending ejaculatory prayer, but I will say one more thing in its favor. I believe it is very suitable to some persons of a peculiar temperament who could not pray for a long time to save their lives. Their minds are rapid and quick. Well, time is not an element in the business, God does not hear us because of the length of our prayer, but because of the sincerity of it. Prayer is not to be measured by the yard, nor weighed by the pound. It is the might and force of it—the truth and reality of it—the energy and the intensity of it. You that are either of so little a mind or of so quick a mind that you cannot use many words, or continue long to think of one thing, it should be to your comfort that ejaculatory prayers are acceptable. And it may be, dear friend, that you are in a condition of body in which you cannot pray any other way. A headache such as some people are frequently affected with the major part of their lives—a state of body which the physician can explain to you—might prevent the mind from concentrating itself long upon one subject. Then it is refreshing to be able again and again and again—fifty or a hundred times a day—to address one's self to God in short, quick sentences, the soul being all on fire. This is a blessed style of praying.

Now, I conclude by mentioning a few of the times *when* I think we ought to resort to this practice of ejaculatory prayer. Mr. Rowland Hill was a remarkable man for the depth of his piety, but when I asked at Wotton-under-Edge for his study, though I rather pressed the question, I did not obtain a satisfactory reply. At length the good minister said, "The fact is, we never found any. Mr. Hill used to study in the garden, in the parlor, in the bedroom, in the streets, in the woods, anywhere." "But where did he retire for prayer?" They said they supposed it was in his chamber, but that he was always praying—that it did not matter where he was, the good old man was always praying. It seemed as if his whole life, though he spent it in the midst of his fellowmen doing good, was passed in perpetual prayer. You know the story of his being in Walworth at Mr. George Clayton's chapel, and of his being seen in the aisles after everybody was gone, while he was waiting for his coachman. There was the old man toddling up and down the aisles, and as someone listened, he heard him singing to himself—

> And when I shall die, receive me I'll cry,
> For Jesus has loved me, I cannot tell why;
> But this thing I find, we two are so joined,
> He won't be in heaven and leave me behind.

And with such rhymes and ditties, and choice words, he would occupy every moment of his life. He has been known to stand in the Blackfriars' road, with his hands under his coat tails, looking in a shop window, and if you listened you might soon perceive that he was breathing out his soul before God. He had got into a constant state of prayer.

I believe it is the best condition in which a man can be—praying always, praying without ceasing, always drawing near to God with these ejaculations.

But if I must give you a selection of suitable times I should mention such as these. Whenever you have a great joy, cry, "Lord, make this a real blessing to me." Do not exclaim with others, "Am I not a lucky fellow?" but say, "Lord, give me more grace, and more gratitude, now that thou dost multiply thy favors." When you have got any arduous undertaking on hand or a heavy piece of business, do not touch it till you have breathed your soul out in a short prayer. When you have a difficulty before you, and you are seriously perplexed, when business has got into a tangle or a confession which you cannot unravel or arrange, breathe a prayer. It need not occupy a minute, but it is wonderful how many snarls come loose after just a word of prayer. Are the children particularly troublesome to you, good woman? Do you seem as if your patience was almost worn out with the worry and harass? Now for an ejaculatory prayer. You will manage them all the better, and you will bear with their naughty tempers all the more quietly. At any rate your own mind will be the less ruffled. Do you think that there is a temptation before you? Do you begin to suspect that somebody is plotting against you? Now for a prayer. "Lead me in a plain path because of mine enemies." Are you at work at the bench, or in a shop, or a warehouse, where lewd conversation and shameful blasphemies assail your ears? Now for a short prayer. Have you noticed some sin that grieves you? Let it move you to prayer. These things ought to remind you to pray. I believe the devil would not let people swear so much if Christian people always prayed every time they heard an oath. He would then see it did not pay. Their blasphemies might somewhat be hushed if they provoked us to supplication. Do you feel your own heart going off the lines? Does sin begin to fascinate you? Now for a prayer—a warm, earnest, passionate cry, "Lord, hold thou me up." Did you see something with your eye, and did that eye infect your heart? Do you feel as if "your feet were almost gone, and your steps had well nigh slipped?" Now for a prayer—"Hold me, Lord, by my right hand." Has something quite unlooked for happened? Has a friend treated you badly? Then like David say, "Lord, put to naught the counsel of Ahithophel." Breathe a prayer now. Are you anxious to do some good? Be sure to have prayer over it. Do you mean to speak to that young man about his soul? Pray first, brother. Do you mean to address yourself to

214 • *Nehemiah: Ejaculatory Prayer*

the members of your class and write them a letter this week about their spiritual welfare? Pray over every line, brother. It is always good to have praying going on while you are talking about Christ.

I always find I can preach the better if I can pray while I am preaching. And the mind is very remarkable in its activities. It can be praying while it is studying: it can be looking up to God while it is talking to man; and there can be one hand held up to receive supplies from God while the other hand is dealing out the same supplies which he is pleased to give. Pray as long as you live. Pray when you are in great pain; the sharper the pang, then the more urgent and importunate should your cry to God be. And when the shadow of death gathers round you, and strange feelings flush or chill you, and plainly tell that you near the journey's end, then pray. Oh! that is a time for ejaculation. Short and pithy prayers like this: "Hide not thy face from me, O Lord"; or this, "Be not far from me, O God"; will doubtless suit you. "Lord Jesus, receive my spirit," were the thrilling words of Stephen in his extremity; and "Father, into thy hands I commend my spirit," were the words that your Master himself uttered just before he bowed his head and gave up the ghost. You may well take up the same strain and imitate him.

These thoughts and counsels are so exclusively addressed to the saints and faithful brethren in Christ that you will be prone to ask. "Is not there anything to be said to the unconverted?" Well, whatever has been spoken in their hearing may be used by them for their own benefit. But let me address myself to you, as pointedly as I can. Though you are not saved, yet you must not say, "I cannot pray." Why, if prayer is thus simple, what excuse can you have for neglecting it? It wants no measurable space of time. Such prayers as these God will hear, and ye have all of you the ability and opportunity to think and to express them, if you have only that elementary faith in God which believes "that he is, and that he is a rewarder of them that diligently seek him." Cornelius had, I suppose, got about as far as this, when he was admonished by the angel to send for Peter, who preached to him peace by Jesus Christ to the conversion of his soul. Is there such a strange being in the Tabernacle as a man or woman that never prays? How shall I expostulate with you? May I steal a passage from a living poet who, though he has contributed nothing to our hymn books, hums a note so suited to my purpose, and so pleasant to my ear that I like to quote it—

More things are wrought by prayer
Than this world dreams of. Wherefore let thy voice
Rise like a fountain, flowing night and day:
For what are men better than sheep or goats,
That nourish a blind life within the brain,
If, knowing God, they lift not hands of prayer,
Both for themselves and those who call them friend?
For so the whole round world is every way
Bound by gold chains about the feet of God.

I do not suspect there is a creature here who never prays, because people generally pray to somebody or other. The man that never prays to God such prayers as he ought, prays to God such prayers as he ought not. It is an awful thing when a man asks God to damn him: and yet there are person that do that. Suppose he were to hear you; he is a prayer-hearing God. If I address one profane swearer here I would like to put this matter clearly to him. Were the Almighty to hear you. If your eyes were blinded and your tongue were struck dumb while you were uttering a wild imprecation, how would you bear the sudden judgment on your impious speech? If some of those prayers of yours were answered for yourself, and some that you have offered in your passion for your wife and for your child, were fulfilled to their hurt and your distraction, what an awful thing it would be. Well, God does answer prayer, and one of these days he may answer your prayers to your shame and everlasting confusion. Would not it be well now, before you leave your seat, to pray, "Lord, have mercy upon me; Lord, save me; Lord, change my heart; Lord, give me to believe in Christ; Lord, give me now an interest in the precious blood of Jesus; Lord, save me now"? Will not each one of you breathe such a prayer as that? May the Holy Spirit lead you so to do, and if you once begin to pray aright I am not afraid that you will ever leave off, for there is a something that holds the soul fast in real prayer.

BOOK II

*Sermons on Women of the
Old Testament*

1

HAGAR

Compassion for Souls

"She went, and sat her down over against him a good way off, as it were a bowshot; for she said, Let me not see the death of the child. And she sat over against him, and lifted up her voice, and wept" (Gen. 21:16).

BRIEFLY let us rehearse the circumstances. The child Isaac was, according to God's Word, to be the heir of Abraham. Ishmael, the elder son of Abraham, by the bondwoman Hagar, resided at home with his father till he was about eighteen years of age; but when he began to mock and scoff at the younger child whom God had ordained to be the heir, it became needful that he and his mother should be sent away from Abraham's encampment. It might have seemed unkind and heartless to have sent them forth, but God, having arranged to provide for them, sent a divine command which at once rendered their expulsion necessary, and certified its success. We may rest assured that whatever God commands he will be quite certain to justify. He knew it would be no cruelty to Hagar or Ishmael to be driven into independence, and he gave a promise which secured them everything which they desired. "Also of the son of the bondwoman will I make a great nation"; and again, "I have blessed him, and will make him fruitful, and will multiply him exceedingly; twelve princes shall he beget, and I will make him a great nation."

Had they both been able to go forth from Abraham's tent in faith they might have trodden the desert with a joyous footstep, fully assured that he who bade them go, and he who promised that he would bless them, would be certain to provide all things needful for them. Early in the morning they were sent forth on their journey, with as much provision as they could carry, and probably they intended to make their way to Egypt, from which Hagar had come. They may have lost their way; at any rate, they are spoken of as wandering. Their store of food became exhausted, the water in the skin bottle was all spent; both of them felt the fatigue of the wilderness, and the heat of the pitiless sand; they were both faint and wary, and the younger utterly failed. As long as the mother could sustain the tottering, fainting footsteps of her boy, she did so; when she could do so no longer, he swooned with weakness, and she laid him down beneath the slight shade of the desert tamarisk, that he might be as far as possible screened from the excessive heat of the sun. Looking into his face and seeing the pallor of coming death gathering upon it, knowing her inability to do anything whatever to revive him, or even to preserve his life, she could not bear to sit and gaze upon his face, but withdrew just far enough to be able still to watch with all a mother's care. She sat down in the brokenness of her spirit, her tears gushed forth in torrents, and heartrending cries of agony startled the rocks around.

It was needful that the high spirit of the mother and her son should be broken down before they received prosperity; the mother had been on a former occasion graciously humbled by being placed in much the same condition, but she had probably relapsed into a haughty spirit, and had encouraged her boy in his insolence to Sarah's son, and therefore she must be chastened yet again; and it was equally needful that the high-spirited lad should for a little bear the yoke in his youth, and that he who would grow up to be the wild man, the father of the unconquerable Arab, should feel the power of God ere he received the fulfillment of the promise given to him in answer to Abraham's prayer. If I read the text aright, while the mother was thus weeping, the child, almost lost to all around, was nevertheless conscious enough of his own helpless condition, and sufficiently mindful of his father's God to cry in his soul to heaven for help; and the Lord heard not so much the mother's weeping (for the feebleness of her faith, which ought to have been stronger in memory of a former deliverance, hindered her prayers), but the silent, unuttered prayers of the fainting lad went up into the ears of Elohim, and the angel of Elohim appeared, and pointed to the well. The child received the needed draft of water, was soon restored, and in him and his posterity the promise of God received and continues to receive a large fulfillment. I am not about to speak upon that narrative except as it serves me with an illustration for the subject which I would now press upon you.

Behold the compassion of a mother for her child expiring with thirst, and remember that such a compassion ought all Christians to feel towards souls that are perishing for lack of Christ, perishing eternally, perishing without hope of salvation. If the mother lifted up her voice and wept, so also should we; and if the contemplation of her dying child was all too painful for her, so may the contemplation of the wrath to come, which is to pass upon every soul that dies impenitent, become too painful for us, but yet at the same time it should stimulate us to earnest prayer and ardent effort for the salvation of our fellow men.

COMPASSION FOR SOULS—THE REASONS WHICH JUSTIFY IT, NAY, COMPEL IT.

It scarce needs that I do more than rehearse in bare outline the reasons why we should tenderly compassionate the perishing sons of men. For first, observe, *the dreadful nature of the calamity which will overwhelm them.* Calamities occurring to our fellow men naturally awaken in us a feeling of commiseration; but what calamity under heaven can be equal to the ruin of a soul? What misery can be equal to that of a man cast away from God, and subject to his wrath world without end? Today your hearts are moved as you hear the harrowing details of war.[†] They have been dreadful indeed; houses burnt, happy families driven as vagabonds upon the face of the earth, domestic circles and quiet households broken up, men wounded, mangled, massacred by thousands, and starved, I was about to say, by millions; but the miseries of war, if they were confined to this world alone were nothing compared with the enormous catastrophe of tens of thousands of spirits accursed by sin, and driven by justice into the place where their worm dieth not, and their fire is not quenched. The edge of the sword grows blunt at last, the flame of war dies out for want of fuel, but, lo! I see before me a sword which is never quiet, a fire unquenchable. Alas! that the souls of men should fall beneath the infinite ire of injustice. All your hearts have been moved of late with the thought of famine, famine in a great city. The dogs of war, and this the fiercest mastiff of them all, have laid hold upon the fair throat of the beautiful city which thought to sit as a lady forever and see no sorrow; you are hastening with your gifts, if possible to remove her urgent want and to avert her starvation; but what is a famine of bread compared with that famine of the soul which our Lord describes when he represents it as pleading in vain for a drop of water to cool its tongue tormented in the

---

† The Franco-Prussian War, 1870–71.

222 • *Hagar (1): Compassion for Souls*

flame? To be without bread for the body is terrible, but to be without the bread of life eternal, none of us can tell the weight of horror which lies there! The evil is so immense that imagination finds no place, and understanding utterly fails. Brethren, if our bowels do not yearn for men who are daily hastening towards destruction, are we men at all?

I could abundantly justify compassion for perishing men even on the ground of *natural feelings*. A mother who did not, like Hagar, weep for her dying child—call her not "mother," call her "monster." A man who passes through the scenes of misery which even this city presents in its more squalid quarters, and yet is never disturbed by them, I venture to say he is unworthy of the name of man. Even the common sorrows of our race may well suffuse our eyes with tears, but the eternal sorrow, the infinite lake of misery—he who grieves not for this, write him down a demon, though he wear the image and semblance of a man. Do not think the less of this argument because I base it upon feelings common to all of woman born, for remember that grace does not destroy our manhood when it elevates it to a higher condition.

In this instance, what nature suggests grace enforces. The more we become what we shall be, the more will compassion rule our hearts. The Lord Jesus Christ, who is the pattern and mirror of perfect manhood, what said he concerning the sins and the woes of Jerusalem? He knew Jerusalem must perish; did he bury his pity beneath the fact of the divine decree, and steel his heart by the thought of the sovereignty or the justice that would be resplendent in the city's destruction? Nay, not he, but with eyes gushing like founts, he cried, "O Jerusalem, Jerusalem, how often would I have gathered thy children together as a hen gathereth her chickens under her wings! and ye would not." If you would be like Jesus, you must be tender and very pitiful. Ye would be as unlike him as possible if ye could sit down in grim content, and, with a Stoic's philosophy, turn all the flesh within you into stone. If it be natural, then, and above all, if it be natural to the higher grace-given nature, I beseech you, let your hearts be moved with pity, do not endure to see the spiritual death of mankind. Be in agony as often as you contemplate the ruin of any soul of the seed of Adam.

Brethren, *the whole run and current, and tenor and spirit of the Gospel* influences us to compassion. Ye are debtors, for what were ye if compassion had not come to your rescue? Divine compassion, all undeserved and free, has redeemed you from your vain conversation.

Surely those who receive mercy should show mercy; those who owe all they have to the pity of God, should not be pitiless to their brethren. The Savior never for a moment tolerates the self-righteous isolation which would make you despise the prodigal, and cavil at his restoration, much less the Cainite spirit which cries, "Am I my brother's keeper?" No doctrine is rightly received by you if it freezes the genial current of your Christian compassion. You may know the truth of the doctrine, but you do not know the doctrine in truth if it makes you gaze on the wrath to come without emotions of pity for immortal souls. You shall find everywhere throughout the Gospel that it rings of brotherly love, tender mercy, and weeping pity. If you have indeed received it in its power, the love of Christ will melt your spirit into compassion for those who are despising Christ, and sealing their own destruction.

Let me beseech you to believe that it is *needful* as well as justifiable that you should feel compassion for the sons of men. You all desire to glorify Christ by becoming soul-winners—I hope you do—and be it remembered that, other things being equal, he is the fittest in God's hand to win souls who pities souls most. I believe he preaches best who loves best, and in the Sunday-school and in private life each soul-seeker shall have the blessing very much in proportion to his yearning for it. Paul becomes a savior of many because his heart's desire and prayer to God is that they may be saved. Oh! I would to God there should come upon us a divine hunger which cannot stay itself except men yield themselves to Jesus; an intense, earnest, longing, panting desire that men should submit themselves to the Gospel of Jesus. This will teach you better than the best college training how to deal with human hearts. This will give the stammering tongue the ready word; the hot heart shall burn the cords which held fast the tongue. You shall become wise to win souls, even though you never exhibit the brilliance of eloquence of the force of logic. Men shall wonder at your power—the secret shall be hidden from them, the fact being that the Holy Ghost shall overshadow you, and your heart shall teach you wisdom, God teaching your heart. Deep feeling in your part for others shall make others feel for themselves, and God shall bless you, and that right early.

We shall pass on to notice THE SIGHT WHICH TRUE COMPASSION DREADS.

Like Hagar, the compassionate spirit says, "Let me not see the death of the child," or as some have read it, "How can I see the death of the child?" To contemplate a soul passing away without hope is too terrible a task! I do not wonder that ingenious persons have invented theories which aim at mitigating the terrors of the world to come to the impenitent. It is natural they should do so, for the facts are so alarming as they are truthfully given us in God's Word, that if desire to preach comfortable doctrine and such as will quiet the consciences of idle professors, we must dilute the awful truth. The revelation of God concerning the doom of the wicked is so overwhelming as to make it penal, nay, I was about to say damnable, to be indifferent and careless in the work of evangelizing the world. I do not wonder that this error in doctrine springs up just now when abounding callousness of heart needs an excuse for itself. What better pillow for idle heads than the doctrine that the finally impenitent become extinct? The logical reasoning of the sinner is, "Let us eat and drink, for tomorrow we die," and the professing Christian is not slow to feel an ease of heart from pressing responsibilities when he accepts so consolatory an opinion. Forbear this sleeping draft, I pray you, for in very deed the sharp stimulant of the truth itself is abundantly needful; even when thus bestirred to duty we are sluggish enough, and need not that these sweet but sleep-producing theories should operate upon us.

The old divines used to speak much of the *poena damni*, or the punishment of loss; there were enough in that phase of the future to make us mourn bitterly, as David did for Absalom. My child shut out of heaven! My husband absent from the seats of the blessed! My sister, my brother not in glory! When the Lord counts up his chosen, my dear companion outside the gates of pearl, outside the jeweled battlements of the New Jerusalem! O God, 'tis a heartbreaking sorrow to think of this. But then comes the punishment added to the loss. What saith the Savior? "Where their worm dieth not, and the fire is not quenched." And yet again, "Into outer darkness: there shall be weeping and gnashing of teeth." "Metaphors," say you. It is true, but not meaningless metaphors. There is a meaning in each expression—and rest assured, though man's metaphors sometimes exaggerate, God's never do; his symbols everywhere are true; never is there an exaggeration in the language of inspiration. Extravaganzas of utterance! He uses them not; his figures are substantial truth. Terrible as the scriptural emblems of punishment are, they set forth matters of undoubted fact, which if a man could look upon this day, the sight might blanch his hair, and quench his eye.

How all this gathers intensity, when it comes to be our own child, our own friend! Hagar might perhaps have looked upon a dying child, but not upon her dying Ishmael. Can you bear not to think for a moment of the perdition of your own flesh and blood? Does not your spirit flinch and draw back with horror instinctively at the idea of one of your own family being lost? Yet, as a matter of stern fact, you know that some of them will be lost if they die as they are now living? At God's right hand they cannot stand unless they be made new creatures in Christ Jesus.

It will greatly add to your feeling of sorrow if you are forced to feel that the ruin of your child or of any other person may have been partly caused by your example. It must be a dreadful thing for a father to feel, "My boy learned to drink from me; my child heard the first blasphemous word from his father's lips." Or mother, if your dying daughter should say, "I was led into temptation by my mother's example," what a grief will this be! O parents, converted late in life, you cannot undo the evil which you have already done; God has forgiven you, but the mischief wrought in your children's characters is indelible, unless the grace of God steps in. I want you to seek after that grace with great earnestness. As you must confess that you have helped to train your child as a servant of sin, will you not long to see your evil work undone before it ends in your child's eternal destruction?

If we shall have to feel that the ruin of any of our friends or relations is partly occasioned by our own personal neglect of religion, it will cause us bitter pangs. If our example has been excellent and admirable in all respects, but that we he forgotten the Lord and his Christ, it will have been none the less injurious to men's souls. I sometimes think that these examples are the very worst in their effect. Immoral, ungodly men can hardly work the same measure of mischief as moral but unchristian men. I will tell you why. The ungodly quote the orderly life of the moralist as an argument that there can be goodness part from Christianity, and this often helps men to rest satisfied apart from Christ Jesus. And what, O moralist, though you never taught your child a vice, if you taught it unbelief, and if your example helped to harden its heart in bold rebellion against God!

I cannot bear the idea of any of my congregation perishing, for in addition to the compassion I hope I feel, I am influenced by a further additional consideration, for I am set as a watchman to your souls. When any die, I ask myself, "Was I faithful? Did I speak all the truth? And did

I speak it from my very soul every time I preached?" John Walsh, the famous Scotch preacher, was often out of bed in the coldest night, by the hour together, in supplication; and when someone wondered that he spent so many hours upon his knees, he said, "Ah, man, I have 3,000 souls to give account of in the day of judgment, and I do not know but what it is going very ill with some of them." Alas! I have more than that to give account of, and well may I cry to God that I may not see you perish. O may it never be that you shall go from these pews to the lowest hell.

Is it not an awful thing that a soul should perish with the Gospel so near? If Ishmael had died, and the water had been within bowshot, and yet unseen till too late, it had been a dreadful reflection for the mother. Would she not have torn her hair with double sorrow? And yet many of you are being lost with the Gospel ringing in your ears; you are perishing while Christ is lifted up before you; you are dying in the camp through the serpent's bite, though the brazen serpent is yonder before your eyes, and with many tears we cry to you, "Look unto Jesus Christ, and live!" Ah, woe is me, woe is me, if you perish when salvation is brought so close to home to you. Some of you are very near the kingdom of God, you are very anxious, very concerned, but you have not believed in Jesus; you have much that is good, but one thing you lack. Will you perish for lack of only one thing? A thousand pities will it be if you make shipwreck in the harbor's mouth and go to hell from the gates of heaven.

In the third place, I would speak upon COMPASSION FOR THE SOULS OF MEN—THE TEMPTATION IT MUST RESIST.

We must not fall into the temptation to imitate the example of Hagar too closely. She put the child under the shrubs and turned away her gaze from the all-too-mournful spectacle. She could not endure to look, but she sat where she could watch in despair. There is temptation with each one of us to try to forget that souls are being lost. I can go home to my house along respectable streets, and naturally should choose that way, for then I need not see the poverty of the lowest quarters of the city, but am I right if I try to forget that there are Bethnal Greens and Kent Streets, and suchlike abodes of poverty? The close courts, the cellars, the crowded garrets, the lodging houses—am I to forget that these exist? Surely the only way for a charitable mind to sleep comfortably in London is to forget how one half of the population lives; but is it our object to live comfortably? Are we such brute beasts that comfort is all we care for, like swine in their sty? Nay, brethren, let us recall to our memories the sins of our great city, its sorrows and griefs, and let us remember also the sins and sorrows of the wide, wide world, and the tens of thousands of our race who are passing constantly into eternity. Nay, look at them! Do not close those eyes! Does the horror of the vision make your eyeballs ache? Then look until your heart aches too, and your spirit breaks forth in vehement agony before the Lord.

Look down into hell a moment; open wide the door; listen, and listen yet again. You say you cannot, it sickens your soul; let it be sickened, and in its swooning let it fall back into the arms of Christ the Savior, and breathe out a cry that he would hasten to save him from the wrath to come. Do not ignore, I pray you, what does exist. It is a matter of fact that in this congregation many are going down to hell, that in this city there are multitudes who are hastening as certainly to perdition as time is hastening to eternity. It is no dream, no fiction of a fevered brain that there is a hell. If you think so, then why dare you call yourselves Christians? Renounce your Bible, renounce your baptism, renounce your profession if one spark of honesty remains in you. Call not yourselves Christians when you deny the teaching of your Master. Since assuredly there is a dreadful hell, shut not your eyes to it, put not the souls of your fellows away among the shrubs, and sit not down in supineness.

I will now speak upon THE PATH WHICH TRUE COMPASSION WILL BE SURE TO FOLLOW; and what is that?

First of all, *true pity does all it can*. Before Hagar sat down and wept, she had done her utmost for her boy; she had given him the last drop from the bottle; she had supported his tottering footsteps, she had sought out the place under the shrubs where he might be a little sheltered; she had laid him down gently with soothing words, and then, but not till then, she sat herself down. Have we done all that it is possible for us to do for the unconverted around us? There are preventable causes of men's ruin. Some causes you and I cannot touch, but there are some we ought at once to remove. For instance, it is certain that many perish through ignorance. It ought never to be that a soul should perish of ignorance within a mile of where a Christian lives. I would even allot a wider area in regions where the people dwell not so thickly. It should at least be the resolve of each Christian. "Within this district where I live, so far as my ability goes, everybody shall know the Gospel by some means or other. If I cannot speak to each one I will send something for him to read; it shall not be said that a man lost his way forever because he had no Bible. The Holy Ghost alone can lead men into the truth, but it is our part to put the letter of the word before all men's eyes.

Prejudice, too, is another preventable cause of unbelief. Some will not hear the Gospel, or listen to it, because of their notions of its sternness, or of the moroseness of its professors. Such a prejudice may effectually close their hearts; be it yours to remove it. Be kind to the ungodly; be loving, be tender, be affable, be generous to them, so that you may remove all unnecessary antipathy to the Gospel of Jesus. Do them all the good you can for their bodies, that they may be the more likely to believe in your life towards their souls. Let it be said by each one here, "If a soul perishes, I, at least, will have done all in my power to reclaim it."

But what next does compassion do? Having done all it can, it sits down and weeps over its own feebleness. I have not the pathos wherewith to describe to you the mother sitting there and pouring out her tears, and lifting up her plaintive voice over her child. The voice of a broken heart cannot be described, it must be heard. But, ah! there is wonderful power with God in the strong crying and tears of his people. If you know how to weep before the Lord, He will yield to tears what He will not yield to anything besides. O ye saints, compassionate sinners; sigh and cry for them; be able to say, as Whitefield could to his congregation, "Sirs, if ye are lost, it is not for want of my weeping for you, for I pour out my soul day and night in petitions unto God that ye may live." When Hagar's compassion had wailed itself out, she looked unto God, and God heard her.

And then what else doth Hagar teach us? She stood there ready to do anything that was needful after the Lord had interposed. The angel opened her eyes, until then she was powerless, and sat and wept, and prayed, but when he pointed to the well, did she linger for a minute? Was she unprepared with the bottle wherewith to draw water? Did she delay to put it to her child's lips? Was she slack in the blessed task? Oh, no! with what alacrity did she spring to the well; with what speed did she fill the bottle; with what motherly joy did she hasten to her child, and give him the saving draft! And so I want every member here to stand ready to mark the faintest indication of grace in any soul. Watch always for the beginning of their conversion, be ready with the bottle of promise to carry a little comfort to their parched lips; watch with a mother's earnestness, watch for the opportunity of doing good to souls, yearn over them, so that when

God shall work you shall work with him *instanter*, and Jesus shall not be hindered because of your carelessness and want of faith. This is the path which the true Christian should pursue. He is earnest for souls, and therefore he lays himself out for them. If we did really know what souls are, and what it is for them to be cast away, those of us who have done very little or nothing would begin to work for Christ directly.

It is said in an old classic story, that a certain king of Lydia had a son who had been dumb from his birth, but when Lydia was captured, a soldier was about to kill the king, when the young man suddenly found a tongue, and cried out, "Soldier, would you kill the king?" He had never spoken a word before, but his astonishment and fear gave him speech. And methinks if ye had been dumb to that moment, if ye indeed saw your own children and neighbors going down into the pit, you would cry out, "Though I never spoke before I will speak now. Poor souls, believe in Christ, and ye shall be saved." You do not know how such an utterance as that, however simple, might be blessed.

A very little child once found herself in company with an old man of eighty, a fine old man who loved little children, and who took the child upon his knee. The little one turning round to him said, "Sir, I got a grandpa just like you, and my grandpa loves Jesus Christ, does you?" He said, "I was eighty-four years of age and have lived always among Christian people, but nobody ever thought it worth his while to say as much as that to me." That little child was the instrument of the old man's conversion.

The last point shall be THE ENCOURAGEMENT WHICH TRUE COMPASSION FOR SOULS WILL ALWAYS RECEIVE.

First, take the case in hand. The mother compassionated, God compassionated too. You pity. God pities. The motions of God's Spirit in the souls of his people are the footfalls of God's eternal purposes about to be fulfilled. It is always a hopeful sign for a man that another man prays for him. There is a difficulty in getting a man to hell whom a child of God is drawing towards heaven by his intercession. Satan is often defeated in his temptations by the intercession of the saints. Have hope then that your personal sense of compassion for souls is an indication that such souls God will bless. Ishmael, whom Hagar pitied, was a lad about whom promises had been made large and broad; he could not die; *she* had forgotten that, but God had not. No thirst could possibly destroy him, for God had said he would make of him a great nation. Let us hope that those for whom you and I are praying and laboring are in God's eternal purpose secured from hell, because the blood of Christ has bought them, and they must be the Lord's. Our prayers are ensigns of the will of God. The Holy Ghost leads us to pray for those whom he intends effectually to call.

Moreover, those we pray for, we may not know it, but there may be in their souls at this time a stirring of divine life. Hagar did not know that her son was praying, but God did. The lad did not speak, but God heard his heart cry. Children are often very reticent to their parents. Often and often have I talked with young lads about their souls, who have told me that they could not talk to their fathers upon such matters. I know it was so with me. When I was under concern of soul, the last persons I should have elected to speak to upon religion would have been my parents, not out of want of love to them, nor absence of love on their part; but so it was. A strange feeling of diffidence pervades a seeking soul, and drives it from its friends. Those whom you are praying for may be praying too, and you do not know it; but the time of love will come when their secret yearnings will be revealed to your earnest endeavors.

The lad was preserved after all, the well of waters was revealed, and the bottle put to his lips. It will be a great comfort to you to believe that God will hear importunate prayers. Your child will be saved, your husband will be brought in yet, good woman, only pray on. Your neighbor shall be brought to hear the truth and be converted, only be earnest about it.

HAGAR

Eyes Opened

"And God opened her eyes, and she saw a well of water"
(Gen. 21:19).

"And their eyes were opened, and they knew him" (Luke
24:31).

THE fall of man was most disastrous in its results to our entire being. "In
the day that thou eatest thereof thou shalt surely die," was no idle
threat; for Adam did die the moment that he transgressed the command—
he died the great spiritual death by which all his spiritual powers became
then and evermore, until God should restore them, absolutely dead. I
said all the spiritual powers, and if I divide them after the analogy of the
senses of the body, my meaning will be still more clear. Through the
fall the spiritual *taste* of man became perverted, so that he puts bitter
for sweet and sweet for bitter; he chooses the poison of hell and loathes
the bread of heaven; he licks the dust of the serpent and rejects the food
of angels. The spiritual *hearing* became grievously injured, for man naturally no longer hears God's Word, but stops his ears at his Maker's voice.
Let the Gospel minister charm never so wisely, yet is the unconverted
soul like the deaf adder which hears not the charmer's voice. The spiritual *feeling* by virtue of our depravity is fearfully deadened. That which
would once have filled the man with alarm and terror no longer excites
emotion. Even the spiritual *smell* with which man should discern between that which is pure and holy and that which is unsavory to the most
High has become defiled, and now man's spiritual nostril, while un-
renewed, derives no enjoyment from the sweet savor which is in Christ
Jesus, but seeks after the putrid joys of sin. As with other senses so is it
with man's *sight*. He is so spiritually blind that things most plain and clear

he cannot and will not see. The understanding, which is the soul's
eye, is covered with scales of ignorance, and when these are removed
by the finger of instruction, the visual orb is still so affected that it only
sees men as trees walking.

Our condition is thus most terrible, but at the same time it affords ample
room for a display of the splendors of divine grace. We are naturally so
entirely ruined, that if saved the whole work must be of God, and the
whole glory must form the head of the Triune Jehovah. There must not
only be a Christ lifted up of whom it can be said, "There is life in a look
at the crucified One," but that very look itself must be given to us, or else
in vain should Christ hang upon the cross; there shall be no salvation
by his death to us.

Taking HAGAR'S CASE first, I shall address myself this morning to
certain unconverted ones who are in a hopeful condition.

Taking Hagar's case as the model to work upon, we may see in her
and in many like her a *preparedness for mercy*. In many respects she was
in a fit state to become an object of mercy's help. She had a *strong sense
of need*. The water was spent in the bottle, she herself was ready to faint,
and her child lay at death's door; and this sense of need was attended
by *vehement desires*. It is a very hard thing to bring a sinner to long after
Christ: so hard, that if a sinner doth really long and thirst after Jesus, the
Spirit of God must have been secretly at work in his soul, begetting, and
fostering those desires. When the invitation is given, "Ho, every one that
thirsteth," you can honestly say, "That means me." That precious
Gospel invitation, "Whosoever will, let him come," is evidently yours,
for you do will it eagerly and vehemently. The Searcher of all hearts knows
that there is no objection in your heart either to be saved or to the way
of being saved; nay, rather you sometimes lift your hands to heaven and
say, "O God! would that I might say, 'Christ for me!' " You know that
the water of life is desirable; you know more than that, you pine with
an inward desire to drink of it. Your soul is now in such a state that if
you do not find Jesus, you never will be happy without him. God has
brought you into such a condition that you are like the magnetized needle, which has been turned away from the pole by the finger of some
passerby, and it cannot rest until it gets back to its place. Your constant
cry is, "Give me Christ! Give me Christ, or else I die!"

This is hopeful, but let me remind you that it alone will not save you.
The discovery of a leak in a vessel may be preparatory to the pumping

of the ship, and to the repair of the leak; but the discovery of the leak will not of itself keep the bark afloat. The fact that you have a fever it is well for you to know; but to groan under that fever will not restore you to health. To desire after Christ is a very blessed symptom, but mere desires will not bring you to heaven. You may be hungering and thirsting after Christ, but hungering and thirsting will not save you; you must have Christ, or your salvation does not lie in your hungering and thirsting, nor in your humblings, nor in your prayings; salvation is in Him who died upon the cross, and not in you.

Like Hagar you are *humbled, and brought to self-despair.* There was a time when you did not admit your need of a Savior; you found comfort enough in ceremonies, and in your own prayers, repentances, and so on. But now the water is spent in your bottle, and you are sitting down with Hagar wringing your hands and weeping in despair—a blessed despair! God bring you all to it! Self-despair is next door to confidence in Christ. Rest assured, until we are empty Jesus will never fill us; till we are stripped he will never clothe us; until self is dead Christ will not live in us.

It is quite certain that in Hagar's case, *the will* was right enough with reference to the water. It would have been preposterous indeed to say to Hagar, "If there be water are you willing to drink?" "Willing?" she would say; "look at my parched lips, hear my dolorous cries, look at my poor panting, dying child! How can you ask a mother if she is willing to have water while her babe is perishing for thirst?" And so with you: if I were to propose to you the question, "Are you willing to be saved?" you might look me in the face and say, "Willing! oh sir. I have long passed beyond that stage, I am panting, groaning, thirsting, fainting, dying to find Christ. If He would come to me this morning I would not only open both the gates of my heart and say, 'Come in,' but the gates are opened now before he comes, and my soul is saying, 'Oh, that I knew where I might find him, that I might even come to his seat!' " All this is hopeful, but I must again remind you that to will to be rich does not make a man rich, and that to will to be saved cannot in itself save you. Panting after health does not restore the sick man, though it may set him upon using the means, and so he may be healed; and with you your panting after salvation cannot save you, you must get beyond all this to the great Physician himself.

In the second place, *mercy was prepared* for Hagar, and is prepared for those in a like state. *There was water.* She thought it was a wilderness without a drop for her to drink, but there was water. Troubled conscience, there is pardon. You think it is all judgment, thunder and thunderbolt, curse and wrath, but it is not so. There is mercy. Jesus died. God is able justly to forgive sinners. God was in Christ reconciling the world unto himself, not imputing their trespasses unto them. He is a God ready to pardon, ready to forgive. There is forgiveness with him that he may be feared. There is water, there is mercy.

What is more, *there is mercy for you;* there is not only that general mercy which we are bound to preach to every creature, but for many of you whom I have described I am persuaded that there is special mercy. Your names are in his book. He has chosen you from before the foundation of the world, though you do not know it. You shall be his, you are his. The hour is not far distant when, washed in the fountain and made clear, you shall cast yourselves at the Savior's feet, and be his captives in the bonds of love forever.

There is mercy for you now, if you trust Jesus. The water was not created as a new thing to supply Hagar's thirst, it was there already. If she could have seen it she might have had it before, but she could not see it. There is mercy, there is mercy for you. All that is wanted is that you should see it, poor troubled conscience; and if you could have seen it there would have been no necessity whatever that you should have been so long a time as you have been in despair, and doubt, and fear.

The water was near to Hagar; and so is Christ near to you. The mercy of God is not a thing to be sought for up yonder among the stars, nor to be discovered in the depths; it is nigh thee, it is even in thy mouth and in thy heart. The Savior who walked along the streets of Jerusalem is in these aisles and in these pews; a God ready to forgive, waiting to be gracious. Do not think of my Master as though he had gone up to heaven out of your reach, and had left no mercy behind him. Let him tell you that he is as near in spirit now as he was to the disciples when he spoke to them at Emmaus. Oh that thou couldst see him! he is "the same yesterday, today, and forever." He is passing by; cry to him, thou blind man, and thou shalt receive thy sight! Call to him, ye deaf; speak, even ye whose lips are dumb, his ear can hear your soul's desires. He is near; only believe in his presence, and trust his grace, and you shall see him. It is a notion abroad that the act of faith is very mysterious. Now faith so far as it is an act of man (and an act of man it most certainly is, as well as the gift of God, for "with the heart *man* believeth") is one of the simplest acts of the human intellect. To trust Jesus, to lean with the soul upon him, just as with my body I am leaning on this rail; to make him all my confidence and all my rest, is what needs no learning, no previous education, needs no straining or mental effort. It is such an action that the babe and the suckling may glorify God by it; while the faith of Sir Isaac Newton, with all his learning, is not a whit more saving or less simple than the faith of the child of three years old, if brought to rest on Christ alone. The moment the dying thief looked to the Crucified and said, "Lord remember me," he was as saved as Paul when he could say, "I have fought a good fight, I have finished my course."

I am very anxious to be understood, and therefore I am trying to speak very simply, and to talk right home to those whom I am driving at. My own case is to the point. I was for some few years, as a child, secretly seeking Jesus. If ever heart knew what the bitter anguish of sin was I did, and when I came to understand the plan of salvation by the simple teaching of a plain, illiterate man, the next thought I had after joy that I was saved, was this: What a fool I was not to trust Jesus Christ before! I concluded that I never could have heard the Gospel, but I think I was mistaken. I think I must have heard the Gospel thousands of times, but did not understand it. I was like Hagar with my eyes closed. We are bound to tell you every Sabbath that trusting Jesus Christ is the way of salvation, but after you have heard that 50,000 times, you really will not even understand what we mean by it, till the Spirit of God reveals the secret; but when you do but know it and trust in Jesus, simply as a child would trust his father's word, you will say of yourself, "How could it be? I was thirsty with the water rippling at my feet. I was famishing and perishing for hunger, and the bread was on the table. I was fretting as though there were no entrance into heaven, but there stood the door wide open right before me, if I could but have seen it." "Trust Christ, and he must save you." I will improve upon it: "Trust him, *you are saved*." The moment you begin to live by faith in his dear Son, there is not a sin left in God's book against you.

We pass on then in the third place to notice that although Hagar was prepared and mercy was prepared, yet *there was an impediment in the way,* for she could not see the water. There is also an impediment in your way. Hagar had a pair of bright beaming eyes, I will be bound to say, and yet she could into see the water; and men may have first-rate understandings, but not understand that simple thing, faith in the Lord Jesus

Christ. You do not suffer so much from want of power to understand faith, as from a kind of haze which hovers over your eye to prevent its looking into the right place. You continue to imagine that there must be something very singular for us to feel in order to eternal life. Now, this is all a mistake. Simple trust in Jesus has this difficulty in it, that it is not difficult, and therefore the human mind refuses to believe that God can intend to save us by so simple a plan. What blindness is this! So foolish and so fatal! Is not this ignorance partly caused by *legal terrors?* Master Bunyan, who had a keen insight into spiritual experience, says that Christian was so troubled with that burden on his back that in running he did not look well to his steps; and therefore being much tumbled up and down in his mind, as he says, he also tumbled into the Slough of Despond. You have heard the thunder of God's law so long, that you cannot hear anything so soft and sweet as the invitation of the loving Jesus. "Come and welcome! Come and welcome!" is unheard because of the din of your sins. The main reason I think why some do not attain early to peace is because they are *looking for more than they will get*, and thus their eyes are dazzled with fancies. You who dare not take Christ because you are not a full-grown Christian yet, be content to be a babe first; be satisfied to go through the seed state, and the blade state, and the ear state, and then you will get to be the full corn in the ear. Be content to begin with Christ and with Christ alone. I verily believe some of you expect that you will experience a galvanic shock, or a superhuman delirium of horror. You have an idea that to be born again is something to make the flesh creep or the bones shiver; an indescribable sensation, quite out of the compass of human feeling. Now believe me, that to be born again involves the ending of superstition and living by feeling, and brings you into the world of plain and simple truth where fools need not err. "Whosoever believeth in him is not condemned." If you can understand that and claim it as your own, you are born again; but though you should understand all human mysteries, if you are not born again you could not truly understand that simplest of all teachings, "He that believeth and is baptized shall be saved."

Again, I am afraid some persons with the water at their feet, do not drink it because of *the bad directions* that are given by ministers. When a minister closes up an address to the unconverted with this exhortation — "Now, my dear friends, go home and pray," that is a very right exhortation; but it is given to the wrong people, and in the wrong place. I do not say to you this morning, I dare not say to you, as though it were the Gospel message, "Go home and pray." I hope you will pray; but there is another matter to come before prayer, namely, faith in Jesus. When Christ told his disciples to go and preach the Gospel to every creature, he did not say to them, "He that prayeth shall be saved," though that would be true if he prayed aright; but "he that believeth shall be saved." Your present duty is, not praying, but believing. You are to look to Jesus Christ upon the cross just as the poor serpent-bitten Israelites looked to the brazen serpent and lived. Your prayings will not do you a farthing's worth of good if you refuse to trust Jesus Christ.

When you have trusted Jesus Christ prayer will become your breath, your native air, you will not be able to live without it; but prayer if put in the place of a childlike trust in Jesus, becomes an antichrist. It is not going to places of worship, or Bible reading which saves. I am not depreciating these duties, but I am putting them in their proper position. It is depending upon the Lord Jesus Christ alone which is the true vital act by which the soul is quickened into spiritual life. If you, trusting in Christ, do not find peace and pardon, the Gospel which I preach is a lie, and I will renounce it; but then that Book would be false also, for it is from that Book my message comes. This is the Gospel which we have received, and which Christ has sent us to preach, that whosoever believeth in him is not condemned.

I feel certain that there are some here upon whom the Lord intends to work this morning; so we will speak, in the fourth place, upon *the divine removal of the impediment.* Hagar's blindness was removed *by God.* No one else could have removed it. God must open a man's eyes to understand practically what belief in Jesus Christ is. That simple verity—salvation by trust in Jesus Christ—still remains a point too hard to be seen; until the whole power of Omnipotence is made to bear upon the intellect, man does not really comprehend it. But while this was divinely removed, *it was removed instrumentally.* An angel spake out of heaven to Hagar. It matters little whether it be an angel or a man, *it is the Word of God* which removes this difficulty. I pray that the Word of God may remove your unbelief. May you see today the light of Jesus Christ by simply trusting him! I believe there are some who are saved who still are afraid they will be lost. Many a man is looking within himself to see the evidence of grace when his anxiety, and the very light by which he looks, ought to be sufficient evidence. I hope there are many of you who are just on the verge of salvation without knowing it. There has been much preparatory work in you, for you are brought to long after a Savior, you are desirous to be saved by him. There he is, take him! take him! The cup of water is put before you. Drink it! no need to wash your mouth first, or to change your garments. Drink it at once. Come to Jesus as you are.

Oh that the Spirit of God would give me power from on high while I try to talk to the saints from THE SECOND CASE, viz. that of the apostles in Luke 24:31. This is no Hagar, but "Cleopas and another disciples." And yet these two suffered under the same spiritual blindness as Hagar, though not of course in the same phase of it. Carefully observe the case of these disciples, for I believe it is often our own. *They ought to have known Jesus* for these reasons. *They were acquainted with him,* they had been with him for years in public and in private, they had heard his voice so often that they ought to have recollected its tones. They had gazed upon that marred face so frequently that they ought to have distinguished its features. They had been admitted into his privacy, and they ought to have known his habits. That Savior walking there ought not to have been *incognito* to them though he was to the rest of men. So it is with us. Perhaps you have not found Jesus Christ lately. You have been to his table, and you have not met him there, and you are in a dark trouble this morning, and though he says, "It is I, be not afraid," yet you cannot see him there. Brother, we ought to know Christ, we ought to discover him at once. We know his voice, we have heard him say, "Rise up, My love, My fair one, and come away." We have looked into his face, we have understood the mystery of his grief, we have leaned our head upon his bosom. Some of us have had an experience of fifteen or twenty years, some of forty or fifty years; and yet, though Christ is near you do not know him this morning, and you are saying, "Oh that I knew where I might find him!"

They ought to have known him, because *he* was close to them; he was walking with them along the same road, he was not up on a mountain at a distance. Even then they ought to have known him, but he was there in the selfsame way with them; and at this hour Jesus is very near to us, sympathizing with all our griefs. He bears and endures with us still, though now exalted in glory's throne in heaven. If he be here, we ought to know him. If he be close to his people every day and in all their affliction is afflicted, we ought to perceive him. Oh! what strange purblindness is this, that Christ should be near, our own well-beloved Redeemer, and yet we should not be able to detect his presence!

They ought to have seen him, because *they had the Scriptures to reflect his image*, and yet how possible it is for us to open that precious Book and turn over page after page of it, and not see Christ. They talked concerning Christ from Moses to the end of the prophets, and yet they did not see Jesus. Dear child of God, are you in that state? He feedeth among the lilies of the Word, and you are among those lilies, and yet you do not see him. He is accustomed to walk through the glades of Scripture and to commune with his people, as the Father did with Adam in the cool of the day, and yet you are in the garden of Scripture but cannot see your Lord, though he is there and is never absent.

What is more, these disciples ought to have seen Jesus, for *they had the Scriptures opened to them*. They not only heard the Word, but they understood it. I am sure they understood it, for *their hearts burned within them* while he spoke with them by the way. I have known what it is, and so have you, to feel our hearts burn when we have been thinking of the precious truth of God, and yet we have said, "Oh that I could get at *him!*" You have heard election, and you have wondered to yourself whether you should ever see again the face of God's first elect One. You have heard of the atonement, and the mournful story of the cross has ravished you, but you have gone from page to page of Scripture doctrine, and have received it and felt its influence, and yet that best of all enjoyments, communion with the Lord Jesus Christ, you have not comfortably possessed.

There was another reason why the disciples ought to have seen him, namely that *they had received testimonies from others* about him. "But we trusted that it had been he which should have redeemed Israel: and beside all this, today is the third day since these things were done. Yea, and certain women also of our company made us astonished, which were early at the sepulcher; and when they found not his body, they came, saying, that they had also seen a vision of angels, which said that he was alive." There he was close to them. Oh! it is so strange that in the ordinances of God's house Jesus should be there, and yet in sad intervals our hearts should get so cold and so worldly that we cannot see him. It is a blessed thing to want to see him; but oh! it is better still to see him. To those who seek him he is sweet; but to those who find him, beyond expression is he dear. In the prayer meeting you have heard some say,

"If ever I loved thee, my Jesus, 'tis now," and your hearts burned within you as they thus spake, and yet you could not say the same yourself. You have been up in the sick-chamber, and you have heard the dying saint sing—

> I will love thee in life, I will love thee in death,
> And praise thee as long as thou lendest me breath;
> And say when the death-dew lies cold on my brow,
> If ever I loved thee, my Jesus, 'tis now.

You have envied that dying saint because you could not just then feel the same confident love; well this is strange, passing strange, it is wonderful—a present Savior, present with his own disciples who have long known, and who long to see him, and yet their eyes are held so that they cannot discover him. *Why do we not see him?* I think it must be ascribed in our case to the same as in theirs, namely, *our unbelief.* They evidently did not expect to see him, and therefore they did not discover him. Brethren, to a great extent in spiritual things we shall get what we expect. The ordinary preacher of the Gospel does not expect to see present conversion, and he does not see it; but there are certain brethren I have known, who have preached with the full faith that God would convert souls, and souls have been converted. Some saints do not expect to see Christ. They read the life of Madame Guyon, and her soul-enchanting hymns, and they say, "Ah! a blessed woman this." They take down the letters of Samuel Rutherford, and when they read them through, they say, "Enchanting epistles! a strange, marvelously good man this." It does not enter into their heads that they may be Madam Guyons, and that they may have as much nearness to Christ, and as much enjoyment as Samuel Rutherford. We have got into the habit of thinking the saints gone by stand up in elevated niches for us to stare at them with solemn awe, and fancy that we can never attain to their elevation. Brethren, they are elevated certainly, but they beckon us to follow them, and point to a something beyond; they invite us to outstrip them, to get greater nearness to Christ, a clearer sense of his love, and a more ravishing enjoyment of his presence. You do not expect to see Christ, and therefore you do not see him, not because he is not there to be seen, but because your eyes are held through your unbelief. I do not know any reason why we should not be full of joy this morning; every believing soul among us. Why hang ye those harps on the willows, beloved? You

have a trial, say you. Yes, but Jesus is in it. He says, "When thou passest through the rivers, I will be with thee, the floods shall not overflow
thee." Why not rejoice then, since the dear Shepherd is with you?
What matters it though there be clouds? They are full of rain when He
is there, and they shall empty themselves upon the earth.

Now, I am sure it is the duty of every Christian, as well as his privilege, to walk in the conscious enjoyment of the love of the Lord Jesus
Christ; and it may be that you came here on purpose that you might begin
such a walk. The disciples had walked a long way without knowing Christ,
but when they sat at his table, it was the breaking of bread that broke
the evil charm, and they saw Jesus clearly at once. Do not neglect that
precious ordinance of the breaking of bread. There is much more in it
than some suppose. Sometimes when the preaching of the Word affords
no joy, the breaking of bread might; and when reading the Word does
not yield consolation, a resort to the Lord's Table might be the means
of comfort. There is nothing in any ordinance of itself, but there may
be much sin in your neglecting it. There is nothing, for instance, in the
ordinance of believers' baptism, and yet, knowing it to be a prescribed
duty in God's Word, it may be that the Lord will never give you a comfortable sense of his presence, till you yield to your conscience in that
matter. But, waiving all that point, what you want is to see him. Faith
alone can bring you to see him. Make it your prayer this morning,
"Lord, open thou mine eyes that I may see my Savior present with
me, and after once seeing him may I never let him go. From this day
forth may I begin like Enoch to walk with God, and may I continue walking with God till I die, that I may then dwell with him forever." I find
it very easy to get near to God, compared with what it is to keep near.
Enoch walked with God 400 years; what a long walk that was! What a
splendid journey through life! Why should not you begin, dear Christian brother, today, if you have not begun, and walk with God through
the few years which remain? Oh to get up above yon mists which dim
the valley! Oh to climb the mountain's top which laughs in the sunlight!
Oh to get away from the heavy atmosphere of worldliness and doubt,
of fear, of care, of fretfulness; to soar away from the worldlings who are
always earth-hunting, digging into its mines and prying after its treasures,
and to get up there where God dwells in the innermost circle of heavenly seclusion; where none can live but men who have been quickened
from among the dead; where none can walk but men who are crucified

with Christ, and who live only in him. Oh to get up there! where no more question concerning our security can molest us; where no carking care can disturb because all is cast upon the Lord, and rests wholly with him. Oh to live in such an entireness of confidence and childlike faith that we will have nothing to do with anything now except with serving him and showing forth the gratitude we owe to him who has done so much for us. Christ has called you to fellowship with himself, and he is not in the grave now. He is risen! rise you! He is ascended! ascend with him and learn what this meaneth, "He hath raised us up together and made us sit together in heavenly places in Christ Jesus."

3

REBEKAH

No Compromise

"And the servant said unto him, Peradventure the woman will not be willing to follow me unto this land: must I needs bring thy son again unto the land from whence thou camest? And Abraham said unto him, Beware thou that thou bring not my son thither again. The Lord God of heaven, which took me from my father's house, and from the land of my kindred, and which spake unto me, and that sware unto me, saying, Unto thy seed will I give this land; he shall send his angel before thee, and thou shalt take a wife unto my son from thence. And if the woman will not be willing to follow thee, then thou shalt be clear from this my oath: only bring not my son thither again." (Gen. 24:5–8).

GENESIS is both the book of beginnings and the book of dispensations. You know what use Paul makes of Sarah and Hagar, of Esau and Jacob, and the like. Genesis is, all through, a book instructing the reader in the dispensations of God towards man. Paul saith, in a certain place, "which things are an allegory," by which he did not mean that they were not literal facts, but that, being literal facts, they might also be used instructively as an allegory. So may I say of this chapter. It records what actually was said and done; but at the same time, it bears within it allegorical instruction with regard to heavenly things. The true minister of Christ is like this Eliezer of Damascus; he is sent to find a wife for his Master's Son. His great desire is that many shall be presented unto Christ in the day of his appearing, as the bride, the Lamb's wife.

The faithful servant of Abraham, before he started, communed with his master; and this is a lesson to us who go on our Lord's errands. Let us, before we engage in actual service, see the Master's face, talk with him, and tell to him any difficulties which occur to our minds. Before we get to work, let us know what we are at, and on what footing we stand. Let us hear from our Lord's own mouth what he expects us to do, and how far he will help us in the doing of it. I charge you, my fellow servants, never to go forth to plead with men for God until you have first pleaded with God for men. Do not attempt to deliver a message which you have not first of all yourself received by his Holy Spirit. Come out of the chamber of fellowship with God into the pulpit of ministry among men, and there will be a freshness and a power about you which none shall be able to resist. Abraham's servant spoke and acted as one who felt bound to do exactly what this master bade him, and to say what his master told him; hence his one anxiety was to know the essence and measure of his commission.

Beginning our sermon, we will ask you, first, to THINK OF THE SERVANT'S JOYFUL BUT WEIGHTY ERRAND. It was a joyful errand: the bells of marriage were ringing around him. The marriage of the heir should be a joyful event. It was an honorable thing for the servant to be entrusted with the finding of a wife for his master's son. Yet it was every way a most responsible business, by no means easy of accomplishment. Blunders might very readily occur before he was aware of it; and he needed to have all his wits about him, and something more than his wits, too, for so delicate a matter. He had to journey far, over lands without track or road; he had to seek out a family which he did not know, and to find out of that family a woman whom he did not know, who nevertheless should be the right person to be the wife of his master's son; all this was a great service.

The work this man undertook was a *business upon which his master's heart was set.* Isaac was now forty years old, and had shown no sign of marrying. He was of a quiet, gentle spirit, and needed a more active spirit to urge him on. The death of Sarah had deprived him of the solace of his life, which he had found in his mother, and had, no doubt, made him desire tender companionship. Abraham himself was old, and well stricken in years; and he very naturally wished to see the promise beginning to be fulfilled, that in Isaac should his seed be called. Therefore, with great anxiety, which is indicated by his making his servant swear an oath of a most solemn kind, he gave him the commission to go to the old family abode in Mesopotamia, and seek for Isaac a bride from thence. Although that family was not all that could be desired, yet it was the best he knew of; and as some heavenly light lingered there, he hoped to find in that place the best wife for his son. The business was, however, a serious one which he committed to his servant.

My brethren, this is nothing compared with the weight which hangs on the true minister of Christ. All the Great Father's heart is set on giving to Christ a Church which shall be His beloved forever. Jesus must not be alone; His Church must be His dear companion. The Father would find a bride for the great Bridegroom, a recompense for the Redeemer, a solace for the Savior: therefore He lays it upon all whom He calls to tell out the Gospel, that we should seek souls for Jesus, and never rest till hearts are wedded to the Son of God. Oh, for grace to carry out this commission!

This message was the more weighty because of the person for whom the spouse was sought. Isaac was an extraordinary personage; indeed, to the servant he was unique. He was a man born according to promise, not after the flesh, but by the power of God; and you know how in Christ, and in all that are one with Christ, the life comes by the promise and the power of God, and springeth not of man. Isaac was himself the fulfillment of promise, and the heir of the promise. Infinitely glorious is our Lord Jesus as the Son of man! Who shall declare his generation? Where shall be found a helpmeet for him? A soul fit to be espoused unto him? Isaac had been sacrificed; he had been laid upon the altar, and although he did not actually die, his father's hand had unsheathed the knife wherewith to slay him. Abraham in spirit had offered up his son; and you know who he is of whom we preach, and for whom we preach, even Jesus, who has laid down his life a sacrifice for sinners. He has been presented as a whole burnt-offering unto God. Oh! by the wounds, and by the bloody sweat, I ask you where shall we find a heart fit to be wedded to him? How shall we find men and women who can worthily recompense love so amazing, so divine, as that of him who died the death of the cross? Isaac had also been, in a figure, raised from the dead. To his father he was "as good as dead," as said the apostle; and he was given back to him from the dead. But our blessed Lord has actually risen from an actual death, and stands before us this day as the Conqueror of death, and the Spoiler of the grave. Who shall be joined to this Conqueror? Who is fit to dwell in glory with this glorious One? One would have thought that every heart would aspire to such happiness, and leap in prospect of such peerless honor, and that none would shrink back except through a sense of great unworthiness. Alas! it is not so, though so it ought to be.

What a weighty errand have we to fulfill to find those who shall be linked forever in holy union with the Heir of the promise, even the sacrificed and risen One! Isaac was everything to Abraham. Abraham would have said to Isaac, "All that I have is thine." So it is true of our blessed Lord, whom he hath made Heir of all things; by whom also he made the worlds, that "it pleased the Father that in him should all fullness dwell." What a dignity will be put upon any of you who are married to Christ! To what a height of eminence will you be uplifted by becoming one with Jesus! O preacher, what a work hast thou to do today, to find out those to whom thou shalt give the bracelet, and upon whose face thou shalt hang the jewel! To whom shall I say, "Wilt thou give thy heart to my Lord? Wilt thou have Jesus to be thy confidence, thy salvation, thine all in all? Art thou willing to become his that he may be thine?"

Said I not truly that it was a joyful, but a weighty errand, when you think *what she must be to whom his master's son should be espoused?* She must, at least, be willing and beautiful. In the day of God's power hearts are made willing. There can be no marriage to Jesus without a heart of love. Where shall we find this willing heart? Only where the grace of God has wrought it. Ah, then I see how I may find beauty, too, among the sons of men! Marred as our nature is by sin, only the Holy Spirit can impart that beauty of holiness which will enable the Lord Jesus to see comeliness in his chosen. Alas! in our hearers there is an aversion to Christ, and an unwillingness to accept of him, and at the same time a terrible unfitness and unworthiness! The Spirit of God implants a love which is of heavenly origin, and renews the heart by a regeneration from above; and then we seek to be one with Jesus, but not till then.

Think what she will become who is to be married to Isaac? She is to be his delight; his loving friend and companion. She is to be partner of all his wealth; and specially is she to be a partaker in the great covenant promise, which was peculiarly entailed upon Abraham and his family. When a sinner comes to Christ, what does Christ make of him? His delight is in him; he communes with him; he hears his prayer, he accepts his praise; he works in him and with him, and glorifies himself in him. He makes the believing man joint-heir with himself of all that he has, and introduces him into the covenant treasure house, wherein the riches and glory of God are stored up for his chosen. Ah, it is a very small business in the esteem of some to preach the Gospel; and yet, if God is with us, ours is more than angels' service. In a humble way you are telling of Jesus to your boys and girls in your classes; and some will despise you as "only Sunday school teachers"; but your work has a spiritual weight about it unknown to conclaves of senators, and absent from the counsels of emperors. Upon what you say, death, and hell, and worlds unknown are hanging. You are working out the destinies of immortal spirits, turning souls from ruin to glory, from sin to holiness.

In carrying out his commission, *this servant must spare no exertion.* It would be required of him to journey to a great distance, having a general indication of direction, but not knowing the way. He must have divine guidance and protection. When he reached the place, he must exercise great common sense, and at the same time a trustful dependence upon the goodness and wisdom of God. It would be a wonder of wonders if he ever met the chosen woman, and only the Lord could bring it to pass. He had all the care and the faith required. We have read the story of how he journeyed, and prayed, and pleaded. We should have cried, "Who is sufficient for these things?" but we see that the Lord Jehovah made him sufficient and his mission was happily carried out. How can we put ourselves into the right position to get at sinners, and win them for Jesus? How can we learn to speak the right words? How shall we suit our teaching to the condition of their hearts? How shall we adapt ourselves to their feelings, their prejudices, their sorrows, and their temptations? Brethren, we who preach the Gospel continually may well cry, "If thy presence go not with me, carry us not up hence." To seek for pearls at the bottom of the sea is child's play compared with seeking for souls in this wicked London. If God be not with us, we may look our eyes out, and wear our tongues away in vain.

Secondly, I would have you CONSIDER THE REASONABLE FEAR WHICH IS MENTIONED. Abraham's servant said, "Peradventure the woman will not be willing to follow me unto this land." This is a very serious, grave, and common difficulty. If the woman be not willing, nothing can be done; force and fraud are out of the question; there must be a true will, or there can be no marriage in this instance. Here was the difficulty: here was a will to be dealt with. Ah, my brethren! this is our difficulty still. Let me describe this difficulty in detail as it appeared to the servant, and appears to us.

She may not believe my report, or be impressed by it. When I come to her and tell her that I am sent by Abraham, she may look me in the face, and say, "There be many deceivers nowadays." If I tell her that my master's son is surpassingly beautiful and rich, and that he would fain take her to himself, she may answer, "Strange tales and romances are common in these days; but the prudent do not quit their homes." Brethren, in our case this is a sad fact. The great evangelical prophet cried of old, "Who hath believed our report?" We also cry in the same words. Men care not for the report of God's great love to the rebellious sons of men. They do not believe that the infinitely glorious Lord is seeking the love of poor, insignificant man, and to win it has laid down his life. Calvary, with its wealth of mercy, grief, love, and merit, is disregarded. Indeed, we tell a wonderful story, and it may well seem too good to be true; but it is sad indeed that the multitude of men go their ways after trifles, and count these grand realities to be but dreams. I am bowed down with dismay that my Lord's great love, which led him even to die for men, should hardly be thought worthy of your hearing, much less of your believing. Here is a heavenly marriage, and right royal nuptials placed within your reach; but with a sneer you turn aside, and prefer the witcheries of sin.

There was another difficulty: *she was expected to feel a love to one she had never seen.* She had only newly heard that there was such a person as Isaac, but yet she must love him enough to leave her kindred, and go to a distant land. This could only be because she recognized the will of Jehovah in the matter. Ah, my dear hearers! all that we tell you is concerning things not seen as yet; and here is our difficulty. You have eyes, and you want to see everything; you have hands, and you want to handle everything; but there is one whom you cannot see as yet, who has won our love because of what we believe concerning him. We can truly say of him, "Whom having not seen, we love: in whom, though now we see Him not, yet believing, we rejoice with joy unspeakable and full of glory." I know that you answer our request thus: "You demand too much of us when you ask us to love a Christ we have never seen." I can only answer, "It is even so: we do ask more of you than we expect to receive." Unless God the Holy Ghost shall work a miracle of grace upon your hearts, you will not be persuaded by us to quit your old associations, and join yourselves to our beloved Lord. And yet, if you did come to him, and love him, he would more than content you; for you would find in him rest unto your souls, and a peace which passeth all understanding.

Abraham's servant may have thought: *She may refuse to make so great a change* as to quit Mesopotamia for Canaan. She had been born and bred away there in a settled country, and all her associations were with her father's house; and to marry Isaac she must tear herself away. So, too, you cannot have Jesus, and have the world too: you must break with sin to be joined to Jesus. You must come away from the licentious world, the fashionable world, the scientific world, and from the (so-called) religious world. If you become a Christian, you must quit old habits, old motives, old ambitions, old pleasures, old boasts, old modes of thought. All things must become new. You must leave the things you have loved, and seek many of those things which you have hitherto despised. There must come to you as great a change as if you had died, and were made over again.

Moreover, it might be a great difficulty to Rebekah, if she had had any difficulties at all, to think that *she must henceforth lead a pilgrim life*. She would quit house and farm for tent and gypsy life. Abraham and Isaac found no city to dwell in, but wandered from place to place, dwelling alone, sojourners with God. Their outward mode of life was typical of the way of faith, by which men live in the world, and are not of it. To all intents and purposes Abraham and Isaac were out of the world, and lived on its surface without lasting connection with it. They were the Lord's men, and the Lord was their possession. He set himself apart for them, and they were set apart for him. Rebekah might well have said, "That will never do for me. I cannot outlaw myself. I cannot quit the comforts of a settled abode to ramble over the fields wherever the flocks may require me to roam.

It does not strike the most of mankind that it would be a good thing to be in the world, and yet not to be of it. They are no strangers in the world, they long to be admitted more fully into its "society." If any man becomes unworldly, and makes spiritual things his one object, they despise him as a dreamy enthusiast. Many men think that the things of religion are merely meant to be read of, and to be preached about; but that to live for them would be to spend a dreamy, unpractical existence. Yet the spiritual is, after all, the only real: the material is in deepest truth the visionary and unsubstantial. Unless the Lord renews the heart, men will always prefer the bird-in-the-hand of this life to the bird-in-the-bush of the life to come.

Moreover, it might be that the woman *might not care for the covenant of promise.* If she had no regard for Jehovah and his revealed will, she was not likely to go with the man, and enter upon marriage with Isaac. He was the heir of the promises, the inheritor of the covenant privileges which the Lord by oath had promised. His chosen would become the mother of that chosen seed in whom God had ordained to bless the world throughout all the ages, even the Messiah, the seed of the woman, who should bruise the serpent's head.

In the third place, I would ENLARGE UPON HIS VERY NATURAL SUGGESTION. This prudent steward said, "Peradventure the woman will not be willing to follow me unto this land: *Must I needs bring thy son again unto the land from whence thou camest?*" If she will not come to Isaac, shall Isaac go down to her? This is the suggestion of the present hour: if the world will not come to Jesus, shall Jesus tone down his teachings to the world? In other words, if the world will not rise to the Church, shall not the Church go down to the world? Instead of bidding men to be converted, and come out from among sinners, and be separate from them, let us join with the ungodly world, enter into union with it, and so pervade it with our influence by allowing it to influence us. Let us have a Christian world.

To this end let us revise our doctrines. Some are old-fashioned, grim, severe, unpopular; let us drop them out! Use the old phrases so as to please the obstinately orthodox, but give them new meanings so as to win philosophical infidels, who are prowling around. Pare off the edges of unpleasant truths, and moderate the dogmatic tone of infallible revelation; say that Abraham and Moses made mistakes, and that the books which have been so long had in reverence are full of errors. Undermine the old faith, and bring in the new doubt; for the times are altered, and the spirit of the age suggests the abandonment of everything that is too severely righteous, and too surely of God.

The deceitful adulteration of doctrine is attended by a falsification of experience. Men are now told that they were born good, and so that great sentence, "Ye must be born again," is deprived of its force. Repentance is ignored, faith is a drug in the market as compared with "honest doubt," and mourning for sin and communion with God are dispensed with, to make way for entertainments, and Socialism, and politics of varying shades. A new creature in Christ Jesus is looked upon as a sour invention of bigoted Puritans. Spiritual religion is despised, and a fashionable morality is set up in its place. Be fashionable, and think with those who profess to be scientific—this is the first and great commandment of the modern school; and the second is like unto it—do not be singular, but be as worldly as your neighbors.

Men seem to say—It is of no use going on in the old way, fetching out one here and another there from the great mass. We want a quicker way. To wait till people are born again, and become followers of Christ, is a long process: let us abolish the separation between the regenerate and unregenerate. Come into the Church, all of you, converted or unconverted. You have good wishes and good resolutions; that will do: don't trouble about more. The new plan is to assimilate the Church to the world and so include a larger area within its bounds. By semi-dramatic performances they make houses of prayer to approximate to the theater; they turn their services into musical displays, and their sermons into political harangues or philosophical essays—in fact, they exchange the temple for the theater, and turn the ministers of God into actors, whose business it is to amuse men. Is it not so, that the Lord's day is becoming more and more a day of recreation or of idleness and the Lord's house either a joss-house full of idols, or a political club, where there is more enthusiasm for a party than zeal for God?

In the fourth place, NOTICE HIS MASTER'S OUTSPOKEN, BELIEVING REPUDIATION OF THE PROPOSAL. He says, shortly and sharply, *"Beware thou that thou bring not my son thither again."* The Lord Jesus Christ heads that grand emigration party which has come right out from the world. Addressing his disciples, he says, "Ye are not of the world, even as I am not of the world. We are not of the world by birth, not of the world in life, not of the world in object, not of the world in spirit, not of the world in any respect whatever. Jesus, and those who are in him, constitute a new race. The proposal to go back to the world is abhorrent to our best instincts; yea, deadly to our noblest life. A voice from heaven cries, "Bring not my son thither again." Let not the people whom the Lord brought up out of Egypt return to the house of bondage; but let their children come out, and be separate, and the Lord Jehovah will be a Father unto them.

Notice how Abraham states the question. In effect, he argues it thus: *this would be to forego the divine order.* "For," says Abraham, "the Lord

God of heaven took me from my father's house, and from the land of my kindred." What, then, if he brought Abraham out, is Isaac to return? This cannot be. Hitherto the way of God with His Church has been to sever a people from the world to be His elect—a people formed for himself, who shall show forth his praise. Beloved, God's plan is not altered. He will still go on calling those whom he did predestinate. Do not let us fly in the teeth of that fact, and suppose that we can save men on a more wholesale scale by ignoring the distinction between the dead in sin and the living in Zion. If God had meant to bless the family at Padan-aram by letting his chosen ones dwell among them, why did he call Abraham out at all? If Isaac may do good by dwelling there, why did Abraham leave? If there is no need of a separate Church now, what have we been at throughout all these ages? Has the martyrs' blood been shed out of mere folly? Have confessors and reformers been mad when contending for doctrines which, it would seem, are of no great account?

Abraham felt that this would be *to renounce the covenant promise.* See how he puts it: "The God that took me from my father's house sware unto me, saying, Unto thy seed will I give this land." Are they, then to leave the land, and go back to the place from which the Lord had called them? Brethren, we also are heirs of the promise of things not seen as yet. For the sake of this we walk by faith, and hence we become separate from those around us. We dwell among men as Abraham dwelt among the Canaanites; but we are of a distinct race: we are born with a new birth, live under different laws, and act from different motives. If we go back to the ways of worldlings, and are numbered with them, we have renounced the covenant of our God, the promise is no longer ours, and the eternal heritage is in other hands. Do you not know this? The moment the Church says, "I will be as the world," she has doomed herself with the world. The covenant promise and the covenant heritage are no longer ours if we go down to the world and quit our sojourning with the Lord.

Besides, *no good can come of trying to conform the world.* Suppose the servant's policy could have been adopted, and Isaac had gone down to Nahor's house, what would have been the motive? To spare the pain of separating from her friends, and the trouble of traveling. If those things could have kept her back, what would she have been worth to Isaac? The test of separation was wholesome, and by no means ought it to be omitted. She is a poor wife who would not take a journey to reach her husband. And all the converts that the Church will ever make by softening down its doctrine, and by becoming worldly, will not be worth one bad farthing a gross. When we get them, the next question will be, "How can we get rid of them?" They would be of no earthly use to us. It swelled the number of Israelites when they came out of Egypt that a great number of the lower order of Egyptians came out with them. Yes, but that mixed multitude became the plague of Israel in the wilderness, and we read that "the mixed multitude fell a lusting." The Israelites were bad enough, but it was the mixed multitude that always led the way in murmuring. Why is there such spiritual death today? Why is false doctrine so rampant in the churches? It is because we have ungodly people in the church and in the ministry. Eagerness for numbers, and especially eagerness to include respectable people, has adulterated many churches, and made them lax in doctrine and practice, and fond of silly amusements. These are the people who despise a prayer meeting, but rush to see "living waxworks" in their schoolrooms. God save us from converts who are made by lowering the standards, and tarnishing the spiritual glory of the Church!

Besides, Abraham felt that *there could be no reason for taking Isaac down there*, for the Lord would assuredly find him a wife. Abraham said, "He shall send His angel before thee, and thou shalt take a wife unto my son from thence." Are you afraid that preaching the Gospel will not win souls? Are you despondent as to success in God's way? Is this why you pine for clever oratory? Is the why you must have music, and architecture, and flowers, and millinery? After all, is it by might and by power, and not by the Spirit of God? It is even so the opinion of many. Where will you find such a multitude as this meeting, Sabbath after Sabbath, for thirty-five years? I have shown you nothing but the cross, the cross without the flowers of oratory, the cross without the blue lights of superstition or excitement, the cross without diamonds of ecclesiastical rank, the cross without the buttresses of a boastful science. It is abundantly sufficient to attract men first to itself and afterwards to eternal life! In this house we have proved successfully, these many years, this great truth, that the Gospel plainly preached will gain an audience, convert sinners, and build up and sustain a church. We beseech the people of God to mark that there is no need to try doubtful expedients and questionable methods. God will save by the Gospel still: only let it be the

Gospel in its purity. To invite the devil to help Christ is shameful. Please God, we shall see prosperity yet, when the Church of God is resolved never to seek it except in God's own way.

And now, fifthly, observe HIS RIGHTEOUS ABSOLUTION OF HIS SERVANT. "If the woman will not be willing to follow thee, then thou shalt be clear from this my oath: only bring not my son thither again."

When we lie a-dying, if we have faithfully preached the Gospel, our conscience will not accuse us for having kept closely to it; we shall not mourn that we did not play the fool or the politician in order to increase our congregation. Oh, no! our Master will give us full absolution, even if few be gathered in, so long as we have been true to him. "If the woman will not be willing to follow thee, then thou shalt be clear from this my oath; only bring not my son thither again." Do not try the dodges which debase religion. Keep to the simple Gospel; and if the people are not converted by it, you will be clear. My dear hearers, how much I long to see you saved! But I would not belie my Lord, even to win your souls, if they could be so won. The true servant of God is responsible for diligence and faithfulness; but he is not responsible for success or non-success. Results are in God's hands. If that dear child in your class is not converted, yet if you have set before him the Gospel of Jesus Christ with loving, prayerful earnestness, you shall not be without your reward. If I preach from any very soul the grand truth that faith in the Lord Jesus Christ will save my hearers, and if I persuade and entreat them to believe in Jesus unto eternal life; if they will not do so, their blood will lie upon their own heads. When I go back to my Master, if I have faithfully told out his message of free grace and dying love, I shall be clear. I have often prayed that I might be able to say at the last what George Fox could so truly say: "I am clear, I am clear!" It is my highest ambition to be clear of the blood of all men. I have preached God's truth, so far as I know it, and I have not been ashamed of its peculiarities.

If Rebekah had not come to Isaac she would have lost her place in the holy line. My beloved hearer, will you have Jesus Christ or not? He has come into the world to save sinners, and he casts out none. Will you accept him? Will you trust him? "He that believeth and is baptized shall be saved." Will you believe him? Will you be baptized into his name? If so, salvation is yours; but if not, he himself hath said it, "He that believeth not shall be damned."

4

REBEKAH

Delay Is Dangerous

*"And her brother and her mother said, Let the damsel abide
with us a few days, at the least ten; after that she shall go"*
(Gen. 24:55).

YOU know the story of which these words form a part. Abraham was anxious to secure a wife for his son, Isaac. He sends, therefore, his well-tried servant to the land of their forefathers, and takes an oath of him that he will bring a maiden from thence, who should be, by her birth and character, suitable to her future destiny. The venerable servant departs on his delicate and difficult errand. He took all precautions, and then commended his case to the wise disposal of his own and his master's God. Success, which was in perfect harmony with his faith, and with the divine promises, at once crowned his efforts. The maiden best adapted above all others to be the spouse of Isaac is sent to meet him. She immediately responded to his wishes, and conducted him to the house of her friends. The aged man was wise in his generation, and knew that a key of gold has the power to open the heart most tightly locked either by prejudice or pride: everything gives way before its subtle influence. He had calculated wisely, and his plans are matured at once into all he had fervently desired and prayed for. No sooner had Abraham's servant exhibited his offerings, jewels of silver and jewels of gold, with earrings and bracelets of precious metal, then he at once won the consent of Laban, Rebekah's brother, and of her mother; for what would not Laban have agreed to do for the sake of such valuable things? The good servant, therefore, when he went to his bed that night, might well have slept soundly, congratulating himself that he had found in his anxious mission an easy task, that he should be able to go back next morning to his master, taking Rebekah with him, and that the whole matter would be carried through with surprising speed.

Judge of his surprise, when the first thing Laban said in answer to the good man's request, "Send me away," was "Oh no! we cannot afford to let you go just yet; we must have the damsel here a little while longer, ten days at the least." I do not know what may have been Laban's particular reason, but I suspect his motives were in keeping with his character. If you observe his subsequent conduct with regard to Jacob, you may rest assured that there was something in the background. He thought, perhaps, that there were more golden bracelets to be had, that he was parting with his sister rather too cheaply, that he must not let the priceless gem go out of his hands too soon, therefore he would keep the account open, and bargain over it again; or, if he could not get more out of the servant, he might at least get ten days more service from the maiden, for she appears to have been the keeper of the sheep of the household, and to have performed the usual menial duties attended to by the young women of the family in the East. So Laban may have thought he might as well have her for ten days longer. It was just like him; he would have as much as he ought to have, and as much more as he could get; that was his honesty. He would get all that it was possible to squeeze out of everybody; that was his generosity.

We shall not, however, have anything more to do with Laban tonight, than to use his desire to retain his good sister Rebekah as an illustration of the way in which this wicked world endeavors to meet the invitations of the Gospel, by trying to retain the awakened sinner a little longer in its grasp. I believe there are many here who have a hope that one day or other they will be saved. They have consented, in their judgment, that it is a right thing to be converted, but not yet. The world says, "Yes, these are weighty considerations; you shall go with that man; you shall have Christ; you shall put your trust in him; but not yet; stop just a little while." Satan's last counsel to his servants seems to have been, "Do not openly oppose the Gospel; give way to it, but suggest delay; do not set men's consciences in opposition to Gospel truth, for that is a hammer, and perhaps it will break their rocky hearts to pieces; but tell them to yield to the hammer; to say, 'Yes, yes, it is all true, quite correct; but we must wait a little longer, at least ten days: there is plenty of time: there is no need to hurry; let the damsel wait a little while, ten days at the least.' "

I want to draw your attention, first of all, to THE WORLD'S PRETEXT FOR THIS DELAY.

I stand knocking tonight at the world's door, and I say, "There is a young heart here I want for Christ"; the world replies, "All right, you shall have it one of these days, but there is time enough yet." I say of another, "Here is a man whose strength and vigor I want for the Savior." "All right," says the world, "do not be in such a fever about it; we are all agreed with you; we all think as you do, that religion is important, but wait awhile, put it off, take time, tarry a little; there is no cause for all this hurry and this fuss." If I ask the world what it means by talking like this, it says, "Well, you see, *some of these people are so young*; it is too young for them to think of giving their hearts to Christ: would you have all the boys and girls turn saints? Would you have all the young men and women walking in the ways of Christ, and following in the footsteps of the Crucified?" I answer, "Yes, indeed, I would"; but I wonder at the world's impudence in putting such a question as this concerning some of you, for some of you are not young. You have passed the period of youth years ago, and yet you are unconverted; and if I might hold parley with the world about some of the youngsters, I cannot about you. Why, surely, the world cannot have the face to tell me that you who are thirty, forty, fifty, or even sixty years of age, are still too young! I should not wonder, indeed, but when it turns round and tells me that you are too old, and that your time of mercy is past, and that I am too late. At any rate, Satan often does play both tunes, and while today he says, "Too soon," tomorrow he cries, "Too late." Too young to be saved! Is any one too young to be happy? Too young to be a Christian! Is anyone too young to get the richest treasure that can make human hearts glad? O young people, do not let the lying world tell you that you are too young. When our Lord was on earth, he said, "let the little ones come unto me, and forbid them not: for of such is the kingdom of God." Do not believe that it is too soon for Christ to welcome you. Your need of him begins with your life, for you are born in sin, and shapen in iniquity; as soon as ever you begin to act, you begin to sin in acting. Your first tendency is to fall as soon as ever you are on your feet. It is never too soon to have the strong arm of a Savior put around you to hold you up, that you may be safe.

Then the world says, "O stop a little longer; *we should like these young people to know something about life.*" Well, but, base world, what dost thou mean by that? What hast thou to do with life? *We*, too, want the young people to know something about life: but what is life? Why, true life is to be found only in the followers of Christ, in whom is life. "Well," says the world, "but we mean the life—" I know what you mean; you mean *the death*. You want the young people to know something about life, you say. I hear you; it is the voice of the same hissing serpent that said, "Ye shall be as gods, knowing good and evil"; and our mother Eve, in order to know evil as well as to know good, has destroyed this race. And many a young man and young woman in trying to know good and to know evil, has come to know that which has made the head to ache, and the heart to palpitate, and the nerves to tingle with exquisite pain, that which has brought the frail body to an early grave, and the doomed soul down to the lowest hell! I pray God that our young people may not know life in that aspect, but that they may know life in the true sense, and search for it where only it is to be found.

> There is life for a look at the crucified One,
> There is life at this moment for thee.

"Ah! then," says the world, putting on its best smiles, "it is all very well for you to talk, *but we do not want our young people to give up all their pleasure.*" And what hast thou to do with pleasure, thou painted Jezebel? what hast thou to do with happiness, false deluder of souls? The world, this canting, hypocritical world, dares to utter and dwell upon that word "pleasure," and it does not know what it means—ask those who have tried its joys. Its princely minds, such as Byron, who, like an angel, flew through the hell of this world's pleasures. Ask them what they have made of it all, and their only answer is in a groan, and with a sign, deep heaving from their inmost spirits, they join in modern times with the verdict of the ancient royal philosopher, who said, "Vanity of vanity, all is vanity!" Pleasure, indeed! Happiness, indeed! Thou base world, what dost thou know about it?

It is because we would have these people possessed of pleasure that we wish them to be converted, and that we desire to see them joined to Christ. It is false, as false as God is true, that religion makes men miserable. Spurious religion may do so. They who worship Moloch may adore him with shrieks and cries, but the worshipers of Jehovah bow before their God with gladness; they come into his presence with thanksgiving, and into his courts with joy. The richest joy, the noblest festivities, the most enchanting mirth that hearts can know, is that which we find at our Father's throne when we adoringly worship him, and do Him active service. When the prodigal came trembling back from the far-off land to his father's house, his misery ceased and his joy began so soon as his father had spoken. What bliss must have thrilled him with the word of his gracious parent's lips! The best robe! the precious ring! The costly shoe! The fatted calf! All for me? Why, it seems too good to be true. But so it is to be; and not only in his case, but with us all. "Religion's ways are ways of pleasantness, and all her paths are peace." Our cup has joy's quintessence distilled into it, and it is filled to the brim. "That your joy may be full," said the Master; and it is full, as full as God's eternal love, as Christ's most precious grace, and the Spirit's blest communion can make it; yes, as full as heaven and eternal bliss can fill it.

Now, I wonder what else the world has to say by way of wishing to keep these people a few more days? Oh! yes: oh! yes; I know it brings out the ledger, and puts the pen behind its ear and it says, "*A young man ought to mind the main chance*, he should get on in business, and then when he has made a competence, he may sit down and think about the world to come; but his first object should be to make money." Yes, my good sir, and if you would but speak the whole of your mind, you would say that he ought in the last place to make money too. I knew your father well. He began life as you would have these young people begin, and he plodded on, and plodded on to the end of his allotted term, never having had time to think about religion. He was such a rare sensible old gentleman, such a wise man! "What I want, is facts and figures," said he, "none of your nonsense; do not tell me about your opinions; I cast my books up on a Sunday—that is the way to spend your Sabbath. I dare say when I have nothing else to do, I shall have time to think about my soul." He was a rare "fine old English gentleman," a very wise old man; howbeit, one night he lifted up his eyes in hell, and with all his accurate bookkeeping and balance of accounts, he had to sum it up: "No profits; I have gained my wealth, but lost my soul." And oh! if he could come back again, he would say to his son, "My son, you have better begin business at the right end; make the soul sure, and then look after the body; hook yourself fast to eternity, and make that right, and then see after the slippery things of time as best you can in subservience to that." At any rate, let Mr. Worldly-Wiseman say what he may; that God, who knows more about us than we do about ourselves, says, "Seek ye first the kingdom of God and his righteousness, and all other things shall be added unto you."

Shall I tell you now WHAT IS THE DRIFT OF ALL THIS WAITING? What the world means is just this, "Ah!" says Madam Bubble, "here is a young person impressed—if we laugh at him it will deepen the impression; but we will say to him, 'Come, come, let the impression go for a little while; this is not the fit time; when you have a more convenient season, you can bring it on again.'" This game the old tempter keeps on playing over and over again. He does it very blandly; he does not oppose religion, but "everything in its proper place," says he, "and this is not just the time for it; wait a little longer." He said this to some of you ten years ago, and he is saying the same to you tonight, and if you live, he will say the same ten years hence; and again when you are on your dying bed; and so with this cunning he will cheat you out of your soul. The world says again to itself, "Every time we get this impression put off, we get the conscience more unlikely to receive it again, for no man stultifies his conscience without suffering injury thereby." If I say to my awakened conscience, "No, I will not hear thee," my ear gets less retentive of the sound, and Mr. Conscience himself grows less able to speak. When the knocking at the door has been heard for sometime and not answered, a man gets to be so in the habit of hearing the alarm, that he could go to sleep and let a man knock all night.

Moreover, the world says, "Well, if they do go at last, yet *we will exact from them as long a time of service as we can.* Suppose they do leave us and engage in the service of Christ, yet we shall have had their help in the work of the devil for a good long time, and they will be poor old lame things when they go limping into Christ's service, and they will not be good for much then." The devil knows that Christ loves the young, and therefore he tries to keep the young from going to him. "No," says he, "if he will have that flower, I will not let him have it in the bud if I can help it; he shall have it when it gets full blown, and much of its beauty has gone from it; I will keep it with me while in its prime as long as I can. Ay, and there is this thing in addition, that while I have it in my power, I can do that to it which it can never get rid of in this life: I will lead it into sins that shall cleave to its memory. I will teach that young man vile songs that shall some day come up in his mind when he begins to pray; I will show him scenes that shall stagger him when he grows old, and make him cry, as though his very bones were broken." That is what the devil says; he wants to have you altogether, or if he cannot do that, he would have you wait a little while. O may God's eternal mercy come to your rescue, and may you be saved from him without waiting the ten days; may your hearts be brought to Jesus now! And how sad the thought, that Satan is getting service out of some who will have to spend much of their afterlife in trying to undo what they have in their blindness been led to perform for the god of this world! What a waste of time and talent, to build up in misery today what you will wish, for very shame, to pull down tomorrow! Some men have written books, or done deeds in early life, which will meet them as long as ever they live, confronting them in the path of service, and proving to be their direst foes. It will be a source of ever recurring grief to find yourself wounded by an arrow feathered thus out of your own wing—to feel yourself crushed by stones your own heads set a rolling in days gone by.

Thirdly, having exposed the pretexts of the world, and tried to show its cruel designs, OUR REAL OBJECT IS TO HAVE OUR HEARERS SAVED, AND TO HAVE THEM SAVED NOW.

I never did come upon this platform desiring that my ministry might be blessed to you months after you had heard the sermon; but I trust I have prayed times without number that it might be blessed at once to the salvation of souls. It is an immediate result that we must look for and labor to achieve.

There were three reasons why Abraham's servant wished Rebekah to go with him at once, and these move me to desire your conversion tonight.

First, *he desired it for his Master's sake.* He knew that Isaac was looking forward to the happy day when he should be married to his chosen bride. And oh! the heart of Jesus is longing after sinners. It is a happy day for the Savior when he welcomes the lost ones. It is one of Christ's wedding days when he gets a soul to come to him. Oh! how the bells of Jesus' heart do ring when he hears a soul say, "God be merciful to me a sinner!" You know how he suffered! See him fastened to the tree! What is to pay him for all his pangs? Nothing—nothing but the love of your hearts when you come to him with all your sins, and say, "Jesus, forgive me!" May you, then, come and trust him now, saying—

> Just as I am, without one plea,
> But that thy blood was shed for me,
> And that thou bidd'st me come to thee,
> O Lamb of God, I come!

Our Lord for the "joy set before him, endured the cross, despising the shame." It is written, that he rejoices over us with joy and singing, so that he reaps the fruit of his pains and groans in our salvation. When the shepherd lays the sheep on his shoulders, he returns home rejoicing, for he has found the sheep which was lost. The joy of finding the strayed one compensates him for all his toil, he forgets the length of the road, the toilsome climb up the mountains in search of it. It is found! It is found! That is enough: that one joyful cry embodies the measure of his satisfaction and rewards. How Christ delights to save! This is how Christ is rewarded for his soul's travail.

Abraham's servant, too, *desired it for his own sake, because he was a faithful steward, and wanted to do his business well. And how we desire your conversion for our sake!* It will make us so happy! There is no bliss that can come to the soul of the Christian minister like the bliss of knowing that he has been made the means of bringing some to Christ. It is in this way that we receive at once the fulfillment of the Scripture, "In keeping his commandments there is exceeding great reward." We get our reward while we are obeying his precept, "Go into all the world, and preach the Gospel unto every creature." Our chief reward is in heaven, but even now, whenever a lost sheep is found, and a prodigal restored by sovereign grace through us, we immediately receive a recompense.

My dear brethren and sisters in the Sunday school, your reward is on high, but do you know what it is to have a crown of rejoicing even here? I am sure you do, if ever you have seen that some young spirits have been by you led to the Savior. Your hearts full weary before, have been refreshed and you have gone back to your labor with more zeal than ever. Your desire has been increased, and you long more intensely after souls. Ask our brethren the city missionaries, and our sisters the Bible-women, "What is your encouragement in your arduous work? They would reply, that next to the Master's presence and the hope of his commendation at last, they placed the joy of doing good, and seeing men, once as heathenish as any found in foreign lands, sitting at the feet of Jesus, all their nature changed, a legion of demons expelled, and now clothed and in their right mind—these once lost ones are found; the dead are alive again.

But the principal reason that the man wished it was *for Rebekah's sake.* He knew that Isaac would make a good husband to her. And we know that Jesus Christ will make a blessed husband to your souls. He will enrich you with all the treasure of his grace. He will clothe you with his robe of righteousness. He will comfort you with his love. He will cheer you in this world. He will take you home to dwell with him in the many mansions above. You will find him to be a precious Christ to you, and when you get to him you will says, "I never knew what happiness meant till I found him." You will be grateful to think that you are saved; and therefore, for your own sakes, we desire that this very night you may give up your sins; that the Spirit of God may draw you by his grace, to cast yourselves upon the finished work of the Lord Jesus, trusting in him to save you, as he will do, if you put your faith in him. Think for a while, I beseech you, how much is to be gained by your im-mediate seeking of the Savior! You at once are free from the guilt and condemnation of sin; you are at once clothed with a peerless robe of right-eousness; immediately "all things are yours": that very moment "all things begin to work together for your good." You have heaven then for your home, and your citizenship is in the kingdom of glory. You shall never more lack any good think. No evil can befall you, or any plague come nigh your dwelling. Time would fail me to try to calculate your immediate blessedness. And then you make the eternal life sure and cer-tain; whereas you may delay and delay, till you lose the life which now is and that which is to come. For your sakes we desire your immediate salvation. Our hearts are filled with joy and gladness, as we sit at the King's table in his banqueting house, and his banner over us is love: but we remember our friends outside, in darkness, poverty, and want, and we would fain call them in to our feast. There is room enough; and our hearts would be yet more filled with joy if we could see the edging com-pletely filled with guests. O all ye hungry ones, come and eat with us of angels' food, and drink with us of cups of salvation! Here is a royal feast: oxen and fatlings are killed: all things are ready: come ye to the wedding; the Master bids you come at once. Why remain in hunger and fear outside? Enter freely.

Now, lastly, WE BELIEVE THAT THIS DESIRE OF OURS IS A VERY REASONABLE ONE, and we think we can prove it without the necessity of entering upon a long argument.

We will put before you, with this view, two or three little pictures. Alexan-der conquered the world, and we should like you to do so, in the best of senses. We will ask Alexander his secret. Alexander, thou hast over-come Darius; thou hast driven the Persians before thee as a lion drives a herd of sheep; how hast thou done it? The very question was once asked of him personally, and his answer was this—"*I never delayed.*" Everybody admits, that in his way, Alexander was a worldly-wise man, and eminently successful, and here was the secret of it—"I never delayed." Do you hear that, young man? You want to be great; you want to be happy. What is your ambition? Learn from Alexander. I think that a greater than he could have said that in his life, I mean the Apostle Paul. How was it that he was able to do so much during that latter part of his life, in which God blessed him? Why, he could have said, "I never delayed."

A number of men are upstairs in a house, amusing themselves with a game of cards. What is that? The window is red! What is that cry in the streets? "*The house is on fire!*" says one. "Oh!" answers another, "Shuffle the cards again, let us finish the game; we have plenty of time." "*Fire! Fire! Fire!*" The cry rises more sharply from the streets, but they keep on. One of them says, "It is all right, I have the key of the door on the roof, and we can get out at the last minute. I know the way over the leads— it is all right." Presently one of them says, "Are you sure we can get through that door?" and he goes to try, but finds it locked. "Never mind," is the answer, "I have the key." "But are you sure you have the key?" "Oh, yes! I am sure I have; here it is, try it for yourself, and do not be such a coward, man, try it." The man tries the key. "It will not turn!" says he. "Let me try," says his friend. He comes and tries, and puts it in the lock, "O God!" he shrieks, "*it is the wrong key!*" Now, sirs, will ye go back to your game again? No, now they will strain every nerve and labor to open the door, only to find, possibly, that it is all too late for them to escape. So, some of your are saying, "Oh, yes! what the man says is well enough, but you know, we can repent whenever we like; we have a key that can turn the grace of God whenever we please; we know the way, has he not told us tonight it is just? Trust Christ, and we can do that whenever we please—we shall get out." Ah! *but suppose you cannot do that whenever you please?* Suppose the day is come when you shall call, and he will not answer, when you shall stretch out your hands, but no man shall regard? Suppose, suppose you should cry, "Lord, Lord, open to us," and the answer should be, "I never knew you; depart, ye cursed!" Besides, if you think that that key will open the door, and you can repent now, *why do you not repent now?* You believe that you have full power to do so! O do it, do it, and do not trifle with that power, lest when the power is gone, you find too late that in one sense it never was there!

Do you want one other picture of the folly of delay? Ah! you heard of it some time back last winter, and I should think you must have heard of it with tears in your eyes—I mean that terrible accident on the ice in Regent's Park. Why did not the people come off the ice when they could see it was rotten? Why did they not leave it when it was beginning to be cut up into such small pieces as to be scarcely larger than paving stones? It was all very well to be on it when it was a solid cake; but why did they not flee at once when there was danger? Nobody can now answer that question; but there is only this to be said: *it is most probable that all those who were there meant to have come off very soon.* Probably nine out of ten of them may have thought to themselves—"Well, it is getting rather dangerous; it is not quite the thing to be here; just one more merry ring; let us just cut another 'figure eight'; and have just one more dash up and down the slide; it will be firm enough for that; let us stand here for two or three minutes at any rate." *They were all coming off, but*—Ah! there is the end of the story; only that it is even till this day continued by other people with the sighs, and cries, and lamentations of husbands and of wives, of children and of parents, who can now only regret the fatal delay, but can do nothing to make amends. Ah! some of you are on the rotten ice of the world's pleasures, and of your own confidence. It is all rotten: why do you not come off? "Oh," say you, "I shall come off by and by." Oh! I see you: there is something fascinating in your pleasures, and a man likes to see his neighbors happy. I see you skating over that dangerous ice; *but why do you not come off?* With some of you life is getting very frail. Ah! those lungs are hardly sound; you are spitting blood. The gray hairs are getting pretty plentiful on your heard. You have had a warning; you have had one fit, and the doctor has told you what will be the consequences of another. *Why do you not come off when the ice is breaking up like this?* You may come off; you may come off tonight. If you perish, it will not be the fault of one who would act the part of a Humane Society man, and say to you, "Now, ere the last breakup comes; now, before the rising of tomorrow's sun, which may bring the final breakup, escape for thy life! Look not behind thee! Stay not until thou hast reached the Savior, and found mercy in him!"

5

RAHAB

The Scarlet Line in the Window

"She bound the scarlet line in the window" (Josh. 2:21).

EVERY little incident in a remarkable conversion like that of the harlot Rahab is worthy of notice. The Apostle James selected her as an illustration of the fact that faith is always attended by good works, and he asks, "Was she not justified by works when she had received the messengers?" while Paul quotes her as an instance of justification by faith, and says, "By faith the harlot Rahab perished not with them that believed not." If both these eminent apostles found an illustration of an important doctrine in her life, we, surely, may do the same. If the hiding of the spies under the flax had some significance, so also had the hanging out of the scarlet line.

The two spies whom Rahab had concealed made an agreement with her that she should hang out a scarlet line in the window by which she had let them down, that they might know, in the day of battle, the house in which she dwelt. She fulfilled their request, and displayed the chosen emblem. In connection with that scarlet line, I observe four things.

First, I see here AN OBEDIENT BELIEVER.

She was told to tie the scarlet thread in the window, and she did it; there was *exact obedience*. It was not merely *a* thread, *a* line, but the *scarlet line*. She did not substitute a blue, or a green, or a white line. The order was *this scarlet line*, not another, and she took that particular one. Obedience to God will be very much seen in small matters. Love always delights to attend to the little things, and thereby makes the little things great. I have heard of a Puritan who was charged with being too precise, but his answer was excellent, "I serve a precise God." The Lord our God is a jealous God, and He is very jealous of His commands.

It appeared a little mistake that Moses made when he struck the rock instead of speaking to it, and yet he could not enter into the promised rest because of his offense. A small action may involve a great principle, and it is for us to be very cautious and careful, searching out what the Master's will is, and then never halting or hesitating for any reason whatever, but doing his will as soon as ever we know it. Christian life should be a mosaic of minute obediences. The soldiers of Christ should be famous for their exact discipline.

I commend scrupulous obedience to all of you, and especially to those young people who have lately made a profession of their faith in Christ. Do not be as your fathers were; for the generation which is now going off the stage neither reads its Bible nor cares to know the Lord's will. If people searched the Scriptures, we should find them come together in union; but the least-read book in all the world, in proportion to its circulation, is the Word of God. It is distributed everywhere, but it is read scarcely anywhere with care and attention, and with a sincere resolve to follow its precepts at all hazards. You come and listen to us, and we give you little bits taken from it here and there, but you do not get a fair notion of it as a whole. How can you? Ministers make mistakes, and you follow them without inquiry. One elects this leader, and another that, to the creation of varieties of opinions and even of sects, which ought not to be, and would not be if all stood fast by the standard of inspired truth. If the Bible were but read, and prayed over, many errors would die a speedy death, and others would be sorely crippled. Had that inspired Book been read in the past, many errors would never have arisen. Search ye, then, the Book of God, I pray you; and whatever you find there, be sure to attend thereto. At all costs, keep to the Word of God.

Notice, next, that hers was *obedience in a very small matter.* She might have said, "I do not think it is essential to tie a piece of line in my window. Can I not be preserved just as well without it, seeing that I believe in the God of Israel? I have faith, and I have shown it by my works by hiding the spies, you cannot suppose for a moment that I shall perish simply because I have not complied with a regulation about a scarlet line." In this way many, nowadays, inquire whether they may not omit those duties which they consider to be nonessential to salvation. Now, this is a question which I never intend to answer for anybody else, because I never intend to ask it on my own account.

Whether or not a believer will perish because some known duty or scriptural ordinance is neglected, is a question which only selfishness would raise. Are we only to do that which will procure our progress, or secure our salvation? Are we so grossly selfish as that? Does a loving child say, "If I refuse to do my father's will, shall I not still be my father's child? Shall I not still be fed and clothed by him?" Only an evil child would talk thus. The true son inquires, "What would my father have me do? I will do it cheerfully for his sake. What doth my father forbid? for what he forbids shall be hateful to me." Rise above all questions concerning essential and non-essential, and learn to obey in all things; if it be only tying a scarlet thread in the window, or washing in water, do as you are bidden, and in nothing rebel against the Word of the Lord.

Remember, too, that this small matter of obedience, as some call it, had *an important symbolical signification.* I am not sure that the spies meant it by that the scarlet thread should be the same to Rahab as the blood on the lintel and on the two side posts had been to Israel in Egypt, but it does strike me as being very probable. Those two men were so acquainted with the Passover, and the sprinkling of the blood, and the consequent preservation of all in the house, that it was very natural that they should give Rahab a sign akin to the token which God had ordained for his people Israel when his angel passed them by in the day of doom. Therefore, trifling as the color of the cord might seem, it had a deep significance; and even so commands of God, which are little in themselves, are great in symbolic teaching.

This woman's obedience also arose out of real faith, and was the exponent of that faith; for, when she tied the scarlet line in the window, she expressed her confidence in the fact that Jericho would be destroyed, and that she would be saved because she had received a promise to that effect. She would not have hidden the spies if she had not believed in their God; and after having done so, if her faith had failed her, she would not have complied with the covenant requirement to hang the scarlet line in the window. Beloved, obey in faith. The obedience of the slave is worth little; the obedience of the child is precious, for it is the fruit of love. That keeping of God's commands which comes of slavish fear lacks the very heart and bowels of obedience, for love is absent; but, as God's dear children, resting alone in Jesus, confiding in your Father's promise, feel that *because you believe you must obey,* not because you dread hell, or expect to win heaven through any works of your own, but because you have believed in Jesus to the salvation of your soul, and therefore, it is your joy to do His bidding.

Now, secondly, I see here AN APPROPRIATED COVENANT.

These men had made a covenant with her that she should have her life spared, and the lives of her family, if she concealed their secret, and if she tied a scarlet line in the window. As she tied up that line she did, as it were, say, "I claim the covenant that you have made with me." Beloved, let us speak about this for a moment, for we want more and more to be able to appropriate covenant blessings. How do we appropriate Jesus? *By simple faith*. Faith is the hand which touches the head of the great sacrifice, and lays sin upon it, that sin may no longer lie upon the sinner. Faith grasps Jesus as the Bread of life, and makes that Bread to be our own, that we may feed upon it, and may live forever. Thus the grand thing for appropriating Christ is to obtain faith, and to gain more and more faith. Do you remember when first of all you tied a scarlet line in your window, and said, "Christ is mine"? I do remember the very hour and the precise spot, but many cannot tell the moment or the occasion, nor need they agitate themselves about it if they still continue to tie that line in its place. Still, you do remember that there was such a time when you could say, "Jesus is mine." You apprehended Christ because he had apprehended you. If such an hour as that has never come to you, may it come even now! Jesus Christ can save you, but He must be appropriated, or He will be no Savior to you. Remember that God the Holy Ghost Himself, though He is the Author of faith, cannot believe for you; you must believe personally for yourself. Certain persons talk very much of repentance as the gift of the Holy Spirit, and their witness would be true if they would not exaggerate it so as to leave the impression on men's minds that the Holy Ghost repents, and that the sinner has little or nothing to do with it, for that is not true, since it is clear that the Holy Spirit has nothing to repent of, that repentance is an act of the repenting sinner's own soul, and faith a personal exercise of the heart, "for with the heart man believeth unto righteousness."

Faith is the first and grandest way of tying the scarlet line in the window, but let your faith follow on in *the use of the ordinances and means of grace*, for these assist her in laying hold upon Jesus. I have often found it most blessed to sit at the communion table, and feel, while I ate the bread and drank the wine, that faith was in active exercise, so that I said to myself, "Yes, as certainly as this bread is put into my mouth, and goes into my bodily system, so as to become a part of myself, so that nobody can ever take it away, even so I have by faith believed on and received into my soul the incarnate God, and in that way he has become mine, so that none can separate him from me, or me from him." The ordinance itself will not give you Christ, but often does the symbol blessedly enable the soul to realize Jesus, and contemplate him so as to partake of him. In that draft of wine, so typical of his blood, how often has our soul said, "I rest entirely upon the Redeemer's bloody sacrifice. His substitutionary pangs, griefs, and merits are all my trust before God, and I receive them as my sole reliance for the remission of sin, and take them into my very self, just as I drink of this cup, and thereby the juice of the vine courses through my veins."

Let *your whole life* be a course of action correspondent to the belief that Christ is yours. I am afraid many believers live as though Jesus Christ did not belong to them at all, nor yet the blessings of the covenant. Do you think that we should be so desponding when we have losses in business if we really believed that all things are ours, and if we had tied the scarlet line in the window, and appropriated all things as ours in Christ? Do you think we should be so soon fluttered, and made to doubt whether we are saved or not, in times of temptation, if our faith took a firm grip of Christ, and tied the scarlet line in the window fast and firm, by claiming the covenant of grace as ours? Beloved, some of you have only appropriated a part of Christ. You believe you are pardoned, but you scarcely know that you are justified. You are justified and covered with his righteousness, but you have not laid hold upon the sanctification which Jesus gives you. You have a measure of grace, but you have not yet believed that Christ can sanctify you wholly, spirit, soul, and body. We are stinted and stunted, lean and lethargic, because of our failure to grasp with holy confidence the infinite treasure which is stored up in our all-sufficient Lord. He is ours, and all things are ours in him.

Here, let me also say, *let us do this by displaying a corresponding restfulness*. After Rahab had tied the line in her window, we do not read that she did anything else, except bring her father, and her mother, and her brethren under her roof. She did not make preparations to defend the house against the siege; there is no notification that she appealed to the king to have a special guard to protect that part of the wall. I do not believe that she had a solitary fear, or a moment's terror; the scarlet line was in the window, and she felt secure: she had appropriated the promise, and she believed it would not be broken. It is a high privilege to dwell peaceably and quietly in the finished work of Christ, and in the sure immutable promise of God, who cannot lie. Why fret ye yourselves, and question ye yourselves, and go about with a thousand anxieties when salvation's work was finished on the accursed tree, and Christ has gone into the glory, and has carried in his perfect work before his Father's face? Why mourn ye, and suspect your safety, when the Lord hath raised us up together, and made us sit together in heavenly places in him? We who have believed do enter into rest; the peace of God is ours; so let us, by our resting, show that we have tied the scarlet line in our window, have claimed the finished work of Christ, and therefore rest henceforth from our own works as God did from his.

Thirdly, I see here AN OPEN DECLARATION.

Rahab tied the scarlet line, not in some secret part of the house, but *in the window*. It was her public declaration of faith. I do not say that everybody understood what she meant by that; only those understood it who were in the secret with her, and that sufficed. She hung out the red signal from the window, where it could be seen by those who needed to see it. It was not that she was ostentatious, and wished to attract attention; but she was bound to make a public sign, and she did it. Now, some of you believe in my Lord Jesus, and yet you have never united with his people. You are resting in him, but you are mightily afraid that anybody should know it. Be not ashamed of Jesus! The wonder is that he is not ashamed of you. If he was not ashamed to take upon him your nature, and die for you, you need never blush to own his name. Come forward, ye trembling ones, tie the scarlet line in your window, and say, "We are his, and we confess it."

Let it be *a scarlet line* that you tie in the window, however, namely an avowal of true faith in his precious blood, a declaration of confidence in atonement by blood; for there are some who profess a sort of faith, but it is not a faith in the substitution of Christ. It is unfashionable, nowadays, to believe in the old doctrine of atonement. Modern "culture" has expunged it, or altered it in such a way that no real atonement is left. There are many who are too advanced to avow the old-fashioned Gospel; but, as for us, we tie forever the scarlet line in our window, and stand by the truth once delivered to the saints. Our declaration of faith is that we believe in the real and literal substitution of Christ, who died, "the Just for the unjust, that he might bring us to God." In the midst of a thousand new gospels, none of them worth the breath that utters them, we hold to that ancient Gospel of the prophet Isaiah, "The chastisement of our peace was upon him; and with his stripes we are healed." Beloved believer, if the doctrine of the sacrifice of Jesus Christ, and his substitutionary atonement, be indeed your hope, avow it; avow it boldly, and let there be no mistake about it in these evil times; tie the scarlet line in your window, and if nobody else will see it, your brethren will mark it, and be encouraged. If nobody else will be pleased with it, your God will smile upon you, and you will be a sweet savor unto him.

Every Christian ought to make his faith in the precious blood visible in many ways. It ought to be manifest in our common conversation; if we are resting in the blood of Jesus, we ought not to be able to talk a quarter of an hour without thoughtful persons perceiving that we are indeed followers of Jesus. I have heard of a man who was so entertaining and instructive in his conversation that it was said that you could not stand under an archway for five minutes with him, to get out of a shower of rain, without learning something from him. Every Christian man ought to be of this sort, in a higher style, so that you cannot be with him many minutes without perceiving him to be a man of God. Of course, in the Church of Christ, the Christian man ought to hang a scarlet line out of his door at once, and let his fellow-worshipers see that he is decided and resolute for the Lord his God; but he ought to do the same in his business. Customers should soon see that in your shop the common tricks of trade are detested. The scarlet line is over this door. In the house, the mistress in the management of her servants, the master as a husband and as a father should be known to be better than others. There is a certain sect of people called "the peculiar people"; I wish we were all peculiar people in this respect, that the blood mark set us apart as not our own, but bought with a price. The Lord grant that it may be so with us!

The last point is this. Here was a DEDICATED HOUSE — a house with a scarlet line in its window.

Coming here, the other afternoon, and walking down one of the back streets, I amused myself by observing how many houses were insured. I noticed the marks of the different Insurance Companies. There was *the sun* on one, with his bright face looking down upon us, as much as to say, "There shall be no loss here." *The globe, the star, the*

Phoenix, all were there as seals of safety. Now, there was only one house in Jericho that was insured, and that had for its symbol and mark of insurance a scarlet line tied in the window. What a mercy it is when houses are insured by the grace of God, and dedicated to the Lord—the very houses, and much more the inhabitants of those houses. How can you dedicate a house? I was reading, the other day, that, in Cromwell's time, you could go down to Cheapside, at a certain hour in the morning, and you would see the blinds down at every house and hear the families singing, all the way along, "for," says an old divine, "in those days, a drawn blind was the scarlet line in the window." People knew, as they passed along, that there was an altar erected to God in that house. I am afraid that there are a great many streets in our towns and cities which you might traverse at any hour of the day, and not discover a solitary sign of *family prayer* going on. The practice has gone out of fashion even among many who profess to be the people of God, and farewell to any progress in godliness till we bring it back again.

I believe that, when the house and the church pull together, things are right; but when religion is made to be a thing of the church, and not of the house, when the priest is looked to instead of the father, when men cease to be priests in their own houses, then the very sinews of vital godliness have been cut. If I had to give up all week-day services, and shut up every place of worship in Christendom from Sunday to Sunday, I would prefer to do that rather than lose the morning and evening gatherings of devout households worshiping God. How much Scotland owes to her family devotions! You need not that I remind you of "The Cotter's Saturday Night." It is the very glory of that country that they do there worship God in their houses. "There is much formality about it," cries one. Well, was there ever anything good which did not degenerate here and there? But I have witnessed, full many a time, the hearty devotion of morning and evening prayer in the North. I wonder how many houses represented by you come up to Matthew Henry's third standard. He says, "Those who pray, do well." You get up to that, I hope. "Those that read the Scriptures and pray, do better. Those that read the Scriptures, and pray, and sing, do best of all." I think so. This is the scarlet line with the threefold cord to it, and I would that every house hung out that scarlet line as meaning, "This house belongs to King Jesus. The devil need not trouble himself to come here, for the strong man armed keeps his goods in peace."

The beauty of it was that *all inside Rahab's house were saved.* "Come in, dear mother," said she. Who among us could bear the thought of our mother being lost? It breaks our hearts to think of such a thing. My mother lost! Oh, no, that must not be! And your father lost! Oh, have you an unconverted father? I beseech you, give no slumber to your eyelids till you have done all you can to set before him the way of peace, and have pleaded for him before God with sighs and tears. And then she said, "Come in, dear brothers and sisters." I delight in Rahab for loving her household. If you have brothers and sisters who are not yet under the scarlet line, pray to God to bring them in, that all your house may be dedicated to the Most High, and, without exception, all may dwell beneath the blessed blood-red token which infallibly preserves all who are sheltered beneath it.

I leave this point to notice that there are other things besides family prayer which should be like the scarlet line in the house. For instance, there should be, in every Christian house, a scarlet line put up in *the selecting of the company that is kept.* The Christian should carefully *select his friends and associates.* He should say, "He that telleth lies shall not tarry in my sight." As for the drunkard and the swearer, and those who use unchaste language, let them be what they may, they shall not visit within our doors, we will not tolerate them. If we are masters of our household, we try to find our children friends whom we should like to be their companions in eternity. Some parents introduce their children to young men and young women who happen to be "very respectable," as they say, but who are worldly and ungodly, and thus they do much to ruin them. It should not be so. Hang the scarlet line over the door, and if they do not love that scarlet line, religious conversation will before long make the place too hot for them. If you talk much of Jesus, the frivolous will consider that they have notice to quit.

A Christian man's house should have a scarlet line over *its reading.* When there are thousands of good and interesting books to be read, it seems a pity that Christian people should give their time to reading which cannot profit them. Let the asses have their thistles, I never grudge them; and so I will not say that worldlings should not read such books; they suit them, let them have them. I have never murmured at a farmer when I have seen him going along with his great mash of all manner of garbage to give to his hogs; so long as he did not give me a basin of it for dinner. I was satisfied to let the swine have their food; and there are a great many romances and a vast mass of literature which it is vain to deny to ungodly people, for it is after their nature; but as for us, let us have none of it.

So let it be with *all amusements*. There are some amusements that we cannot say are absolutely bad in themselves, but they lead to evil. They go up to the edge of the precipice, and there are many who only need to get so far and they are sure to fall over. Besides, they make the Christian so like the worldling that nobody could tell which is which. Now, tie the scarlet line up. I would do so even as to what *pictures* I would hang up in my house. If you have a bad picture, no matter how good a work of art it is, burn it; and if you have a bad book, no matter how much it may be worth, do not sell it for somebody else to read, tear it in pieces.

Let the Christian hang up the scarlet line, and make certain that nobody shall be debauched in mind or body by anything that he tolerates in his house. I may seem to be too severe; but if my Master were to speak out of heaven, he would not rebuke that as a sin on my part; far rather would he say that we need to be much more precise and decided about evil things.

Well, you shall do what you please, you have your own liberty; but, "as for me and my house, we will serve the Lord," and the blood-red line shall be in my window. My father's father, do I not remember how, when I was a child, I used to hear his prayers for my father and for me? Well do I remember my father's conversion in answer to my grandfather's prayers. And my father, can I ever forget how he wrestled for us at the mercy-seat; and God forbid it should happen that in my son's house, in years to come, there should be no altar to my God! I would sooner be without a tent for myself than without an altar for the Lord. Wherever we are, we must hang up the scarlet line. We cannot expect a blessing if we do not. Of course, I am not speaking to those who are not fathers or heads of households. If they are servants, they cannot help what is done in the house. If they are underlings who have not the power, they cannot arrange as they would; but I am speaking to those who fear the Lord, and can do it. Do, beloved, dedicate your house to God from the garret to the cellar. Let there be nothing about the house but what shall be so ordered that, if your Lord should come, you could open your door, and say, "Come and welcome, Master, there is nothing here that thy servant desires to conceal."

Believe in Jesus, O ye who know him not; and ye who know him, practice what you know; and God bless you!

6

MANOAH'S WIFE

Her Excellent Argument

> *"And Manoah said unto his wife, We shall surely die, because we have seen God. But his wife said unto him, If the Lord were pleased to kill us, he would not have received a burnt offering and a meat offering at our hands, neither would He have showed us all these things, nor would us at this time have told us such things as these"* (Judg. 13:22, 23).

THE first remark arising out the story of Manoah and his wife is this — that *oftentimes we pray for blessings which will make us tremble when we receive them.* Manoah had asked that he might see the angel, and he saw him: in answer to his request the wonderful One condescended to reveal himself a second time, but the consequence was that the good man was filled with astonishment and dismay, and turning to his wife, he exclaimed, "We shall surely die, because we have seen God." Brethren, do we always know what we are asking for when we pray? We are imploring an undoubted blessing, and yet if we knew the way in which such blessing must necessarily come, we should, perhaps, hesitate before we pressed our suit. You have been entreating very much for growth in holiness. Do you know, brother, that in almost every case that means increased affliction? for we do not make much progress in the divine life except when the Lord is pleased to try us in the furnace and purge us with many fires. Do you desire the mercy on that condition? Are you willing to take it as God pleases to send it, and to say, "Lord, if spiritual growth implies trial, if it signifies a long sickness of body, if it means deep depression of soul, if it entails the loss of property, if it involves the taking away of my dearest friends, yet I make no reserve, but include in the prayer all that is needful to the good end. When I say, sanctify me wholly, spirit, soul, and body, I leave the process to thy discretion.

Suppose you really knew all that it would bring upon you, would you not pray, at any rate, with more solemn tones? I hope you would not hesitate, but, counting all the cost, would still desire to be delivered from sin; but, at any rate, you would put up your petition with deliberation, weighing every syllable, and then when the answer came you would not be so astonished at its peculiar form. Often and often the blessing which we used so eagerly to *im*plore is the occasion of the suffering which we *de*plore. We do not know God's methods.

This is the Lord's way of answering prayer for faith and grace. He comes with rods of chastisement, and makes us smart for our follies, for thus alone can he deliver our childish spirits from them. He comes with sharp plowshares and tears up the soil, for thus only can we be made to yield him a harvest. He comes with hot irons and burns us to the heart; and when we inquire, "Why all this?" the answer comes to us, "This is what you asked for, this is the way in which the Lord answers your requests." Perhaps, at this moment, the fainting feeling that some you are now experiencing, which makes you fear that you will surely die, may be accounted for by your own prayers. I should like you to look at your present sorrows in that light, and say, "After all, I can see that now My God has given to me exactly what I sought at his hands. I asked to see the angel, and I have seen him, and now it is that my spirit is cast down within me."

A second remark is this—*Very frequently deep prostration of spirit is the forerunner of some remarkable blessing.* It was to Manoah and to his wife the highest conceivable joy of life, the climax of their ambition, that they should be the parents of a son by whom the Lord should begin to deliver Israel. Joy filled them—inexpressible joy—at the thought of it; but, at the time when the good news was first communicated, Manoah, at least, was made so heavy in spirit that he said, "We shall surely die, for we have seen an angel of the Lord." Take it as a general rule that dull skies foretell a shower of mercy. Expect sweet favor when you experience sharp affliction. Do you not remember, concerning the apostles, that they feared as they entered into the cloud on Mount Tabor? And yet it was in that cloud that they saw their Master transfigured; and you and I have had many a fear about the cloud we were entering, although we were therein to see more of Christ and his glory than we had ever beheld before. The cloud which you fear makes the external wall of that secret chamber wherein the Lord reveals himself.

Before thou canst carry Samson in thy arms, Manoah, thou must be made to say, "We shall surely die." Before the minister shall preach the word to thousands, he must be emptied and made to tremble under a sense of inability. Before the Sunday-school teacher shall bring her girls to Christ, she shall be led to see how weak and insufficient she is. I do believe that whenever the Lord is about to use us in his household, he takes us like a dish and wipes us right out and sets us on the shelf, and then afterwards he takes us down and puts thereon his own heavenly meat, with which to fill the souls of others. There must as a rule be an emptying, a turning upside down, and a putting on one side, before the very greatest blessing comes. Manoah felt that he must die, and yet die he could not, for he was to be the father of Samson, the deliverer of Israel and the terror of Philistia.

Let me offer a third remark, which is this—*great faith is in many instances subject to fits.* What great faith Manoah had! His wife was barren, yet when she was told by the angel that she should bear a child, he believed it, although no heavenly messenger had come to himself personally—so believed it that he did not want to see the man of God a second time to be told that it would be so, but only to be informed how to bring up the child: that was all. "Well," says old Bishop Hall, "might he be the father of strong Samson, that had such a strong faith." He had a strong faith indeed, and yet here he is saying in alarm, "We shall surely die, because we have seen God." Do not judge a man by any solitary word or act, for if you do you will surely mistake him. Cowards are occasionally brave, and the bravest men are sometimes cowards; and there are men who would be worse cowards practically if they were a little less cowardly than they are. A man may be too much a coward to confess that he is timid. Trembling Manoah was so outspoken, honest, and sincere that he expressed his feelings, which a more politic person might have concealed. Though fully believing what had been spoken from God, yet at the same time this doubt was on him, as the result of his belief in tradition: "We shall surely die, because we have seen God."

Once again, another remark is that *it is a great mercy to have a Christian companion to go to for counsel and comfort whenever your soul is depressed.* Manoah had married a capital wife. She was the better one of the two in sound judgment. She was the weaker vessel by nature, but she was the stronger believer, and probably that was why the angel was sent to her, for the angels are best pleased to speak with those who have faith, and if they have the pick of their company, and the wife has more faith than the husband, they will visit the wife sooner than her spouse, for they love to take God's messages to those who will receive them with confidence. She was full of faith, evidently, and so when her husband tremblingly said, "We shall surely die," she did not believe in such a mistrustful inference. Moreover, though they say that women cannot reason, yet here was a woman whose arguments were logical and overwhelming. Certain it is that women's perceptions are generally far clearer than men's reasonings; they look at once into a truth, while we are hunting for our spectacles. Their instincts are generally as safe as our reasonings, and therefore when they have in addition a clear logical mind they make the wisest of counselors.

Well, Manoah's wife not only had clear perceptions, but she had capital reasoning faculties. She argued, according to the language of the text, that it was not possible that God should kill them after what they had seen and heard. Oh that every man had such a prudent, gracious wife as Manoah had! Oh that whenever a man is cast down a Christian brother or sister stands ready to cheer him with some reminder of the Lord's past goodness, or with some gracious promise from the divine word! It may happen to be the husband who cheers the wife, and in such a case it is equally beautiful. We have known a Christian sister to be very nervous and very often depressed and troubled: what a mercy to her to have a Christian husband whose strength of faith can encourage her to smile away her griefs, by resting in the everlasting faithfulness and goodness of the Lord.

God the Holy Spirit shall help us, we will take up the argument of Manoah's wife, and see whether it will not also comfort our hearts. She had three strings to her bow, good woman. One was—The Lord does not mean to kill us, because he has accepted our sacrifices. The second was—he does not mean to kill us, or else he would not, as at this time, have told us such things as these. So the three strings to her bow were *accepted sacrifices, gracious revelations*, and *precious promises*. Let us dwell upon each of them.

And, first, ACCEPTED SACRIFICES. I will suppose that I am addressing a brother who is sadly tried, and terribly cast down, and who therefore has begun to lament—

The Lord has forsaken me quite;
My God will be gracious no more.

Brother, is that possible? Has not God of old accepted on you behalf the
offering of his Son Jesus Christ? You have believed in Jesus, dear friend.
You do not believe in him now. Lay your hand on your heart, and put
the question solemnly to yourself, "Dost thou believe on the Son of God?"
You are able to say, "Yes, Lord, notwithstanding all my unhappiness, I
do believe in thee, and rest the stress and weight of my soul's interests
on thy power to save." Well, then, you have God's own word, recorded
in his own infallible Book, assuring you that Jesus Christ was accepted
of God on your behalf, for He laid down his life for as many as believe
in him, that they might never perish. He stood as their surety, and suffered as their substitute, is it possible that this should be unavailing, and
that after all they may be cast away? The argument of Manoah's wife was
just this—"Did we not put the kid on the rock, and as we put it there
was it not consumed? It was consumed instead of us; we shall not die,
for the victim has been consumed. The fire will not burn us: it has spent
itself upon the sacrifice. Did you not see it go up in smoke, and see the
angel ascend with it? The fire is gone; it cannot fall on us to destroy us."
    This being interpreted into the Gospel is just this—Have we not
seen the Lord Jesus Christ fastened to the cross? Have we not beheld
him in agonies extreme? Has not the fire of God consumed him? Have
we not seen him rising, as it were, from that sacred fire in the resurrection
and the ascension, to go into the glory? Because the fire of Jehovah's wrath
had spent itself on him we shall not die. He has died instead of us. It cannot be that the Lord has made him suffer, the Just for the unjust, and
now will make the believer suffer too. It cannot be that Christ loved His
Church, and gave himself for it, and that now the Church must perish
also. It cannot be that the Lord has laid on him the iniquity of us all,
and now will lay our iniquity on us too. It were not consistent with justice. It would make the vicarious sacrifice of Christ to be a nullity, a superfluity of cruelty which achieved nothing. The atonement cannot be
made of none effect, the very supposition would be blasphemy. O,
look, my soul, look to the redeemer's cross, and as thou seest how God
accepts Christ, be thou filled with content. Hear how the "It is finished"
of Jesus on earth is echoed from the throne of God himself, as he raises
up His Son from the dead, and bestows glory upon him: hear this, I say,

and as thou hearest, attend to the power of this argument—If the Lord had been pleased to kill us, he would not have accepted his Son for us. If he meant *us* to die, would he have put him to death too? How can it be? The sacrifice of Jesus must effectually prevent the destruction of those for whom he offered up himself as a sacrifice. Jesus dying for sinners, and yet the sinners denied mercy! Inconceivable and impossible! My soul, whatever thy inward feelings and the tumult of thy thoughts, the accepted sacrifice shows that God is not pleased to kill thee.

But, if you notice, in the case of Manoah, they had offered a burnt sacrifice and a meat offering too. Well, now, in addition to the great, grand sacrifice of Christ, which is our trust, we, dear brothers and sisters, have offered other sacrifices to God, and in consequence of his acceptance of such sacrifice we cannot imagine that he intends to destroy us.

First, let me conduct your thoughts back to the offering of *prayer* which you have presented. I will speak for myself. I recall now, running over my diary mentally, full many an instance in which I have sought the Lord in prayer and he has most graciously heard me. I am as sure that my requests have been heard as ever Manoah could have been sure that his sacrifice was consumed upon the rock. May I not infer from this that the Lord does not mean to destroy you? You know that it had been so with you, dear brother. You are down in the dumps today, you are beginning to raise many questions about divine love; but there have been times—you know there have—when you have sought the Lord and he has heard you. You can say, "This poor man cried, and the Lord heard him, and delivered him from all his fears." Perhaps you have not jotted down the fact in a book, but your memory holds the indelible record. Your soul has made her personal boast in the Lord concerning his fidelity to his promise in helping his people in the hour of need, for you have happily proved it in your own case. Now, brother, if the Lord had been pleased to kill you, would he have heard your prayers? If he had meant to cast you out after all, would he have heard you so many times? If he had sought a quarrel against you he might have had cause for that quarrel many years ago, and have said to you, "When you make many prayers I will not hear." But since he has listened to your cries and tears, and many a time answered your petitions, he cannot intend to kill you.

Again, you brought to him, years ago, not only your prayers but *yourself*. You gave yourself over to Christ, body, soul, spirit, all your goods,

all your hours, all your talents, every faculty, and every possible ac-
quirement, and you said, "Lord, I am not my own, but I am bought with
a price." Now, at that time did not the Lord accept you? You have at this
very moment a lively recollection of the sweet sense of acceptance
you had at that time. Though you are at this time sorely troubled, yet
you would not wish to withdraw from the consecration which you then
made, but on the contrary you declare,

> High heaven, that heard the solemn vow,
> That vow renewed shall daily hear,
> Till, in life's latest hour, I bow,
> And bless in death a bond so dear.

Now, would the Lord have accepted the offering of yourself to him
if he meant to destroy you? Would he have let you say, "I am thy servant
and the son of thy handmaid: thou hast loosed my bond?" Would he have
permitted you to declare as you can boldly assert tonight, "I bear in my
body the marks of the Lord Jesus," delighting to remember the time of
your baptism into him, whereby your body washed with his pure body,
was declared to be the Lord's forever? Would he enable you to feel a joy
in the very mark of your consecration, as well as in the consecration itself, if he meant to slay you? Oh, surely not! He does not let a man give
himself up to him and then cast him away. That cannot be.

Some of us, dear friends, can recollect how, growing out of this last
sacrifice, there have been others. The Lord has accepted our offerings
at other times too, for our works, faith, and labors of love have been owned
of his Spirit. There are some of you, I am leased to remember, whom
God has blest to the conversion of little children whom you brought to
the Savior, and there are others on earth whom you can look upon with
great joy because God was pleased to make you the instrument of their
conviction and their after conversion. Some of you, I perceive, are
ministers of the Gospel, others of you preach at the corners of the
streets, and there have been times in your lives—I am sure that you wish
they were ten times as many—in which God has been pleased to succeed your efforts, so that hearts have yielded to the sway of Jesus. Now,
you do not put any trust in those things, nor do you claim any merit for
having served your Master, but still I think they may be thrown in as a
matter of consolation, and you may say, If the Lord had meant to destroy me, would he have enabled me to preach his Gospel? Would he

have helped me to weep over men's souls? Would he have enabled me to gather those dear children like lambs to his bosom? Would he have granted me my longing desire to bear fruit in his vineyard, if he did not mean to bless me.?

Now, the second argument was that they had received GRACIOUS REVELATIONS. "If the Lord were pleased to kill us, he would not have showed us all these things." Now, what has the Lord shown you, my dear brother? I will mention one or two things.

First, the Lord has shown you, perhaps years ago, or possibly at this moment he is showing you for the first time—*your sin*. What a sight that was when we first had it. Some of you never saw your sins, but yours sins are there all the same. In an old house, perhaps, there is a cellar into which nobody goes, and no light ever comes in. You live in the house comfortably enough, not knowing what is there; but one day you take a candle, and go down the steps, and open that moldy door, and when it is opened, dear me! What a damp, pestilential smell! How foul the floor is! All sorts of living creatures hop away from under your feet. There are growths on the very walls—a heap of roots in the corner, sending out those long yellow growths which look like the fingers of death. And there is a spider, and there are a hundred like him, of such a size as cannot be grown, except in such horrible places. You get out as quickly as ever you can. You do not like the look of it. Now, the candle did not make that cellar bad; the candle did not make it filthy. No, the candle only showed what there was. And when you get in the carpenter to take down that shutter which you could not open anyhow, for it had not been opened for years, and when the daylight comes in, it seems more horrible than it did by candlelight, and you wonder, indeed, however you did go across it with all those dreadful things all around you and you cannot be satisfied to live upstairs now till that cellar downstairs has been perfectly cleansed. That is just like our heart; it is full of sin, but we do not know it. It is a den of unclean birds, a menagerie of everything that is fearful, and fierce, and furious—a little hell stocked with devils. Such is our nature; such is our heart. Now, the Lord showed me mine years ago, as he did some of you and the result of sight of one's heart is horrible. Well does Dr. Young say, "God spares all eyes but his own that fearful sight, a naked human heart." Nobody ever did see all his heart as it really is. You have only seen a part, but when seen, it is so horrible that it is enough to drive a man out of his senses to see the evil of his nature.

Now, let us gather some honey out of this dead lion. Brother, if the Lord had meant to destroy us, he would not have shown us our sin, because we were happy enough previously, were we not? In our own poor way we were content enough, and if he did not mean to pardon us, it was not like the Lord to show us our sin, and so to torment us before our time, unless he meant to take it away. We were swine, but we were satisfied enough with the husks we ate; and why not let us remain swine? What was the good of letting us see our filthiness if he did not purpose to take it away? It never can be possible that God sets himself studiously to torture the human mind by making it conscious of its evil, if he never intends to supply a remedy. Oh no! A deep sense of sin will not save you, but it is a pledge that there is something begun in your soul which may lead to salvation; for that deep sense of sin does as good as say, "The Lord is laying bare the disease that he may cure it. He is letting you see the foulness of that underground cellar of your corruption, because he means to cleanse it for you."

But He has shown us more than this, for he has made us see *the hollowness and emptiness of the world*. There are some here present, who at one time, were very gratified with the pleasures and amusements of the world. The theater was a great delight to them. The ballroom afforded them supreme satisfaction. To be able to dress just after their own fancy, and to spend money on their own whims, were the very acme of delight; but there came a time when across all these the soul perceived a mysterious handwriting, which being interpreted ran thus: "Vanity of vanities; all is vanity." These very people went to the same amusements, but they seemed so dull and stupid that they came away saying, "We do not care a bit for them. The joys are all gone. What seemed gold turns out to be gilt; and what we thought marble was only white paint. The varnish is cracked, the tinsel is faded, the coloring has vanished. Mirth laughs like an idiot, and pleasure grins like madness."

We have heard the words, "Vanity of vanities; all is vanity," sounding in our hearts; and now do you think that, if the Lord had meant to kill us, he would have taught us this? Why, no; he would have said, "Let them alone, they are given unto idols. They are only going to have one world in which they can rejoice; let them enjoy it." He would have let the swine go on with their husks if he had not meant to turn them into his children, and bring them to his own bosom.

But he has taught us something better than this—namely, *the preciousness of Christ*. Unless we are awfully deceived—self-deceived, I mean—we have known what it is to lose the burden of our sin at the foot of the cross. We have known what it is to see the suitability and all-sufficiency of the merit of our dear Redeemer, and we have rejoiced in him with joy unspeakable and full of glory. If he had meant to destroy us he would not have shown us Christ.

Sometimes also we have strong desires after *God!* What pinings after communion with him have we felt! What longings to be delivered from sin! What yearnings to be perfect! What aspirations to be with him in heaven, and what desires to be like him while we are here! Now these longings, cravings, desirings, yearnings, do you think the Lord would have put them into our hearts if he had meant to destroy us? What would be the good of it? Would it not be tormenting us as Tantalus was tormented? Would it not, indeed, be a superfluity of cruelty thus to make us wish for what we could never have, and pine after what we should never gain? O beloved, let us be comforted about these things. If he had meant to kill us, he would not have shown us such things as these.

I shall have no time to dwell upon the last source of comfort, which is what the Lord has spoken to us—MANY PRECIOUS PROMISES. "Nor would he have told us such things as these." At almost any time when a child of God is depressed, if he goes to the Word of God and to prayer, and looks up, he will generally get a hold of some promise or other. I know I generally do. I could not tell you, dear brother, tonight, what promise would suit your case, but the Lord always knows how to apply the right word at the right time; and when a promise is applied with great power to the soul, and you are enabled to plead it at the mercy-seat, you may say, "If the Lord had meant to kill us, he would not have made us such a promise as this." I have a promise that hangs up before my eyes whenever I wake every morning, and it has continued in its place for years. It is a stay to my soul. It is this: "I will not fail thee nor forsake thee." Difficulties arise, funds run short, sickness comes; but somehow or other my text always seems to flow like a fountain—"I will not fail thee nor forsake thee." If the Lord had meant to kill us, he would not have said that to us.

What is your promise, brother? What have you got a hold of? If you have not laid hold of any, and feel as if none belonged to you, yet there are such words as these, "This is a faithful saying and worthy of all acceptation, that Christ Jesus came not the world to save sinners," and you are one. Ah, if he had meant to destroy you, he would not have spoken a text of such a wide character on purpose to include your case. A thousand promises go down to the lowest deep into which a heart can ever descend, and if the Lord had meant to destroy a soul in the deeps, he would not have sent a gospel promise down even to that extreme.

I should like to say these two or three words to you who are unconverted, but who are troubled in your souls. You think that God means to destroy you. Now, dear friend, I take it that if the Lord had meant to kill you, He would not have sent the Gospel to you. If there had been a purpose and a decree to destroy you, He would not have brought you here. Now you are sitting to hear that Jesus has died to save such as you are. You are sitting where you are bidden to trust Him and be saved. If the Lord had meant to slay you I do not think He would haven sent me on such a fruitless errand as to tell you of a Christ who could not save you. Some of you have had your lives spared very remarkably. You have been in accidents on land or on sea—perhaps in battle and shipwreck. You have been raised from a sickbed. If the Lord had meant to destroy you, surely He would have let you die then; but He has spared you, and you are getting on in years; surely it is time that you yielded to His mercy and gave yourself up into the hands of grace. If the Lord had meant to destroy you, surely, He would not have brought you here, for, possibly, I am addressing one who has come here, wondering why. All the time that he has been sitting here he has been saying to himself, "I do not know how I got into this place, but here I am." God means to bless you tonight, I trust, and He will, if you breathe this prayer to heaven, "Father, forgive me! I have sinned against heaven and before thee, but for Christ's sake forgive me! I put my trust in thy Son." You shall find eternal life, rejoicing in the sacrifice which God has accepted. You shall one of these days rejoice in the revelations of His love, and in the promises which He gives you, and say as we say tonight, "If the Lord were pleased to kill us He would not have showed us all these things."

7

DELILAH

Samson Conquered

"And she said, The Philistines be upon thee, Samson. And he awoke out of his sleep, and said, I will go out as at other times before, and shake myself. And he knew not that the Lord was departed from him. But the Philistines took him, and put out his eyes, and brought him down to Gaza, and bound him with fetters of brass; and he did grind in the prison house" (Judg. 16:20, 21).

SAMSON is, in many respects, one of the most remarkable men whose history is recorded in the pages of inspiration. He enjoyed a singular privilege only accorded to one other person in the Old Testament. His birth was foretold to his parents by an angel. Isaac was promised to Abraham and Sarah by angels whom they entertained unawares; but save Isaac, Samson was the only one whose birth was foretold by an angelic messenger before the opening of the Gospel dispensation. Before his birth he was dedicated to God, and set apart as a Nazarite. Now, a Nazarite was a person who was entirely consecrated to God, and in token of his consecration he drank no wine; and allowed his hair to grow, untouched by the razor. Samson, you may therefore understand, was entirely consecrated to God, and when any saw him, they would say, "That man is God's man, a Nazarite, set apart." God endowed Samson with supernatural strength, a strength which never could have been the result of mere muscles and sinews. It was not the fashioning of Samson's body that made him strong; it was not the arm, or the fist with which he smote the Philistines; it was a miracle that dwelt with him, a continued going forth of the omnipotence of God, which made him mightier than thousands of his enemies.

Samson appears very early to have discovered in himself this great strength, for "the Spirit of the Lord began to move him at times in the camp of Dan." He judged Israel for thirty years, and gloriously did he deliver them. What a noble being he must have been! See him, when he steps into the vineyard for a moment from his parents. A lion that has been crouching there springs upon him, but he meets him all unarmed, receives him upon his brawny arms and rends him like a kid. See him afterwards, when his countrymen have bound him and taken him down from the top of the rock, and delivered him up to the thousands of the Philistines. He has scarcely come near them, when, without a weapon, with his own foot, he begins to spurn them; and seeing there the jawbone of an ass, he takes that ignoble weapon, and sweeps away the men that had helmets about their heads and were girded with greaves of brass. Nor did his vigor fail him in his later life, for he died in the very prime of his days. One of his greatest exploits was performed at this very season. He is entrapped in the city of Gaza. He remains there till midnight; so confident is he in his strength that he is in no hurry to depart, and instead of assailing the guard, and making them draw the bolts, he wrenches up the two posts, and takes away the gate, bar and all, and carries his mighty burden for miles to the top of a hill that is before Hebron.

Every way it must have been a great thing to see this man, especially if one had him for a friend. Had one been his foe, the more distant the sight the better, for none could escape from him but those who fled; but to have him for a friend and to stand with him in the day of battle, was to feel that you had an army in a single man, and had in one frame that which would strike thousands with terror.

Samson, however, though he had great physical strength, had but little mental force, and even less spiritual power. His whole life is a scene of miracles and follies. He had but little grace, and was easily overcome by temptation. He is enticed and led astray. Often corrected; still he sins again. At last he falls into the hands of Delilah. She is bribed with an enormous sum, and she endeavors to get from him the secret of his strength. He foolishly toys with the danger, and plays with his own destruction. At last, goaded by her importunity, he lets out the secret which he ought to have confided to no one but himself. The secret of his strength lay in his locks. Not that his hair made him strong; but that his hair was the symbol of his consecration, and was the pledge of

God's favor to him. While his hair was untouched he was a consecrated man; as soon as that was cut away, he was no longer perfectly consecrated, and then his strength departed from him. His hair is cut away; the locks that covered him once are taken from him, and there he stands a shaveling, weak as other men. Now the Philistines begin to oppress him, and his eyes are burned out with hot iron. How are the mighty fallen! How are the great ones taken in the net!

Samson the great hero of Israel, is seen with a shuffling gait walking towards Gaza. A shuffling gait, I said, because he had just received blindness, which was a new thing to him; therefore, he had not as yet learned to walk as well as those who, having been blind for years, at least learn to set their feet firmly upon the earth. With his feet bound together with brazen fetters—an unusual mode of binding a prisoner, but adopted in this case because Samson was supposed to be still so strong, that any other kind of fetter would have been insufficient— you see him walking along in the midst of a small escort towards Gaza. And now he comes to the very city out of which he had walked in all his pride with the gates and bolts upon his shoulders; and the little children come out, the lower orders of the people come round about him, and point at him—"Samson, the great hero, has fallen! let us make sport of him!" What a spectacle! The hot sun is beating upon his bare head, which had once been protected by those luxuriant locks. Look at the escorts who guard him, a mere handful of men, how they would have bled before him in his brighter days; but now a child might overcome him. They take him to a place where an ass is grinding at the mill, and Samson must to the same ignoble work. Why, he must be the sport and jest of every passerby, and of every fool who shall step in to see this great wonder—the destroyer of the Philistines made to toil at the mill. Ah, what a fall was there, my brethren! We might indeed stand and weep over poor blind Samson. That he should have lost his eyes was terrible; that he should have lost his strength was worse; but that he should have lost the favor of God for a while; that he should become the sport of God's enemies, was the worst of all. Over this indeed we might weep.

Now, why have I narrated this story? Why should I direct your attention to Samson? For this reason. *Every child of God is a consecrated man.* His consecration is not typified by any outward symbol; we are not commanded to let our hair grow forever, nor to abstain from meats or drinks. The Christian is a consecrated man, but his consecration is unseen by his fellows, except in the outward deeds which are the result thereof.

And now I want to speak to you as consecrated men, as Nazarites, and I think I shall find a lesson for you in the history of Samson.

First, THE STRENGTH OF THE CONSECRATED MAN. Do you know that the strongest man in all the world is a consecrated man? Even though he may consecrate himself to a wrong object, yet if it be a thorough consecration, he will have strength—strength, for evil, it may be, but still strength. In the old Roman wars with Pyrrhus, you remember an ancient story of self-devotion. There was an oracle which said that victory would attend that army whose leader should give himself up to death. Decius the Roman Consul, knowing this, rushed into the thickest of the battle, that his army might overcome by his dying. The prodigies of valor which he performed are proofs of the power of consecration. The Romans at that time seemed to be every man a hero, because every man was a consecrated man. They went to battle with this thought—"I will conquer or die; the name of Rome is written on my heart; for my country I am prepared to live, or for that to shed my blood." And no enemies could ever stand against them. If a Roman fell there were no wounds in his back, but all in his breast. His face, even in cold death, was like the face of a lion, and when looked upon it was of terrible aspect. They were men consecrated to their country; they were ambitious to make the name of Rome the noblest word in human language; and consequently the Roman became a giant. And to this day let a man get a purpose within him, I care not what his purpose is, and let his whole soul be absorbed by it, and what will he not do? You that are "everything by turns and nothing long," that have nothing to live for, soulless carcasses that walk this earth and waste its air, what can you do? Why nothing. But the man who knows what he is at, and has his mark, speeds to it "like an arrow from a bowshot by an archer strong." Nought can turn him aside from his design. How much more is this true if I limit the description to that which is peculiar to the Christian—consecration to God! Oh! what strength that man has who is dedicated to God! Is there such a one here? I know there is.

Need I tell you of the wonders that have been done by consecrated men? You have read the stories of olden times, when our religion was hunted like a partridge on the mountains. Did you never hear how consecrated men and women endured unheard-of pangs and agonies? Have you not read how they were cast to the lions, how they were sawn in sunder, how they languished in prisons, or met with the swifter death of the sword? Have you not heard how they wandered about in sheeps' skins and goat's skins, destitute, afflicted, tormented, of whom the world was not worthy? Have you not heard how they defied tyrants to their face, how, when they were threatened, they dared most boldly to laugh at all the threats of the foe—how at the stake they clapped their hands in the fire, and sang psalms of triumph, when men, worse than fiends, were jeering at their miseries? How as this? What made women stronger than men, and men stronger than angels? Why this—they were consecrated to God. They felt that every pang which rent their heart was giving glory to God, that all the pains they endured in their bodies were but the marks of the Lord Jesus, whereby they were proven to be wholly dedicated unto him. Nor in this alone has the power of the consecrated ones been proved. Have you never heard how the sanctified ones have done wonders? Read the stories of those who counted not their lives dear to them, that they might honor their Lord and Master by preaching his Word, by telling forth the Gospel in foreign lands. Have you not heard how men have left their kindred and their friends, and all that life held dear—have crossed the stormy sea, and have gone into the lands of the heathen, where men were devouring one another? Have you not known how they have put their foot upon that country, and have seen the ship that conveyed them there fading away in the distance, and yet without a fear have dwelt amongst the wild savages of the woods, have walked into the midst of them, and told them, the simple story of the God that loved and died for man? You must know how those men have conquered, how those, who seemed to be fiercer than lions, have crouched before them, have listened to their words, and have been converted by the majesty of the Gospel which they preached.

What made these men heroes? What enabled them to rend themselves away from all their kith and kin, and banish themselves into the land of the stranger? It was because they were consecrated, thoroughly consecrated to the Lord Jesus Christ. What is there in the world which the consecrated man cannot do? Tempt him; offer him gold and silver; carry him to the mountain top, and show him all the kingdoms of the world, and tell him he shall have all these if he will bow down and worship the god of this world. What saith this consecrated man? "Get thee behind me, Satan; I have more than all this which thou dost offer me; this world is mine, and worlds to come; I despise the temptation; I will not bow before thee." Let men threaten a consecrated man, what does he say? "I fear God, and, therefore, I cannot fear you; if it be right in your sight to obey man rather than God, judge ye; but, as for me, I will serve none but God."

"But," says someone, "can we be consecrated to Christ? I thought that was for ministers only." Oh, no, my brethren; all God's children must be consecrated men. What are you? Are you engaged in business? If you are what you profess to be, your business must be consecrated to God. Perhaps you have no family whatever, and you are engaged in trade, and are saving some considerable sum a year; let me tell you the example of a man thoroughly consecrated to God. There lives in Bristol, (name unknown), a man whose income is large; and what does he do with it? He labors in business continually that this income may come to him, but of it, every farthing every year is expended in the Lord's cause except that which he requires for the necessaries of life. He makes his necessities as few as possible, that he may have the more to give away. He is God's man in his business. I do not exhort you to do the same. You may be in a different position; but a man who has a family, and is in business, should be able to say—"Now, I make so much from my business; my family must be provided for—but I seek not to amass riches. I will make money for God and I will spend it in his cause."

If I have said, "I am Christ's," by his grace I will be Christ's. Brethren, you in business may be as much consecrated to Christ as the minister in his pulpit; you may make your ordinary transactions in life a solemn service of God. Happy the man who is consecrated unto the Lord; where'er he is, he is a consecrated man, and he shall do wonders.

The littleness of Christians of this age results from the littleness of their consecration to Christ. The age of John Owen was the day of great preachers; but let me tell you, that that was the age of great consecration. Those great preachers whose names we remember, were men who counted nothing their own: they were driven out from their benefices, because they could not conform to the Established Church, and they gave up all they had willingly to the Lord. They were hunted from place to place; the disgraceful Five-Mile-Act would not permit them to come within five miles of any market town; they wandered here and there to preach the Gospel to a few poor sheep, being fully given up to their Lord. Those were foul times; but they promised they would walk the road fair or foul, and they did walk it knee-deep in mud; and they would have walked it if it had been knee-deep in blood, too. They became great men; and if we were, as they were, wholly given up to God–if we could say of ourselves, "From the crown of my head to the sole of my foot, there is not a drop of blood that is not wholly God's; all my time, all my talents, everything I have is God's"—if we could say that, we should be strong like Samson, for the *consecrated must be strong.*

Now, in the second place, THE SECRET OF THEIR STRENGTH. What makes the consecrated man strong? Ah! beloved; there is no strength in man of himself. Samson without his God was but a poor fool indeed. The secret of Samson's strength was this—as long as he was consecrated he should be strong; so long as he was thoroughly devoted to his God, and had no object but to serve God, (and that was to be indicated by the growing of his hair) so long, and no longer, would God be with him to help him. And now you see that if you have any strength to serve God, the secret of your strength lies in the same place. What strength have you save in God? Ah! I have heard some men talk as if the strength of free will, of human nature, was sufficient to carry men to heaven. Free will has carried many souls to hell, but never a soul to heaven yet. No strength of nature can suffice to serve the Lord aright. No man can say that Jesus is the Christ but by the Holy Ghost. No man can come to Christ except the Father that hath sent Christ doth draw him. If, then, the first act of Christian life is beyond all human strength, how much more are those higher steps far beyond any one of us? Do we not utter a certain truth when we say in the words of Scripture, "Not that we are sufficient of ourselves to think anything as of ourselves; but our sufficiency is of God." I think everyone who has a really quickened soul will sooner or later be made to feel this. Ay! I question whether a man can be converted a day without finding out his own weakness. It is but a little space before the child finds that he can stand alone so long as God his Father takes him by the arms and teaches him to go, but that if his Father's hand be taken away he has no power to stand, but down he falls at once. See Samson without his God, going out against a thousand men. Would they not laugh at him? and with scarcely time to express is terror, he would flee, or be rent in pieces. Imagine him without his God, locked up in Gaza, the gates fast closed. He goes out into the streets to escape; but how can he clear a passage? He is caught like a wild bull in a net; he may go round and round the walls, but where shall be his deliverance? without his God he is but as other men. The secret of his strength lies in his consecration, and in the strength which is its results. Remember, then, the secret of your strength. Never think that you have any power of your own; rely wholly upon the God of Israel; and remember that the channel through which that strength must come to you must be your entire consecration to God.

In the third place, What is THE PECULIAR DANGER OF A CONSECRATED MAN? His danger is that his locks may be shorn, that is to say, that his consecration may be broken. As long as he is consecrated he is strong; break that, he is weak as water. Now there are a thousand razors with which the devil can shave off the locks of a consecrated man without his knowing it. Samson is sound asleep; so clever is the barber that he even lulls him to sleep as his fingers move across the pate, the fool's pate, which he is making bare. The devil is cleverer far than even the skillful barber; he can shave the believer's locks while he scarcely knows it.

Shall I tell you with what razors he can accomplish this work? Sometimes he takes the sharp *razor of pride,* and when the Christian falls asleep and is not vigilant, he comes with it and begins to run his fingers upon the Christian's locks, and says, "What a fine fellow you are! What wonders you have done! Didn't you rend that lion finely? Wasn't it a great feat to smite those Philistines hip and thigh? Ah! you will be talked of as long as time endures for carrying those gates of Gaza away. You need not be afraid of anybody." And so on goes the razor, lock after lock falling off, and Samson knows it not. He is just thinking within himself, "How brave am I! How great am I!" Thus works the razor of pride—cut, cut, cut away—and he wakes up to find himself bald, and all his strength gone. Have you never had that razor upon your head? I confess I have on mine. Have you never, after you have been able to endure afflictions, heard a voice saying to you, "How patient you were!" After you have cast aside some temptation, and have been able to keep to the unswerving course of integrity, has not Satan said to you, "That is a fine thing you have done; that was bravely done." And all the while you little knew that it was the cunning hand of the evil one taking away your locks with the sharp razor of pride. For mark, pride is a breach of our consecration. As soon as I begin to get proud of what I do, or what I am, what am I proud of? Why, there is in that pride the act of taking away from God his glory. For I promised that God should have all the glory, and is not that part of my consecration? And I am taking it to myself. I have broken my consecration; my locks are gone, and I become weak. Mark this, Christian—God will never give thee strength to glorify thyself with. God will give thee a crown, but not to put on thine own head. As sure as ever a Christian begins to write his feats and his triumphs upon his own escutcheon, and take to himself the glory, God will lay him level with the dust.

Another razor he also uses is *self-sufficiency*. "Ah," saith the devil as he is shaving away your locks. "you have done a very great deal. You see they bound you with green withers, and you snapped them in sunder, they merely smelt the fire and they burst. Then they took new ropes to bind you; ah! you overcame even them; for you snapped the ropes in sunder as if they had been a thread. Then they wove the seven locks of your head, but you walked away with loom and web too, beam and all. You can do anything, don't be afraid; you have strength enough to do anything; you can accomplish any feat you set our will upon." How softly the devil will do all that; how will he be rubbing the poll while the razor is moving softly along and the locks are dropping off, and he is treading them in the dust. "You have done all this, and you can do anything else." Every drop of grace distills from heaven. O my brethren, what have we that we have not received? Let us not imagine that we can create might wherewith to gird ourselves. "All my springs are in *thee*." The moment we begin to think that it is our own arm that has gotten us the victory, it will be all over with us—our locks of strength shall be taken away, and the glory shall depart from us. So, you see, self-sufficiency, as well as pride, may be the razor with which the enemy may shave away our strength.

There is yet another, and a more palpable danger still. When a consecrated man begins to *change his purpose in life and live for himself*— that razor shaves clean indeed. There is a minister; when he first began his ministry he could say, "God is my witness I have but one object, that I may free my skirts from the blood of every one of my hearers, that I may preach the Gospel faithfully and honor my Master." In a little time, tempted by Satan, he changes his tone and talks like this, "I must keep my congregation up. If I preach such hard doctrine, they won't come. Did not one of the newspapers criticize me, and did not some of my people go away from me because of it? I must mind what I am at. I must keep this going. I must look out a little sharper, and prune my speech down. I must adopt a little gentler style, or preach a new-fashioned doctrine; for I must keep my popularity up. What is to become of me if I go down? People will say, 'Up like a rocket, down like the stick'; and then all my enemies laugh." Ah, when once a man begins to care so much as a snap of the finger about the world, it is all over with him. If he can go to his pulpit, and say, "I have got a message to deliver; and whether they will hear or whether they will not hear, I will deliver it as God puts it into my mouth; I will not change the dot of an 'i', or the cross of a 't' for the biggest man that lives, or to bring in the mightiest congregation that ever sat at minister's feet"—that man is mighty. He does not let human judgments move him, and he will move the world.

But let him turn aside, and think about his congregation, and how that shall be kept up; ah Samson! How are thy locks shorn! What canst thy do now? That false Delilah has destroyed thee—thine eyes are put out, thy comfort is taken away, and thy future ministry shall be like the grinding of an ass around the continually revolving mill; thou shalt have no rest or peace ever afterwards. Or let him turn aside another way. Suppose he should say, "I must get preferment, or wealth, I must look well to myself, I must see my next feathered, that must be the object of my life." I am not now speaking of the ministry merely, but of all the consecrated; and as sure as ever we begin to make *self* the primary object of our existence our locks are shorn. "Now," says the Lord, "I gave that man strength, but not to use it for himself. Then I put him into a high position, but not that he might clothe himself about with glory; I put him there that he might look to my cause, to my interests; and if he does not do that first, down he shall go.

And so, if you live in this world, and God prospers you, you get perhaps into some position, and you say, "Here I am; I will look out for myself; I have been serving the church before, but now I will look to myself a little." "Come, come," says human nature, "you must look after your family," (which means, you must look after yourself). Very well, do it, sir, as your main object, and you are a ruined man. "Seek first the kingdom of God and his righteousness, and all these shall be added to you." If you keep your eye single, your whole body shall be full of light. Though you seemed as if you had shut out half the light by having that single eye, yet your body shall be full of light. But begin to have two masters, and two objects to serve, and you shall serve neither; you shall neither prosper for this world, nor for that which is to come. Oh,

Christian, above all things take care of thy consecration. Ever feel that thou art wholly given up to God, and to God alone.

And now, lastly, there is THE CHRISTIAN'S DISGRACE. His locks are cut off. I have seen him, young as I am, and you with gray hairs upon your brows have seen him oftener than I; I have seen him in the ministry. He spake like an angel of God; many there were that regarded him, and did hang upon his lips; he seemed to be sound in doctrine and earnest in manner. I have seen him turn aside; it was but a little thing—some slight deviation from the ancient orthodoxy of his fathers, some slight violation of the law of his church. I have seen him, till he has given up doctrine after doctrine until, at last, the very place wherein he preached has become a byword and a proverb; and the man is pointed out by the gray-headed sire to his child as a man who is to be looked upon with suspicion; who, if he lectures, is to be heard with caution; and if he preaches, is not to be listened to at all. Have you not seen him? What disgrace was there! What a fall! The man who came out in the camps of Dan, and seemed to be moved by the Spirit of the Lord, has become the slave of error. He has gone into the very camps of the enemy, and there he is now, grinding in the mill for the Philistine, whom he ought to have been striking with his arm.

Now these men who have turned aside and broken their consecration vow, are pointed at as a disgrace to themselves and dishonor to the Church. And you who are members of Christ's Church, you have seen men who stood in your ranks as firm soldiers of the cross, and you have noticed them go out, from us, "because they were not of us," or like poor Samson, you have seen them go to their graves with the eyes of their comfort put out, with the feet of their usefulness bound with brazen fetters, and with the strength of their arms entirely departed from them. Now, do any of you wish to be backsliders? Do you wish to betray the holy profession of your religion? My brethren, is there one among you who this day makes a profession of love to Christ, who desires to be an apostate? Is there one of you who desires like Samson to have his eyes put out, and to be made to grind in the mill? Would you, like David, commit a great sin, and go with broken bones to the grave? Would you, like Lot, be drunken, and fall into lust? No, I know what you say, "Lord, let my path be like the eagle's flight; let me fly upwards to the sun, and never stay and never turn aside. Oh, give me grace that I may serve thee like Caleb, with a perfect heart, and that from the beginning even to the end of my days, my course may be as the shining light, which shineth more and more unto the perfect day." Ay, I know what is your desire. How, then, shall it be accomplished? Look well to your consecration; see that it is sincere; see that you mean it, and then look up to the Holy Spirit, after you have looked to your consecration, and beg of him to give you daily grace; for as day-by-day the manna fell, so must you receive daily food from on high. And, remember, it is not by any grace you have in you, but by the grace that is in Christ, and that must be given to you hour by hour, that you are to stand, and having done all, to be crowned at last as a faithful one, who has endured unto the end. I ask your prayers that I may be kept faithful to my Lord; and on the other hand, I will offer my earnest prayers, that you may serve him while he lends you breath, that when your voice is lost in death, you may throughout a never-ending immortality, praise him in louder and sweeter strains.

And as for you that have not given yourselves to God, and you are not consecrated to him, I can only speak to you as to Philistines, and warn you, that the day shall come when Israel shall be avenged upon the Philistines. You may be one day assembled upon the roof of your plea-sures, enjoying yourselves in health and strength; but there is a Samson — called Death, who shall pull down the pillars of your tabernacle, and you must fall and be destroyed — and great shall be the ruin. May God give you grace that you may be consecrated to Christ; so that living or dying, you may rejoice in him, and may share with him the glory of his Father.

8

RUTH

Deciding for God

"And Ruth said, Intreat me not to leave thee, or to return from following after thee: for whither thou goest, I will go; and where thou lodgest, I will lodge: thy people shall be my people, and thy God my God" (Ruth 1:16).

THIS was a very brave, outspoken confession of faith. Please to notice that it was made by a woman, a young woman, a poor woman, a widow woman, and a foreigner. Remembering all that, I should think there is no condition of gentleness, or of obscurity, or of poverty, or of sorrow, which should prevent anybody from making an open confession of allegiance to God when faith in the Lord Jesus Christ has been exercised. If that is your experience, then whoever you may be, you will find an opportunity, somewhere or other, of declaring that you are on the Lord's side. I am glad that all candidates for membership in our church make their confession of faith at our church meetings. It does the man, the woman, the boy, or the girl, whoever it is, so much good for once, at least, to say right out straight, "I am a believer in the Lord Jesus Christ, and I am not ashamed of it," that I do not think we shall ever deviate from our custom. I have also noticed that, when people have once confessed Christ before men, they are very apt to do it again somewhere else; and they thus acquire a kind of boldness and outspokenness upon religious matters, and a holy courage as followers of Christ, which more than make up for any self-denial and trembling which the effort may have cost them.

I think Naomi was quite right to drive Ruth, as it were, to take this brave stand, in which it became an absolute necessity for her to speak right straight out, and say, in the worlds of our text, "Intreat me not to leave thee, or to return from following after thee: for whither thou goest, I will go; and where thou lodgest, I will lodge: thy people shall be my people, and thy God my God." What is there for any of us to be ashamed of in acknowledging that we belong to the Lord Jesus Christ? What can there be that should cause us to be ashamed of Jesus, or make us blush to own his name?

> Ashamed of Jesus! that dear Friend
> On whom my hopes of heaven depend!
> No; when I blush, be this my shame,
> That I no more revere his name.

We ought to be ashamed of being ashamed of Jesus; we ought to be afraid of being afraid to own him; we ought to tremble at trembling to confess him, and to resolve that we will take all suitable opportunities that we can find of saying, first to relatives, and then to all others with whom we come into contact, "We serve the Lord Christ."

I should think that Naomi was—certainly she ought to have been—greatly cheered by hearing this declaration from Ruth, especially the last part of it: "Thy people shall be my people, and thy God my God." Naomi had suffered great temporal loss; she had lost her husband and her two sons; but now she had found the soul of her daughter-in-law; and I believe that, according to the scales of true judgment, there ought to have been more joy in her heart at the conversion of Ruth's soul than grief over the death of her husband and her sons. Our Lord Jesus has told us that "there is joy in the presence of the angels of God over one sinner that repenteth"; and I always understand, by that expression, that there is joy in the heart of God himself over every sinner's repentance. Well, then, if Naomi's husband and sons were true believers—if they had been walking aright before the Lord—as, let us hope, they had done—she need not have felt such sorrow for them as could at all compare with the joy of her daughter-in-law being saved.

Perhaps, some of you have had bereavements in your homes; but if the death—the temporal death—of one should be the means of the spiritual life of another, there is a clear gain, I am sure there is; and though you may have gone weeping to the grave, yet, if you have evidence that, with those tears, there were also tears of repentance on the part of others of your family, and with that sad glance into the grave there was also a believing look at the dying, risen, and living Savior, you are decidedly a gainer, and you need not say, with Naomi, "I went out full, and the Lord hath brought me home again empty." Really Naomi, with her converted daughter-in-law at her side, if she had only been able to look into the future, might have been a happier woman than when she went away with her husband and her boys, for now she had with her one who was to be in the direct line of the progenitors of Christ, a right royal woman; for I count that the line of Christ is the true imperial line, and that they were the most highly honored among men and women who were in any way associated with the birth of the Savior into this world; and Ruth, though a Moabitess, was one of those who were elected to share in this high privilege.

Another thought strikes me here; that is, that it was when Naomi returned to the land which she ought never to have left, it was when she came out from the idolatrous Moabites among whom she had, as you see, relatives, and friends, and acquaintances—it was when she said, "I will go back to my own country, and people, and God,"—that then the Lord gave her the soul of this young woman who was so closely related to her. It may be that some of you professedly Christian people he been living at a distance from God. You have not led the separated life; you have tried to be friendly with the world as well as with Christ, and your children are not growing up as you wish they would. You say that your sons are not turning out well, and that your girls are dressy, and flighty, and worldly. Do you wonder that it is so? "Oh!" you say, "I have gone a good way to try to please them, thinking that, perhaps, by so doing, I might win them for Christ." Ah! you will never win any soul to the right by a compromise with the wrong. It is decision for Christ and his truth that has the greatest power in the family, and the greatest power in the world, too.

My first observation is, that AFFECTION FOR THE GODLY SHOULD INFLUENCE US TO GODLINESS.

It did so in this case. Affection for their godly mother-in-law influenced both Orpah and Ruth for a time, "and they said unto her, Surely we will return with thee unto thy people." They were both drawn part of the way towards Canaan; but, alas! natural affection has not sufficient power in itself to draw anybody to decision for God. It may be helpful to that end; it may be one of the "cords of a man" and "bands of love" which God, in his infinite mercy, often uses in drawing sinners to himself; but there has to be something more than that mere human affection. Still, it ought to be of some service in leading to decision; and it is a very dreadful thing when those who have godly parents seem to be the worse rather than the better for that fact, or when men, who have Christian wives, rebel against the light, and become all the more wicked because God has blessed their homes with godly women who speak to them lovingly and tenderly, concerning the claims of the religion of Jesus. That is a terrible state of affairs, for it ought always to be the case that our affection for godly people should help to draw us towards godliness. In Ruth's case, by the grace of God, it was the means of leading her to the decision expressed in our text, "Thy people shall be my people, and thy God my God."

Many forces may be combined to bring others to this decision. First, *there is the influence of companionship.* Nobody doubts that evil company tends to make a man bad, and it is equally sure that good companionship has a tendency to influence men towards that which is good. It is a happy thing to have side by side with you one whose heart is full of love to God. It is a great blessing to have as a mother a true saint, or to have as a brother or a sister one who fears the Lord; and it is a special privilege to be linked for life, in the closest bonds, with one whose prayers may rise with ours, and whose praises may also mingle with ours. There is something about Christian companionship which must tell in the right direction unless the heart be resolutely bent on mischief.

There is something more than this, however, and that is, *the influence of admiration.* There can be no doubt whatever that Ruth looked with loving reverence and admiration upon Naomi, for she saw in her a character which won her heart's esteem and affection. The few glimpses which we have of that godly woman, in this Book of Ruth, show us that she was a most disinterested and unselfish person, not one who, because of her own great sorrow, would burden others with it, and pull them down to her own level in order that they might in some way assist her. She was one who considered the interests of others rather than her own; and all such persons are sure to win admiration and esteem. When a Christian man so lives that others see something about him which they do not perceive in themselves, that is one way in which they are often attracted towards the Christian life. When the sick Christian is patient, when the poor Christian is cheerful, when the believer in Christ is forgiving, generous, tenderhearted, sympathetic, honest, upright, then it is that observers say, "Here is something worth looking at; whence came all this excellence?"

Nor is it only by companionship and admiration that people are won to the Savior; there is also *the influence of instruction*. I have no doubt that Naomi gave her daughter-in-law much helpful teaching. Ruth would want to know about Naomi's God, and Naomi would be only too glad to tell her all she knew. We should make people want to know what our religion really is, and then be ready to tell them. I have no doubt that, many a time, in the land of Moab, when her daughters-in-law ran in to see her, Naomi would begin telling them about the deliverance at the Red Sea, and how the Lord brought his people through the wilderness, and how the goodly land, which flowed with milk and honey, had been given to them by the hand of Joshua. Then she would tell them about the tabernacle and its worship, and talk to them about the lamb, and the red heifer, and the bullock, and the sin offering, and son on; and it was thus, probably, that Ruth's heart had been won to Jehovah the God of Israel. And, perhaps, for that reason—because of Naomi's instruction— Ruth said to her, " 'Thy people shall be my people;' I know so much about them, that I want to be numbered with them; 'and thy God shall be my God.' Thou hast told me about him, what wonders he has wrought, and I have resolved to trust myself under the shadow of his wings."

I think, too, that there was another thing which had great influence over Ruth, as it has had over a great many other people. That is, *the fear of separation*. "Ah!" said one to me, only last week, "it used to trouble me greatly when my wife went downstairs to the communion, and I had to go home, or to remain with the spectators in the gallery. I did not like to be separated from her even here; and then, sir, the thought stole over me, 'What if I have to be divided from her forever and ever?' " I think that a similar reflection ought, with the blessing of God, to impress a good many. Young man, if you live and die impenitent, you will see your mother no more, except it be from an awful distance, with a great gulf fixed between her and you, so that she cannot cross over to you, or you go over to her. There will come a day when one shall be taken and another left; and before the great separation takes place, at the judgment seat of Christ, when there shall be a sundering made between the goats and the sheep, and between the tares and the wheat, I do implore you to let the influence of the godly whom you love help to draw you towards decision for God and His Christ.

My time would fail me if I dwelt longer on this point, though it is a very interesting one, so I must pass on to my second observation, which is, that RESOLVES TO GODLINESS WILL BE TESTED. Ruth speaks very positively: "Thy people shall be my people, and thy God my God." This was her resolve, but it was a resolve which had already been put to the test, and had in great measure satisfactorily passed through it.

First, *it had been tested by the poverty and the sorrow of her mother-in-law*. Naomi said, "The Almighty hath dealt very bitterly with me"; yet Ruth says, "Thy God shall be my God." I like that brave resolution of the young Moabitess. Some people say, "We should like to be converted, for we want to be happy." Yes, but suppose you knew that you would not be happy after conversion, you ought still to wish to have this God to be your God. Naomi has lost her husband, she has lost her sons, she has lost everything; she is going back penniless to Bethlehem, and yet her daughter-in-law says to her, "Thy God shall be my God." Oh, if you can share the lot of Christians when they are in trouble, if you can take God and affliction, if you can accept Christ and a cross, then your decision to be His follower is true and real. It has been tested by the afflictions and the trials which you know belong to the people of God, yet you are content to suffer with them in taking their God to be your God, too.

Next, Ruth's decision had been tested when *she was bidden to count the cost*. Naomi had put the whole case before her. She had told her daughter-in-law that there was no hope that she should ever bear a son who could become a husband to Ruth, and that she had better stay and find a husband in her own land. She set before her the dark side of the case — possibly too earnestly. She seemed as if she wanted to persuade her to go back, though I do not think that, in her heart she could really have wished her to do so. But, my young friend, before you say to any Christian, "Thy people shall be my people, and thy God my God," count the cost. Recollect, if you are following an evil trade, you will have to give it up; if you have formed bad habits, you will have to forsake them; and if you had bad companions, you will have to leave them. There are a great many things which have afforded you pleasure, which must become painful to you, and must be renounced. Are you prepared to follow Christ through the mire and the slough, as well as along the high road, and down in the valley as well as upon the hills? Are you ready to carry his cross as you hope, afterwards, to share his crown? If you can stand the test in detail — such a test as Christ set before those who wanted to be his followers on earth, then is your decision a right one, but not else.

Ruth had been tried, too, by *the apparent coldness of one in whom she trusted*, and whom she had a right to rust, for Naomi did not at all encourage her; indeed, she seemed to discourage her. I am not sure that Naomi is to be blamed for that, and I am not certain that she is to be much praised. You know, it is quite possible for you to encourage people too much. I have known some encouraged in their doubts and fears till they never could get out of them. At the same time, you can certainly very easily chill inquirers and seekers. And though Naomi showed her love to Ruth, yet she did not seem to have any very great desire to bring her to follow Jehovah. This is a test that many young people find to be very trying; but this young woman said to her mother-in-law, "Intreat me not to leave thee, or to return from following after thee: for whither thou goest, I will go; and where thou lodgest, I will lodge: thy people shall be my people, and thy God my God."

Another trial for Ruth was *the drawing back of her sister-in-law*. Orpah kissed Naomi, and left her; and you know the influence of one young person upon another when they are of the same age, or when they are related as these two were. You went to the revival meeting with a friend, and she was as much impressed as you were. She has gone back to the world, and the temptation is for you to do the same. Can you stand out against it? You two young men went to hear the same preacher, and you both felt the force of the Word; but your companion has gone back to where he used to be. Can you hold out now, and say, "I will follow Christ alone if I cannot find a companion to go with me?" If so, it is well with you.

But one of the worst trials that Ruth had was *the silence of Naomi*. I think that is what is meant, for after she had solemnly declared that she would follow the Lord, we read, "When she saw that she was steadfastly minded to go with her, then she left speaking unto her." She left off stating the black side of the case, but she does not appear to have talked to her about the bright side. "She left speaking unto her." The good woman was so sorrowful that she could not talk, her heartbreak was so great that she could not converse, but such silence must have been very trying to Ruth; and when a young person had just joined the people of God, it is a severe test to be brought face to face with a very mournful Christian, and not to get one encouraging word. Sometimes, brethren and sisters, we must swallow our own bitter pills as fast as ever we can, that we may not discourage others by making a wry face over them. It is sometimes the very best thing a sorrowful person can do to say, "I must not be sad; here is young So-and-so coming in. I must be cheerful now, for here comes one who might be discouraged by my grief." You remember how the psalmist, when he was in a very mournful state of mind, said, "If I say, I will speak thus; behold, I should offend against the generation of thy children. When I thought to know this, it was too painful for me." Let it be too painful for us to give any cause for stumbling or disquietude to those who have just come to the Savior, but let us cheer and encourage them all we can. Still, Naomi's silence did not discourage Ruth; she was evidently a strong-minded though gentle young woman, and she gave herself up to God and his people without any reserve. Even though she might not be helped much by the older believer, and might even be discouraged by her, and still more by the departure of her sister-in-law, Orpah, yet still she pressed on in the course she had chosen. Well, you do the same, Mary; and you, Jane, and John and Thomas. Will you be like Mr. Pliable, and go back to the City of Destruction? Or will you, like Christian, pursue your way, and steadfastly hold on through the Slough of Despond, or whatever else may be in your pathway to the Celestial City?

Now, thirdly, and very briefly, TRUE GODLINESS MUST MAINLY LIE IN THE CHOICE OF GOD. That is the very pith of the text: "Thy God shall be my God."

First, *God is the believer's choicest possession*; indeed, it is the distinguishing mark of a Christian that he owns a God. Naomi had not much else—no husband, no son, no lands, no gold, no silver, no pleasure even; but she had a God. Come now, my friend, are you determined that, henceforth, and forever, the Lord shall be your chief possession? Can you say, "God shall be mine; my faith shall grasp him now, and hold him fast"?

Next, *God was, henceforth, to Ruth, as he had been to Naomi, her Ruler and Lawgiver.* When anyone truthfully says, "God shall be my God," there is some practical meaning about that declaration; it means, "He shall influence me; he shall direct me; he shall lead me; he shall govern me; he shall be my King. I will yield to him and obey him in everything. I will endeavor to do all things according to his will. God shall be my God." You must not want to take God to be your helper, in the sense of making him to be your servant; but to be your Master, and so to help you. Dear friends, does the Holy Spirit lead you to make this blessed choice, and to declare, "This God shall be mine, my Lawgiver and Ruler from this time forth"?

Well, then, *he must also be your Instructor*. At the present day, I am afraid that nine people out of ten do not believe in the God who is revealed to us in the Bible. "What?" you say. It is so, I grieve to say. I can point you to newspapers, to magazines, to periodicals, and also to pulpits by the score, in which there is a new god set up to be worshiped; not the God of the Old Testament, he is said to be too strict, too severe, too stern for our modern teachers. They do not believe in him. The God of Abraham is dethroned by many nowadays; and in his place they have a molluscous god, like those of whom Moses spoke, "new gods that come newly up, whom your fathers feared not." They shudder at the very mention of the God of the Puritans. If Jonathan Edwards were to rise from the dead, they would not listen to him for a minute, they would say that they had quite a new god since his day; but brethren, I believe in the God of Abraham, and of Isaac, and of Jacob; this God is my God— ay, the God that drowned Pharaoh and his host at the Red Sea, and moved his people to sing "Hallelujah" as he did it; the God that caused the earth to open, and swallow up Korah, Dathan, and Abiram, and all their company—a terrible God is the God whom I adore—he is the God and Father of our Lord and Savior Jesus Christ, full of mercy, compassion, and grace, tender and gentle, yet just and dreadful in his holiness, and terrible out of his holy places. This is the God whom we worship, and he who come to him in Christ, and trusts in him, will take him to be his Instructor, and so shall he learn aright all that he needs to know. But woe unto the men of this day, we have made unto themselves a calf of their own devising, which has no power to bless or to save them! "Thy God" says Ruth to Naomi, not another god, not Chemosh or Moloch, but Jehovah "shall be my God"; and so she took him to be her Instructor, as we also must do.

Then, let us take him to be *our entire trust and stay*. O my beloved friends, the happiest thing in life is to trust God, first to trust him with your soul through Jesus Christ the Savior, and then to trust him with everything, and in everything. I am speaking what I do know. The life of sense is death, but the life of faith is life indeed. Trust God about temporals—nay, I do not know any division between temporals and spirituals; trust God about everything, about your daily livelihood, about your health, about your wife, about your children; live a life of faith in God, and you will truly live, and all things will be right about you. It is because we get partly trusting God and partly trusting ourselves that we are often so unhappy. But when, by simple faith, you just cast yourselves on God, then you find the highest joy and bliss that is possible on earth, and a whole series of wonders is spread out before you; your life becomes like a miracle, or a succession of miracles, God hearing your prayers, and answering you out of heaven, delivering you in the time of trial, supplying your every need, and leading you ever onward by a matchless way which you know not, which every moment shall cause you greater astonishment and delight as you see the unfoldings of the character of God. Oh, that each one of you would say, "This God shall be my God; I will trust him; by his grace, I will trust him now."

The last thing is, that THIS DECISION SHOULD LEAD US TO CAST IN OUR LOT WITH GOD'S PEOPLE AS WELL AS WITH HIMSELF, for Ruth said, "Thy people shall be my people."

She might have said, "You are not well spoken of, you Jews, you Israelites; the Moabites, among whom I have lived, hated you." But in effect, she said, "I am no Moabitess now. I am going to belong to Israel, and to be spoken against, too. They have all manner of bad things to say in Moab about Bethlehem-Judah; but I do not mind that, for I am going to be henceforth an inhabitant of Bethlehem, and to be reckoned in the number of the Bethlehemites, for no longer am I of Moab and the Moabites."

Now, will you thus cast in your lot with God's people; and though they are spoken against, will you be willing to be spoken against, too? I daresay that the Bethlehemites were not all that Ruth could have wished them to be. Even Naomi was not; she was too sad and sorrowful; but, still, I expect that Ruth thought that her mother-in-law was a be0tter woman than she was herself. I have heard people find fault with the members of our churches, and say that they cannot join with them, for they are such inferior sort of people. Well, I know a great many different sorts of people; and, after all, I shall be quite content to be numbered with God's people, as I see them even in his visible Church, rather than to be. numbered with any other persons in the whole world. I count the despised people of God the best company I have ever met with.

"Oh!" says one, "I will join the church when I can find a perfect one." Then you will never join any. "Ah!" you say, "but perhaps I may." Well, but it will not be a perfect church the moment after you have joined it, for it will cease to be perfect as soon as it receives you into its membership. I think that, if a church is such as Christ can love, it is such as I can love; and if it is such that Christ counts it as his Church, I may well be thankful to be a member of it. Christ "loved the Church, and gave himself for it"; then may I not think it an honor to be allowed to give myself to it?

Ruth was not joining a people out of whom she expected to get much. Shame on those who think to join the Church for what they can get! Yet the loaves and fishes are always a bait for some people. But there was Ruth, going with Naomi to Bethlehem, and all that the townsfolk would do would be to turn out and stare at them, and say, "Is this Naomi? And pray who is this young woman that has come with her? This Naomi—dear me! How altered she is! How worn she looks! Quite the old woman to what she was when she left us." Not much sympathy was given to them, as far as I gather from that remark; yet Ruth seemed to say, "I do not care how they treat me; they are God's people, even if they have a great many faults and imperfections, and I am going to join them." And I invite all of you who can say to us, "Your God is our God," to join with the people of God, openly, visibly, manifestly, decidedly, without any hesitancy, even though you may gain nothing by it. Perhaps you will not; but, on the other hand, you will bring a good deal to it, for that is the true spirit of Christ. "It is more blessed to give than to receive." Yet, in any case, cast in your lot with the people of God, and share and share alike with them.

I conclude by saying that, whatever the other Bethlehemites might be, there was among them one notable being, and it was worthwhile to join the nation for the sake of union with him. Ruth found it all out by degrees. There was a near kinsman among those people, and his name was Boaz. She went to glean in his field; and, by and by, she was married to him. Ah! that was the reason why I cast in my lot with the people of God, for I said to myself, "There is One among them who, whatever faults they may have, is so fair and lovely that he more than makes up for all their imperfections. My Lord Jesus Christ, in the midst of his people, makes them all fair in his fairness; and makes me feel that, to be poor with the poorest and most illiterate of the Church of Christ, meeting in a village barn, is an unspeakable honor, since he is among them." Our Lord Jesus Christ himself is always present wherever two or three are gathered together in his name. If his name is in the list, there may be a number of odds and ends put down with him, members of different denominations, some queer persons, some very old people; but as long as his name is in the list, I do not mind about what others are there, put my name down.

Oh, that I might have the eternal honor of having it written even at the bottom of the page beneath the name of Jesus, my Lord, the Lamb! As Boaz was there, it was enough for Ruth; and as Christ is here, that is quite enough for me. So I hope I have said sufficient to persuade you, who say that our God is your God, to come and join with us, or with some other part of Christ's Church, and so to make his people to be your people. And mind you do it at once, and in the scriptural fashion, and God bless you in the doing of it, for Christ's sake!

9

RUTH

Reward; or, Cheer for Converts

"The Lord recompense thy work, and a full reward be given thee of the Lord God of Israel, under whose wings thou art come to trust" (Ruth 2:12).

THIS was the language of Boaz, a man of substance and of note in Bethlehem, to a poor stranger of whom he had heard that she had left her kindred, and the idols of her nation, that she might become a worshiper of the living and true God. He acted a noble part when he cheered her, and bade her be of good courage now that she was casting in her lot with Naomi and the chosen nation. Observe that he saluted her with words of tender encouragement; for this is precisely what I want all the elder Christians among you to do to those who are the counterparts of Ruth. You who have long been believers in the Lord Jesus, who have grown rich in experience, who know the love and faithfulness of our covenant God, and who are strong in the Lord, and in the power of his might; I want you to make a point of looking out the young converts, and speaking to them goodly words, and comfortable words, whereby they may be cheered and strengthened.

There is a text, a very short one, which I would like often to preach from in reference to those who are newly saved, and I would invite you continually to be practicing it: that text is, *"Encourage him."* So many will throw cold water upon the aspirant after holiness, that I would urge others of you heartily to cheer him.

I have no doubt that much sorrow might be prevented if words of encouragement were more frequently spoken fitly and in season; and therefore to withhold them is sin. I am afraid that many poor souls have remained in darkness, shut in within themselves, when two or three

313

minutes' brotherly cheer might have taken down the shutters, and let in the light of day. Many matters are real difficulties to young believers, which are no difficulties to us who have been longer in the way. You and I could clear up in ten minutes' conversation questions and doubts which cause our uninstructed friends months of misery. Why are we so reticent when a word would send our weaker brethren on their way rejoicing? Therefore, I do entreat all of you whom God has greatly blessed, to look after those that are of low estate in spiritual things, and try to cheer and encourage them. As you do this, God will bless you in return; but, if you neglect this tender duty, it may be that you yourselves will grow despondent, and be yourselves in need of friendly succor.

I think I can say for every Christian here, that the young converts among us have our very best wishes. We desire for them every good and spiritual gift. See how Boaz, wishing well as he did to the humble maiden from Moab, spoke with her, and then spoke with God in prayer for her. I take it that my text is a prayer as well as a benediction: "Jehovah recompense thy work, and a full reward be given thee of Jehovah, God of Israel, under whose wings thou art come to trust." Let us pray more than ever for the feeble-minded and the young.

We should, in all probability, see a much more rapid growth in grace among our young converts if they were better nursed and watched over. Some of us owed much to old-experienced Christians in our younger days. I know I did. I shall forever respect the memory of a humble servant in the school wherein I was usher, at Newmarket; an old woman, who talked with me concerning the things of the kingdom, and taught me the way of the Lord more perfectly. She knew the doctrines of grace better than many a doctor of divinity; and she held them with the tenacious grasp of one who found her life in them. It was my great privilege to help her in her old age; and but a little while ago she passed away to heaven. Many things did I learn of her, which today I delight to preach. Let it be said of us, when we, too, grow old, that those who were children when we were young were helped by us to become useful in their riper years.

First, then, WHAT HAS THE YOUNG CONVERT DONE? We illustrate the subject by the instance of Ruth.

Many young converts deserve encouragement because *they have left all their old associates.* Ruth, no doubt, had many friends in her native country, but she tore herself away to cling to Naomi and her God.

Perhaps she parted from a mother and a father; if they were alive she certainly left them to go to the Israelites' country. Possibly she bade adieu to brothers and sisters, certainly she quitted old friends and neighbors; for she resolved to go with Naomi, and share her lot. She said, "Intreat me not to leave thee, or to return from following after thee: for whither thou goest, I will go: and where thou lodgest, I will lodge: thy people shall be my people, and thy God my God: where thou diest, will I die, and there will I be buried: the Lord do so to me, and more also, if ought but death part thee and me."

The young convert is an emigrant from the world; and has become, for Christ's sake, an alien. Possibly he had many companions, friends who made him merry after their fashion, men of fascinating manners, who could easily provoke his laughter, and make the hours dance by; but, because he found in them no savor of Christ, he has forsaken them, and for Christ's sake they have forsaken him. Among his old associates he has become as a speckled bird, and they are all against him. You may, perhaps, have seen a canary which has flown from its home, where it enjoyed the fondness of its mistress: you have seen it out among the sparrows. They pursue it as though they would tear it into pieces, and they give it no rest anywhere. Just so the young convert, being no longer of the same feather as his comrades, is the subject of their persecution. He endures trials of cruel mockings, and these are as hot irons to the soul. He is now to them a hypocrite, and a fanatic; they honor him with ridiculous names by which they express their scorn. In their hearts they crown him with a fool's cap, and write him down as both idiot and knave. He will need to exhibit years of holy living before they will be forced into respect for him; and all this because he is quitting their Moab to join with Israel. Why should he leave them? Has he grown better than they? Does he pretend to be a saint? Can he not drink with them as he once did? He is a protest against their excesses, and men don't care for such protests. Can he not sing a jolly song as they do? Forsooth, he has turned saint; and what is a saint but a hypocrite? He is a deal too precise and Puritanical, and is not to be endured in their free society. According to the grade in life, this opposition takes one form or another, but in no case does Moab admire the Ruth who deserts her idols to worship the God of Israel.

Is it not most meet that you older Christian people, who have long been separated from the world, and are hardened against its jeers, should step in and defend the newcomers? Should you not say, "Come you with us, and we will do you good: we will be better friends to you than those you have left. We will accompany you on a better road than that from which you have turned; and we will find you better joys than worldlings can ever know"? When our great King is represented as saying to his spouse, "Forget also thine own people, and thy father's house," he adds, "so shall the king greatly desire thy beauty: for he is thy Lord"; thus he gives her new company to supply the place of that which she gives up. Let us gather a hint from this, and make society for those whom the world casts out. When Ruth had quitted her former connections, it was wise and kind for Boaz to address her in the words of comfort which I will again quote to you: "The Lord recompense thy work, and a full reward be given thee of the Lord God of Israel, under whose wings thou art come to trust."

Next, Ruth, having left her old companions, had *come amongst strangers*. She was not yet at home in the land of Israel, but confessed herself "a stranger." She knew Naomi, but in the whole town of Bethlehem she knew no one else. When she came into the harvest field the neighbors were there gleaning, but they were no neighbors of hers; no glance of sympathy fell upon her from them; perhaps they looked at her with cold curiosity. They may have thought, "What business has this Moabitess to come here to take away a part of the gleaning which belongs to the poor of Israel?" I know that such feelings do arise among country people when a stranger from another parish comes gleaning in the field. Ruth was a foreigner, and, of course, in their eyes an intruder. She felt herself to be alone, though under the wings of Israel's God. Boaz very properly felt that she should not think that courtesy and kindness had died out of Israel; and he made a point though he was by far her superior in station, to go to her and speak a word of encouragement to her. Should not certain of you follow the same practice? May I not call you to do so at once? There will come into our assemblies those that have been lately impressed with a sense of their guilt, or have newly sought and found the Savior; should they be suffered to remain strangers among us long? Should not recognition, companionship, and hospitality be extended to them to make them feel at home with us? Do let us try with all our hearts so to look every man upon the things of others that no single seeking soul shall feel itself deserted. Seekers should be spared the agony of crying, "No man careth for my soul." Are you a believer? Then you are my brother. We are no more strangers and foreigners, but fellow citizens with the saints, and of the household of God. We would lay ourselves out to bring our fellowmen to Jesus, and to aid new converts in finding perfect peace at his feet. Let us learn the art of personal address. Do not let us be so bashful and retiring that we leave others in sorrow because we cannot screw up our courage to say a kind and tender word in the name of the Lord Jesus.

The new convert is like Ruth in another respect: he is *very lowly in his own eyes.* Ruth said to Boaz, "Why have I found grace in thine eyes, that thou shouldest take knowledge of me, seeing I am a stranger?" She said again, "Let me find favor in thy sight, my lord; for that thou hast comforted me, and for that thou hast spoken friendly unto thine handmaid, though I be not like unto one of thine handmaidens." She had little self-esteem, and therefore she won the esteem of others. She felt herself to be a very inconsiderable person, to whom any kindness was a great favor; and so do young converts, if they are real and true. I remember when I first went to the house of God as a Christian youth who had lately come to know the Lord, that I looked with veneration on every officer and member of the church. I thought them all, if not quite angels, yet very nearly as good; at any rate, I had no disposition to criticize *them,* for I felt myself to be so undeserving. I do not think that I have quite so high an idea of all professed Christians as I had then, for I am afraid that I could not truthfully entertain it; but for all that, I think far better of them than many are apt to do. I believe that young people, when first brought to Christ, have so deep a sense of their own imperfection, and know so little of the infirmities of others, that they look up to the members of the church with a very high esteem, and this fixes upon such members, officers, and pastors a great responsibility. Since these converts are lowly in their own eyes it is proper and safe to encourage them; moreover, it is kind and needful to do so. Never be critical and severe with them, but deal tenderly with their budding graces; a frosty sentence may nip them; a genial word will develop them. Our Lord bids you feed the lambs; act the shepherd towards them, and never overdrive them, lest they faint by the way.

Once more, the young convert is like Ruth because he has *come to trust under the wings of Jehovah, the God of Israel.* Herein is a beautiful metaphor. You know that the wing of a strong bird especially, and of any bird relatively, is strong. It makes a kind of arch, and from the outer side you have the architectural idea of strength. Under the wings, even of so feeble a creature as a hen, there is a complete and perfect refuge for her little chicks, judging from without. And then the inside of the wing is lined with soft feathers for the comfort of the young. The interior of the wing is arranged as though it would prevent any friction from the strength of the wing to the weakness of the little bird. I do not know of a more snug place than under the wing feathers of the hen. Have you never thought of this? Would not the Lord have us in time of trouble come and cower down under the great wing of His omnipotent love, just as the chicks do under the mother? Here is the Scripture—"He shall cover thee with his feathers, and under his wings shalt thou trust: his truth shall be thy shield and buckler." What a warm defense! When I have seen the little birds put their heads out from under the feathers of their mother's breast it has looked like the perfection of happiness; and when they have chirped their little notes, they have seemed to tell how warm and safe they were, though there may have been a rough wind blowing around the bend. They could not be happier than they are. If they run a little way, they are soon back again to the wing, for it is house and home to them; it is their shield and succor, defense and delight. This is what our young converts have done: they have come, not to trust themselves, but to trust in Jesus. They have come to find a righteousness in Christ—ay, to find everything in him, and so they are trusting, trusting under the wings of God. Is not this what you are doing? You full-grown saints—is not this your condition? I know it is. Very well then; encourage the younger sort to do what you delight to do: say to them, "There is no place like this: let us joyously abide together under the wing of God." There is no rest, no peace, no calm, no perfect quiet, like that of giving up all care, because you cast your care on God; renouncing all fear, because your only fear is a fear of offending God.

But now I must come closer to the text. Having shown you what these converts have done to need encouragement, I want, in the second place, to answer the question, WHAT IS THE FULL REWARD OF THOSE WHO COME TO TRUST UNDER THE WINGS OF GOD?

I would answer that a full reward will come to us in that day when we lay down these bodies of flesh and blood, that they may sleep in Jesus, while our unclothed spirits are absent from the body but present with the Lord. In the disembodied state we shall enjoy perfect happiness of spirit; but a fuller reward will be ours when the Lord shall come a second time, and our bodies shall rise from the grave to share in the glorious reign of the descended King. Then in our perfect manhood we shall behold the face of him we love, and shall be like him. Then shall come the adoption, to wit, the redemption of our body; and we, as body, soul, and spirit, a trinity in unity, shall be forever with Father, Son, and Holy Ghost, our triune God. This unspeakable bliss is the full reward of trusting beneath the wings of Jehovah.

But there is a present reward, and to that Boaz referred. There is in this world a present recompense for the godly, notwithstanding the fact that many are the afflictions of the righteous. Years ago a brother minister printed a book, "How to Make the Best of Both Worlds," which contained much wisdom; but at the same time many of us objected to the title, as diving the pursuit of the believer, and putting the two worlds too much on a level. Assuredly, it would be wrong for any godly man to make it his object in life to make the best of both worlds in the way which the title is likely to suggest. This present world must be subordinate to the world to come, and is to be cheerfully sacrificed to it, if need be. Yet, be it never forgotten, if any man will live unto God he will make the best of both worlds, for godliness has the promise of the life that now is as well as of that which is to come. Even in losing the present life for Christ's sake we are saving it, and self-denial and taking up the cross are but forms of blessedness. If we seek first the kingdom of God and his righteousness, all other things shall be added to us.

Do you ask me, "How shall we be rewarded for trusting in the Lord?" I answer, first, by the *deep peace of conscience* which he will grant you. Can any reward be better than this? When a man can say, "I have sinned, but I am forgiven," is not that forgiveness an unspeakable boon? My sins were laid on Jesus, and he took them away as my scapegoat, so that they are gone forever, and I am consciously absolved. Is not this a glorious assurance? Is it not worth worlds? A calm settles down upon the heart which is under the power of the blood of sprinkling; a voice within proclaims the peace of God, and the Holy Spirit seals that peace by his own witness; and thus all is rest. If you were to offer all that you have to buy this peace, you could not purchase it; but were it purchasable it were worthwhile to forego the dowry of a myriad worlds to win it. If you had all riches and power and honor you could not reach the price of the pearl of peace. The revenues of kingdoms could not purchase so much as a glance at this jewel. A guilty conscience is the undying worm of hell; the torture of remorse is the fire that never can be quenched: he that hath that worm gnawing at his heart and that fire burning in his bosom is lost already. On the other hand, he that trusts in God through Christ Jesus is delivered from inward hell-pangs: the burning fever of unrest is cured. He may well sing for joy of soul, for heaven is born within him and lies in his heart like the Christ in the manger.

That, however, is only the beginning of the believer's reward. He that has come to trust in God shall be *"quiet from fear of evil."* What a blessing that must be! "He shall not be afraid of evil tidings; his heart is fixed, trusting in the Lord." When a man is at his very highest as to this world's joy, he hears the whisper of a dark spirit saying, "Will it last?" He peers into the morrow with apprehension, for he knows not what may be lurking in his path. But, when a man is no longer afraid, but is prepared to welcome whatever comes, because he sees it in the appointment of a loving Father, why, then he is in a happy state.

More than this: the man who trusts in God *rests in him with respect to all the supplies he now needs, or shall ever need.* What happy music gladdens the green pastures of that twenty-third psalm! I am half inclined to ask you to rise and sing it, for my heart is leaping for joy while I rehearse the first stanza of it:

> The Lord my Shepherd is
> I shall be well supplied.
> Since he is mine and I am his,
> What can I want beside?

Usually man is made up of wants; and *he* must have reached the land of abounding wealth who boldly asks, "What can I want beside?" We are never quite content; it always needs a little more to fill the cup to the brim; but only think of singing, "What can I want beside?" Is not this sweet content a full reward from the Lord in whom we trust? Human nature has swallowed a horse-leech, and henceforth it crieth night and day, "Give, give, give": who but the Lord can stay this craving? The vortex of dissatisfaction threatens to suck in the main ocean and still to remain unfilled; but the Lord rewards faith by satisfying its mouth with good things.

Another part of the believer's great gain lies in *the consciousness that all things are working together for his good.* Nothing is, after all, able to injure us. Neither pains of body, nor sufferings of mind, nor losses in business, nor cruel blows of death, can work us real ill. The thefts of robbers, the mutterings of slanderers, the changes of trade, the rage of the elements, shall all be overruled for good. These many drugs and poisons, compounded in the mortar of the unerring Chemist, shall produce a healthy potion for our souls: "we know that all things work together for good to them that love God, to them who are the called according to his purpose." It is a great joy to know this to be an unquestionable fact, and to watch with expectation to see it repeated in our own case.

Then, let me tell you, they that trust in God and follow him have another full reward, and that is, *the bliss of doing good.* Can any happiness excel this? This joy is a diamond of the first water. Match me, if you can, the joy of helping the widow and the fatherless! Find me the equal of the delight of saving a soul from death and covering a multitude of sins! It were worth worlds to have faith in God even if we lived here for ever, if our sojourn could be filled up with doing good to the poor and needy, and rescuing the erring and fallen. If you desire to taste the purest joy that ever flowed from the founts of Paradise, drink of the unselfish bliss of saving a lost soul. When faith in God teaches you to forego self, and live wholly to glorify God and benefit your fellowmen, it puts you on the track of the Lord of angels, and by following it you will come to reign with him.

Brothers and sisters, there remains the singular and refined joy which comes of a humble *perception of personal growth.* Children rejoice when they find that they are growing more like their parents and may soon hope to be strong and full-grown. Most of us recollect our childish mirth when we began to wear garments which we thought would make us look like men. When I first wore boots and walked through the stubble with my big uncle, I felt that I was somebody. That, of course, was childish pride; but it has its commendable analogy in the pleasure of gathering spiritual strength, and becoming equal to higher labors and deeper experiences. When you find that you do not lose your temper under provocation, as you did a year ago, you are humble thankful. When an evil lust is driven away, and no longer haunts you, you are quietly joyful, rejoicing with trembling. When you have sustained a trial which once would have crushed you, the victory is exceedingly sweet. Every advance in holiness is an advance in secret happiness. To be a little more meet for heaven is to have a little more of heaven in the heart. As we mellow for the celestial garner we are conscious of a more pervading sweetness, which in itself is no mean reward of virtue.

Let me tell you another splendid part of this full reward, and that is, to have *prevalence with God in prayer*. Somebody called me, in print, a hypocrite, because I said that God had heard my prayers. This was evidently malicious: a man might be called fanatical for such a statement, but I cannot see the justice of imputing hypocrisy on that account. If by hypocrisy he meant a sincere conviction that the great God answers prayer, I will be more and more hypocritical as long as I live. I will glory in the name of God—the God that heareth my prayer. If that writer had claimed that *he* prayed and had been heard, it is possible that he would have been guilty of hypocrisy: of that matter he is personally the best informed, and I leave the question with himself; but he had no right to measure my corn with his bushel. Certainly, I shall not use his bushel to measure my corn, but I shall speak what I know and am persuaded of. In deep sincerity I can bear testimony that the Lord hears prayer, and that it is his wont so to do. Many a saint of God has but to ask and have. When such men wrestle with God in prayer they always prevail, like Israel of old at Jabbok when he grasped the angel, and would not let him go without a blessing. If you have got this power to the full you will often say to yourself, "If I had nothing else but power at the throne of grace I have more than enough to recompense me for every self-denial." What are the jests and jeers of an ungodly and ignorant world in comparison with the honor of being favored of the Lord to ask what we will, and receive the utmost of our desires?

Many other items make up the full of the reward; but perhaps the chief of all is *communion with God*—to be permitted to speak with him as a man speaketh with his friend—to be led by the divine Bridegroom to sit down in the banqueting house while his banner over us is love. Those who dwell outside the palace of love know nothing about our secret ecstasies and raptures. We cannot tell them much about our spiritual delights, for they would only turn again and rend us. The delights of heavenly fellowship are too sacred to be commonly displayed. There is a joy, the clearest foretaste of heaven below, when the soul becomes as the chariot of Amminadib by the energy of the Holy Spirit. I believe, brethren, that our lot, even when we are poor and sorrowful and cast down, is infinitely to be preferred to that of the loftiest emperor who does not know the Savior. Oh, poor kings, poor princes, poor peers, poor gentry, that do not know Christ! But happy paupers that know him! Happy slaves that love him! Happy dying men and women that rejoice in him! Those have solid joy and lasting pleasure who have God to be their all in all. Come, then, and put your trust under the wings of God, and you shall be blessed in your body and in your soul, blessed in your house and in your family, blessed in your basket and in your store, blessed in your sickness and in your health, blessed in time and in eternity; for the righteous are blessed of the Lord, and their offspring with them.

Finally, WHAT FIGURE SETS FORTH THIS FULL REWARD? What was the full reward that Ruth obtained? I do not think that Boaz knew the full meaning of what he said. He could not foresee all that was appointed of the Lord. In the light of Ruth's history we will read the good man's blessing. This poor stranger, Ruth, in coming to put her trust in the God of Israel was giving up everything: yes, but she was also gaining everything. If she could have looked behind the veil which hides the future, she could not have conducted herself more to her own advantage than she did. She had no prospect of gain; she followed Naomi, expecting poverty and obscurity; but in doing that which was right, she found the blessing which maketh rich. She lost her Moabitish kindred, but she found a noble kinsman in Israel. She quitted the home of her fathers in the other land to find a heritage among the chosen tribes, a heritage redeemed by one who loved her. Ah! when you come to trust in Christ, you find in the Lord Jesus Christ one who is next of kin to you, who redeems your heritage, and unites you to himself. You thought that he was a stranger; you were afraid to approach him; but he comes near to you, and you find yourself near to his heart, and one with him forever.

Yes, this is a fair picture of each convert's reward. Ruth found what she did not look for, she found a husband. It was exactly what was for her comfort and her joy, for she find rest in the house of her husband, and she became possessed of his large estate by virtue of her marriage union with him. When a poor sinner trusts in God he does not expect so great a boon, but, to his surprise, his heart finds a husband, and a home, and an inheritance priceless beyond all conception; and all this is found in Christ Jesus our Lord. Then is the soul brought into loving, living, lasting, indissoluble union with the Well-beloved, the unrivaled Lord of love. We are one with Jesus. What a glorious mystery is this!

Ruth obtained an inheritance among the chosen people of Jehovah. She could not have obtained it except through Boaz, who redeemed it for her; but thus she came into indisputable possession of it. When a poor soul comes to God, he thinks that he is flying to Him only for a refuge, but, indeed, he is coming for much more; he is coming for a heritage undefiled, and that fadeth not away. He becomes an heir of God, a joint-heir with Jesus Christ.

10

RUTH

Mealtime in the Cornfields

"And Boaz said unto her, At mealtime come thou hither, and eat of the bread, and dip thy morsel in the vinegar. And she sat beside the reapers: and he reached her parched corn, and she did eat, and was sufficed, and left" (Ruth 2:14).

WE are going to the cornfields, as we did last year, not however, so much to glean, as to rest with the reapers and the gleaners, when under some wide-spreading oak they sit down to take refreshment. We hope there will be found some timid gleaner here, who will accept our invitation to come and eat with us.

Our first point is this—THAT GOD'S REAPERS HAVE THEIR MEALTIMES.

Those who work for God will find him a good Master. He cares for oxen, and has commanded his Israel, "Thou shalt not muzzle the ox when he treadeth out the corn." Much more doth he care of his servants who serve him. "He hath given meat unto them that fear him: he will ever be mindful of his covenant." The reapers in Jesus' fields shall not only receive a blessed reward at the last, but they shall have plenteous comforts by the way.

God has ordained certain mealtimes for his reapers; and he has appointed that one of these shall be *when they come together to listen to the Word preached.* If God be with our ministers, they act as the disciples did of old, for they received the barley loaves and fishes from Christ as He multiplied them, and handed them to the people. We, of ourselves, cannot feed one soul, much less thousands; but when the Lord is with us, we can keep as good a table as Solomon himself, with all his fine flour, and fat oxen, and roebucks, and fallow deer. When the Lord blesses the provisions of his House, no matter how many thousands there may be, all his poor shall be filled with bread. I hope, beloved, you know what it is to sit under the shadow of the Word with great delight, and find the fruit thereof sweet unto your taste. Where the doctrines of grace are boldly and plainly delivered to you in connection with the other truths of revelation; where Jesus Christ upon his cross is *ever* lifted up; where the work of the Spirit is not forgotten; where the glorious purpose of the Father is never despised, there is sure to be food for the children of God.

We have learned not to feed upon oratorical flourishes, or philo-sophical refining; we leave these fine things, these twelfth-cake ornaments, to be eaten by those little children who can find delight in such unhealthy dainties: we prefer to hear truth, even when roughly spoken, to the fine garnishings of eloquence without the truth. We care little about how the table is served, or of what ware the dishes are made, so long as the covenant bread and water, and the promised oil and wine, are given us.

Certain grumblers among the Lord's reapers do not feed under the preached Word, because they do not intend to feed; they come to the House of Bread on purpose to find fault, and therefore they go away empty. My verdict is, "It serves them right." Little care I to please such hearers. I would as soon feed bears and jackals, as attempt to supply the wants of grumbling professors. How much mischief is done by observations made upon the preacher! How often do we censure where our God ap-proves! We have heard of a high doctrinal deacon, who said to a young minister who was supplying the pulpit on probation, "I should have en-joyed your sermon very much, sir, if it had not been for that last appeal to the sinner. I do not think that dead sinners should be exhorted to be-lieve in Jesus." When that deacon reached home, he found his own daugh-ter in tears. She became converted to God, and united with the Church of which that young man ultimately became the minister. How was she converted, think you? By that address at the close of the sermon, which her father did not like. Take heed of railing at that by which the Holy Ghost saves souls. There may be much in the sermon which may not suit you or me, but then we are not the only persons to be considered. There is a wide variety of characters, and all our hearers must have "their portion of meat in due season." Is it not a selfishness very unlike the spirit of a Christian, which would make me find fault with the provisions, be-cause *I* cannot eat them all? There should be the unadulterated milk for the babe in grace, as well as the strong substantial meat for the full-grown believer. Beloved, I know that however murmurers may call our manna "light bread," yet our gracious God does "in this mountain make unto all people a feast of fat things, a feast of wines on the lees, of fat things full of marrow, of wines on the lees well refined."

Often, too, our gracious Lord appoints us mealtimes *in our private readings and meditations.* Here it is that his "paths drop fatness." Nothing can be more fattening to the soul of the believer than feeding upon the Word, and digesting it by frequent meditations. No wonder that some grow so little, when they meditate so little. Cattle must chew the cud; it is not what they crop with their teeth, but that which is masticated, and afterwards digested by rumination, that nourishes them. We must take the truth, and roll it over and over again in the inward parts of our spirit, and so we shall extract divine nourishment therefrom. Have you not, my brethren, frequently found a Benjamin's mess prepared for you in a choice promise of your God? Is not meditation the land of Goshen to you? If men once said, "There is corn in Egypt" may they not always say, that the finest of the wheat is to be found in secret prayer? Private devotion is a land which floweth with milk and honey; a paradise yielding all manner of fruits; a banqueting house of choice wines. Ahasuerus might make a great feast, but all his 120 provinces could not furnish such dainties as the closet offers to the spiritual mind. Where can we feed and lie down in green pastures in so sweet a sense as we do in our musings on the Word? Meditation distills the quintessence from the Scriptures, and gladdens our mouth with a sweetness which exceeds the virgin honey dropping from the honeycomb. Your retired seasons and occasions of prayer, should be to you regal entertainments, or at least refreshing seasons, in which, like the reapers at noonday, you sit with Boaz and eat of your Master's generous provisions.

Let us not forget, that there is one specially ordained mealtime which ought to occur oftener, but which, even monthly, is very refreshing to us, I mean *the Supper of the Lord.* There you have literally, as well as spiritually, a meal. The table is richly spread; it has upon it both meat and drink; there is the bread and the wine, and looking at what these symbolize, we have before us a table richer than that which kings could furnish. There we have the flesh and the blood of our Lord Jesus Christ, whereof if a man eat, he shall never hunger and never thirst, for that bread shall be unto him everlasting life. Oh! the sweet seasons we have known at the Lord's Supper. If some of you really did understand the enjoyment of feeding upon Christ in that ordinance, you would chide yourselves for not having united with the Church in fellowship. In keeping the Master's commandments there is a "great reward," and consequently in neglecting them there is a great loss of reward. Christ is not so tied to the Sacramental table as to be always found of those who partake thereat, but still it is in the way that we may expect the Lord to meet with us.

Besides these regular mealtimes, there are others which God gives us, *at seasons when perhaps we little expect them.* You have been walking the street, and suddenly you have felt a holy flowing-out of your soul toward God; or, in the middle of business your heart has been melted with love and made to leap for joy, even as the brooks which have been bound with winter's ice leap to fell the touch of spring. Seasons too you have had on your sickbeds, when you would have been content to be sick always, if you could have your bed so well made, and your head so softly pillowed.

Our blessed Redeemer comes to us in the morning, and wakes us up with such sweet thoughts upon our soul, we know not how they came; as if, when the dew was visiting the flowers, a few drops of heaven's dew had fallen upon us. In the cool eventide, too, as we have gone to our beds, our meditation of him has been sweet. Nay, in the night watches, when we tossed to and fro, and could not sleep, he has been pleased to become our song in the night.

God's reapers find it hard work to reap; but they find a blessed solace when they sit down and eat of their Master's rich provisions; then, with renewed strength, they go with sharpened sickle, to reap again in the noontide heat.

Let me observe, that while these mealtimes come, we know not exactly when, there are *certain seasons when we may expect them.* The Eastern reapers generally sit down under the shelter of a tree, or a booth, to take refreshment during the heat of the day. And certain I am, that when trouble, affliction, persecution, and bereavement, become the most painful to us, it is then that the Lord hands out to us the sweetest comforts. We must work till the hot sun forces the sweat from our face; we must bear the burden and heat of the day before we can expect to be invited to those choice meals which the Lord prepares for those who are diligent in his work. When thy day of trouble is the hottest, then the love of Jesus shall be sweetest; when thy night of trial is the darkest, then will his candle shine most brightly about thee; when thy head aches most heavily—when thy heart palpitates most terribly—when heart and flesh fail thee, then he will be the strength of thy life, and thy portion forever.

Again, these mealtimes frequently occur *before* a trial. Elijah must be entertained beneath a juniper tree, for he is to go a forty-day journey in the strength of that meat. You may suspect some danger nigh when your delights are overflowing. If you see a ship taking in great quantities of provision, it is bound for a distant port. And when God gives you extraordinary seasons of communion with Jesus, you may look for long leagues of tempestuous sea. Sweet cordials prepare for stern conflicts. Times of refreshing also occur *after* trouble or arduous service. Christ was tempted of the devil, and *afterwards* angels came and ministered unto him. Abraham wars with the kings, and returns from their slaughter; then is it that Melchisedec refreshes him with bread and wine. After conflict, content; after battle, banquet. When thou hast waited on thy Lord, then thou shalt sit down, and thy Master will gird himself and wait upon thee. Yes, let the worldling say what he will about the hardness of religion, we do not find it so. We do confess that reaping is no child's play; that toiling for Christ has its difficulties and its troubles; but still the bread which we eat is *very* sweet, and the wine which we drink is crushed from celestial clusters—

> I would not change my bless'd estate
> For all the world calls good or great;
> And while my faith can keep her hold,
> I envy not the sinner's gold.

Follow me while we turn to a second point. TO THESE MEALS THE GLEANER IS AFFECTIONATELY INVITED. That is to say, the poor, trembling stranger who has not strength enough to reap; who has no right to be in the field, except the right of charity—the poor, trembling sinner, conscious of his own demerit, and feeling but little hope and little joy. To the meals of the strong-handed, fully-assured reaper, the *gleaner* is invited.

The gleaner is invited, in the text, to *come*. "At mealtime, come thou hither." We have known some who felt ashamed to come to the House of God; but we trust you will none of you be kept away from the place of feasting by any shame on account of your dress, or your personal character, or your poverty; nay, nor even on account of your physical infirmities. "At mealtime come thou hither." I have heard of a deaf woman who could never hear a sound, and yet she was always in the House of God, and when asked why, her reply was, "Because a friend found her the text, and then God was pleased to give her many a sweet thought upon the text while she sat in his House; beside," she said, "she felt that as a believer, she ought to honor God by her *presence* in his courts, and recognizing her union with his people; and, better still, she always liked to be in the best of company, and as the presence of God was there, and the holy angels, and the saints of the Most High, whether she could hear or not, she would go." There is a brother whose face I seldom miss from this house, who, I believe, has never in his life heard a sound, and cannot make an articulate utterance, yet he is a joyful believer, and loves the place where God's honor dwelleth. Well, now, I think if *such* persons find pleasure in coming, we who *can hear*, though we feel our unworthiness, though we are conscious that we are not fit to come, should be desirous to be *laid* in the House of God, as the sick were at the pool of Bethesda, hoping that the waters may be stirred, and that we may step in and be healed. Trembling soul, never let the temptations of the devil keep thee from God's House. "At mealtime come thou hither."

Moreover, she was bidden not only to come, but to *eat*. Now, whatever there is sweet and comfortable in the Word of God, ye that are of a broken and contrite spirit, are invited to partake of it. "Jesus Christ came into the world to save *sinners*"—sinners such as you are. "In due time Christ died for the *ungodly*"—for such ungodly ones as you feel yourselves to be. You are desiring this morning to be Christ's. Well, you *may* be Christ's. You are saying in your heart, "Oh that I could eat the children's bread!" You *may* eat it. You say, "I have no right." But he gives you the invitation! Come without any other right than the right of his invitation. I know you will say how unworthy you are.

> Let not conscience make you linger,
> Nor of fitness fondly dream.

But since he bids you "come," take him at his Word; and if there be a promise, believe it; if there be rich consolation, drink it; if there be an encouraging word, accept it, and let the sweetness of it be yours.

Note further, that she was not only invited to eat the bread, but to *dip her morsel in the vinegar*. We must not look upon this as being some sour stuff. No doubt there are crabbed souls in the Church, who always dip their morsel in the sourest imaginable vinegar, and with a grim liberality invite others to share a little comfortable misery with them; but the vinegar in my text is altogether another thing. This was either a compound of various sweets expressed from fruits, or else it was that weak kind of wine mingled with water which is still commonly used in the harvest fields of Italy, and the warmer parts of the world—a drink not exceedingly strong, but excellently cooling, and good enough to impart a relish to the reapers' food. It was, to use the only word which will give the meaning, a sauce, which the Orientals used with their bread. As we use butter, or as they on other occasions used oil, so in the harvest field, believing it to have cooling properties, they used what is here called vinegar. Beloved, the Lord's reapers have sauce with their bread; they have sweet consolations; they have not merely doctrines, but the holy unction which is the essence of doctrines; they have not merely truths, but a hallowed and ravishing delight accompanies the truths. Take, for instance, the doctrine of election, which is like the bread; there is a sauce to dip that in. When I can say, "He loved *me* before the foundations of the world," the personal application, the personal enjoyment of my interest in the truth becomes a sauce into which I dip my morsel. And you, poor gleaner, are invited to dip your morsel in it too. I used to hear people sing that hymn of Toplady's, which begins—

> A debtor to mercy alone,
> Of covenant mercy I sing;
> Nor fear with thy righteousness on,
> My person and offerings to bring.

And rises to its climax—

> Yes, I to the end shall endure,
> As sure as the earnest is given;
> More happy, but not more secure,
> The glorified spirits in heaven.

And I used to think I could never sing that hymn. It was the sauce, you know. I might manage to eat some of the plain bread, but I could not dip it in that sauce. It was too high doctrine, too sweet, too consoling. But I thank God I have since ventured to dip my morsel in it, and now I hardly like my bread without it.

332 • *Ruth (3): Mealtime in the Cornfields*

Now I think I see her, and she is half prepared to come, for she is very hungry, and she has brought nothing with her this morning; but she begins to say, "I have no right to come, for I am not a reaper; I do nothing for Christ; I did not even come here this morning to honor him; I came here, as gleaners go into a cornfield, from a selfish motive, to pick up what I could for myself; and all the religion that I have lies in this—the hope that I may be saved; I do not glorify God; I do not good to other people; I am only a selfish gleaner; I am not a reaper." Ah! but thou art *invited* to come. Make no questions about it. Boaz bids thee. Take thou his invitation and enter at once. But, you say, "I am such a *poor* gleaner; though it is all for myself, yet it is little I get at it; I get a few thoughts while the sermon is being preached, but I lose them before I reach home." I know you do, poor weak-handed woman. But still, Jesus invites thee. Come! Take thou the sweet promise as He presents it to thee, and let no bashfulness of thine send thee home hungry. "But," you say, "I am a stranger; you do not know my sins, my sinfulness, and the waywardness of my heart." But Jesus does; and yet Jesus invites you! he knows you are but a Moabitess, a stranger from the commonwealth of Israel; but he bids you. Is not that enough? Will you refuse Boaz? Shall Jesus' lips give the invitation, and will you say me nay? Come, now, come. Remember that the little which Ruth could eat did not make Boaz any the poorer; and all that thou wantest will make Christ none the less glorious, or full of grace. What! are thy necessities large? Yes, but His supplies are larger. Dost thou require great mercy? He is a great Savior. I tell thee, that His mercy is no more to be exhausted than the sea is to be drained; or than the sun is to be rendered dim by the excess of the light which He pours forth today.

Moreover, let me tell thee a secret—Jesus *loves* thee; therefore it is that he would have thee feed at his table. If thou are not a longing, trembling sinner, willing to be saved, but conscious that thou deservest it not, Jesus loves thee, sinner, and he will take more delight in seeing thee eat than thou wilt take in the eating. Let the sweet love he feels in his soul toward thee draw thee to him. And what is more—but this is a great secret, and must only be whispered in your ear—he *intends to be married to you*; and when you are married to him, why, the fields will be yours; for, of course, if you are the spouse, you are joint-proprietor with him. Is it not so? Doth not the wife share with the husband? All those promises which are "yea and Amen in Christ" shall be yours; nay, they all *are* yours now, for "the man is next of kin unto you," and ere long he will spread his skirt over you and take you unto himself forever, espousing you in faithfulness, and truth, and righteousness.

Now, thirdly, and here is a very sweet point in the narrative: BOAZ REACHED HER THE PARCHED CORN. "She did come and eat." Where did she eat? You notice she "sat beside the reapers." She did not feel that she was one of them—she "sat beside" them. Just as some of you do, who do not come down here this evening to the Lord's Supper, but sit in the gallery. You are sitting "beside the reapers." You are sitting as if you were not one of us—had no right to be among the people of God; still you will sit beside us. If there is a good thing to be had, and you cannot get it, you will get as near as you can to those who *do*; you think there is some comfort even in looking on at the gracious feast. "She sat beside the reapers." And while she was sitting there, what happened? Did she stretch forth her hand and get the food herself? No, it is written, "HE reached her the parched corn." Ah! that is it. I give the invitation, brother, today; I give it earnestly, affectionately, sincerely; but I know very well, that while I give it, no trembling heart will accept it, unless the King himself comes near, and feasts his saints today. He must reach the parched corn; *he* must give you to drink of the "juice of the spiced wine of his pomegranate." How does he do this? By his gracious spirit, he first of all inspires your faith. You are afraid to think it can be true that such a sinner as you are accepted in the Beloved; he breathes upon you, and your faint hope becomes an expectancy, and that expectation buds and blossoms into an appropriating faith, which says, "Yes, my beloved is *mine*, and his desire is toward *me*." Having done this, the Savior does more; *he sheds abroad the love of God in your heart.* The love of Christ is like sweet perfume in a box. Now, he who put the pefume in the box is the only Person that knows how to take the lid off. He, with His own skillful hand, takes the lid from the box; then it is "shed abroad" like "ointment poured forth." You know it may be there, and yet not be shed abroad.

But Jesus does more than this; he reaches the parched corn with his own hand, when *he gives us close communion with him.* Do not think that this is a dream; I tell you there is such a thing as talking with Christ today. As certainly as I can talk with my dearest friend, or find solace in the company of my beloved wife, so surely may I speak with Jesus, and find intense delight in the company of Immanuel. It is not a fiction. We do not worship a far-off Savior; he is a God right at hand. We do not adore him as One who has gone away to heaven, and who never can be approached; but he is nigh us, in our mouth and in our heart, and we do today walk with him as the elect did of old, and commune with him as his apostles did on earth; not after the flesh, it is true, but spiritual men value spiritual communion better than any carnal fellowship.

Yet once more let me add, the Lord Jesus is pleased to reach the parched corn, in the best sense, when *the Spirit gives us the infallible witness within, that we are "born of God."* A man may know that he is a Christian infallibly. Philip de Morny, who lived in the time of Prince Henry of Navarre, was wont to say that the Holy Spirit had made his own salvation to him as clear a point as ever a problem proved to a demonstration in Euclid could be. You know with what mathematical precision the scholar of Euclid solves a problem or proves a proposition, and just the same, with as absolute a precision, as certainly as twice two are four, we may "know that we have passed from death unto life." The sun in the heavens is not more clear to the eye than his own salvation to an assured believer; such a man would as soon doubt his own existence, and suspect his interest in eternal life.

After Boaz had reached the parched corn, we are told that "SHE DID EAT, AND WAS SUFFICED, AND LEFT." So shall it be with every Ruth. Sooner or later every penitent shall become a believer. There may be a space of deep conviction, and a period of much hesitation; but there shall come a season, when the soul decides for the Lord. If I perish, I perish. I will go as I am to Jesus. I will not play the fool any longer with my *buts* and *ifs*, but since he bids me believe that he died for me, I *will* believe it, and will trust his cross for my salvation. And oh! whenever you shall be privileged to do this, you shall be *"satisfied."* She did eat, and was satisifed. Your *head* shall be satisifed with the precious truth which Christ reveals; you *heart* shall be content with Jesus, as the altogether lovely object of affection; your *hope* shall be satisfied, for whom have you in heaven but Christ? Your *desire* shall be satiated, for what can even the hunger of your desire wish for more than "to know Christ, and to be found in him." You shall find Jesus fill your *conscience*, till it is at perfect peace; he shall fill your *judgment*, till you know the certainty of his teachings; he shall fill your *memory* with recollections of what he did, and fill your *imagination* with the prospects of what he is yet to do. You shall be "satisfied." Still, still it shall be true, that you shall leave something. "She was satisfied, and she left." Some of us have had deep drafts; we have thought that we could take in all of Christ; but when we have done our best, we have had to leave a vast remainder. We have sat down with a ravenous appetite at the table of the Lord's love, and said, "Now, nothing but the Infinite can ever satisfy me; I am such a great sinner that I must have infinite merit to wash my sin away"; but we have had our sin removed, and found that there was merit to spare; we have had our hunger relieved, and found that there was a redundance for others who were in a similar case. There are certain sweet things in the Word of God which you and I have not enjoyed yet, and which we cannot enjoy yet; we are obliged to leave them for a while. "I have yet many things to say unto you, but ye cannot bear them now." There is a knowledge to which we have not attained — a place of fellowship nearer yet to Christ. There are heights of communion which as yet our feet have not climbed — virgin snows upon the mountain untrodden by the foot of man. There is a yet beyond, and there will be forever.

But please to notice: it is not in the text, but it is recorded a verse or two further on, what she did with her leavings. It is a very bad habit, I believe, at feasts, to carry anything home with you; but *she* did, for that which was left she took home; and when she reached Naomi, and showed her the quantity of wheat in her apron, after she had asked, "Where hast thou gleaned today" and had received the answer, she gave to Naomi a portion of that which she had reserved after she was sufficed. So it shall be even with you, poor tremblers, who think you have no right to any for yourselves; you shall be able to eat and be quite satisfied, and what is more, you shall have a morsel to carry to others in a like condition. I am always pleased to find the young believer beginning to pocket something for other poeple. When you hear a sermon, you think, "Well, poor mother cannot get out today, I will tell her something about it. There now, that point will just suit her: I will take that, if I forget anything else; I will tell her that by the bedside. There is my brother William, who will not come with me to chapel; I wish he would; but now, there was something which struck me in the sermon, and when I get close to him, I will tell him *that*, and I will say, 'Will you not come this evening?' I will tell him those portions which interested me; perhaps they will interest him." There are your children in the Sunday school class. You say, "That illustration will do for them." I think sometimes, when I see you putting down my metaphors on little scraps of paper, that you may recollect to tell somebody else; I would fain give more where they are so well used; I would let fall an extra handful, on purpose that there may be enough for you and for your friends.

Cultivate an unselfish spirit. Seek to love as you have been loved. Remember that "the law and the prophets" lie in this, to "love the Lord your God with all your heart, and your neighbor as yourself." How can you love him as yourself, if you do not love his soul? You *have* loved your own soul; through grace you have been led to lay hold on Jesus. Love your neighbor's soul, and never be satisified till you see him in the enjoyment of those things which are the charm of your life and the joy of your spirit. I do not know how to give my invitation in a more comfortable way; but as we are sitting down to feed at his table in the evening of this day, I pray the Master to reach a large handful of parched corn to some trembling sinner, and enable him to eat and be satisfied.

11

RUTH

A Sermon for Gleaners

"Boaz commanded his young men, saying, Let her glean even among the sheaves, and reproach her not: and let fall also some of the handfuls of purpose for her, and leave them, that she may glean them, and rebuke her not" (Ruth 2:15, 16).

ALL the world dependeth upon the labor of the field, and the king himself is served of the plow and of the sickle. The dwellers in the country who watch the up-springing blade through all its perils, who mark the ear as it bursts from its sheath, and who anxiously observe it until it hangeth downward through ripeness, and becometh yellow in the sun— these, being brought constantly into contact wit clods and crops, are not able to forget their entire dependence upon "the staff of life." One can hardly live where the operations of husbandry are carried on, without often looking up to the God of Providence in anxious prayer, and anon, lifting up the heart in grateful praise. But the most of us are condemned to live in this huge wilderness of bricks, where scarcely a green thing salutes our eyes; where, if we try to rear a plant, it is but a sickly thing, neither tempting for beauty, nor fragrant with perfume. In the absence of the bright-eyed flowers, it is small wonder if we grow a little blind towards our mother earth. We are too apt to think that *we* are independent of the operations of the country; that our trade, our commerce, our manufacturers are sufficient to support us; forgetting all the while, that in vain is yonder forest of masts unless the earth shall yield her fruit; in vain the emporium, the exchange, and the places of merchandise, unless the land be plowed and harrowed, and at last yield to the husbandman his reward.

I would that I could recall to your memories, O ye dwellers in the city, how much ye depend upon the Lord God of the earth for your daily bread. Doth your food fall like manna from the skies? Do ye create it at the forge, or fashion it in the loom or on the wheel? Cometh it not of the earth, and is it not the Lord who giveth to the fertile womb of earth the power to yield its harvests? Cometh now the dew from heaven, and the sunshine from above, and do not these bring to *us* our bread as well as to those who abide in the midst of the fields? Let us not forget this time of the harvest, nor be unthankful for the bounty of the wheatsheaf; let us not forget to plead with God that he would be pleased to give us suitable weather for the ingathering of the precious grain, and when it shall be ingathered, let us not sullenly keep silence, but with the toiling swains who, well-pleased, behold the waving yellow crop, let us lift up the shout of harvest-home, and thank the God who covereth the valleys with corn, and crowneth the year with his goodness.

Tell me not that this is not a proper theme for the Sabbath day. I wot ye know not what ye say. Did not the disciples of Jesus walk though the cornfields on the Sabbath, and did not the Master make the fields themselves the subjects of his sermons? I fear not his disapprobation when I say, on this hallowed day, "Lift up now your eyes, and behold the fields are ripe already unto the harvest." Do you think that the outward creation is sinful, and that God would be worshiped on Sabbaths with closed eyes, and vacant faces, which must not look on flowers and fields? There is no impurity in green grass, or flowers, or sailing-clouds, or rippling waves, or ripening corn. To the believing ear, the footsteps of the Bountiful Father are everywhere audible, and the revolving seasons do but reveal the varied attributes of God. We may gather from every rustling ear a son, and listen in every harvest-field to a sermon which angels might stoop to hear. 'Tis no unhallowed theme. Come with me to the harvest-field—may the Master come with us—and let us talk awhile of other things than harvests, though the harvest shall be the metaphor on which we will fashion our speech.

I have now to invite you to other fields than these. I would bring you to the field of Gospel truth. My Master is the Boaz. See here, in this precious book is a field full of truthful promises, of blessings rich and ripe. The Master standeth at the gate, and affords us welcome. Strong men, full of faith, like reapers, reap their sheaves and gather in their armfuls. Would you were all reapers, for the harvest truly is plenteous. But if not reapers, may ye be as the maidens of Boaz. I see some servants who do not so much reap themselves as partake of that which others have reaped; I know we have many in this Church who are glad to eat the sweets and feed upon the fat things of the kingdom when they are brought forth each Sabbath-day, in the ministry of the Word. But I see trembling yonder, outside the gate, a little company to whom I am to address myself today; they are not reapers, they have not strength enough of faith to take the big sheaves; they are not as yet like household servants; they are not peaceful enough in their consciences to sit down and eat, and dip their morsel in the vinegar and be satisfied; but they are *gleaners*, and they are saying as they stand at the gate, "Would that I might find favor in the sight of my Lord, that I might even glean in this field, for I should then be content if I might gather here and there an ear of gospel grace." I am sent to you. My Master sendeth me as one of his young men, and thus he biddeth me say unto you, "Come into the field and glean wheresoever you will, and if in the gleaning you should grow strong and become reapers, reap and carry home the sheaves for yourselves."

First then, like Boaz, I shall ask the question, "WHO IS THIS DAMSEL?" in order that I may find out who these gleaners are who are invited into the field of Christ, that they may glean the handfuls that are let fall on purpose for them.

"Who is this damsel?" The first answer is, *she is a Moabitess and a stranger.* Ah! I know thee, poor timid heart. Thou sayest, "I am sprang of an evil stock, an heir of wrath even as others; my nature is depraved and vile; how can I hope, such a one as I am, that I should ever be allowed to go into the Master's field, and glean of his good corn of grace? Oh! sir, did you know what I feel of my lost and helpless state, could you but perceive how base I am in my own eyes, because I have been so long a stranger to God, and an alien from the commonwealth of Israel. I think you would scarce invite me to glean in the field at all." Verily, my sister, thou art the very person to whom I am sent, for it was a Moabitish damsel upon whom Boaz set his heart, and it was to her that he sent his message. "Abide thou fast by my maidens; go not in any other field."

But I ask again who this damsel is, and she answers, "I am not only by nature a stranger, *but I must confess that I am now in my condition miserable and poor;* I cannot buy Christ's grace; I can do nothing to win his love. Once I thought I had some good works, but now I have none.

Once I relied upon ceremonies, but I have given them up, for I find no comfort in them. I am utterly poor—so poor, that I despair of ever in the future being richer than I am now. I am helpless; I am hopeless; I am nothing; yea, I am less than nothing. Alas! I am such a miserable beggar, that I am not worthy of the least of all his mercies." Dost thou say this? Right glad am I, then, to hear thee use such language, for unto thee, again, am I sent, and unto thee am I bidden to give the gracious invitation—"Come into the field and glean even among the sheaves."

Now the gleaner whom I describe is not only in her experience an alien and a stranger, and in her own present condition naked and poor, and miserable, *but she hath, despite all this, a decision for the Lord God of Israel.* I think I hear her say, "If I perish, I will perish looking to the cross of Christ; I have nothing of my own to bring, but I come just as I am. The Lord knoweth I have no other dependence but upon the blood and the finished righteousness of Jesus Christ. I forswear the gods of Moab in whom I once trusted; the world is now nothing to me; the pomps and vanities thereof have lost all their glory; as to myself, I abhor myself in dust and ashes. I would be Christ's and if he will not have me, if I may not glean in his fields, I will never go elsewhere.

It is marvelous the tenacity with which some of these timid souls will hold to Christ. Just as a man, the more fearful he is of sinking, clutches the plant with a more terrible earnestness; so have I seen some of these fearful souls lay hold on Jesus with a grip which neither death nor hell could unloose. Were the times of burning to come back again, many a wavering soul, that can scarce say, "I know that my Redeemer liveth," would go singing to the stake; while many of those who are bold in words would prove cowardly in acts, and withdraw from Christ when it came to burning for him.

Our description, however, is far from being complete. *This gleaner is one who is exceedingly humble and self-emptied.* Just observe what she saith when Boaz takes notice of her—"Who am I, that I should find grace in thy sight, seeing that I am a stranger?" Ah! and the woman to whom I would speak this morning has such a low estimate of herself, that when she gets a grain of hope she thinks, "Ah! it is too good for me." When, sometimes, you half hope that Christ hath loved you and given himself for you, a sight of your unworthiness comes in, and you say, "No, this can hardly be, that such an one, so mean and so despicable as I, should ever be regarded by the lovely eyes of Christ, my Lord." I know you think not yourself to be pure, or fair, or lovely; and when you read such a passage as that, where Christ saith of His spouse, "Thou art all fair, my love, there is no spot in thee," tears come in your eyes, for you say, "Alas! He will never say that of me, for 'I am all defiled with sin, all unholy and unclean.' Should he search the world through, he would not find a more worthless one than I, and should he turn the heap over again and again, he could not find one that less deserved to be the object of his pity than I, poor unworthy I." Aye, but thou art just the person to whom I am sent! Thy Lord Jesus hath heard of thee, and he loveth such as thou art, for when thou art little in thine own eyes, then art thou great in his, and when thou talkest thus bashfully of thyself then he loves to hear thy words, for they are words of truth. In very deed, thou art what thou sayest thou art, nothing but loathesomeness, and corruption, and depravity; and yet he who hath loved thee, notwithstanding all this, will never leave thee till thy corruption has been removed, till thy loathesomeness has been washed away, till for deformity thou hast matchless beauty, and for unholiness his perfect righteousness.

Once again, *these gleaners have a very high opinion of those who are true Christians.* You notice, Ruth says, "I am not like unto one of thy hand-maidens." No, and my poor gleaner yonder, she thinks the saints of God are such a blessed people, she is not like one of them. When she gets into her black experience she says, "If I were a child of God I would never be like this." Knowing her vileness and her imperfections she cries, "Ah! if I were one of Christ's chosen I should be much holier than I am; though I love his saints, I cannot dare to hope that I shall ever be numbered with them; my goodness can never reach so high as to be joined with them in visible fellowship." Ah! I know some of you feel that if you ever did get to heaven you would creep through some cranny in the door, and hide yourselves in some mousehole far away, where none could see you; and today, though in truth you are the best of the saints, you think yourselves the vilest of the vile; for many there be that are very rich in grace who think themselves miserably poor; while, on the other hand, many who say "I am rich and increased in goods, and have need of nothing," are naked and poor, and miserable. Poor Moabitess, long an alien, having gone far into sin, and now decided for Christ, with a sort of despairing hope that maybe he will look upon thee, today—even today, he speaketh to thee. Open thine ear and hear him; forget thy kindred and thy father's house, for he greatly desireth thee, and he would have thee even now come to him and be espoused unto him forever.

Having beckoned to the gleaner, I shall now, like Boaz, ADDRESS THE REAPERS. The ministers are the reapers, and thus speaks Boaz to them—"Let her glean, even among the sheaves, and reproach her not; let fall some of the handfuls of purpose for her, and leave them that she may glean them, and rebuke her not."

The first command Christ gives to his ministers is—"Rebuke her not." Ah! I fear me, my brethren in the ministry, that we have often rebuked where we ought to have comforted, and perhaps our unwise speeches, when we did not mean to do it, have been very hard blows to the afflicted in Zion. I know some preachers who never went to Martin Luther's school; they may have prayer and meditation, but they have never been schooled by temptation; and if we are not much tempted ourselves, if we are not emptied from vessel to vessel ourselves, we are in very great danger when we are dealing with these Ruths, lest we be hard with them, and rebuke and reproach them, when instead thereof we should hear the Master say, "Comfort ye, comfort ye my people; speak ye comfortably unto Jerusalem."

Now I take it that we do very much reproach these tender ones *when we set up standards in our ministry to which we tell them they must come or else perish.* Some do it in *experience.* I have heard old divines, and, like Elihu, I have been ready to rebuke my seniors when they have taught their experience, in all its length and breadth, as necessary for all the people of God. The experience of the advanced saint must never be set up as a standard for the young beginner. There are mountains for us to climb when our bones are firm, but these mountains are not for babes. There are depths into which we are to dive when we have learned the art of plunging into them, but these are not for little children, who must be dandled on the knee and nourished at the breast. When we describe some dark passage in our lives and say to the young convert—"You must have felt all this or you are not a child of God," we are reproaching where we ought to have comforted, and rebuking where we ought to have consoled. So have I seen a standard of *grace* set up. Some Christians are eminent in their graces; their faith is valorous; their courage defies all danger; their hope is bright and sparkling like a diamond; but if in our preaching we tell young converts that their graces must be equal in luster to the fathers in the Church, what do we but rebuke Ruth when we ought to have let fall handfuls of corn for her to gather?

And so, too, with regard to *doctrinal knowledge*. I have known some Christians well-schooled in these matters, and deeply read in theology who, when they meet with one who knows no more than this, that he is a sinner, and that Christ came to save sinners, will ask hard, wrinkled questions, which are more fit for an assembly of divines than for a babe in Christ; and because, truly, the little child cannot untie a Gordian knot, because the babe cannot crack the hard shells of these theological nuts, they send him away and say, "The root of the matter is not in thee; thou hast not passed from death unto life." Oh! let us not do this, dear brother-reapers; let us sooner cut ourselves with our own sickle than cut Ruths therewith; let us rather be patient and very tender, and receive the weak in the faith, as Christ hath received them. Let us, like our Master, not overdrive the lambs, but carry them in our bosom, and gently lead them when they need our tenderness and our care.

There is also another way in which some rebuke these gleaners, who should rather be invited and comforted—that is, by denying their faith when it is mixed with unbelief. It is marvelous, it is miraculous, that a spark of faith can live in the midst of an ocean of unbelief. You will find men who, at times, fear that they believe nothing; in their own apprehension they are so beclouded and bemisted that they have lost their way, and do not know where they are; and yet they are true believers for all that. Some of us have passed through crisis of our being in which, if we had been asked our very name, we could hardly have told it, for we were so utterly distressed, so lost and cast away by reason of overwhelming blasphemies, or incessant temptations, that we could scarce tell our right hand from our left. And were we therefore without faith? Nay, there was a little faith still; there was an undying principle still within us when death had made us wretched men. So we must not talk to these young beginners as though the uprising of their corruption disproved the indwelling of the Holy Spirit, but we must succor them. We may tell them of the dragons we have fought, and the giants we have slain, but we must use discretion even in this; and when they are in the Slough of Despond, we must not leave them to sink there up to their very necks, but go like Help in the *Pilgrim's Progress*, and lend them our hand to pull them out, for they may be in the right road even in the slough, and they may still have their faces to Zion though those faces may be

besmeared with the mire and filth of that dreadful bog. Let us never rebuke or reproach these timid ones, but help and sustain them.

But further; Boaz gave another exhortation to the reapers — "*Let fall
handfuls of purpose for her.*" In our ministry there should always be a corner cupboard for the tired and timid saints. I think there should never
be a sermon without a Benjamin's mess for the children. There should
be strong meat for the men, but there should always be milk for the babes.
Ready to adapt our ministry to all sorts of people, if we forget any we should
never forget these. My brother, wouldest thou minister to these gleaners? Let me remind thee, first, that our ministry must be *plain*, for
these timid souls cannot feed on hard words. Dr. Manton once preached
in St. Paul's Cathedral, and a great crowd went to listen to him. A poor
man who had walked fifty miles to hear the good doctor, afterwards plucked
him by the sleeve and said — "There was nothing for me this morning."
The doctor had preached a very learned sermon, full of Greek and Latin
quotations which the poor countryman could not understand; but the
doctor had not expected him, and there was nothing for him. I think there
should always be in our ministry some things for poor Ruth; so plain and
so simple that the wiseacres will turn up their noses and say, "What plat-
itudes!" Never mind, if Ruth gets a handful of corn, our Master at the
last shall know who did his errand best, and served him with a perfect
heart.

And then, if plain, we must remember, too, that it must be very *elementary*. We must be often laying again the foundation-stone; teaching
faith in Christ again and again; as Luther says, repeating justification
by faith every Sunday, because men are so apt to forget it. Oh! ye fine
preachers who elaborate your learned essays, who work all the week long
to addle your own brains, and then spend the Sunday in muddling
your hearers, would that ye would remember these poor gleaners, who
want none of your fine stuff, none of our glorious fights, none of your
rounded periods; but who will be better far content if you will tell
them that Jesus Christ came into the world to save sinners, and will point
their eyes to Calvary and bid them look and live. We must let fall handfuls on purpose for the weak and ignorant.

And then again, our preaching must be *evangelical*. Seeing eyes
need Christ to dry them; tender hearts need Jesus' wounds to make them
whole. A man who lives without temptation may enjoy a Sunday's sermon without Christ in it, but give me a man who is tempted in the week

and I know he wants Christ; give me a man who has lost money in the week, or that has been subjected to ridicule for Christ's sake, and I know that you might as well offer him the husks that swine do eat as offer him anything but Christ crucified visibly set forth before his eyes. Oh! we must get back to this, all of us who are preachers; we must forget what we learned at college; we must leave behind what we pick up from learned books, and come out to tell to Ruth just that which she most wants to hear, that Boaz welcomes her to the field, and bids her glean till her hands are full.

But then, brethren, you will notice that these reapers were to let handfuls fall *on purpose for her*. Well, then, ye reapers in God's field, let your preaching be very *personal*. Oh! I love when I draw the bow not to do it at a venture, but to single out some troubled heart and speak to you all as though there were but one here; not pouring the oil over the wound, but coming up to the edge of the gaping sore to pour *in* the oil and wine. These poor Ruths will not dare to take the corn unless we put it right in their way. They are so fearful, so timorous, that though it seem to be scattered for everybody, they think it cannot be for them; but if it be *there*, put *there*, so that they cannot mistake it, then they say — "Well, that is for me; ay, that is what *I* have felt; that is what *I* want"; and they cannot, unbelieving though they be, they cannot help stooping down and picking up the handful that is let fall *on purpose* for them. Then, if it be so, our preaching must always be very *affectionate*, for if we let fall a handful with a scowling face, our Ruth will go to the other end of the field rather than pick it up.

Oh! brethren in Christ, it is after all our sympathy with our fellow-men which is the great engine the Holy Ghost uses in converting them. It is not merely telling out the truth which is the power. God, if he had willed it, might have made statues which could preach, and they could have preached as well as we do, and infinitely better if the Lord had poured the words out of their cold lips; but he made *men* preachers that men might feel for men, and that our words might come out from our hearts, and so go glowing into the hearts of the afflicted. Oh! let *us*, then, who are reapers for Christ, be very tender with poor Ruth, and often when we forget the strong and leave the mighty man to take care of himself, let us go to the gate to pull in the fainting Mercy, and to invite Christiana and her little children to sit down and rest. So would I do this morning, and therefore I pass on to our third point.

As myself a reaper for Christ, I must try to follow the example of the reapers of Boaz, and let fall handfuls on purpose for the gleaner.

I am afraid I shall not be able to give you such handfuls as I would, but they shall come out of the right field. Oh! thou timid and troubled heart, let me drop before thee now *a handful of precious promises.* "He will not break the risen reed, or quench the smoking flax." Doth not that suit thy case? A reed, helpless, insignificant, and weak; a bruised reed, out of which no music can come; weaker than weakness itself; a reed, and that reed bruised! He will not break thee; he who broke Rahab by his right hand will not break thee. Thou art like the smoking flax; no light, no warmth, come from thee; thou art on the contrary, like flax that smokes, giving forth a foul, offensive smell. But he will not quench thee; he will blow with his sweet breath of mercy, till he fans thee to a flame. Dost thou need another? "Come unto me all ye that labor and are heavy laden, and I will give you rest; take my yoke upon you, and learn of me, for I am meek and lowly in heart, and ye shall find rest unto your souls." What soft words! Thy heart is tender and the Master knows it, and therefore he speaketh so gently to thee. Wilt thou not listen, and obey him, and come to him, come to him even now? Hear him yet again—"Fear not, thou worn Jacob, I will help thee, saith the Lord, and thy Redeemer, the Holy One of Israel." Or wouldest thou hear Jesus Christ speak to thee again?—"Let not your heart be troubled: ye believe in God, believe also in me." Or, again, "He is able to save unto the uttermost them that come unto God by him."

Dost thou not remember ten thousand such passages as these? "When thou passest through the rivers I will be with thee, and the floods shall not overflow thee; when thou goest through the fires thou shalt not be burned; neither shall the flame kindle upon thee." Or this, "Can a woman forget her sucking child that she should not have compassion on the son of her womb? Yea, she may forget, yet will I not forget thee." Or this, "I have blotted out thy sins like a cloud, and like a thick cloud thy transgressions." Or this, "Though your sins be as scarlet they shall be as wool; though they be red like crimson they shall be whiter than snow." Or this, "The Spirit and the bride say Come, and let him that is athirst come, and whosoever will, let him come and take the water of life freely." Or this, again, "Ho, every one that thirsteth, come ye to the waters, and ye that have no money, come and eat; yea, come, buy wine and milk, without money and without price." Oh! my Master's field is very rich; behold the handfuls. See, there they lie before thee, poor timid soul! Gather them up, make them thine own, for Jesus bids thee take them. Be not thou too bashful; but take them, feed on them, and go on in the strength of this meat all thy days.

Well, I have dropped a handful of promises; now let me try to scatter a *handful of doctrines.* But Ruth starts back, for she is afraid to glean in the wheat fields of doctrine. Nay, but, Ruth, here is the doctrine of election; come and glean that. Fear thee not, poor timid soul, 'tis a sweet and blessed truth. Hear it—"God hath chosen the weak things of this world, and the things that are not hath God chosen to bring to naught the things that are." "I thank thee, O Father of heaven and earth, that thou hast hid these things from the wise and prudent, and hast revealed them unto babes." Doth not that suit thee, timid soul? Art not thou as a babe, as a weak thing, and as a foolish thing? Oh, there is a handful on purpose for thee, in the doctrine of electing love. Hear thou another, the doctrine of justification by faith; not by works of righteousness which we have done he saveth us, but through Christ Jesus; we are saved through what Jesus hath done on our behalf. "He that believeth on him is not condemned, but hath everlasting life." What sayest thou? Doth not that suit thee? Thou hast no good works; canst thou not trust Christ and *his* good works on thy behalf? Is not this a handful on purpose for thee? "Yes, but I fear me," saith one, "that if I were saved I should yet fall away, for I am so weak." There is another handful for thee, "I give unto my sheep eternal life, and they shall never perish, neither shall any pluck them out of my hand." "For I am persuaded, that neither death, nor life, nor angels, nor principalities, nor powers, nor things present, nor things to come, nor height, nor depth, nor any other creature shall be able to separate us from the love of God, which is in Christ Jesus." Is not this a handful on purpose for thee? "I have made and I will bear, even I will carry; even unto hoar hairs I am he, and unto old age will I carry thee." What more dost thou want. I tell thee, Ruth, there is not a single doctrine in Scripture which, if it be rightly understood, will not yield handfuls on purpose *for thee.* Indeed, my Master's gospel, though it be a chariot in which a king may ride, is like an ambulance used on the field of battle, in which a man with broken limbs may ride comfortably too.

Once more, we have some handfuls to drop that we have gathered in another field; we have been to promise-field and to doctrine-field, *now*

348 • *Ruth (4): A Sermon for Gleaners*

let us go to the field of experience. Dost thou not know, Ruth, that thy experience is no exception to the rule? There are thousands such as thou art; and I, too, who speak to thee this morning, that thou mayest know the truth of this matter, I tell thee that once upon a time I stood like thyself shivering at the gate, and I said in my soul, "His mercy is clean gone forever; he will be mindful of his covenant no more." For years I cried for mercy but did not find it, and I wrote my name among the damned, and said I must perish, for God had shut up the bowels of his compassion. But he hath not despised the cry of his prisoner. I looked unto him and was lightened, and I am not ashamed to confess that there is light nowhere but in him. "Oh," say you, "then your experience is something like mine! Just so, it is; and so there is a handful on purpose *for you.* I know the devil tells you, you are lost in a byroad where Christ's mercy never travels; but it is a mistake; you are in the midst of the king's highway. I know he tells you, you have got to the ends of the earth; but my Lord puts it—"Look unto me and be ye saved, all ye ends of the earth." Oh, but you think you are the last man! Ah! but Christ loveth to take the last and make them first, while the first he often leaveth to be last. Yes, but you have written bitter things against yourself! Never mind what you have written; what a mercy it is Christ did not write them, and that, on the contrary, he has written sweet things of you, and hath said, "Return unto me, saith the Lord, for I am reconciled unto thee." My Master woos thee this morning. Instead of offering thee a gleaning, he offers thee himself. Thou camest to be a gleaner; he would make thee his spouse. See, Boaz comes to thee. Wilt thou have him? The ring is in his hand; come, stretch out the finger of thy little faith, and let the deed be done. Say, "Unworthy though I be, I hope, my Lord, I am thine; no other would I have to serve, to love, to trust; Jesu, just as I am take thou me, and make me what thou wouldest have me to be." 'Tis done; the marriage is ratified, and by and by it shall be consummated before the eternal throne in thine everlasting bliss.

I close, then, by stirring up timid and troubled ones to do what I know grace will make them do ere long. I say, then to you who are thus troubled in your consciences, since the field is open to you, and we bid you glean; since Boaz himself commands us to let fall handfuls on purpose for you, do your duty, and be bold to believe today. You have been afraid to trust Christ hitherto; trust him now. Venture on him; 'tis a poor word to use, but do it.

Ruth, we are told, threshed her corn and left the straw behind, and took home the good wheat. Do thou the same. There is much straw in all our sermons, much that our Master would not have us say, for we are poor, poor creatures, and but fallible like yourselves, but do you leave the straw behind, and take home the good wheat; and do us this service — do not take home the straw and leave the wheat as some do. And, lastly, while on your knees in prayer you are beating out the sermon by meditation, turn your eye to my Master; go you to him and say to him, "Lord, I am content to glean though I get but one ear of mercy; but oh! that I had thyself! Oh! that thou wouldest give me thyself! I have no beauty, but oh! Thou dost not love us for *our* beauty, but for *thy* beauty which thou dost cast on us; Lord, look on me; all I can say is that if thou wilt save me I will praise thee on earth and I'll praise thee in heaven, and there shall not be one before the throne more grateful than I, because there shall be none who shall owe so much to thine unmerited, rich, free, sovereign grace."

12

HANNAH

A Woman of a Sorrowful Spirit

"Hannah answered and said, No, my lord, I am a woman of a sorrowful spirit" (1 Sam. 1:15).

THE special cause of Hannah's sorrow arose from the institution of polygamy, which, although it was tolerated under the old law, is always exhibited to us in practical action as a most fruitful source of sorrow and sin. In no one recorded instance in Holy Scripture is it set forth as admirable; and in most cases the proofs of its evil effects lie open to the sun. We ought to be grateful that under the Christian religion that abomination has been wiped away; for even with such husbands as Abraham, Jacob, David, and Solomon it did not work towards happiness or righteousness. The husband found the system a heavy burden, grievous to be borne, for he soon found out the truth of the wise man's advice to the Sultan, "First learn to live with two tigresses, and then expect to live happily with two wives." The wife must in nearly every case have felt the wretchedness of sharing a love which ought to be all her own. What miseries Eastern women have suffered in the harem none can tell, or perhaps imagine.

In the case before us, Elkanah had trouble enough through wearing the double chain, but still the heaviest burden fell upon his beloved Hannah, the better of his two wives. The worse the woman the better she could get on with the system of many wives, but the good woman, the true woman, was sure to smart under it. Though dearly loved by her husband, the jealousy of the rival wife embittered Hannah's life, and made her "a woman of a sorrowful spirit." We thank God that no longer is the altar of God covered with tears, with weeping, and with crying out, of those wives of youth who find their husbands' hearts estranged and divided by

351

other wives. Because of the hardness of their hearts the evil was tolerated for a while, but the many evils which sprang of it should suffice to put a ban upon it among all who seek the welfare of our race. In the beginning the Lord made for man but one wife. And wherefore one? For he had the residue of the spirit, and could have breathed into as many as he pleased. Malachi answers, "That he might seek a godly seed." As if it was quite clear that the children of polygamy would be ungodly, and only in the house of one man and one wife would godliness be found. This witness is of the Lord, and is true.

But enough sources of grief remain; more than enough; and there is not in any household, I suppose, however joyous, the utter absence of the cross. The worldling says, "There is a skeleton in every house." I know little about such dead things, but I know that a cross of some sort or other must be borne by every child of God. All the true-born heirs of heaven must pass under the rod of the covenant. What son is there whom the Father chasteneth not? The smoking furnace is part of the insignia of the heavenly family, without which a man may well question whether he stands in covenant relationship to God at all. Probably some Hannah is now before me, smarting under the chastening hand of God, some child of light walking in darkness, some daughter of Abraham bowed down by Satan, and it may not be amiss to remind her that she is not the first of her kind, but that in years gone by there stood at the door of God's house one like to her, who said of herself, "No, my lord, I am a woman of a sorrowful spirit." May the ever-blessed Comforter, whose work lies mainly with the sorrowful, fill our meditation with consolation at this time.

In speaking of this "woman of a sorrowful spirit" we shall make this first remark—that THAT MUCH IS PRECIOUS MAY BE CONNECTED WITH A SORROWFUL SPIRIT. In itself, a sorrowful spirit is not to be desired. Give us the bright eye, the cheerful smile, the vivacious manner, the genial tone. If we do not desire mirth and merriment, yet give us at least that calm peace, that quiet composure, that restful happiness which makes home happy wherever it pervades the atmosphere. There are wives, mothers, and daughters who should exhibit more of these cheerful graces than they now do, and they are very blameable for being petulant, unkind, and irritable; but there are others, I doubt not, who labor to their utmost to be all that is delightful, and yet fail in the attempt, because, like Hannah, they are of a sorrowful spirit, and cannot shake off the grief which burdens their heart. Now, it is idle to tell the night that it should be brilliant as the day, or bid the winter put on the flowers of summer; and equally vain is it to chide the broken heart. The bird of night cannot sing at heaven's gate, nor can the crushed worm leap like a hart up on the mountains. It is of little use exhorting the willow whose branches weep by the river to lift up its head like the palm, or spread its branches like the cedar: everything must act according to its kind; each nature hath its own appropriate ways, nor can it escape the bonds of its fashioning. There are circumstances of constitution, education, and surroundings which render it difficult for some very excellent persons to be cheerful: they are predestined to be known by such a name as this—"A woman of a sorrowful spirit."

Note well the precious things which went in Hannah's case with a sorrowful spirit. The first was true godliness; *she was a godly woman.* As we read the chapter, we are thoroughly certified that her heart was right with God. We cannot raise any question about the sincerity of her prayer, or the prevalence of it. We do not doubt for a moment the truthfulness of her consecration. She was one that feared God above many, an eminently gracious woman, and yet "a woman of a sorrowful spirit." Never draw the inference from sorrow that the subject of it is not beloved of God. You might more safely reason in the opposite way, though it would not be always safe to do so, for outward circumstances are poor tests of a man's spiritual state. Certainly Dives, in his scarlet and fine linen, was not beloved of God, while Lazarus, with the dogs licking his sores, was a favorite of heaven; and yet it is not every rich man that is cast away, or every beggar that will be borne aloft by angels. Outward condition can lead us to no determination one way or another. Hearts must be judged, conduct and action must be weighed, and a verdict given otherwise than by the outward appearance. Many persons feel very happy, but they must not therefore infer that God loves them; while certain others are sadly depressed, it would be most cruel to suggest to them that God is angry with them. It is never said, "whom the Lord loveth he enricheth," but it is said, "whom the Lord loveth he chasteneth."

Affliction and suffering are not proofs of sonship, for "many sorrows shall be to the wicked"; and yet, where there are great tribulations, it often happens that there are great manifestations of the divine favor. There is a sorrow of the world that worketh death—a sorrow which springs from self-will, and is nurtured in rebellion, and is therefore an evil thing, because it is opposed to the divine will. There is a sorrow which eats as doth a canker, and breeds yet greater sorrows, so that such mourners descend with their sorrowful spirits down to the place where sorrow reigns supreme, and hope shall never come. Think of this, but never doubt the fact that a sorrowful spirit is in perfect consistency with the love of God, and the possession of true godliness. It is freely admitted that godliness ought to cheer many a sorrowful spirit more than it does. It is also admitted that much of the experience of Christians is no Christian experience, but a mournful departure from what true believers ought to be and feel.

There is very much that Christians experience which they never ought to experience. Half the troubles of life are homemade, and utterly unnecessary. We afflict ourselves perhaps, ten times more than God afflicts us. We add many thongs to God's whip: when there would be but one we must needs make nine. God sends one cloud by his providence, and we raise a score by our unbelief. But taking all that off, and making the still further abatement that the Gospel commands us to rejoice in the Lord always, and that it would never bid us do so if there were not abundant causes and arguments for it, yet, for all that, a sorrowful spirit may be possessed by one who most truly and deeply fears the Lord. Never judge those whom you see sad, and write them down as under the divine anger, for you might err most grievously and most cruelly in making so rash a judgment. Fools despise the afflicted, but wise men prize them. Many of the sweetest flowers in the garden of grace grow in the shade, and flourish in the drip. I am persuaded that he "who feedeth among the lilies" has rare plants in his flora, fair and fragrant, choice and comely, which are more at home in the damps of mourning than in the glaring sun of joy. I have known such, who have been a living lesson to us all, from their broken-hearted penitence, their solemn earnestness, their jealous watchfulness, their sweet humility, and their gentle love. These are lilies of the valley, bearing a wealth of beauty pleasant even to the King himself. Feeble as to assurance, and to be pitied for their timidity, yet have they been lovely in their despondencies, and graceful in their holy anxieties. Hannah, then, possessed godliness despite her sorrow.

In connection with this sorrowful spirit of hers Hannah was *a lovable woman.* Her husband greatly delighted in her. That she had no children was to him no depreciation of her value. He said, "Am I not better to thee than ten sons?" He evidently felt that he would do anything in his power to uplift the gloom from her spirit. This fact is worth noting, for it does so happen that many sorrowful people are far from being lovable people. In too many instances their griefs have soured them. Their affliction has generated acid in their hearts, and with that acrid acid they bite into everything they touch; their temper has more of the oil of vitriol in it than of the oil of brotherly love. Nobody ever had any trouble except themselves, they brook no rival in the realm of suffering, but persecute their fellow sufferers with a kind of jealousy, as if they alone were the brides of suffering, and others were mere intruders. Every other person's sorrow is a mere fancy, or make-believe, compared with theirs. They sit alone, and keep silence; or when they speak, their silence would have been preferable.

It is a pity it should be so, and yet so it is that men and women of a sorrowful spirit are frequently to be met with those who are unloving and unlovable. The more heartily, therefore, do I admire in true Christian people the grace which sweetens them so that the more they suffer themselves the more gentle and patient they become with other sufferers, and the more ready to bear whatever trouble may be involved in the necessities of compassion. Beloved, if you are much tried and troubled, and if you are much depressed in spirit, entreat the Lord to prevent your becoming a kill-joy to others. Remember your Master's rule, "And thou, when thou fastest, anoint thy head, and wash thy face, that thou appear not unto men to fast." I say not that our Lord spoke the word with the exact meaning I am now giving to it, but it is a kindred sense. Be cheerful even when your heart is sad. It is not necessary that every heart should be heavy because I am burdened; of what use would that be to me or to anyone else? No, let us try to be cheerful that we may be lovable, even if we still remain of a sorrowful spirit. Self and our own personal woes must not be our life-psalm, nor our daily discourse. Others must be thought of, and in their joys we must try to sympathize.

In Hannah's case, too, the woman of a sorrowful spirit was *a very gentle woman*. Peninnah with her harsh, and haughty, and arrogant speech vexed her sore to make her fret, but we do not find that she answered her. At the annual festival, when Peninnah had provoked her most, she stole away to the sanctuary to weep alone, for she was very tender and submissive. When Eli said, "How long wilt thou be drunken? Put away thy wine from thee," she did not answer him tartly, as she might well have done. Her answer to the aged priest is a model of well have done. Her answer to the aged priest is a model of gentleness. She most effectually cleared herself, and plainly refuted the harsh imputation, but she made no retort, and murmured no charge of injustice. She did not tell him that he was ungenerous in having though so harshly, nor was there anger in her grief. She excused his mistake. He was an old man. It was his duty to see that worship was fitly conducted, and, if he judged her to be in a wrong state, it was but faithfulness on his part to make the remark; and she took it, therefore, in the spirit in which she thought he offered it. At any rate, she bore the rebuke without resentment or repining.

Now, some sad people are very tart, very sharp, very severe, and, if you misjudge them at all, they inveigh against your cruelty with the utmost bitterness. You are the unkindest of men if you think them less than perfect. With what an air and tone of injured innocence will they vindicate themselves! You have committed worse than blasphemy if you have ventured to hint a fault. I am not about to blame them, for we might be as ungentle as they if we were to be too severe in our criticism on the sharpness which springs of sorrow; but it is very beautiful when the afflicted are full of sweetness and light, and like the sycamore figs are ripened by their bruising. When their own bleeding wound makes them tender of wounding others, and their own hurt makes them more ready to bear what of hurt may come through the mistakes of others, then have we a lovely proof that "sweet are the uses of adversity." Look at your Lord. Oh that we all would look at him, who when he was reviled reviled not again, and who, when they mocked him, had not a word of upbraiding, but answered by his prayers, saying, "Father, forgive them, for they know not what they do." See you not that much that is precious may go with a sorrowful spirit?

There was more, however, than I have shown you, for Hannah was *a thoughtful woman,* for her sorrow drove her first within herself, and next into much communion with her God. That she was a highly thoughtful woman appears in everything she says. She does not pour out that which first comes to hand. The product of her mind is evidently that which only a cultivated soil could yield. I will not just now speak of her son, further than to say that for loftiness of majesty and fullness of true poetry it is equal to anything from the pen of that sweet psalmist of Israel, David himself. The Virgin Mary evidently followed in the wake of this great poetess, this mistress of the lyric art.

Remember, also, that though she was a woman of a sorrowful spirit, she was *a blessed woman*. I might fitly say of her, "Hail, thou that art highly favored! The Lord is with thee. Blessed art thou among women." The daughters of Belial could laugh and make merry, and regard her as the dust beneath their feet, but yet had she with her sorrowful spirit found grace in the sight of the Lord. There was Peninnah, with her quiver full of children, exulting over the barren mourner, yet was not Peninnah blessed, while Hannah, with all her griefs, was dear unto the Lord. She seems to be somewhat like him of another age, of whom we read that Jabez was more honorable than his brethren because his mother bare him with sorrow. Sorrow brings a wealth of blessing with it when the Lord consecrates it; and if one had to take his position with the merry, or with the mournful, he would do well to take counsel of Solomon, who said, "It is better to go to the house of mourning than to the house of feasting." A present flash is seen in the mirth of the world, but there is vastly more true light to be found in the griefs of Christians. When you see how the Lord sustains and sanctifies his people by their afflictions, the darkness glows into noonday.

We come now to a second remark, which is that MUCH THAT IS PRE-CIOUS MAY COME OUT OF A SORROWFUL SPIRIT: it is not only to be found with it, but may even grow out of it.

Observe, first, that through her sorrowful spirit Hannah *had learned to pray*. I will not say but what she prayed before this great sorrow struck her, but this I know, she prayed with more intensity than before when she heard her rival talk so exceeding proudly, and saw herself to be utterly despised. Oh! brothers and sisters, if you have a secret grief, learn where to carry it, and delay not to take it there. Learn from Hannah. Her appeal was to the Lord. She poured not out the secret of her soul into mortal ear, but spread her grief before God in his own house, and in his own appointed manner. She was in bitterness of soul, and prayed to the Lord. Bitterness of soul should always be thus sweetened. Many are in bitterness of soul, but they do not pray, and therefore the taste of the wormwood remains: O that they were wise, and looked upon their sorrows as the divine call for prayer, the cloud which brings a shower of supplication! Our troubles should be steeds upon which we ride to God; rough winds which hurry our bark into the haven of all-prayer. When the heart is merry we may sing psalms, but concerning the afflicted it is written, "Let him pray." Thus, bitterness of spirit may be an index of our need of prayer, and an incentive to that holy exercise.

O daughter of sorrow, if in thy darkened chamber thou shalt learn the art of prevailing with the Well-beloved, you bright-eyed maidens, adown whose cheeks no tears have ever rushed, may well envy you, for to be proficient in the art and mystery of prayer is to be as a prince with God. May God grant that if we are of a sorrowful spirit, we may in the same proportion be of a prayerful spirit; and we need scarcely desire a change.

In the next place, Hannah *had learned self-denial.* This is clear, since the very prayer by which she hoped to escape out of her great grief was a self-denying one. She desired a son, that her reproach might be removed; but if her eyes might be blessed with such a sight she would cheerfully resign her darling to be the Lord's as long as he lived. Mothers wish to keep their children about them. It is natural that they should wish to see them often. But Hannah, when most eager for a manchild, asking, but for one, and that one as the special gift of God, yet does not seek him for herself, but for her God. She has it on her heart, that as soon as she has weaned him, she will take him up to the house of God and leave him there, as a dedicated child whom she can only see at certain festivals. Read her own words: "O Lord of hosts, if thou wilt indeed look on the affliction of thine handmaid, and remember me, and not forget thine handmaid, but wilt give unto thine handmaid a man-child, then I will give him unto the Lord all the days of his life, and there shall no razor come upon his head." Her heart longs not to see her boy at home, his father's daily pride, and her own hourly solace, but to see him serving as a Levite in the house of the Lord. She thus proved that she had learned self-denial.

Brethren and sisters, this is one of our hardest lessons: to learn to give up what we most prize at the command of God, and to do so cheerfully. This is real self-denial, when we ourselves make the proposition, and offer the sacrifice freely, as she did. To desire a blessing that we may have the opportunity of parting with it, this is self-conquest: have we reached it? O thou of a sorrowful spirit, if thou hast learned to crucify the flesh, if thou hast learned to keep under the body, if thou hast learned to cast all thy desires and wills at his feet, thou hast gained what a thousand times repays thee for all the losses and crosses thou hast suffered. Personally, I bless God for joy, I think I could sometimes do with a little more of it; but I fear, when I take stock of my whole life, that I have very seldom made any real growth in grace except as the result of being digged about and dunged by the stern husbandry of pain. My leaf is greenest in showery weather: my fruit is sweetest when it has been frosted by a winter's night.

Another precious thing had come to this woman, and that was, *she had learned faith.* She had become proficient in believing promises. It is very beautiful to note how at one moment she was in bitterness, but as soon as Eli had said, "Go in peace: and the God of Israel grant thee thy petition that thou hast asked of him," "the woman went her way and did eat, and her countenance was no more sad." She had not yet obtained the blessing, but she was persuaded of the promise, and embraced it, after that Christly fashion which our Lord taught us when he said, "Believe that ye have the petitions which ye have asked, and ye shall have them," she wiped her tears, and smoothed the wrinkles from her brow, knowing that she was heard. By faith she held a man-child in her arms, and presented it to the Lord. This is no small virtue to attain. When a sorrowful spirit has learned to believe God, to roll its burden upon him, and bravely to expect succor and help from him, it has learned by its losses how to make its best gains—by its griefs how to unfold its richest joys. Hannah is one of the honored band who through faith "received promises," therefore, O you who are of a sorrowful spirit, there is no reason why you should not also be of a believing spirit, even as she was.

Still more of preciousness this woman of a sorrowful spirit found growing out of her sorrow, but with one invaluable item I shall close the list: she had evidently *learned much of God.* Driven from common family joys she had been drawn near to God, and in that heavenly fellowship she had remained a humble waiter and watcher. In seasons of sacred nearness to the Lord she had made many heavenly discoveries of his name and nature, as her son makes us perceive.

First, she now knew that the heart's truest joy is not in children, nor even in mercies given in answer to prayer, for she began to sing, "My heart rejoiceth in the Lord"—not "in Samuel," but in Jehovah her chief delight was found. "Mine horn is exalted in the Lord"—not "in that little one whom I have so gladly brought up to the sanctuary." No. She says in the first verse, "I rejoice in thy salvation," and it was even so. God was her exceeding joy, and his salvation her delight. Oh! it is a great thing to be taught to put earthly things in their proper places, and when they make you glad yet to feel, "My gladness is in God; not in corn and wine and oil, but in the Lord himself; all my fresh springs are in him."

Next, she had also discovered the Lord's glorious *holiness*, for she sang, "There is none holy as the Lord." The wholeness of his perfect character charmed and impressed her, and she sang of him as far above all others in his goodness.

She had perceived his *all-sufficiency*, she saw that he is all in all, for she sang, "There is none beside thee; neither is there any rock like our God."

She had found out *God's method in providence*, for how sweetly she sings, "The bows of the mighty men are broken, and they that stumbled are girded with strength." She knew that this was always God's way—to overturn those who are strong in self, and to set up those who are weak. It is God's way to unite the strong with weakness, and to bless the weak with strength. It is God's peculiar way, and he abides by it. The full he empties, and the empty he fills. Those who boast of the power to live he slays; and those who faint before him as dead, he makes alive.

She had also been taught *the way and method of his grace* as well as of his providence, for never did a woman show more acquaintance with the wonders of divine grace than she did when she sang, "He raiseth up the poor out of the dust, and lifteth up the beggar from the dunghill, to set them among princes, and to make them inherit the throne of glory." This, too, is another of those ways of the Lord which are only understood by his people.

She had also seen the *Lord's faithfulness* to his people. Some Christians, even in these Gospel days, do not believe in the doctrine of the final perseverance of the saints, but she did. She sang, "He will keep the feet of his saints"; and, beloved, so he will, or none of them will ever stand.

She had foreseen also somewhat of *his kingdom*, and of the glory of it. Her prophetic eye, made brighter and clearer by her holy tears, enabled her to look into the future, and looking, her joyful heart made her sing, "He shall give strength unto his King, and exalt the horn of his Anointed."

And now, lastly, MUCH THAT IS PRECIOUS WILL YET BE GIVEN TO THOSE WHO ARE TRULY THE LORD'S, EVEN THOUGH THEY HAVE A SORROWFUL SPIRIT.

For, first, Hannah had *her prayers answered*. Ah! little could she have imagined when Eli was rebuking her for drunkenness, that within a short time she should be there, and the same priest should look at her with deep respect and delight because the Lord had favored her. And you, my dear friend of a sorrowful spirit, would not weep so much tonight if you knew what is in store for you. You would not weep at all if you guessed how soon all will change, and like Sarah you will laugh for very joy. You are very poor; you scarcely know where you will place your head tonight; but if you knew in how short a time you will be amongst the angels, your penury would not cause you much distress. You are sickening and pining away, and will soon go to your long home. You would not be so depressed if you remembered how bright around your head will shine the starry diadem, and how sweetly your tongue shall pour forth heavenly sonnets such as none can sing but those who, like you, have tasted of the bitter waters of grief. It is better on before! It is better on before! Let these things cheer you if you are of a sorrowful spirit. There shall be a fulfillment of the things which God has promised to you. Eye hath not seen, nor ear heard, the things he hath laid up for you, but his Spirit reveals them to you at this hour.

Not only did there come to Hannah after her sorrow an answered prayer, but *grace to use that answer*. I do not think that Hannah would have been a fit mother for Samuel if she had not first of all been of a sorrowful spirit. It is not everybody that can be trusted to educate a young prophet. Many a fool of a woman has made a fool of her child. He was so much her "duck" that he grew up to be a goose. It needs a wise woman to train up a wise son, and therefore I regard Samuel's eminent character and career as largely the fruit of his mother's sorrow, and as a reward for her griefs. Hannah was a thoughtful mother, which was something, and her thought induced diligence. She had slender space in which to educate her boy, for he left her early to wear the little coat, and minister before the Lord; but in that space her work was effectually done, for the child Samuel worshiped the very day she took him up to the temple. In many of our homes we have a well-drawn picture of a child at prayer, and such I doubt not was the very image of the youthful Samuel. I like to think of him with that little coat on—that linen ephod—coming forth in solemn style, as a child-servant of God, to help in the services of the temple.

Hannah had acquired another blessing, and that was the *power to magnify the Lord*. Those sweet songs of hers, especially that precious one which we have been reading—where did she get it from? I will tell you. You have picked up a shell, have you not, by the seaside, and you have put it to your ear, and heard it sing of the wild waves? Where did it learn this music? In the deeps. It had been tossed to and fro in the rough sea until it learned to talk with a deep, soft meaning of mysterious things, which only the salt sea caves can communicate. Hannah's poesy was born of her sorrow; and if everyone here that is of a sorrowful spirit can but learn to tune his harp as sweetly as she tuned hers, he may be right glad to have passed through such griefs as she endured.

Moreover, her sorrow *prepared her to receive further blessings,* for after the birth of Samuel she had three more sons and two daughters, God thus giving her five for the one that she had dedicated to him. This was grand interest for her loan: five hundred percent. Parting with Samuel was the necessary preface to the reception of other little ones. God cannot bless some of us till first of all he has tried us. Many of us are not fit to receive a great blessing till we have gone through the fire. Half the men that have been ruined by popularity have been so ruined because they did not undergo a preparatory course of opprobrium and shame. Half the men who perish by riches do so because they had not toiled to earn them, but made a lucky hit, and became wealthy in an hour. Passing through the fire anneals the weapon which afterwards is to be used in the conflict; and Hannah gained grace to be greatly favored by being greatly sorrowing. Her name stands amongst the highly-favored women because she was deeply sorrowing.

Last of all, it was by suffering in patience that she became so brave a witness for the Lord, and could so sweetly sing, "There is none holy as the Lord, neither is there any rock like our God." We cannot bear testimony unless we test the promise, and therefore happy is the man whom the Lord tests and qualifies to heave a testimony to the world that God is true. To that witness I would set my own personal seal.

13

THE QUEEN OF SHEBA

A Sign

"The queen of the south shall rise up in the judgment with this generation, and shall condemn it: for she came from the uttermost parts of the earth to hear the wisdom of Solomon; and, behold, a greater than Solomon is here" (Matt. 12:42).

THE scribes and Pharisees might easily have ascertained that Jesus was the promised Messiah if they had only taken the trouble to examine his credentials. They had the law and the testimony at their finger's ends, and they might also have made an appeal to the prophets; and, then, they could scarcely have failed to note the many wonderful points of resemblance between Jesus of Nazareth and the Messiah who was to come; but they refused to thoroughly investigate his claims, took it for granted that he was an impostor, and therefore rejected him. When they were driven up into a corner by the truth that he spoke, they demanded of him a sign; and there again they showed that they were not sincere, for he had given them many signs—some of which they must have recognized, because their anger had been excited by them, as, for instance, when Jesus went into their synagogue, and healed, on the Sabbath-day, a man who had his hand withered. They had condemned him as a Sabbath-breaker because he wrought this miracle, so it must certainly have come to their knowledge; yet, while this and multitudes of other miracle were constantly being reported of him, they still continued to reject him, disdaining to confess that he was the Christ, even though he proved it to their faces.

They asked him for a sign, but the Savior tells them that they shall have no signs beyond those they had already had. One of those signs was the prophet Jonah coming up from the belly of the fish after having lain there three days. Christ himself would rise again, the third day, and, by his resurrection, he would fulfill the type of Jonah; this would be such a sign as they could not gainsay. Then there were the signs of the men of Nineveh, repenting at the preaching of Jonah, and the Queen of the South coming to Solomon. The Gentiles, the far-off ones, should be signs to the unbelieving Jews; they would see that Jesus was the Christ because he called unto himself a people who knew him not, and they ran unto him because of the Lord his God, who had sent him as his Messenger. If the scribes and Pharisees would continue to reject these infallible signs, no others would be given to them; but the great King's signet would be set to the writ of execution, condemning Jerusalem to destruction and the people to be scattered abroad.

I think we may truly say that the Queen of Sheba is a sign even to this generation; for each generation, though differing in some respects from others, has many points of resemblance to them. When you perceive what other men have been, you see very much what you yourself are. It is a commonly admitted truth that history repeats itself, and it does so because it is the result of the same sort of passions, the same sinful tendencies in wicked human hearts. So I believe that the present age is, in many points, very like the one in which Christ himself appeared; and if he were corporeally here, at this moment, he could with great accuracy say, "The Queen of the South shall rise up in the judgment with this generation, and shall condemn it: for she came from the uttermost parts of the earth to hear the wisdom of Solomon; and, behold, a greater than Solomon is here."

First, then, THE CONDUCT OF THE QUEEN OF SHEBA CONDEMNS UNBELIEVERS.

For, first of all, *she was interested in the report of Solomon's wisdom.* We do not know much about her, except that she came from a great distance, constrained by her desire after knowledge, her wish "to hear the wisdom of Solomon." I suppose she was a woman of intelligence and thoughtfulness, and therefore she sought the king who was of the same way of thinking. A man of taste, living in a city, or only visiting it, very soon knows all about its sculpture and paintings, and he very naturally gets reports concerning its chief artists brought to him. Even in a little village, a lover of science and art very soon finds people informing him of details and facts which bear upon scientific and artistic matters. He attracts to himself those who are somewhat like himself; and, in similar fashion, Solomon attracted this woman because she was evidently the possessor of some wisdom, and she desired to have more.

Her action is a strong condemnation of the many people in the world whose thoughts never rise above their bodies, and whose only questions are, "What shall we eat? What shall we drink? Wherewithal shall we be clothed?" There are thousands who would not go half a mile to obtain even the ordinary kind of wisdom, they shun all forms of education; they have no idea beyond their usual day labor, or the pursuits in which they occupy their time; but this Queen of Sheba longed for wisdom, and traveled far to obtain it. In contrast to her, look at the great majority of people in this vast city of London, and in various parts of our own and other lands. Some are interested in science, art, politics, and such matters; but as for the higher things, which he who is "greater than Solomon" would teach them, they seem to have no inclination for them. You may build a chapel or mission hall in some dark neighborhood, and it may be by self-denial that you provide the means for its erection; you may feel intense anxiety about the people in that region, and use all lawful inducements to bring them inside the place you have built; yet you cannot stir them, or interest them.

Oftentimes, it is the very hardest task in the world to get even a moment's hearing for the Gospel of Jesus Christ our Lord and Savior. Plenty of people will read the newspaper through from the first word of the title to the last advertisement, but they will scarcely deign to look at a gracious treatise, or tract, or their Bibles; there is nothing there to interest them. Anything about war, or the wreck of a ship, or an accident in a coal mine; or, worse still, the story of some foul crime, or the details with which the Divorce Court is familiar—there are many who are quite sure to read all that through; but as to that which concerns the soul, eternity, heaven, hell, the Christ of God—all this appears to be a matter of perfect indifference to a large mass of our fellow creatures. Oh, how will this Queen of Sheba, who was so interested in the best things that she knew of, and who sought them as a merchant seeketh goodly pearls, how will she rise up in the judgment, and condemn multitudes of careless folk in this worldly generation.

She will also condemn many because *she believed the report of Solomon's wisdom when she heard it.* She was not only interested in hearing it; but what she heard she believed. I do not know who brought the report to her, but Solomon was a great merchant, and traders came from all parts to do business with him. So one and another, who had stayed at Jerusalem, and heard of the marvelous wisdom of the great king, and had seen some of his matchless architectural feats, his vast reservoirs, his wonderful ascent by which he went up to the house of the Lord, carried the report of all this to the Queen of Sheba, and she believed it. I do not say that it was very wonderful that she should believe it; yet her belief condemns the skepticism of this age, and condemns it all the more because, in some respects, this is a very credulous age. We readily believe what travelers tell us. There have been some very extraordinary stories told, which once were not believed, yet afterwards were found to be true; and, now, we generally accept the testimony of a man who comes back, and says that he has seen such and such things. Our learned Societies invite these men to visit them, and tell their story. There may be some who doubt; but, on the whole, they are believed. Yet, when we give our report concerning the Lord Jesus, we have often to ask, "Who hath believed our report, and to whom is the arm of the Lord revealed?" We tell men, not only what God says in his Word, but what we ourselves have tasted, and handled, and felt; yet even when we get them interested in our message, they do not always believe it.

Nothing appears to be more popular, at this present time, than the casting of doubts upon everything that is sacred; and he seems to be reckoned the cleverest man who takes a tarbrush, and goes through the sanctuary daubing all the holy vessels thereof; and whereas, of old, "a man was famous according as he had lifted up axes upon the thick trees," that he might use them in building for God, it seems now as if every man's axes were for breaking down the carved work, and damaging the cedar of which the temple of the Lord is constructed. The Queen of Sheba, in her belief of the report which, I do not doubt, bore upon its face some degree of improbability—for marvelous stories were told about Solomon— yet, believing it because it came to her upon good, fair, honest testimony of men who had no object in deceiving her—she shall rise up in condemnation of the people of this generation who will not believe Christ himself, nor God himself, but even say that this Book is God's, and then deny the things which are most plainly taught therein, and so make God himself to be a liar.

This Queen of Sheba will condemn the unbelief of this generation, in the next place, because she was not only interested in the highest things that came in her way, and believed the honest report that was brought to her, but also because *she acted upon it.* She determined to go where she could hear more of the wisdom of which she had been told. She loved wisdom, and sought for it as for rubies. She, therefore, made up her mind to take the long and perilous journey, and to go and find Solomon, that she might hear his wisdom. She so believed the report that she set out upon her journey; and a journey in those days was a different thing from what it is now. Even a century or so ago, our grandfathers made their wills before they went 100 miles, so what must it have been for the Queen of Sheba to go to Jerusalem to see the great and wise king who reigned there? She believed that she would be fully rewarded for all the trouble she was taking, so she went.

This is a very important point, for we have, in our congregations, a large number of persons who profess to believe everything that they hear; yet, in their hearts, they cannot really be believing anything, for they do not act upon it. O sirs, if you do believe yourselves to be sinful, why do you not seek forgiveness? If you believe yourselves to be in danger, why do you not bestir yourselves, and search for a way of escape? If you believe that there is a God, why do you not ask how you may be reconciled to him? If you believe the words of Jesus, why do you not trust in him, and obey him? It will go very hard with those of you who have been believers in the Bible and lovers of orthodoxy all your lives, and who very earnestly condemn anything like doubt, yet who prove that you do not yourselves truly believe because your belief does not lead you to action. God grant that, if any of you are guilty of such a sin as this, the arrow of conviction may pierce your conscience now!

The Queen of Sheba will also rise up in judgment against unbelievers because she not only acted upon the report she received and believed, but *she persevered in doing so under very great difficulties.* I have already said that a journey to Jerusalem was no small thing for her to accomplish. We little know what were the difficulties of traveling at that time. She may not have been afraid of thieves and other evildoers who were in the way, for Solomon's great power, I do not doubt, kept a wide district very much more quiet than it would otherwise have been; but still, it was a serious task for her to undertake. Yet now, alas! there are many who would like to hear of the wisdom of Christ, but they fear that it would cost them too much, and that there would be too many hardships to be borne. They would have Christ if he could be had by a careless soul, or by one who is living in sin; but the idea of starting out to seek for Christ, and facing difficulties—which, indeed, would soon vanish if they had but resolute hearts—that idea daunts them. Like Pliable, they cannot push their way through the Slough of Despond; anybody else may have the Celestial City, but they cannot go to it through such a foul place as that.

Another point that is worth noticing is, that *this Queen of the South had to stoop from a high position.* Her position, at any rate, involved her in greater difficulty than many others would have experienced. Was she to leave her throne? Then, what would become of her dominions during her absence? Perhaps there would be plots to overthrow her; she might not be able to trust her counselors in power. Shall she, a woman, nursed in luxury as she has been, brave all these dangers to make such a journey as that to Solomon's court? Well, she did all that, so she condemns those who will not do likewise. There is something to be said for those who are in high places, and who fear not God. I would not say anything to apologize for their neglect of Christ, yet I remember his own words, "How hardly shall they that have riches enter into the Kingdom of God!" But the most of you have not that kind of hindrance; you could not say that you have a kingdom to rule, or a large business to manage. You have your cares; but, still, they are not such as to be an excuse for you if you do not seek the Lord. This woman, with a kingdom's cares about her, went to Solomon for wisdom; how she condemns those who have very little to do, yet who say that they have not time to think about these things! You have not to step down from a throne, which is a very trying position for any of the Lord's people to occupy; you have not to shake off the manners of the court, the vices of the court, the pomp of the court, to come down and listen to some poor minister of the Gospel—no, you know that you are not at all demeaned when you are sitting here, listening to a plain preacher like myself. There is no necessity for you to have the Archbishop of Canterbury to preach to you; I am quite big enough for you in that respect. Well, now, there is an advantage in all this, and it is still true that "the poor have the Gospel preached to them." Oh, then, when Jesus, the "greater than Solomon," is near, should not the poor, to whom he delighted to preach, the common people, like the most of us here, should not we feel that there is nothing in our way to keep us from coming to him?

One thing more about this wise queen is, that *she made great use of Solomon when she reached his court,* for she asked him hard questions, and searched and pried into everything that she could. Now, in this, I think she rebukes a great many half-believing professors. You have come to him who is "greater than Solomon," you have come to the infinite wisdom of our great Lord; yet there is many a hard question that you puzzle over, instead of taking it to him. You do not commune with him concerning all that is in your heart as the Queen of Sheba did with Solomon. You do not get from Christ rich gifts as she received from Solomon. Oh, when you do get to Jesus, make use of him! It is no good for you to have a Savior if you do not use him. If God, in his great grace, has given him to you, get out of him all that you can, and do not think that he will consider you to be intruding. It is the delight of his heart to give out of his fullness to his needy people; he is best satisfied with you when you are best satisfied with him; he gets most from you when you get most from him. Do remember that, and never, never, never, start back from a golden promise as though you must get it changed before you spend it. Some Christians seem as if they could not touch the sovereigns that lie before them in heaps, but they must take only a half-crown at a time, and think they have taken a great deal then. There is a blessed prodigality in grace; you may spend as much as you please, yet you shall not be considered a spendthrift.

Now, secondly, THE QUEEN OF SHEBA'S CONDEMNATION IS STRENGTHENED BY MANY CIRCUMSTANCES CONNECTED WITH HER HISTORY.

The first of those circumstances is this—*the report, which came to her, could not have come with the same force as the report which comes to us.* As I have already said, it is probable that the merchants, who traded with Solomon, told what they had seen; and some of their servants no doubt, talked to some of the Queen of Sheba's servants, and, possibly, they told very extraordinary tales, and drew the long bow, as we say. In this case, however, they might draw the longest bow they could get; because, when they had said all they did say, the half was not told. Solomon was wiser than they thought he was, yet they thought him to be almost impossible sage. The report of his wisdom could not have come to the queen, one would think, from many who had been eyewitnesses; yet it was sufficient to convince her. But the report concerning Christ comes to you, in the Word of God, from many witnesses; and it is repeated to you by many ministers of the Gospel, and by many others of God's servants, living men and living women, who tell you what they know, what they have felt, what they have experienced.

Ah! some of you had the report, first of all, from one whose word you never doubted. Your mother told it to you when you were quite a child. Is she dead? Then I feel sure that, among the last words that she spoke, she told you that report again, and bade you seek him who is "greater than Solomon." Perhaps I am addressing some, whose dear grandfather, now in heaven, told them the report when they were little children; and your brother, your sister, your friend, and several of your acquaintances have again and again said to you, "It is true; I have tried it, and proved it; I know it is so." There are very many converted people around some of you, and if you do not believe their report, you practically make them out to be liars; and, as I have already reminded you, you make God himself a liar. The Queen of Sheba had no divine witness, she had only the testimony of men; but you believe this bible to be the Book of God, and the witness of God is greater than the witness of men. Beware, therefore, lest ye reject the testimony of God against yourselves, and the witness of all his people, age after age, and the witness of your kinsfolk and acquaintance now.

I do not wish to have a congregation that will accept teaching simply upon my bare word. No, dear friends, "let the Word of Christ dwell in you." There is always a tendency to follow this divine or that; but I charge you to do nothing of the kind. Go to the Book for yourselves, go to Christ, and to his inspired Word on your own account. We will teach you the truth, as far as we know it; but we will never bear the responsibility of being the standard for other men's beliefs. It may suit so-called "priests" to take away the Bible from the people, but true preachers of the Gospel ever push the Bible to the front. Therefore, we urge you to search the Scriptures; and we pray God to grant that, as you search them, they may search you, and, as you dwell upon the reading of them, that what you read may dwell in your hearts to your permanent profit, making you wise unto salvation.

The report that comes to you, also, *concerns much weightier matters than the Queen of Sheba heard of.* Solomon's wisdom interested the Queen of Sheba because she loved all kinds of wisdom; but it did not matter much to her after all. Her country would still have been as productive of its wondrous spices and gold if she had never gone to Solomon; why, then, should she go to him? But the matters about which God's Word reports to you, and God's Spirit reports to you, and God's servants report to you, unbelievers, concern your souls, yourselves, your sins, your fears, your hopes. It is about your everlasting destruction from the presence of the Lord, and the glory of his power, or your eternal happiness in Christ Jesus. I cannot make some of you out. You are not fools in secular matters. Jingle a guinea near you, and you quickly hear the sound of it, and are pretty sharp to catch it. You are shrewd traders, keep your books correctly, and look well to your accounts, yet you neglect your souls. If a man had a bag full of bank notes, and he went down the borough with it, and got into a crowd, it would be strange if all his anxiety was lest he should lose a cotton pocket handkerchief, while he never thought about his bank notes.

The Queen of Sheba will, next, condemn unbelievers very seriously, *because the report that came to her was not nearly so touching as that which comes to us.* There was no report like this—that Solomon had died for her. There was no message of love, there were no tidings of self-sacrifice, which indicated a heart of pity. No, simply that he was wise; so she resolved to go and see him. O sirs, what a different report I have to bring to you! I have not to set before careless souls merely a wise Savior, but a loving, condescending, self-sacrificing, dying Savior; and if that report does not lead men to seek him, they will be fearfully condemned by this Queen of Sheba who came to see Solomon because of the report she had heard of him in her own land.

Then, again, *this report was, in her case, accompanied by no divine command.* She heard a report about Solomon, but there was no law, either human or divine, ordering her to go to Solomon. She could do precisely as she pleased about it. But when you hear about Christ, O sinners, it is not left to your own option whether you will come to him, or not; but "God now commandeth all men everywhere to repent"; and he hath bidden us go into all the world, and preach the Gospel to every creature, and to say to them, "He that believeth and is baptized shall be saved; but he that believeth not shall be damned."

Beside that, *the Queen of Sheba had no invitation to go to Solomon.* He did not send to her, and say, "Come, and hear my wisdom." She came uninvited; but, O sons and daughters of men, you have been invited again and again! "Come unto me," is Christ's constant message. You are invited to come to him, yet you will not come.

And again, *the Queen of Sheba had no promise that she should be welcomed if she did come.* She could not tell that Solomon would receive her; yet she came, believing that he would, and he did; but you have the Savior's gracious assurance, "Him that cometh to me I will in no wise cast out." Oh, with what readiness and promptness ought you to respond to the sacred invitation of love, backed by the divine command, and confirmed by the sacred promise!

And then again, dear friends, this woman came simply through a report; but, *in your case, it is not merely by report.* When I tell you about what Christ has done, which is written in the Word, that is a report; but when you see—and many of you have seen—the finger of God upon some of your friends, that is not a report. I put it to some here present who are unconverted, but who have had godly mothers, was not your mother's life one of the things you never could get over when you tried to doubt your Bible? And is it not still to you a very wonderful life as you look back upon it? How calm, how joyous, she was in suffering or in poverty! How quiet, how patient, she was in putting up with you! Then, as to her death, was there not something almost divine about that patient waiting for her Lord, and that dying smile, and that last triumphant hymn? Why, if ever I doubted the Word of God, some of the deathbeds that I have witnessed would bring me back to faith directly.

And then, when this woman heard the report, *she had not the opportunity of testing it at once without along journey.* She had to go all the way to Jerusalem; but you, sirs, have not to go an inch in order to find Christ. What saith the apostle? "The word is nigh thee, even in thy mouth." Note that expression, "in thy mouth." Why, hungry man, if I say to you, "There is bread on the table, take as much as you need"; it is your own fault if you do not eat it. But if I can say, "Man, it is in thy mouth," you will have to exert yourself to reject it. It will cost you more pains to spit Christ out than to feed upon him.

I cannot help saying that *the Queen of Sheba, in coming to Solomon, did not have anything like the inducements which are put before you in coming to Christ.* Solomon could prove to her his own possession of wisdom, but he could not make her wise; though I think that, generally, people learn a good deal of wisdom by seeing and hearing it in others. But, in coming to Christ, you have not the inducement of merely learning how much he knows, but he will make you wise unto salvation, and he will give you unspeakably precious gifts. Solomon gave to the Queen of Sheba great gifts, yet he had never promised that he would do so; but you may come to Christ, with the confident expectation that of his fullness you shall receive, grace for grace, for this is his way of welcoming all who come unto him.

Who will come to my Lord and Master for the first time? It is now many years since I first came to him, but I have never once regretted that step. Blessed was the day, and blessed was the hour, when I came unto him. Oh, if I had not come to him, methinks that my soul would never rest until it had found him! If it had all to be done over again—aye, if the coming had to be continually repeated, as indeed it has—"to whom coming, as unto a living stone"—I would delight to do it all over again; and if I had to begin preaching the Gospel to you, I would still preach the same Gospel that I have preached to you. I would seek to preach it better, but it should be the same "old, old story of Jesus and his love." I love it so much because I know that it is true; I prove it, every day, by happy personal experience. Believe it, O ye careless ones, who now are found at the post of Wisdom's doors; and come in to see him, the Lord Jesus, who, in his dominion, and in his person, and in his wealth, and in his grace, is "greater than Solomon"!

I have only time for just a few closing words upon the third point, which is that THE CONDEMNATION OF SUCH A WITNESS MUST BE SOLEMN AND OVERWHELMING.

I have shown you that all along; that is the point at which I have continually been aiming. Surely, you will none of you wish to be condemned by a heathen queen. It is bad enough to be condemned by the example of Christian people, and by what they say; but this heathen queen, with swarthy countenance, will rise up in the judgment, and condemn you who do not believe in Jesus, though you live in the midst of Christian light, and even call yourselves Christians, and talk about being inhabitants of a Christian country. The Queen of Sheba lived in a dark age; but this, you know, is a very wonderful age. Some people are never weary of crying it up; according to them, this is the most marvelous generation that has ever existed on the face of the earth. We are wonderful people, yet a heathen queen, of the dark ages, will rise up in the judgment, and condemn us, if we do not believe, because she acted better with her little light than we do with our far greater light. When God teaches us more about his works, some of us think less about their Maker; and when he reveals more of the secrets of nature, some care less about the secrets of his grace.

Verily, the Queen of Sheba will condemn this generation. Christ will call her up as a witness; and at the sight of her—albeit his condemnation will also come, yet, at the sight of her—this heathen queen, the unbelieving world will stand condemned. Looking into her dark face, their own faces will turn deadly pale, for her faith, and her coming to Solomon, will condemn all unbelieving ones, and especially those who only pretended to believe, yet who never acted upon the faith they professed to possess.

14

THE QUEEN OF SHEBA
Consulting with Jesus

"And when the queen of Sheba heard of the fame of Solomon concerning the name of the LORD, she came to prove him with hard questions. . . . And Solomon told her all her questions: there was not any thing hid from the king, which he told her not" (1 Kgs. 10:1–3).

As our Lord has given the Queen of Sheba for a sign, it would be unbecoming if we did not try to learn all that we can from that sign. She came "to hear the wisdom of Solomon"; but Christ is "greater than Solomon" in every respect. He is greater in wisdom; for, though Solomon was wise, he was not Wisdom itself, and that Jesus is. In the Book of Proverbs he is referred to under the name of Wisdom, and the Apostle Paul tells us that he is made of God unto us wisdom. They who really know him know something of how wise he is, and how truly he may be called Wisdom. Because he is with the Father, and knows the Father, he has such wisdom as no one else can have. "No man knoweth the Son, but the Father; neither knoweth any man the Father, save the Son, and he to whomsoever the Son will reveal him." He knows the deep things of God, for he came down from heaven bringing his Father's greatest secrets in his heart. To him, therefore, men ought to come if they wish to be wise, and ought we not to wish for wisdom? To whom else can we go if we go not to him "in whom are hid all the treasures of wisdom and knowledge"?

First, then I call upon you to ADMIRE THIS QUEEN'S MODE OF PROCEDURE WHEN SHE CAME TO SOLOMON. We are told, in the text, that "she came to prove him with hard questions."

375

She wanted to prove whether he was as wise as she had been led to believe, and her mode of proving it was by *endeavoring to learn from him.* She put difficult questions to him in order that she might be instructed by his wisdom; and if you want to ascertain what the wisdom of Christ is, the way to know it is to come and sit at his feet, and learn of him. I know of no other method; it is a very sure one, and it will be a very profitable and blessed one if you adopt it. He has himself said, "Take my yoke upon you, and learn of me; for I am meek and lowly in heart: and ye shall find rest unto your souls."

Jesus came forth from God to be "the faithful Witness" to the truth, and therefore we are bound to believe what he says; and, certainly, we shall never fully appreciate his wisdom unless we are willing to receive his testimony. The psalmist says, "O taste and see that the Lord is good"; but, in this case, we must test and prove that the Lord is wise. There are some who despise the wisdom of Christ; and if you probe them, you will discover that they were never willing to learn of him. His own words are, "Except ye be converted, and become as little children, ye shall not enter into the kingdom of heaven." The wisdom of Christ cannot be known by those who refuse to be disciples, that is, learners. We must learn of him before we are competent to judge whether Christ is wise, or not; and never did a disciple sit humbly at his feet, never did one, in the spirit of a little child, sit with Mary at the feet of the great Teacher, without saying, as he listened to the gracious words that proceeded out of his mouth, "The half was not told me. Oh, the depth of the riches both of the wisdom and the knowledge that are to be found in him!"

The Queen of Sheba is also to be admired in that, wishing to learn from Solomon, *she asked him many questions* — not simply one or two, but many. Some people say, though I do not know how true it is, that curiosity is largely developed in women. I think I have known some men who have had a tolerably large share of it also. In this case, however, the woman's curiosity was wise and right; it was a wise thing, on her part, when she was in the presence of such a man of wisdom, to try to learn all that she could from him; and therefore she questioned him about all sorts of things. Very likely she brought before him the difficulties connected with her government, various schemes relating to trade, the modes of war, or the arts of peace; possibly she talked to him concerning the beasts of the field, and the fish of the sea, and the fowls of the air; but I am persuaded that she also talked about higher things—the things of God; and I am led to that conclusion by the expression in the first verse of my text, "When the Queen of Sheba heard of the name of Solomon *concerning the name of the Lord,* she came to prove him with hard questions." The report that came to her had to do with Jehovah, the God of Israel, as well as with Solomon; so we may rest assured that she put to him many difficult questions concerning the state of her heart, her character, her present position before God, and her future relationship to Israel's God. Questions on those points are not easy to answer, but she took care to ask them so that, when she reached her home, she might not have to say, "I wish I had asked Solomon about that matter; then I should no longer be in doubt."

Now, beloved, if you want to know the wisdom of Christ, you must ask him many questions. Come and inquire of him about anything you please. There is nothing which he does not now of earth, of heaven, and of hell. He knows the past, the present, the future; the things of every day, and the things of that last great day of days. He knows the things of God as nobody else knows them, for he is one with the Father, and with the Spirit, and he can tell us all that we need to know. Come to him, then, with every question that has ever puzzled you, and with every doubt that has ever staggered you. Resort not so much to your own thoughts, or to the counsels and arguments of your fellow creatures; but consult with him who spake as never man spake, and whose wisdom, like Alexander's sword, can cut each Gordian knot, and end in a moment all the difficulties that trouble your spirit.

But the main point, for which I admire the Queen of Sheba, is that *she proved Solomon "with hard questions."* Was she not wise? If she had asked Solomon questions which a schoolboy could reply to, it would have been almost an insult to him. No, if Solomon's wisdom is to be tested, let him be proved with "hard questions." If a man is really wise, he likes to have inquiries put to him which a man with less wisdom could not answer. If the queen's questions had been such as she could herself answer, why need she have gone all that long way to ask Solomon to reply to them? Or if she had somebody at her home, wherever it was, who could have replied to her questions, why need she have gone to Jerusalem? It was because she had no one else to help her that she brought her questions to the one who, because of his superlative wisdom, would be able to answer them. This would relieve her mind, and send her home satisfied upon many points that had previously troubled her; so she did well to bring her "hard questions" to Solomon.

But I have known some — I think I know some still — who seem as if they could not ask Christ a hard question. For instance, they feel that they are great sinners; and they think that, if they had not sinned so much, he might be better able to forgive them, so they do not like to bring their hard questions to King Jesus. Others have a hard struggle to conquer some fierce passion, or some reigning lust, and they think they must overcome that evil themselves. Then, do you think that my Master is only a little Savior? He is the great Physician; will you only bring to him a cut finger or an aching tooth to cure? Oh, he is such a Savior that you may bring to him the worst, the most abject and depraved of men, for they are those who can best prove his power to save! When you feel yourselves most lost, then come to him; when you are at your worst state, when you think you are almost damned, and wonder that you are not altogether so, then come to him. If yours is a hard case, bring it to the almighty Savior. Do you think he only came into the world to save those who are decent and good? You know what he himself said, "They that are whole have no need of the physician, but they that are sick: I came not to call the righteous, but sinners to repentance."

And, beloved, hearken yet again. Are you in some very sharp trial? Is your spirit terribly depressed, and have you, because of that, kept away from Christ? Have you felt that you could go to him with your everyday burdens, but not with that special load? But why not take that also to him? Prove him with hard questions; the harder, the better. Do you not remember the Indian nurse, who said to the invalid lady who seemed as if she did not like to lean too heavily upon her, "If you love me, lean hard." That is what your Lord says to you, "if you love me, lean hard upon me." The more of your weight you rest upon him, the better pleased will he be. The more you trust him, the more you prove your confidence in him, the closer will be the union between you. Christ is the Bearer of a world's iniquities; so he may readily enough be the Bearer of your most extraordinary griefs. Prove the Lord Jesus in every possible way for he loves so to be proved. The more needy the outcast, the louder does the Gospel trumpet blow that they, who are ready to perish, may come and be saved.

Now, secondly, LET US IMITATE HER EXAMPLE, IN REFERENCE TO CHRIST, WHO IS "GREATER THAN SOLOMON." Let us prove him with hard questions. Let us bring to him some nuts to be cracked some diamonds to be cut, some difficulties to be solved. I do not know what hard question may be resting upon the mind of any of you, but I will briefly mention ten hard questions which Jesus answers. They are only ten out of ten thousand that might be put to him, for there is no hard question which he cannot answer.

Here is the first hard question. *How can a man be just with God?* It stands in the Book of Job, and it seems to stand there unanswered: "How should man be just with God?" There is nobody, on the face of the earth, who could have answered that question if it had not been made possible by our Lord Jesus Christ. There is no way of being just in the sight of God except through him. But if we come to him, he will tell us that we ourselves must stand in the place of condemnation, and confess that, for our sin, we deserve the wrath of God. We must always admit that no merits of ours can ever win his favor; that, in fact, we have no merits of our own, but are undeserving, ill-deserving, hell-deserving sinners; and when we occupy that position, then, of his own abounding grace and mercy, God will reckon us as just through Christ Jesus.

Our Lord Jesus also tells us how a man can be just with God as he reminds us that he is the covenant head of his believing people, that, as in Adam, the first head, all men fell, so those who are in him who is the second Adam, the Lord from heaven, all rise again. "As by one man's disobedience many were made righteous." Righteousness in the sigh of God comes, through the headship of Christ, to all who are in him. Christ has honored the law of God, he has obeyed every jot and tittle of it; and his obedience is reckoned as the obedience of all who are in him. The question, "How can a man be just with God?" is, therefore, answered thus. Jesus saith, "I have stood in the place of the guilty, and have rendered to God's law a perfect obedience. This is imputed to all who believe, and God regards them as just through my righteousness." Oh, glorious doctrine of imputation! Happy are all they who believe it, and rejoice in it.

Here is another hard question. *How can God be just, and yet the Justifier of the ungodly?* If he be just, surely he must condemn the ungodly; yet we know, of a certainty, many who have been ungodly, whom God has been pleased to meet with, and to justify so completely that they have been heard to say, "Who shall lay anything to the charge of God's elect? It is God that justifieth." How can this be? Only Jesus can answer the question, and he answers it thus. "I have borne the penalty that was due to sin; I have stood in the sinner's place, and suffered that which has fully satisfied the claims of divine justice on his behalf; I have paid the sinner's debt, so the law may well let him go free." "He was wounded for our transgressions, he was bruised for our iniquities: the chastisement of our peace was upon him; and with his stripes we are healed. All we like sheep have gone astray; we have turned every one to his own way; and the Lord hath laid on him the iniquity of us all." The great Sin-bearer has suffered in the sinner's stead; the sword of divine justice smote him, for He stood in the sinner's place, willingly bearing the sinner's penalty; and, now that sin has been punished upon him, God can be just, and yet be the Justifier of all who believe in his dear Son.

The next question is one which has puzzled many. *How can a man be saved by faith alone without works, and yet no man can be saved by a faith that is without works?* If you are puzzled by this question, our Lord Jesus Christ will tell you, in this Book, through which he still speaks to us, that we are to believe in him for salvation, and not to bring any works of our own as the ground of our trust; not even our own faith, so far as it is a work, for a man is saved by grace, that is, by God's free favor, not by works of righteousness which he has himself done. "For by grace are ye saved through faith; and that not of yourselves; it is the gift of God; not of works, lest any man should boast." That truth is as clearly taught in Scripture as it can possibly be; but then it is equally true that no man may claim that he is saved unless the faith, which he professes to have, is an active, living faith, which makes him love God, and, consequently, do that which is well pleasing in his sight. If I say that I believe in God, yet continue to live in sin willfully and knowingly, then I have not so good a faith as the devils have, for they "believe and tremble." There are some men who profess to believe in God, yet who do not tremble before him, but are impudent and presumptuous. That is not the kind of faith that saves the soul; saving faith is that which produces good works, which leads to repentance, or is accompanied by it, and leads to love of God, and to holiness, and to a desire to be made like unto the Savior. Good works are not the root of faith, but they are its fruit. A house does not rest upon the slates on its roof, yet it would not be fit to live in if it had not a roof; and, in like manner, our faith does not rest upon our good works, yet it would be a poor and useless faith if it had not some of the fruit of the Spirit to prove that it had come from God. Jesus

Christ can tell us how a man can aim at being as holy as God is holy, and yet never talk about his holiness, or dream of trusting in it. We would live as if we were to be saved by our own works, yet place no reliance whatever upon them, but count them as dross, that we may win Christ, and be found in him, not having our own righteousness, which is of the law, but that which is through the faith of Christ, the righteousness which is God by faith.

Here is another hard question, which once greatly puzzled a ruler of the Jews. You know his name, Nicodemus: "the same came to Jesus by night." This was his hard question: "*How can a man be born when he is old?*" At first sight, it seems as if that were unanswerable; but Jesus Christ has said, "Behold, I make all things new." Even under the old dispensation, God's promise to his people was, "A new heart also will I give you, and a new spirit will I put within you: and I will take away the stony heart out of your flesh, and I will give you a heart of flesh." All this is impossible with man, but it is possible with God. The Holy Spirit regenerates a man, causes him to be born again, so that, though his bodily frame remains the same, yet his inner spirit becometh like that of a little child, and as a newborn babe, he desires the unadulterated milk of the Word that he may grow thereby. Yes, there is a total change wrought in men when they believe in Jesus Christ. He said to Nicodemus, "Except a man be born again, he cannot see the kingdom of God"; but men, who are old, can be born again, "by the Word of God, which liveth and abideth forever." Greybeard, thou canst be born again; leaning on thy staff for very age, though thou hast outnumbered three score years and ten, thou canst be born again; and if thou wert a hundred years of age, yet if thou shouldst believe in Jesus, by the power of the Eternal Spirit, thou wouldst at once be made a new creature in Christ Jesus.

Here is another hard question. *How can God, who sees all things, no longer see any sin in believers?* That is a puzzle which many cannot understand. God is everywhere, and everything is present to his all-seeing eye, yet he says, through the prophet Jeremiah, "In those days, and in that time, saith the Lord, the iniquity of Israel shall be sought for, and there shall be none." I venture to say that even God himself cannot see that which no longer exists; even his eye resteth not on a thing that is not; and thus is it with the sin of those who have believed in Jesus; it has ceased to be. God himself has declared, "I will remember their sin no more." But can God forget? Of course he can, as he says that he will.

The work of the Messiah was described to Daniel in these remarkable words, "to finish the transgression, and to make an end of sins, and to make reconciliation for iniquity, and to bring in everlasting righteousness." To make an end of sins? Well, then, there *is* an end of them, according to that other gracious, divine declaration, "I have blotted out, as a thick cloud, thy transgressions, and, as a cloud, thy sins." Oh, what blessed words! Hence, they are gone, they have ceased to be, Christ has obliterated them; and, therefore, God no longer sees them. Oh, the splendor of the pardon which God has bestowed upon all believers, making a clean sweep of all their sins forever!

Here is another hard question. *How can a man see the invisible God?* Yet Christ said, "Blessed are the pure in heart: for they shall see God"; and the angel said to John: "His servants shall serve him, and they shall see his face." This hard question is putting in another form the difficulty which Philip brought to Jesus: "Lord, shew us the Father, and it sufficeth us." Jesus answered him, "Have I been so long time with you, and yet hast thou not known me, Philip? He that hath seen me hath seen the Father." In the person of his dear Son, God the Father has displayed himself before the eyes of men, as John says, "The Word was made flesh, and dwelt among us, (and we beheld his glory, the glory as of the only begotten of the Father), full of grace and truth." Jesus himself said, "I and my Father are One"; so that we can see the invisible Father in the person of Jesus Christ his Son.

Moving upward in Christian experience, here is another hard question. *How can it be true that "whosoever is born of God sinneth not," yet men who are born of God do sin?* Ah! that is a question which has puzzled man; but we must remember that every man of God is two men in one. That new part of him, which is born of God, that new nature which was implanted in regeneration, cannot sin because it is born of God. It is the incorruptible seed, which liveth and abideth forever; but, as far as the man is still in the flesh, it is true that "the carnal mind is enmity against God: for it is not subject to the law of God, neither indeed can be." The old nature sinneth through the force of nature; but the new nature sinneth not, because it is born of God.

This helps also to answer another hard question. *How can a man be a new man, and yet be constantly sighing because he finds in himself so much of the old man?* The Holy Spirit guided the Apostle Paul to instruct us upon this matter. There is the new man within us, which leaps for joy because of the heavenly life; but, alas! there is also the old man. Paul calls it "the body of this death." There it is, and you know that it is the older of the two, and that it will not go out if it can help it. It says to the new nature, "What right have you here?" "I have the right of grace," answers the new nature; "God put me here, and here I mean to stay." "Not if I can prevent it," cries the old nature; "I will stamp you out, or I will smother you with doubts, or puff you up with pride, or kill you with the poison of unbelief; but out you shall go somehow." "No," replies the new nature; "out I never will go, for I have come to stay here. I came in the name and under the authority of Jesus; and where Jesus comes, he comes to reign, and I mean to reign over you." He deals some heavy blows at the old nature, and smites him to the dust; but it is not easy to keep him under. That old nature is such a horrible companion for the new nature, that it often makes him cry, "O wretched man that I am! who shall deliver me from the body of this death?" But even while he is thus crying out, he is not afraid of the ultimate issue; he feels sure of victory. The new nature sits and sings; even, as it were, within the ribs of death, with the stench of corruption in its nostrils, it still sits and sings, "I thank God though Jesus Christ our Lord," and triumphs still in him. We are not going to be overcome, beloved. "Sin shall not have dominion over you: for ye are not under the law, but under grace." But, my brethren, it is a tremendous struggle; and if our Lord had not instructed his servant Paul to tell us about his own experience, some of us would have been obliged to cry, "If it be so, why am I thus?" Christ knows all about the inner life of his people, and his Word explains what may appear mysterious to you; so, when next you feel this conflict raging within your spirit, you will understand it, and say, "It is not because I am dead in sin; for, if I were dead, I should not have this fighting. It is because I have been quickened that this battle is going on."

Here is one more of these hard questions. *How can a man be sorrowful, yet always rejoicing?* That is one of the Apostle Paul's riddles, of which he gives us a great number, such as these. How can a man be poor, yet make many rich? How can a man be cast down, yet not destroyed; persecuted, yet not forsaken? How can a man be less than nothing, and yet possess all things? The explanation is that, while we are in this body, we must suffer, and smart, and pine; but thanks be to God! He has taught us to glory in tribulation also, and to expect the great reward that awaits us by and by; so that if we are full of sorrow, we accept the sorrow joyfully; if we are made to smart, we bow beneath the rod, and look for the after blessed results from it. So we can sigh, yet at the same time sing.

I have one more hard question. *How can a man's life be in heaven while he still lives on earth?* May you all understand this riddle by learning what Paul means when he says, "For ye are dead, and your life is hid with Christ in God"; who "hath raised us up together, and made us sit together in heavenly places in Christ Jesus"! Even now, the heavenly life may be enjoyed by us, although we still live upon earth; and, sometimes, we are half inclined to say, with the apostle, "Whether in the body, or out of the body, I cannot tell: God knoweth." Yet we soon discover that we are in the body, for we have physical wants, temptations, and trials; and then we cry, "Woe is me, that I sojourn in Mesech, that I dwell in the tents of Kedar!" Yet, perhaps, the next moment, we say, "My treasure is all packed up, and gone on before me; and I stand on tiptoe, waiting to be called away; for, where my treasure is, there my heart is also, and they are both above the skies with my dear Lord and Savior."

Now in closing, let us ANSWER CERTAIN QUESTIONS OF A PRACTICAL CHARACTER.

Answer, first, this question: *How can we come to Christ?* He is in heaven, so we cannot climb up to him there. Yes, but he has graciously said, "Lo, I am with you alway, even unto the end of the world." And though we see him not, and hear him not, yet in spirit he is among us at this moment. You need not stir even a step in order to get to him. If Jesus were again upon earth, he could not, in his bodily presence, be in all places at once. Suppose he were in London, what would they do who live in Australia, and wanted to get to him? They might die on the voyage. Or if he were at Jerusalem, how many poor people would never be able to get to Palestine! It is much better that he is not on earth; it is more expedient for us, because his Spirit is everywhere; and, desiring to think about him, wishing to know him, seeking him, and, above all, trusting him, we have come to him.

"Well," says one, "supposing that is done, *how can we ask Christ hard questions?*" You may ask anything of him just the same as if you could see him. You need not even speak the question; if you think it, he hears it. Pray to him, for he hears prayer. Wherever there is the praying lip of a sinner, there is the hearing ear of the Savior.

"But," you say, "*if I ask of him, how will he answer me?*" Do not expect that he will answer you in a dream, or by any vocal sound. He has spoken all you need to know in this Book. Read it, study it, that you may learn what he has revealed. We who preach are not worth hearing unless what we say is taken out of the Bible. Listen to us when we do so preach, because, oftentimes, the words of the Book may seem cold to you; but, if we translate them into warm lip-language, they will go home to your heart. You will understand them better, and feel them better, as coming from one who loves you, and who is a man of flesh and blood like yourselves.

"Ay," says one, "I would fain come to Christ with my doubts and difficulties, and here is one question that I want him to answer now. *How is it that I read, in the Word of God, that he hath limited a day, and yet you bid me come to him now?*" Yes, I do bid you come to him now; and what is more, I tell you that his own word is "Him that cometh to me I will in no wise cast out." "But is it not also true that he limiteth a day?" Yes, he does; but shall I tell you how he limits it? "Again, he limiteth a certain day, saying in David, Today, after so long a time, as it is said, Today if ye will hear his voice, harden not your hearts." Blessed be his holy name, if he has limited you, he has limited you to today; and if I live to see your face tomorrow, I will still say the same to you. The limit is a very gracious one; it is "today." If ever a soul does come to Christ, when he does come, it is today; and if you come this day, you will be within the limit, for he hath said, "Today if ye will hear his voice, harden not your hearts." Today then, dear soul, is within the boundary; this night, ere you go to your home, you are just within the limit. "Today if ye will hear his voice, harden not your hearts." Accept him now; trust him now; come to him with your hard questions now; come to him with your hard doubts, come with your hard infidelity, come with your hard obstinacy; come just as you are, and cast yourself at those dear pierced feet of his, for there is not a question that he will not answer, not a difficulty that he will not overcome, nor a sin that he will not pardon, and send you away rejoicing.

I think I hear someone say, "What is all this about? Are there really any people in the world who want God in this fashion?" Yes, there are; and we are grieved if you are not one of them; for, believe me, friend, all who are living as if there were no God are missing everything that truly makes up life. I heard a young man say, "I should like to see a little life."

Yes, I hope you will, and a great deal of life, too; but there is no life in the purlieus of vice; that is death, rottenness, stench, corruption, like the valley of Hinnom and the burning of Tophet. Flee from it. But life is to be found by coming to God; and by trusting Jesus you get to God, and so become the possessor of eternal life. Then, getting to know God, you help to make the world all alive. The very times and season seem to have changed to you, for things are not what they once were. The wilderness and the solitary places rejoice, and the desert blooms as the rose. If I could live ten thousand years on earth without my God, and perpetually swim in a sea of sensual delights, I would beg to be annihilated sooner than have to undergo such a doom. But let God send or withhold whatever he pleases of temporal favors, if he will but give me to know that he is mine, and that I am his, it shall be all I will ask of him. I mean what I say, and I believe that every child of God, who has once enjoyed the full light of his countenance, will say the same.

15

THE QUEEN OF SHEBA

Heart-Communing

"She communed with him of all that was in her heart"
(1 Kgs. 10:2).

IT appears that the Queen of Sheba, when she had once obtained an
interview with the great and wise king of Israel, was not content with merely
putting to him various difficult questions. for she unbosomed herself to
him, told out all that lay concealed in her heart; and Solomon listened attentively to her, and, no doubt, so spoke to her that he sent her
away rejoicing.

It is not generally a wise thing to tell all that is in your heart. Solomon
himself said, "A fool uttereth all his mind; but a wise man keepeth it in
till afterwards." There are many things which you had better not tell to
anybody. Make no one your confidant completely. If you do, you run
great risks of making an Ahithophel or a Judas for yourself. David said,
in his haste, that all men were liars. That was not quite true; probably,
what he meant was that, if we trust all men, we shall soon find ourselves
deceived; but if we could meet with a Solomon—one who had been divinely endowed with wisdom, as he was, it might be safe for us to bring
all our questions and tell all our troubles to him. At any rate, we know
of One, who is "greater than Solomon," to whom it is most safe and blessed
to tell out all that is in our heart. He is willing to listen to us, and to commune with us; and the more frank and open we are with him, the better will he be pleased, and the better will it be for us. That is to be our
subject, heart-communing with Jesus, spiritualizing the action of the Queen
of Sheba, when she came to Solomon, and "communed with him of all
that was in her heart."

We will begin by saying that WE OUGHT TO COMMUNE WITH JESUS OF ALL THAT IS IN OUR HEART.

I do not mean all of you who are present; I mean all those who have been redeemed from among men by his most precious blood all those who are believing in him, and who call him their Savior, their Master, their Lord. You are bound to tell him all that is in your heart, and to have no secrets hidden away from him within your soul.

Tell Jesus all that is in your heart, for *neglect of intercourse with Christ, of the most intimate kind is ungenerous towards him.* Are there any professing Christians here, who have lived for a month without conscious communion with Christ? If I were to speak of a longer period, and to ask, "Are there not some professing Christians here, who have lived for three months without conscious communion with Christ," I am afraid there are some who, if they were honest and truthful, would have to reply, "That is the case with us." If so, think what that means; you profess to belong to Jesus, and to be his disciple, yet you confess that you have lived all this while without real, intimate communication with him who is your Master and Lord. What is more, you profess to be, not only one of His disciples, but one of his friends. "Is this thy kindness to thy Friend?" I may go further than that, for you believe yourself to be married to Christ, for that is the union which exists between himself and his people. That would be a strange kind of marriage union in which the wife should be in the presence of her husband, and, and not even speak to him by the week, by the month, by the three months, by the six months together. For them to have no fellowship with one another, no mutual interchange of love, no communications with each other, would be regarded as unnatural, and would be rightly condemned; but do we not, sometimes, act towards our heavenly Bridegroom in just that manner? Are we not, too often, like the men of the world who do not know him? Do we not live as if we did not know him, or as if he were no longer present with us? It ought not to be thus; unless we would act contrary to all the dictates of our higher nature, we must be continually holding intimate intercourse with our Lord Jesus Christ.

And we must tell him all that is in our heart, because *to conceal anything from so true a Friend betrays the sad fact that there is something wrong to be concealed.* Is there anything that you do that you could not tell to Jesus? Is there anything you love that you could not ask him to bless? Is there any plan now before you that you could not ask him to sanction?

Is there anything in your heart which you would wish to hide from him? Then it is a wrong thing; be you sure of that. The thing must be evil, or else you would not wish to conceal it from him whom, I trust, you do really love. O my Lord, wherefore should I desire to hide anything from thee? If I do want to hide it, then, surely, it must be because it is something of which I have cause to be ashamed; so help me to get rid of it. O Christian brothers and sisters, I beseech you to live just as you would do if Christ Jesus were in your room, in your bedchamber, in your shop, or walking along the street with you, for his spiritual presence is there! May there never be anything about you which you wish to conceal from him!

If we cannot tell Jesus all that is in our heart, *it shows a want of confidence in his love, or his sympathy, or his wisdom, or his power.* When there is something that the wife cannot tell to her husband, or there begin to be some secret things on the part of one of them, that cannot be revealed to the other, there will soon be an end of mutual love, and peace, and joy. Things cannot go on well in the home while there has to be concealment. O beloved, I beseech you to love Christ too much to keep anything back from him! Love him so much that you can trust him even with the little frivolous things which so often worry and vex you. Love him so much that you can tell him all that is in your heart, nor ever for a moment wish to keep back anything from him.

If we do not tell it all to Jesus, it looks as if we had not confidence in his love, and therefore thought that he would not bear with us; or else that we had not confidence in his sympathy, and fancied that he would not take any notice of us; or else that we had not confidence in his wisdom, and thought that our trouble was too perplexing to bring to him; or else, that we had not confidence in his power, and dreamt that he could not help us in such an emergency. Let this never be the case with any of you; but, every day, unburden your heart to Christ, and never let him think that you even begin to distrust him. So shall you keep up a frank, and open, and blessed fellowship between Christ and your own soul.

I am quite certain that if you will carry out the plan I am commending to you, *it will bring you great ease of mind;* whereas, if you do not, you will continue to have much uneasiness. Is there anything that I have not told to Jesus—anything in which I could not have fellowship with him? Then, there is something wrong with me. Are you keeping your trouble to yourself, and trying to manage without consulting with

Jesus? Well, then, if anything goes wrong, you will have the responsibility of it; but if you take it all to him, and leave it with him, it cannot go wrong whatever happens; and even if it should seem to do so, you would not have the responsibility of it.

I believe that our trials usually come out of the things that we do not take to the Lord; and, moreover, I am sure that we make greater blunders in what we consider to be simple matters, which we need not take to the Lord, than we do in far more difficult matters which we take to him. The men of Israel were deceived by the Gibeonites because they had on old shoes and clouted, and had moldy bread in their wallets, and the Israelites said, "It is perfectly clear that these men must have come from a long distance; look at their old boots and their ragged garments"; so they make a covenant with them, and inquired not the will of the Lord. If it had not appeared to them to be quite so clear a case, they would have asked the Lord for direction, and then they would have been rightly guided. It is when you think you can see your way that you go wrong; when you cannot see your way, but trust to God to lead you by a way that you know not, you will go perfectly right. I am persuaded that it is so—that the simplest and plainest matter kept away from Christ, will turn out to be a maze, while the most intricate labyrinth, under the guidance of Christ, will prove to have in it straight road for the feet of all those who trust in the infallible wisdom of their Lord and Savior.

On the other hand, if you do not come to Jesus, and commune with him of all that is in your heart, *you will lose his counsel and help, and the comfort that comes from them.* I do not suppose anybody here knows what he has lost in this way, and I can hardly imagine how you are to calculate what you have lost of spiritual good that you might have had. There is many a child of God, who might be rich in all the intents of bliss, who continues to be as poor as Lazarus the beggar; he has hardly a crumb of comfort to feed upon, and is full of doubts and fears, when he might have had full assurance long ago. There is many an heir of heaven who is living upon the mere husks of Gospel food when he might be eating the rich fare of which Moses speaks: "Butter of kine, and milk of sheep, with fat of lambs, and rams of the breed of Bashan, and goats, with the fat of kidneys of wheat." Very often, beloved, you have not because you ask not; or because you believe not, or because you do not confide in Jesus, and commune with him. How strong the weakling might be if he would go to Jesus more frequently! How rich the poor soul might be if it would draw continually from Christ's inexhaustible treasury! Oh, what might we not be if we would but live up to our privileges! Might we not live in the suburbs of heaven, and often, as it were, be close to the pearly gates, if we would but go and tell all to Jesus, and commune with him concerning all that is in our hearts?

Sometimes, our naughty habit of *reticence towards Jesus is aggravated by our eagerness to tell our troubles to others.* In the time of trial, we often imitate King Asa, who, when he was sick, "sought not to the Lord, but to the physicians." It was not wrong to go to the physicians, but he should have gone to the Lord first. It is the same with many of you as it was with Asa, away you go to your neighbor over the fence, or you call in a friend, and have a talk with him in your own drawing room, or you go to some great one, and tell him all your trouble; yet how much have you gained by doing so? Have you not often found that you would have been wiser if you had followed Solomon's advice, "Go not into thy brother's house in the day of thy calamity?" Have you not also frequently discovered that, when you have talked over your griefs with your friends, they still remain?

You say that you want a friend; yet he who is the Friend that sticketh closer than a brother is neglected by you. Suppose the Lord Jesus Christ were to meet some of you, and you were to say to him, "Good Master, we are in trouble"; and suppose he should say to you, "Where have you been with your trouble? You have not been to me"; and you were to reply, "No, Lord, we have been consulting with flesh and blood; we have been asking our friends to help us"; and suppose he were to say to you, "And have they disappointed you?" and you had to reply, "Yea, Lord, they have"; suppose he looked at you severely, and said, "Where you have already gone, you had better go again. You went to your friends first; are you coming to me last? Am I to play the lackey to you, and do you only come to me after having tried all the others?" Ah! if he did talk like that, what could you reply? Why, I think your only answer could be, and I trust your answer now will be, "Jesus, Master, I have too much forgotten thee. I have not regarded thee as a real present friend. I have gone to my neighbors because I could see them, and speak with them, and hear what they had to say to me; but I have thought of thee as if thou wert a myth, or, perhaps, I have not thought of thee at all. Forgive me, Lord, for I do believe that thou art, and that thy Word is true, which declares that thou are ever with thy people, and help me, hence-forth, by thy grace, always to come to thee."

Secondly, WE NEED NOT CEASE COMMUNING WITH CHRIST FOR WANT OF TOPICS.

The Queen of Sheba and Solomon came at last to an end of their talk; they could not go on speaking to one another forever. But with regard to ourselves and our Lord, there need never be any end to our communion with him, for the subjects upon which we can have fellowship with him are almost innumerable. Let me mention just a few of them.

There are, first, *your sorrows.* Are you very grieved? Are you smitten of God, and afflicted? Then, brother, sister, you may well go to Jesus with your sorrows, for he is the Man of sorrows and acquainted with grief. He knows all about you, and all about your sorrows, too. There is not a pang that you have ever felt but he has felt the like. If you will only talk with him, you will find an open ear, and a sympathetic heart, and a ready hand, all placed at your disposal. "What do you mean, sir? Do you mean that I am to sit down in my room, and tell Jesus all about my troubles?" Yes, I do mean just that; and as you would do if you could see him sitting in the chair on the other side of the fire, sit down, and tell it all to him. If you have a quiet and secluded chamber, speak aloud if that will help you; but, anyhow, tell it all to him, pour into his ear and heart the story which you cannot disclose to anyone else. "But it seems so fanciful to imagine that I can really speak to Jesus." Try it, beloved; if you have faith in God, you will discover that it is not a matter of fancy, but the most blessed reality in the world. If you can only see what your eye perceives, it is no use for you to do as I say; in fact, you cannot do it. But if you have the inner eyes that have been enlightened by the Holy Spirit, and if your heart discerns the invisible presence of the once-crucified but now glorified Savior, tell him the whole story of your grief. Oftentimes, after you have done, you will find that it will cease to grieve you any more.

Then, also, tell him *your joys,* for he can have as much true fellowship with the joyous as with the sad. Go, young sister, young brother, in the gladness of your first youthful joy, and tell it all to Jesus. He rejoiced in spirit when he was upon the earth; and, now, he has the joy that was set before him when he endured the cross, and despised the shame. If you tell him your joys, he will sober them—not sour them. He will take away from them their earthly effervescence, and impart to them a spiritual flavor, and an abiding sweetness, so that, even in common things, your joy shall not become idolatrous and sinful. You who are bereft of creature comforts should pray that you may find all things in God; but you who have such comforts, and are full of joy, should pray this prayer—that you may find God in all things. They are both good prayers. That latter petition, you joyous souls may well pray to Jesus, and he will answer it, and you shall find that the marriage feast is all the better for Jesus being there to turn the water into wine, and that to all earthly joys he adds a bliss which they could not otherwise possess.

Some people say that we Christians get into ecstasies and raptures, and then we hardly know our head from our heels, and we are so excited that we are not fair witnesses as to matters of fact. I do not think that the Church has often had too much excitement, the fault has usually been something quite in the opposite direction; but my own conviction is that we do not see the glory of Christ when we are excited, or when we are in an ecstasy, one half so well as we do in our cool, calm, reflective moments. I know a great many Christian people who are by no means fools; if you try to do business with them, you will find that they are as shrewd and wide-awake as any men. I should like to appeal to them about this matter. I believe that I have myself a certain degree of common sense, and I venture to say that Christ never appears to me so glorious as when I am perfectly cool and collected, just as I should be if I were sitting down to write out some statistics, or to work out a mathematical problem, or to make up an account, and strike a balance. Whenever, in the very calmest and quietest manner, I begin to think of my Lord and Master, he then most of all strikes me as glorious. Our religion does not require the excitements and stimulants upon which some seem to live; but when we are in the most serene state of mind and heart, then we can best see the glories of Christ. O sirs, my Master would have you sit down, and count the cost of being his servants! He would make you arithmeticians, that, after you have counted the cost, you may see that he is worth ten thousand times more than he could ever cost you. He would have you survey him, and look upon him from all points of view—look at his person, his work, his offices, his promises, his achievements—that in all things you may see how glorious he is. I ask you calmly to see what kind of Lord and Master he is, and what sort of glory it is that surrounds him; and if you will do so—that is, if your hearts have really been changed by his grace—you will say, "Oh, yes! tell it, the wide world over, that it is simple common sense to believe in Christ, that it is irrational to reject him, that the best use of your reason is to lay it at his feet, and that the truest wisdom is to count yourself but a fool in comparison with him, and to sit with Mary, and listen to his wondrous words."

You may, also, go to Jesus, and tell him all about *your service*. You have begun to work for the Lord, and you are very pleased with the opportunity of doing something for him; but you do not find it to be all sweetness. perhaps you are like Martha who was "cumbered" with her service for Christ. When she was preparing a dinner for him, she was greatly worried over it. The servants would burn the meat, or she was afraid that one very special delicacy would be spoiled altogether. Besides, somebody had broken the best dish, and the tablecloth did not look a white as she liked to see it. Martha was also troubled because Mary did not help her, so she went to the Master about it, which was the most sensible thing she could do. I can speak very sympathetically about this matter, for I get worrying concerning it sometimes. I want to see Christ served with the best that I have, and with the best that all his people have; and if things go a little awry, and will not work quite rightly, I am apt to become fidgety; but this will not do, either for me or for you. We must go and tell the Master about it. He will set it all right, and make us see that it is all right. Suppose any of you have not been treated kindly by your fellow members even when you were trying to do good, suppose that the girls in your class have grieved you, suppose that you have been rapped over the knuckles when you really meant to be serving your Lord, what are you to do? Again I say, "Tell it all to Jesus, comfort or complaint." Do not come and tell me. If I could help you, I would; but there is One who is far better than any pastor on earth to go to, even the great Shepherd and Bishop of souls, our Lord Jesus Christ.

Then, next, go and tell Jesus all *your plans*. You think you will do something for him, do you not? Do not begin till you have told him all about what you mean to do. He had great plans for the redemption of his people, but he communicated them all to his Father; nay, I would rather say that he drew them out of his Father's eternal decrees. Go and tell him what you are planning for the glory of God, and the good of men, and you may, perhaps, discover that some of it would be a mistake.

When you have any *successes*, go and tell him. The seventy disciples returned to Jesus with joy, saying, "Lord, even the devils are subject unto us through thy name." If you have the high honor of winning a soul, tell

Jesus, and be sure to give God all the glory of it. Sing, "*Non nobis, Domine*"—"Not unto us, O Lord, not unto us, but unto thy name give glory, for thy mercy, and for thy truth's sake."

And when you have any *failures*—when your hopes are disappointed—go and tell it all to Jesus. I do not know whether I make myself clearly understood upon all these points; but I feel that working side by side with Christ is the only style of working at which a man can keep on year after year. If you get alone away from your Master—if you have sorrows or joys which are all your own, and which you do not tell to him, you will get into a sad state; but if you feel, "He is near me, he is with me," and if you act upon that belief by constantly communicating with him concerning what you feel, and what you believe, and what you do, you will lead a holy, and blessed and useful, and happy life.

I have not time to complete the long list of topics on which were to commune with Jesus; but, in brief, let me urge you to tell him all *your desires*. If thou desirest anything that thou oughtest to desire, and mayest desire, let him know it. Tell him also, all *your fears*. Tell him that you are sometimes afraid to die. Tell him every fear that distresses you; for, as a nurse is tender with her child, so is Christ with his people.

Tell him all *your loves*. Bring before him, in prayer, all upon whom your love is set. Tell him especially all you can about your love to himself; and ask him to make it firmer, stronger, more abiding, more potent over the whole of your life. Often sing a song to Jesus, your Best-beloved; and say, "Now will I sing to my Well-beloved a song touching my Beloved." Sing and speak often to him; and whenever you have any *mysteries* which you cannot explain or tell to anyone else, go and ask him to read the inscription that is engraved upon your heart, and to decipher the strange hieroglyphics which no one else can read.

Now I will close when I have briefly shown you, in the third place, that WE SHALL NEVER CEASE COMMUNING WITH CHRIST FOR WANT OF REASONS.

I am not speaking now to those who have never communed with my Lord. I have often communed with him, I do still commune with him, and so do many of you; and I say that, we shall never cease communing with him for lack of reasons.

For, first, *it is most ennobling to have fellowship with the Son of God;* "and truly our fellowship is with the Father, and with his Son Jesus Christ." I have heard it said of some men that, to know them, is a liberal education. If you are only slightly acquainted with them, you are sure to learn much from them; but to know Christ is to know everything that is worth knowing, and he is our All-in-all.

It is also *highly beneficial to commune with Christ.* I know of nothing that can lift you up so much above the evil influences of an ungodly world as constantly abiding in close fellowship with Christ, and telling out to him all that you feel in your heart of hearts.

How *consoling* it is to do this! You forget your griefs while you commune with him. How *sanctifying* it is! A man cannot take delight in sin while he walks with Christ. Communion with him will make a man leave off sinning, or else sinning will make him leave off communing. You will not be perfect while you are in this world, but the nearest way to perfection lies along the pathway where Jesus walks. How *delightful* it is, too, to commune with Jesus! There is no other joy that is at all comparable with it, and it prepares us for the higher joys above. When those who walk with Christ on earth come to live with him above, there will certainly be a change in some respects, but it will be no new experience to them. Did he not love his saints, and seek their fellowship while they wee here below? Then they shall have that fellowship continued above. Did thy not walk with God here? They shall walk with Jesus up there.

Are there any of Christ's followers who seldom commune with him? Beloved, shall I not chide you if that is true of you? My Master is looking down upon you at this moment. Does he need to speak to you? He did not speak to Peter when the boastful apostle had denied his Lord. Jesus turned, and looked upon Peter; and I trust he will look upon you; that those dear eyes, which wept for you, will gaze right down into your would; and that his blessed heart, that bled for you, will look out of those eyes of his upon you. He seems to say, "Dost thou indeed love me, as thou dost never wish for my company? *Canst* thou love me?"

And then, methinks that my Master looks upon some here who have never had any communion with him at all, and he says, "Is it nothing to you that I loved mankind, and came to earth, and died to save sinners? Is it nothing to you that I bid you trust me, and that I promise to save you if you do so? Will you still refuse to trust me? Will you turn upon your heel away from me? Oh, why will ye die? Why will ye die?

16

ESTHER

The Hand of Providence

"Though it was turned to the contrary, that the Jews had rule over them that hated them" (Esth. 9:1).

YOU are probably aware that some persons have denied the inspiration of the Book of Esther because the name of God does not occur in it. They might with equal justice deny the inspiration of a great number of chapters in the Bible, and of a far greater number of verses. Although the name of God does not occur in the Book of Esther, the Lord himself is there most conspicuously in every incident which it relates. I have seen portraits bearing the names of persons for whom they were intended, and they certainly needed them, but we have all seen others which required no name, because they were such striking likenesses that the moment you looked upon them you knew them. In the Book of Esther, as much as in any other part of the Word of God, and I had almost committed myself by saying—more than anywhere else, the hand of Providence is manifestly to be seen.

To condense the whole story of the Book of Esther into one sermon would be impossible, and therefore I must rely upon your previous acquaintance with it; I must also ask your patience if there should be more of history in the sermon than is usual with me. All Scripture is given by inspiration, and is profitable, whether it be history or doctrine. God never meant the Book of Esther to lie dumb, and whatever it seemed good to him to teach us by it, it ought to be our earnest endeavor to learn.

The Lord intended by the narrative of Esther's history to set before us a wonderful instance of his providence, that when we had viewed it with interest and pleasure, we might praise his name, and then go on to acquire the habit of observing his hand in other histories, and especially in our own lives. Well does Flavel say, that he who observes providence will never be long without a providence to observe. The man who can walk through the world and see no God, is said upon inspired authority to be a fool; but the wise man's eyes are in his head, he sees with an inner sight, and discovers God everywhere at work. It is his joy to perceive that the Lord is working according to his will in heaven, and earth, and in all deep places.

It has pleased God at different times in history to startle the heathen world into a conviction of his presence. He had a chosen people, to whom he committed the true light, and to these he revealed himself continually: the rest of the world was left in darkness, but every now and then the divine glory flamed through the gloom, as the lightning pierces the blackness of tempest. Some by that sudden light were led to seek after God, and found him; others were rendered uneasy, and without excuse, though they continued in their blind idolatry. The wonderful destruction of Pharaoh and his armies at the Red Sea was a burst of light, which startled the midnight of the world by giving proof to mankind that the Lord lived, and could accomplish his purposes by suspending the laws of nature and working miracles. The marvelous drama enacted at Shushan, the capital of Persia, was intended to be another manifestation of the being and glory of God, working not as formerly, by a miracle, but in the usual methods of his providence, and yet accomplishing all his designs. It has been well said that the Book of Esther is a record of wonders without a miracle, and therefore, though equally revealing the glory of the Lord, it sets it forth in another fashion from that which is displayed in the overthrow of Pharaoh by miraculous power.

Let us come now to the story. There were two races, one of which God had blessed promised to preserve, and another of which he had said that he would utterly put out the remembrance of it from under heaven. Israel was to be blessed and made a blessing, but of Amalek the Lord had sworn that "The Lord will war with Amalek from generation to generation." These two peoples were therefore in deadly hostility, like the seed of the woman and the seed of the serpent, between whom the Lord himself has put an enmity. Many years had rolled away; the chosen people were in great distress, and at this far-off time there still existed upon the face of the earth some relics of the race of Amalek; among them was one descended of the royal line of Agag, whose name was Haman, and he was in supreme power at the court of Ahasuerus, the Persian monarch.

Now it was God's intent that a last conflict should take place between Israel and Amalek; the conflict which began with Joshua in the desert was to be finished by Mordecai in the king's palace.

This last struggle began with great disadvantage to God's people. Haman was prime minister of the far-extending empire of Persia, the favorite of a despotic monarch, who was pliant to his will. Mordecai, a Jew in the employment of the king, sat in the king's gate; and when he saw proud Haman go to and for, he refused to pay to him the homage which others rendered obsequiously. He would not bow his head or bend his knee to him, and this galled Haman exceedingly. It came into his mind that his Mordecai was of the seed of the Jews, and with the remembrance came the high ambition to avenge the quarrel of his race. He thought it scorn to touch one man, and resolved that in himself he would incarnate all the hate of generations, and at one blow weep the accursed Jews, as he thought them, from off the face of the earth. He went in to the king, with whom his word was power, and told him that there was a singular people scattered up and down the Persian empire, different from all others, and opposed to the king's laws, and that it was not for the king's profit to suffer them. He asked that they might all be destroyed, and he would pay into the king's treasury an enormous sum of money to compensate for any loss of revenue by their destruction. He intended that the spoil which would be taken from the Jews should tempt their neighbors to kill them, and that the part allotted to himself should repay the amount which he advanced, thus he would make the Jews pay for their own murder. He had no sooner asked for this horrible grant than the monarch conceded it; taking his signet ring from off his finger, he bade him do with the Jews as seemed good to him. Thus the chosen seed are in the hands of the Agagite, who thirsts to annihilate them. Only one thing stands in the way, the Lord has said, "No weapon that is formed against thee shall prosper, and every tongue that riseth against thee in judgment thou shalt condemn." We shall see what happens, and learn from it.

First, we shall learn from the narrative that GOD PLACES HIS AGENTS IN FITTING PLACES FOR DOING HIS WORK. The Lord was not taken by surprise by this plot of Haman; He had foreseen it and forestalled it. It was needful, in order to match this cunning, malicious design of Haman, that someone of Jewish race should possess great influence with the king. How was this to be effected? Should a Jewess become Queen of Persia, the power she would possess would be useful in counteracting the enemy's design. This had been all arranged years before Haman had concocted in his wicked heart the scheme of murdering the Jews. Esther, whose sweet name signifies myrtle, had been elevated to the position of Queen of Persia by a singular course of events. It happened that Ahasuerus, at a certain drinking bout, was so far gone with wine as to forget all the proprieties of Eastern life, and sent for his queen, Vashti, to exhibit herself to the people and the princes. No one dreamed in those days of disobeying the tyrant's word, and therefore all stood aghast when Vashti, evidently a woman of right royal spirit, refused to degrade herself by being made a spectacle before that ribald rout of drinking princes, and refused to come. For her courage Vashti was divorced, and a new queen was sought for. We cannot commend Mordecai for putting his adopted daughter in competition for the monarch's choice; it was contrary to the law of God, and dangerous to her soul in the highest degree. It would have been better for Esther to have been the wife of the poorest man of the house of Israel than to have gone into the den of the Persian despot. The Scripture does not excuse, much less commend, the wrongdoing of Esther and Mordecai in thus acting, but simply tells us how divine wisdom brought good out of evil, even as the chemist distills healing drugs from poisonous plants. The high position of Esther, though gained contrary to the wisest of laws, was overruled for the best interests of her people. Esther in the king's house was the means of defeating the malicious adversary.

But Esther alone would not suffice; she is shut up in the harem, surrounded by her chamberlains and her maids of honor, but quite secluded from the outside world. A watchman is needed outside the palace to guard the people of the Lord, and to urge Esther to action when help is wanted. Mordecai, her cousin and foster father, obtained an office which placed him at the palace gate. Where could he be better posted? He is where much of the royal business will come under his eye, and he is both quick, courageous and unflinching: never had Israel a better sentinel than Mordecai, the son of Kish, a Benjamite—a very different man from that other son of Kish, who had suffered Amalek to escape in former times. His relationship to the queen allowed him to communicate with her through Hatach, her chamberlain, and, when Haman's evil decree was published, it was not long before intelligence of it reached her ear, and she felt the danger to which Mordecai and all her people were exposed. By singular providences did the Lord place those two most efficient instruments in their places. Mordecai would have been of little use without Esther, and Esther could have rendered no aid had it not been for Mordecai. Meanwhile, there is a conspiracy hatched against the king, which Mordecai discovers, and communicates to the highest authority, and so puts the king under obligation to him, which was a needful part of the Lord's plan.

Now, brethren, whatever mischief may be brewing against the cause of God and truth, and I dare say there is very much gong on at this moment, for neither the devil, nor the Jesuits, nor the atheists are long quiet, this we are sure of, the Lord knows all about it, and he has his Esther and his Mordecai ready at their posts to frustrate their designs. The Lord has his men well placed, and his ambushes hidden in their coverts, to surprise his foes. We need never be afraid but what the Lord has forestalled his enemies, and provided against their mischief.

Every child of God is where God has placed him for some purpose, and the practical use of this first point is to lead you to inquire, for what practical purpose has God placed each one of you where you now are? You have been wishing for another position where you could do something for Jesus: do not wish anything of the kind, but serve him where you are. If you are sitting at the King's gate there is something for you to do there, and if you were on the queen's throne, there would be something for you to do there; do not ask either to be gatekeeper or queen, but whichever you are, serve God therein. Brother, are you rich? God has made you a steward, take care that you are a good steward. Brother, are you poor? God has thrown you into a position where you will be better able to give a word of sympathy to poor saints. Are you doing your allotted work? Do you live in a godly family? God has a motive for placing you in so happy a position. Are you in an ungodly house? You are a lamp hung up in a dark place; mind you shine there. Esther did well, because she acted as an Esther should, and Mordecai did well, because he acted as a Mordecai should. I like to think, as I look over you all — God has put each one of them in the right place, even as a good captain well arranges the different parts of his army, and though we do not know his plan of battle, it will be seen during the conflict that he has placed each soldier where he should be. Our wisdom is not to desire another place, nor to judge those who are in another position, but each one being redeemed with the precious blood of Jesus, should consecrate himself fully to the Lord, and say, "Lord, what wilt thou have *me* to do, for here I am, and by thy grace I am ready to do it." Forget not then the fact that God in his providence places his servants in positions where he can make use of them.

Secondly, the Lord not only arranges his servants, but HE RESTRAINS HIS ENEMIES. I would call your attention particularly to the fact that Haman, having gained a decree for the destruction of all the Jews upon a certain day, was very anxious to have his cruel work done thoroughly, and therefore, being very superstitious and believing in astrology, he bade his magicians cast lots that he might find a lucky day for his great undertaking. The lots were cast for the various months, but not a single fortunate day could be found till hard by the close of the year, and then the chosen day was the thirteenth of the twelfth month. On that day the magicians told their dupe that the heavens would be propitious, and the star of Haman would be in the ascendant. Truly the lot was cast into the lap, but the disposal of it was of the Lord. See ye not that there were eleven clear months left before the Jews would be put to death, and that would give Mordecai and Esther time to turn round, and if anything could be done to reverse the cruel decree they had space to do it in. Suppose that the lot had fallen on the second or third month, the swift dromedaries and camels and messengers would scarcely have been able to reach the extremity of the Persian dominions, certainly a second set of messengers to counteract the decree could not have done so, and, humanely speaking, the Jews must have been destroyed; but oh, in that secret council chamber where sit the sorcerers and the man who asks counsel at the hands of the infernal powers, the Lord himself is present, frustrating the tokens of the liars and making diviners mad. Vain were their enchantments and the multitude of their sorceries; the astrologers, the star gazers, and the monthly prognosticators were all fools together, and led the superstitious Haman to destruction. "Surely there is no enchantment against Jacob, nor divination against Israel." Trust ye in the Lord, ye righteous and in patience possess your souls. Leave your adversaries in the hands of God, for he can make them fall into the snare which they have privily laid for you.

Notice attentively that Haman selected a mode of destroying the Jews which was wonderfully overruled for their preservation. They were to be slain by any of the people among whom they lived who chose to do so, and their plunder was to reward their slayers. Now, this was a very cunning drive, for greed would naturally incite the baser sort of men to murder the thrifty Jews, and no doubt there were debtors would also be glad to see their creditors disposed of: but see the loophole for escape which this afforded! If the decree had enacted that the Jews should be slain by the soldiery of the Persian empire it must have been done, and it is not easy to see how they could have escaped, but, the matter being left in private hands, the subsequent decree that they might defend themselves, was a sufficient counteraction of the first edict. Thus the Lord arranged that the wisdom of Haman should turn out to be folly after all.

In another point, also, we mark the restraining hand of God: namely, that Mordecai, though he had provoked Haman to the utmost, was not put to death at once. Haman "refrained himself." Why did he do so? Proud men are usually in a mighty tiff if they consider themselves insulted, and are ready at once to take revenge; but Haman "refrained himself"; until that day in which his anger burned furiously, and he set up the gallows, he smothered his passion. I marvel at this; it shows how God makes the wrath of man to praise him, and the remainder he doth restrain. Mordecai must not die a violent death by Haman's hand. The enemies of the Church of God, and of his people, can never do more than the Lord permits; they cannot go a hair's breadth beyond the divine license, and when they are permitted to do their worst there is always some weak point about all that they do, some extreme folly which renders their fury vain. The wicked carry about them the weapons of their own destruction, and when they rage most against the Most High, the Lord of all brings out of it good for his people and glory to himself. Judge not providence in little pieces, it is a grand mosaic, and must be seen as a whole. Say not of any one hour "This is dark," — it may be so, but that darkness will minister to the light, even as the ebony gloom of midnight makes the stars appear the more effulgent. Trust ye in the Lord forever, for in the Lord Jehovah there is everlasting strength. His wisdom will undermine the mines of cunning, his skill will overtop the climbings of craft; "He taketh the wise in their own craftiness, and the counsel of the froward is carried headlong."

Next we will notice that GOD IN HIS PROVIDENCE TRIES HIS PEOPLE. You must not suppose that those who are God's servants will be screened from trial; that is no part of the design of providence. "If ye be without chastisement," says the apostle, "then are ye bastards and not sons." God's

intent is to educate his people by affliction, and we must not therefore
dream that an event is not providential because it is grievous, nay, ye may
count it to be all the more so, for "the Lord trieth the righteous." Observe that God tried Mordecai; he was a quiet old man, I have no
doubt, and it must have been a daily trial for him to stand erect, or to
sit in his place when that proud peer of the realm went strutting by. His
fellow servants told him that the King has commanded all men to pay
homage to Haman, but he held his own, not, however, without knowing what it might cost him to be so sternly independent. Haman was an
Amalekite, and the Jew would not bow before him. But what a trouble
it must have been to the heart of Mordecai, when he saw the proclamation
that all the Jews must die: the good man must have bitterly lamented
his unhappy fate in being the innocent cause of the destruction of his
nation. "Perhaps," he thought within himself, "I have been too obstinate.
Woe is me; my whole house, and my whole people are to be lain because
of what I have done." He put on sackcloth and cast ashes on his head,
and was full of sorrow, a sorrow which we can hardly realize; for even
if you know you have done right, yet if you bring down trouble, and especially destruction, upon the heads of others it cuts you to the quick.
You could bear martyrdom for yourself, but it is sad to see others suffer
through your firmness.

Esther also had to be tried. Amid the glitter of the Persian court she
might have grown forgetful of her God, but the sad news comes to
her, "Your cousin and your nation are to be destroyed." Sorrow and dread
filled her heart. There was no hope for her people, unless she would go
in unto the king—that despot from whom one angry look would be death;
he must risk all, and go unbidden into his presence, and plead for her
nation. Do you wonder that she trembled? Do you marvel that she
asked the prayers of the faithful? Are you surprised to see both herself
and her maids of honor fasting and lamenting before God? Do nothing, my prosperous friend, that the Lord has given you a high place that
you may escape the trials which belong to all his people: yours is no position of ease, but one of the hottest parts of the battle. Neither the lowest and most quiet position, nor the most public and exposed condition
will enable you to escape the "much tribulation" through which the
Church militant must fight its way to glory. Why should we wish it? Should
not the gold be tested in the crucible? Should not the strong pillar
sustain great weights? When the Menai bridge was first flung across the

straits the engineer did not stipulate that his tube should never be tried with great weights; on the contrary, I can imagine his saying, "Bring up your heaviest trains and load the bridge as much as ever you will, for it will bear every strain." The Lord trieth the righteous because he has made them of metal which will endure the test, and he knows that by the sustaining power of his Holy Spirit they will be held up and made more than conquerors; therefore is it a part of the operation of providence to try the saints. Let that comfort those of you who are in trouble at this time.

But we must pass on to note, fourthly, that the LORD'S WISDOM IS SEEN IN ARRANGING THE SMALLEST EVENTS SO AS TO PRODUCE GREAT RESULTS. We frequently hear persons say of a pleasant or a great event, "What a providence!" While they are silent as to anything which appears less important, or has an unpleasant savor. Everything, the most minute as well as the most magnificent, is ordered by the Lord who has prepared his throne in the heavens, whose kingdom ruleth over all. The history before us furnishes proof of this.

We have reached the point where Esther is to go in unto the king and plead for her people. Strengthened by prayer, but doubtless trembling still, Esther entered the inner court, and the king's affection led him instantly to stretch out the golden scepter. Being told to ask what she leases, she invites the king to come to a banquet, and bring Haman with him. He comes, and for the second time invites her to ask what she wills to the half of his kingdom. Why, when the king was in so kind a spirit, did not Esther speak? He was charmed with her beauty, and his royal word was given to deny her nothing, why not speak out? But no, she merely asks that he and Haman will come to another banquet of wine tomorrow. O, daughter of Abraham, what an opportunity hast thou lost! Wherefore didst thou not plead for thy people? Their very existence hangs upon thy entreaty, and the king has said, "What wilt thou?" and yet thou art backward! Was it timidity? It is possible. Did she think that Haman stood too high in the king's favor for her to prevail? It would be hard to say. Some of us are very unaccountable, but on that woman's unaccountable silence far more was hanging than appears at first sight. Doubtless she longed to bring out her secret, but the words came not. God was in it; it was not the right time to speak, and therefore she was led to put off her disclosure. I dare say he regretted it, and wondered when she should be able to come to the point, but the Lord knew best. After that banquet Haman went out joyfully at the palace gate, but being mortified beyond measure by Mordecai's unbending posture, he called for his wife and his friends, and told them that his riches and honors availed him nothing so long as Mordecai, the Jew, sat in the king's gate. They might have told him, "You will destroy Mordecai and all his people in a few months, and the man is already fretting himself over the decree; let him live, and be you content to watch his miseries and gloat over his despair!" But no, they counsel speedy revenge. Let Mordecai be hanged on a gibbet on the top of the house, and let the gallows be set up at once, and let Haman early in the morning ask for the Jew's life, and let his insolence be punished. Go, call the workman, and let the gallows be set up at a great height that very night. It seemed a small matter that Haman should be so enraged just at that hour, but it was a very important item in the whole transaction, for had he not been so hasty he would not have gone so early in the morning to the palace, and would not have been at hand when the king said, "Who is in the court?"

But what has happened? Why, that very night, when Haman was devising to hang up Mordecai, the king could not sleep. What caused the monarch's restlessness? Why happened it on that night of all others? Ahasuerus is master of 127 provinces, but not master of ten minutes' sleep. What shall he do? Shall he call for soothing instruments of music, or beguile the hours with a tale that is told, or with a merry ballad of the minstrel? No, he calls for a book. Who would have thought that this luxurious prince must listen to a reader at dead of night? "Bring a book!" What book? A volume perfumed with roses, musical with songs, sweet as the notes of the nightingale? "No, bring the chronicles of the empire." Dull reading, that! But there are 127 provinces—which volume shall the page bring from the recorder's shelves? He chose the record of Shushan the royal city. That is the center of the empire, and its record is lengthy, in which section shall the reader make a beginning? He may begin where he pleases, but ere he closes the book the story of the discovery of a conspiracy by Mordecai has been read in the king's hearing. Was not this a singular accident? Singular if you like, but no accident. Out of 10,000 other records the reader pitches upon that one of all others. The Jews tell us that he began at another place, but that the book closed and fell open at the chapter upon Mordecai. Be that as it may, this is certain, that the Lord knew where the record was, and guided the reader to the right page. Speaking after the manner of men, there were a million chances against one that the king of Persia should, in the dead of the night, be reading the chronicle of his own kingdom, and that he should light upon this particular part of it. But that was not all, the king is interested, he had desired to go to sleep, but that wish is gone, and he is in haste to act. He says, "This man Mordecai has done me good service, has he been rewarded?" "No." Then cries the impulsive monarch, "He shall be rewarded at once. Who is in the court?" It was the most unlikely thing in the world for the luxurious Ahasuerus to be in haste to do justice, for he had done injustice thousands of times without remorse, and chiefly on that day when he wantonly signed the death warrant of that very Mordecai and his people. For once, the king is intent on being just, and at the door stands Haman—but you know the rest of the story, and how he had to lead Mordecai in state through the streets. It seems a very small matter whether you or I shall sleep tonight or toss restlessly on our beds, but God will be in our rest or in our wakefulness; we know not what his purpose may be, but his hand will be in it, neither doth nay man sleep or wake but according to the decree of the Lord.

Observe well how this matter prepared the way for the queen at the next banquet; for when she unfolded her sorrow and told of the threatened destruction of the Jews, and pointed to that wicked Haman, the king must have been the more interested and ready to grant her request, from the fact that the man who had saved his life was a Jew, and that he had already awarded the highest honors to a man in every way fitted to supersede his worthless favorite. All was well, the plotter was unmasked, the gibbet ready, and he who ordered it was made to try his own arrangements.

Our next remark is THE LORD IN HIS PROVIDENCE CALLS HIS OWN SERVANTS TO BE ACTIVE. The business was done, and well done, by divine providence, but those concerned had to pray about it. Mordecai and all the Jews outside in Shushan fasted, and cried unto the Lord. Unbelievers inquire, "What difference could prayer make?" My brethren, prayer is an essential part of the providence of God, so essential, that you will always find that when God delivers his people, his people have been praying for that deliverance. They tell us that prayer does not affect the Most High, and cannot alter his purposes. We never thought it did; but prayer is a part of the purpose and plan, and a most effective wheel in the machinery of providence. The Lord sets his people praying, and then he blesses them. Moreover, Mordecai was quite sure the Lord would deliver his people, and he expressed that confidence, but he did not therefore sit still: he stirred up Esther, and when she seemed a little slack, he put it very strongly, "If thou altogether holdest thy peace at this time, then enlargement and deliverance will arise from another place, but thou and thy father's house shall be destroyed." Nerved by this message, Esther braced herself to the effort. She did not sit still and say, "The Lord will arrange this business, there is nothing for me to do," but she both pleaded with God, and ventured her life and her all for her people's sake, and then acted very wisely and discreetly in her interviews with the king. So, my brethren, we rest confidently in providence, but we are not idle. We believe that God has an elect people, and therefore do we preach in the hope that we may be the means in the hands of his Spirit, of bringing this select people to Christ. We believe that God has appointed for his people both holiness here and heaven hereafter; therefore do we strive against sin, and press forward to the rest which remaineth for the people of God. Faith in God's providence, instead of repressing our energies, excites us to diligence. We labor as if all depended upon us, and then fall back upon the Lord with the calm faith which knows that all depends upon him.

Now must we close our historical review with the remark that in the end THE LORD ACHIEVES THE TOTAL DEFEAT OF HIS FOES AND THE SAFETY OF HIS PEOPLE. Never was a man so utterly defeated as Haman, never was a project so altogether turned aside. He was taken in his own trap, and he and his sons were hanged up on the gibbet set up for Mordecai. As for the Jews, they were in this special danger, that they were to be destroyed on a certain day, and though Esther pleaded with the king for their lives, he was not able to alter his decree, though willing to do so, for it was a rule of the constitution that the law of the Medes and Persians altered not. The king might determine what he pleased, but when he had once decreed it he could not change it, the people feeling it better to submit to the worse established law than to be left utterly to every capricious whim of their master. Now, what was to be done? The decree was given that the Jews might be slain, and it could not be reversed. Here was the door of escape—another decree was issued giving the Jews permission to defend themselves, and take the property of any who dared to attack them; thus one decree effectually neutralized the other. With great haste this mandate was sent all over the kingdom, and on the appointed day the Jews stood up for themselves and slew their foes. According to their tradition nobody attempted to attack them except the Amalekites, and consequently only Amalekites were slain, and the ace of Amalek was on that day swept from off the face of the earth. God thus gave to the Jews a high position in the empire and we are told that many became Jews, or were proselytes of the God of Abraham, because they saw what God had done. As I commenced by saying that God sometimes darted flashes of light through the thick darkness, you will now see what a flash this must have been. All the people were perplexed when they found that the Hebrews might be put to death, but they must have been far more astonished when the decree came that they might defend themselves. All the word inquired, "Why is this?" and the answer was "The living God whom the Jews worship, has displayed his wisdom and rescued his people." All nations were compelled to feel that there was a God in Israel, and thus the divine purpose was fully accomplished, his people were secured, and his name was glorified to the world's end.

From the whole we learn the following lessons.

First, it is clear that *the divine will is accomplished, and yet men are perfectly free agents.* Haman acted according to his own will, Ahasuerus did whatever he pleased, Mordecai behaved as his heart moved him, and so did Esther. We see no interference with them, no force or coercion; hence the entire sin and responsibility rest with each guilty one, yet, acting with perfect freedom, none of them acts otherwise than divine providence had foreseen. "I cannot understand it," says one. My dear friend, I am compelled to say the same—I do not understand it either. I have known many who think they comprehend all things, but I fancy they had a higher opinion of themselves than truth would endorse. Certain of my brethren deny free agency, and so get out of the difficulty; others assert that there is no predestination, and so cut the knot. As I do not wish to get out of the difficulty, and have no wish to shut my eyes to any part of the truth, I believe both free agency and predestination to be facts. How they can be made to agree I do not know, or care to know; I am satisfied to know anything which God chooses to reveal to me, and equally content not to know what he does not reveal. There it is; man is a free agent in what he does, responsible for his actions, and verily guilty when he does wrong, and he will be justly punished, too, and if he be lost the blame will rest with himself alone: but yet there is One who ruleth over all, who, without complicity in their sin, makes even the actions of wicked men to subserve his holy and righteous purposes. Believe these two truths and you will see them in practical agreement in daily life, though you will not be able to devise a theory for harmonizing them on paper.

Next, we learn *what wonders can be wrought without miracles*. When God does a wonderful thing by suspending the laws of nature men are greatly astonished and say, "This is the finger of God," but nowadays they say to us, "Where is your God? He never suspends his laws now!' Now, I see God in the history of Pharaoh, but I must confess I see him quite as clearly in the history of Haman, and I think I see him in even a grander light; for (I say it with reverence to his holy name) it is a somewhat rough method of accomplishing a purpose to stop the wheel of nature and reverse wise and admirable laws; certainly it reveals his power, but it does not so clearly display his immutability. When, however, the Lord allows everything to go on in the usual way, and gives mind and thought, ambition and passion their full liberty, and yet achieves his purpose, it is doubly wonderful. In the miracles of Pharaoh we see the finger of God, but in the wonders of providence, without miracle, we see the hand of God. Today, whenever the event may be, the attentive eye will as clearly see the Lord as if by miraculous power the hills had leaped from their places, or the floods had stood upright as a heap. I am sure that God is in the world, aye, and is at my own fireside, and in my chamber, and manages my affairs, and orders all things for me, and for each one of his children. We want no miracles to convince us of his working, the wonders of his providence are as great marvels as miracles themselves.

Next we learn *how safe the Church of God is*. At one time the people of God seemed to be altogether in Haman's power. Nero once said that he wished his enemies had but one neck that he might destroy them all at a blow, and Haman seemed to have realized just such power. yet the chosen nation was delivered, the Jewish people lived on until the Messiah came, and does exist, and will exist till they shall enjoy the bright future which is decreed for them. So is it with the Church of God today. The foes of truth can never put out the candle which God has lit, never crush the living seed which the Lord Jesus has sown in his own blood-bought people. Brethren, be ye not afraid, but stablish your hearts to God.

Again, we see that *the wicked will surely come to an ill end*. They may be very powerful, but God will bring them down. They may be very crafty, and may plot and plan, and may think that even God himself is their accomplice, because everything goes as they desire; but they may be sure their sin will find them out. They may dig deep as hell, but God will undermine them, and they may climb as high as the stars, but God will be above them to hurl them down. Wicked man, I charge you if you be wise, turn you from your career of opposition to the Most High, you cannot stand against him, neither can you outwit him. Cease, I beseech you, from this idle opposition, and hear the voice of his Gospel which says, "Confess your sin and forsake it. Believe in Jesus, the Son of God, the great atoning sacrifice, and even you shall yet be saved." If you do not do so, upon your own head shall your iniquities fall.

Last of all, let each child of God rejoice that *we have a guardian so near the throne.* Every Jew in Shushan must have felt hope when he remembered that the queen was a Jewess. Today let us be glad that Jesus is exalted.

> He is at the Father's side,
> The Man of love, the crucified.

How safe are all his people, for "if any man sin, we have an advocate with the Father, Jesus Christ the righteous." There is one that lieth in the bosom of God who will plead for all those who put their trust in him. Therefore be ye not dismayed, but let your souls rest in God, and wait patiently for him, for sooner shall heaven and earth pass away than those who trust the Lord shall perish. "They shall not be ashamed nor confounded, world without end."

17

THE BRIDE AND BRIDEGROOM

The Good Shepherdess

"Tell me, O thou whom my soul loveth, where thou feedest, where thou makest thy flock to rest at noon: for why should I be as one that turneth aside by the flocks of thy companions? If thou know not, O thou fairest among women, go thy way forth by the footsteps of the flock, and feed thy kids beside the shepherds' tents" (Song 1:7, 8).

THE bride is most unhappy and ashamed, because her personal beauty has been sorely marred by the heat of the sun. The fairest among women has become swarthy as a sunburnt slave. Spiritually it is so with a chosen soul full often. The Lord's grace has made her fair to look upon, even as the lily; but she has been so busy about earthly things that the sun of worldliness has injured her beauty. She says, "Look not upon me, for I am black, because the sun hath looked upon me." In her distress she turns to her beloved, and this is one index of a gracious soul—that whereas the ungodly rush to and fro, and know not where to look for consolation, the believing heart naturally flies to the Well-beloved, knowing that in him is its only rest.

It would appear from the preceding verse that the bride was also in trouble about a certain charge which had been given to her, which burdened her, and in the discharge of which she had become negligent of herself. She says, "They made me the keeper of the vineyards," and she would wish to have kept them well, but she felt she had not done so, and that, moreover, she had failed in a more immediate duty—"Mine own vineyard have I not kept." Under this sense of double unworthiness and failure, feeling her omissions and her commissions to be weighing her down, she turned round to her Beloved and asked instruction at his hands.

This was well. She was wise thus to appeal to her Lord against herself. Beloved, never let sin part you from Jesus. Under a sense of sin do not fly from him; that were foolishness. Sin may drive you *from* Sinai; it ought to draw you *to* Calvary. To the fountain we should fly with all the greater alacrity when we feel that we are foul; and to the dear wounds of Jesus, whence all our life and healing must come, we should resort with the greater earnestness when we feel our soul to be sick, even though we feel that sickness to be unto death. The bride, in the present case, takes to Jesus her two troubles, her distress about herself, and her confession concerning her work. She brings before him her double charge, the keeping of her own vineyard, and the keeping of the vineyards of others. It may be I shall be speaking to many who are busy in serving their Lord; I know I am; but it may be that they feel great anxiety because they cannot keep their own hearts near to Jesus: they do not feel themselves warm and lively in the divine service; they plod on, but they are very much in the condition of those who are described as "faint, yet pursuing." They cannot give up working for Jesus; they love him too well for that, but they pine for his company while they are working for him; they wish they could enjoy sweet communion with him while they are actively engaged in his cause. Indeed, beloved, this is most important to all of us. I do not know of any point which Christian workers need more often to think upon than the subject of keeping their work and themselves near to the Master's hand.

Here is A QUESTION ASKED. Every word of the inquiry is worthy of our careful meditation. You will observe, first, concerning it, that it is *asked in love*. She calls him to whom she speaks by the endearing title, "O thou whom my soul loveth." Whatever she may feel herself to be, she knows that she loves *him*. She is black, and shamed to have her face gazed upon, but she still loves him. She has not kept her own vineyard as she ought to have done, but still she loves him; that she is sure of, and therefore boldly declares it. She loves him as she loves none other in all the world. He only is to be called "him whom my soul loveth." She knows none at all worthy to be compared with him, none who can rival him. He is her bosom's Lord, sole prince and monarch of all her affections. She feels also that she loves him intensely—from her inmost *soul* loveth. The life of her existence is bound up with him: if there be any force and power and vitality in her, it is but as fuel to the great flame of her love, which burns alone for him.

Mark well that it is not "O thou whom my soul believe in." That would be true, but she has passed further. It is not "O thou whom my soul honors." That is true, too, but she has passed beyond that stage. Nor is it merely "O thou whom my soul trusts and obeys." She is doing that, but she has reached something warmer, more tender, more full of fire and enthusiasm, and it is "O thou whom my soul *loveth*." Now, beloved, I trust many of us can speak so to Jesus. He is to us the Well-beloved, the chief amongst a myriad: "His mouth is every sweetness, yea, all of him is loveliness," and our soul is wrapped up in him, our heart is altogether taken up with him. We shall never serve him aright unless it be so. Before our Lord said to Peter, "Feed my lambs," and "Feed my sheep," he put the question, "Simon, son of Jonas, lovest thou me?" and this he repeated three times; for until that question is settled we are unfit for his service. So the bride here, having both herself and her little flock to care for, avows that she loves the spouse as if she felt that she would not dare to have a part of his flock to look after if she did not love himself; as if she saw that her right to be shepherdess at all depended upon her love *to* the Great Shepherd. She could not expect his help in her work, much less his fellowship in the work, unless there was first in her that all-essential fitness of love to his person. The question therefore becomes instructive to us, because it is addressed to Christ under that title; and I ask every worker here to take care that he always does his work in a spirit of love, and always regards the Lord Jesus not as a taskmaster, not as one who has given us work to do from which we would fain escape, but as our dear Lord, whom to serve is bliss, and for whom to die is gain. "O thou whom my soul loveth," is the right name by which a worker for Jesus should address his Lord.

Now note that the question, as it is asked in love, is also *asked of him*. "tell me, O thou whom my soul loveth, where thou feedest." She asked him to tell her, as if she feared that none but himself would give her the correct answer; others might be mistaken, but he could not be. She asked of him because she was quite sure that he would give her the kindest answer. Others might be indifferent, and might scarcely take the trouble to reply; but if Jesus would tell her himself, with his own lips, he would mingle love with every word, and so console as well as instruct her. Perhaps she felt that nobody else could tell her as he could, for others speak to the ear, but he speaks to the heart: others speak with lower degrees of influence; we hear their speech but are not moved thereby; but Jesus speaks, and the Spirit goes with every word he utters, and therefore we hear to profit when He instructs us. I do not know how it may be with you, my brethren, but I feel that if I could get a word from Christ it would satisfy my soul for many a day. I love to hear the Gospel and to read it, and to preach it; but to hear it fresh from himself, applied by the energy of the Holy Spirit! O, this were refreshment! This were energy and power! Therefore, Savior, when thy workers desire to know where thou feedest, tell them thyself, speak to their hearts by thine own Spirit, and let them feel as though it were a new revelation to their inmost nature. "Tell me, O thou whom my soul loveth." It is asked in love: it is asked of him.

Now, observe what the question is. She wishes to know how Jesus does his work, and where he does it. It appears, from the eighth verse, that she herself has a flock of kids to tend. She is a shepherdess, and would fain feed her flock; hence her question, "Tell me where thou feedest?" She desires those little ones of hers to obtain rest as well as food, and she is troubled about them; therefore she says, "Tell me where thou makest thy flock to rest," for if she can see how Jesus does his work, and where he does it, and in what way, then she will be satisfied that she is doing it in the right way, if she abides in fellowship with him. The question seems to be just this: "Lord, tell me what are the truths with which thou dost feed thy people's souls; tell me what are the doctrines which make the strong ones weak and the sad ones glad: tell me what is that precious meat which thou art wont to give to hungry and fainting spirits, to revive them and keep them alive: for if thou tell me, then I will give my flock the same food: tell me where the pasture is wherein thou dost feel thy sheep, and straightway I will lead mine to the self-same happy fields. Then tell me how thou makest thy people to rest. What are those promises which thou doest apply to the consolation of their spirit, so that their cares and doubts and fears and agitations all subside? Thou hast sweet meadows where thou makest thy beloved flock to lie calmly down and slumber, tell me where those meadows are that I may go and fetch the flock committed to my charge, the mourners whom I ought to comfort, the distressed ones whom I am bound to relive, the desponding whom I have endeavored to encourage; tell me, Lord, where thou makest thy flock to lie down, for then, under thy help, I will go and make my flock to lie down too. It is for myself, but yet far more for others, that I ask the question, 'Tell me where thou feedest, where thou makest them to rest at noon.' "

But it does not strike me that this is all the meaning of the passage by a very long way. The bride says, "Tell me where thou feedest thy flock," as if she would wish to feed with the flock; "where thou makest thy flock to rest," as if she wanted to rest there too: but it strikes me the very gist of the thing is this, that she wishes to bring her flock to feed where Christ's flock feeds, and to lead her kids to lie down where Christ's little lambs were reposing; she desired, in fact, to do her work in his company; she wanted to mix up her flock with the Lord's flock, her work with his work, and to feel that what she was doing she was doing for him, yea, and with him and through him. She had evidently met with a great many difficulties in what she had tried to do. She wished to feed her flock of kids, but could not find them pasture. Perhaps when she began her work as a shepherdess she thought herself quite equal to the task, but now the same sun which had bronzed her face had dried up the pasture, and so she says, "O thou that knowest all the pastures, tell me where thou feedest, for I cannot find grass for my flock"; and suffering herself from the noontide heat, she finds her little flock suffering too; and she inquires "Where dost thou make thy flock to rest at noon? Where are cool shadows of great rocks which screen off the sultry rays when the sun is in its zenith and pours down torrents of heat? For I cannot shade my poor flock and give them comfort in their many trials and troubles. I wish I could. O Lord, tell me the secret art of consolation; then will I try to console my own charge by the self-same means." We would know the groves of promise and the cool streams of peace, that we may lead others into rest. If we can follow Jesus we can guide others, and so both we and they will find comfort and peace. That is the meaning of the request before us.

Note that she said most particularly, "Tell *me*," "O Master, do not merely tell thy sheep where thou feedest, though they want to know; but tell me where thou feedest, for I would fain instruct others." She would fain know many things, but chiefly she says, "Tell me *where Thou feedest*," for she wished to feed others. We want practical knowledge, for our desire is to be helped to bring others into rest; to be the means of speaking peace to the consciences of others, as the Lord has spoken peace to ours. Therefore the prayer is, "Tell me." "Thou art my model, O Great shepherd; thou art my wisdom. If I be a shepherd to thy sheep, yet am I also a sheep beneath thy Shepherd, therefore teach thou me, that I may teach others."

I do not know whether I make myself plain to you, but I wish to put it very simply. I am preaching to myself perhaps a great deal more than to you. I am preaching to my own heart. I feel I have to come, Sabbath after Sabbath, and weekday after weekday, and tell you a great many precious things about Christ, and sometimes I enjoy them myself; and if nobody else gets blessed by them, I do, and I go home and praise the Lord for it; but my daily fear is lest I should be a handler of texts for you, and a preacher of good things for others, and yet remain unprofited in my own heart. My prayer is that the Lord Jesus will show me where he feeds his people, and let me feed with them, that then I may conduct you to the pastures where he is, and be with him myself at the same time that I bring you to him. You Sabbath-school teachers and evangelists, and others, my dear, earnest comrades, for whom I thank God at every remembrance, I feel that the main point you have to watch about is that you do not lose your own spirituality while trying to make others spiritual. The great point is to live near to God. It would be a dreadful thing for you to be very busy about other men's souls and neglect your own. Appeal to the Well-beloved, and entreat him to let you feed your flock where he is feeding his people, that he would let you sit at his feet, like Mary, even while you are working in the house, like Martha. Do not do less, but rather more; but ask to do it in such communion with him that your work shall be melted into his work, and what you are doing shall be really only his working in you, and you rejoicing to pour out to others what he pours into your own soul.

Secondly, here is AN ARGUMENT USED. The bride says, "Why should I be as one that turneth aside by the flocks of they companions?" If she should lead her flock into distant meadows, far away from the place where Jesus is feeding His flock—suppose she should join herself to some other flock, as a shepherdess would naturally be rather dependent, and would need to associate herself for protection with others; suppose she should turn aside with other shepherds, and leave her Bridegroom, would it be right? She speaks of it as a thing most abhorrent to her mind, and well might it be. For, first, would it not look very unseemly that the bride should be associating with others than the Bridegroom? They have each a flock: there is he with his great flock, and here is she with her little one. Shall they seek pastures far off from one another? Will there not be talk about this? Will not onlookers say, "This is not comely: there must be some lack of love here, or else these two would not be so divided?"

Stress may be put, if you like, upon that little word "I". Why should I, thy blood-bought spouse; I, betrothed unto thee, as even the earth was, I whom thou hast loved—why should I turn after others and forget thee? Beloved, you had better put the emphasis in your own reading of it just there. Why should I, whom the Lord has pardoned, whom the Lord has loved, whom the Lord has favored so much—I, who have enjoyed fellowship with him for many years—I, who know that his love is better than wine—I, who have aforetime been inebriated with his sweetness—why should I turn aside? Let others do so if they will, but it would be uncomely and unseemly for me.

I pray you, brother and sister, try to feel that—that for you to work apart from Christ would have a bad look about it; that for your work to take you away from fellowship with Jesus would have a very ugly appearance: it would not be among the things that are honest and of good repute. For the bride to feed her flock in other company would look like unfaithfulness to her husband. What, shall the bride of Christ forsake her Beloved? Shall she be unchaste towards her Lord? Yet it would seem so if she makes companions of others and forgets her Beloved. Our hearts may grow unchaste to Christ even while they are zealous in Christian work. I dread very much the tendency to do Christ's work in a cold, mechanical spirit; but above even that I tremble lest I should be able to have warmth for Christ's work and yet should be cold towards the Lord himself. I fear that such a condition of heart is possible—that we may burn great bonfires in the streets for public display, and scarcely keep a live coal upon our hearth for Jesus to warm his hands at. When we meet in the great assembly the good company helps to warm our hearts, and when we are working for the Lord with others they stimulate us and cause us to put forth all our energy and strength, and then we think, "Surely my heart is in a healthy condition towards God." But, beloved, such excitement may be a poor index of our real state. I love that quiet, holy fire which will glow in the closet and flame forth in the chamber when I am alone, and that is the point I am more fearful about than anything else, both for myself and for you, lest we should be doing Christ's work without Christ; having much to do but not thinking much of *him*; cumbered about much serving and forgetting him. Why, that would soon grow into making a Christ out of our own service, an Antichrist out of our own labors. Beware of that! Love your work, but love your Master better; love your flock, but love the great Shepherd better still, and ever keep close to him, for it will be a token of unfaithfulness if you do not.

And mark again, "Why should I be as one that turneth aside by the flocks of thy companions?" We may read this as meaning, "Why should I be so unhappy as to have to work for thee, and yet be out of communion with thee?" It is a very unhappy thing to lose fellowship with Jesus, and yet to have to go on with religious exercises. If the wheels are taken off your chariot it is no great matter if nobody wants to ride, but how if you are called upon to drive on? Drive on? When a man's foot is lamed he may not so much regret it if he can sit still, but if he is bound to run a race he is greatly to be pitied. It made the spouse doubly unhappy even to suppose that she, with her flock to feed and herself needing feeding too, should have to turn aside by the flocks of others and miss the presence of her Lord. In fact, the question seems to be put in this shape: "What reason is there why I should leave my Lord? What apology could I make, what excuse could I offer for so doing? Is there any argument why I should not abide in constant fellowship with him? Why should I be as one that turneth aside? Perhaps it may be said that others turn aside, but why should *I* be as one of them? There may be excuses for such an act in others, but there can be none for me: thy rich love, thy free love, thy undeserved love, thy special love to me, hath bound me hand and foot; how can I turn aside? There may be some professors who owe thee little, but I, once the chief of sinners, owe thee so much, how can I turn aside? There may be some with whom thou hast dealt hardly who may turn aside, but thou hast been so tender, so kind to me, how can I forget thee? There may be some who know but little of thee, whose experience of thee is so slender that their turning aside is not to be wondered at; but how can I turn aside when thou hast showed me thy love, and revealed thy heart to me? Oh, by the banqueting house where I have feasted with thee, by the Hermonites and the hill Mizar, where thou hast manifested thy love, by the place where deep called to deep, and then mercy called to mercy; by those mighty storms and sweeping hurricanes in which thou wast the shelter of my head, by ten thousand thousand mercies past which have been my blessed portion, why should *I* be as one that turneth aside by the flocks of thy companions?"

Let me address the members of this church, and say to you, if all the churches in Christendom were to go aside from the Gospel, why should you? If in every other place the Gospel should be neglected, and an uncertain sound should be given forth; if Ritualism should swallow up half the churches, and Rationalism the rest, yet why should *you* turn aside? You have been peculiarly a people of prayer; you have also followed the Lord fully in doctrine and in ordinance; and consequently you have enjoyed the divine presence, and have prospered beyond measure. We have cast ourselves upon the Holy Ghost for strength, and have not relied upon human eloquence, music, or beauties of color, or architecture. Our only weapon has been the simple, plain, full Gospel, and why should we turn aside? Have we not been favored for these many years with unexampled success? Has not the Lord added unto our numbers so abundantly that we have not had room enough to receive them? Has he not multiplied the people, and increased the joy? Hold fast to your first love, and let no man take your crown. I thank God there are churches still, a few in England and yet more in Scotland, that hold fast the doctrines of the Gospel and will not let them go. To them I would say, why should ye turn aside? Should not your history, both in its troublous and its joyous chapters teach you to hold fast the form of sound words?

Above all, should we not try to live as a church, and individually, also in abiding fellowship with Jesus; for if we turn aside from him we shall rob the truth of its aroma, yea, of its essential fragrance. If we lose fellowship with Jesus we shall have the standard, but where will be the standard bearer? We may retain the candlestick, but where shall be the light? We shall be shorn of our strength, our joy, our comfort, our all, if we miss fellowship with him. God grant, therefore, that we may never be as one that turneth aside.

Thirdly, we have here AN ANSWER GIVEN by the Bridegroom to his beloved. She asked him where he fed, where he made his flock to rest, and he answered her. Observe carefully that this answer is *given in tenderness to her infirmity*, not ignoring her ignorance, but dealing very gently with it. "If thou know not" —a hint that she ought to have known, but such a hint as kind lovers give when they would fain forbear to chide. Our Lord is very tender to our ignorance. There are many things which we do not know, but ought to have known. We are children when we should be men, and have to be spoken to as unto carnal —unto babes in Christ, when we should have become fathers. Is there one among us who can say, "I am not faulty in my knowledge"? I am afraid the most of us must confess that if we had done the Lord's will better we should have known his doctrine better; if we had lived more closely to him we should have known more of him. Still, how very gentle the rebuke is. The Lord forgives our ignorance, and condescends to instruct it.

Note next that the answer is *given in great love.* He says, "O thou fairest among women." That is a blessed cordial for her distress. She said, "I am black"; but he says, "O thou fairest among women." I would rather trust Christ's eyes than mine. If my eyes tell me I am black I will weep, but if he assures me I am fair I will believe him and rejoice. Some saints are more apt to remember their sinfulness, and grieve over it, than to believe in their righteousness in Christ, and triumph in it. Remember, beloved, it is quite as true today that you are all fair and without spot as that you are black, because the sun hath looked upon you. It must be true, because Jesus says so. Let me give you one of the sayings of the Bridegroom to his bride: "Thou art all fair, my love; there is no spot in thee." "Ah, that is a figure," say you. Well, I will give you one that is not a figure. The Lord Jesus, after he had washed his disciples' feet, said, "he that is washed needeth not except to wash his feet, for he is clean every whit"; and then he added, "And ye are clean." If you desire an apostolic word to the same effect, let me give you this: "Who shall lay anything to the charge of God's elect?" — *anything* — any little thing or any great thing either. Jesus has washed them so clean that there is no spot, no wrinkle, nor any such thing upon them in the matter of justification before God.

How glorious is this! Jesus does not exaggerate when he thus commands his Church. He speaks plain, sober truth. "O thou fairest among women," saith he. My soul, dost thou not feel love to Christ when thou rememberest that he thinks thee beautiful? I cannot see anything in myself to love, but he does, and calls me "all fair." I think it must be that he looks into our eyes and sees, himself, or else this, that he knows what we are going to be, and judges us on that scale.

The answer contains much sacred wisdom. The bride is directed where to go that she may find her beloved and lead her flock to him. "Go thy way forth by the footprints of the flock." If thou wilt find Jesus, thou wilt find him in the way the holy prophets went, in the way of the patriarchs and the way of the apostles. And if thy next desire be to find thy flock and to make them lie down, very well, go thou and feed them as other shepherds have done—Christ's own shepherds whom he has sent in other days to feed his chosen.

I feel very glad, in speaking from this text, that the Lord does not give to his bride in answer to her question some singular directions of great difficulty, some novel prescription singular and remarkable. Just as the Gospel itself is simple and homely, so is this exhortation and direction for the renewal of communion. It is simple, it is plain. You want to get to Jesus, and you want to bring those under your charge to him. Very well, then, do not seek out a new road, but simply go the way which all other saints have gone. If you want to walk with Jesus, walk where other saints have walked; and if you want to lead others into communion with him, lead them by your example where others have gone. What is that? If you want to be with Jesus, go where Abraham went in the path of separation. See how he lived as a pilgrim and a sojourner with His God. If you would see Jesus, "Come ye out from among them, be ye separate, touch not the unclean thing." You shall find Jesus when you have left the world. If you would walk with Jesus, follow the path of obedience. Saints have never had fellowship with Jesus when they have disobeyed him. Keep his statutes and observe his testimonies, be jealous over your conduct and character; for the path of obedience is the path of communion. Be sure that you follow the ancient ways with regard to the Christian ordinances: do not alter them, but keep to the good old paths. Stand and inquire what apostles did, and do the same. Above all, if you would walk with Jesus, continue in the way of holiness; persevere in the way of grace. Make the Lord Jesus your model and example; and by treading where the footprints of the flock are to be seen, you will both save yourself and them that hear you; you shall find Jesus, and they shall find Jesus too.

Then the Spouse added, "Feed thy kids beside the shepherds' tents." Now, who are these shepherds? There be many in these days who set up for shepherds, who feed their sheep in poisonous pastures. Keep away from them; but there are others whom it is safe to follow. Let me take you to the twelve principal shepherds who came after the great Shepherd of all. You want to bless your children, to save their souls, and have fellowship with Christ in the doing of it; then teach them the truths which the apostles taught. And what were they? Take Paul as an example. "I determined not to now anything among you save Jesus Christ, and him crucified." That is feeding the kids beside the shepherds' tents, when you teach your children Christ, much of Christ, all of Christ, and nothing else but Christ. Mind you stick to that blessed subject. And when you are teaching Christ, teach them all about his life, his death, his resurrection; teach them his godhead and his manhood. You will never enjoy Christ's company if you doubt his divinity. Take care that you feed your flock upon the doctrine of the atonement. Christ will have no fellowship with a worker unless he represents him fairly, and you cannot represent Christ truthfully unless you see the ruddy hue of his atoning blood as well as the lily purity of his life. "Feed thy kids beside the shepherds' tents," then wilt thou teach them the atoning sacrifice, and justification by faith, and imputed righteousness, and union with the risen Head, and the coming of the great One, wherein we shall receive the adoption, to wit, the redemption of the body from the grave.

I speak the truth and lie not when I say that if we want to teach a congregation so as to bless them, and keep in fellowship with Christ at the same time ourselves, we must be very particular to teach nothing but the truth—not a part of it, but all of it. Preach that blessed doctrine of election. Oh, the deeps of divine love which are continued in that blessed truth! Do not shirk it, or keep it in the background. You cannot expect Christ's presence if you do. Teach the doctrine of man's depravity. Lay the sinner low. God will not bless a ministry that exalts men. Preach the doctrine of the Holy Spirit's effectual calling, for if we do not magnify the Spirit of God, we cannot expect that he will make our work to stand. Preach regeneration. Let it be seen how thorough the change is, that we may glorify God's work. Preach the final perseverance of the saints. Teach that the Lord is not changeable—casting away his people, living them today and hating them tomorrow. Preach, in fact, the doctrines of grace as you find them in the Book.

Feed them beside the shepherds' tents. Aye, and feed the kids there— the little children. I begin to feel more and more that it is a mistake to divide the children from the congregation. I believe in special services for children, but I would also have them worship with us. If our preaching does not teach children, it lacks some element which it ought to possess. The kind of preaching that is best of all for grown-up people is that in which children also will take delight. I like to see the congregation made up not all of the young, nor all of the old; not all of the mature nor all of the inexperienced, but some of all sorts gathered together. Feed the kids with the same Gospel as the grown-up ones—not exactly in the same terms; let your language be appropriate to them, but let it be the same truth. The same truth for all; and you cannot expect Christ to be with you in the feeding of your little flocks unless you feed them where Christ feeds us. Where does he feed us but where the truth grows? Give me the doctrines of grace, and I am in clover. If you have to feed others, take them there. Do not conduct them to the starved pastures of modern thought and culture. Preachers are starving God's people nowadays. O for the good old corn of the kingdom; we want that, and I am persuaded that when the churches get back to the old food again, when they begin to feed their flocks beside the shepherds' tents, and when in practical living Christians get back to the old Puritan method, and follow once again the tracks of the sheep, and the sheep follow the tracks of Christ, then we shall get the Church into fellowship with Jesus, and Jesus will do wonders in our midst.

18

THE BRIDE AND BRIDEGROOM

Heavenly Love-Sickness

"I charge you, O daughters of Jerusalem, if ye find my beloved, that ye tell him that I am sick of love " (Song 5:8).

Sɪᴄᴋ! that is a sad thing; it moves your pity. Sick of love—lovesick! that stirs up other emotions which we shall presently attempt to explain. No doubt certain sicknesses are peculiar to the saints: the ungodly are never visited with them. Strange to say, these sicknesses, to which the refined sensibilities of the children of God render them peculiarly liable, are signs of vigorous health. Who but the beloved of the Lord ever experience that *sin-sickness* in which the soul loathes the very name of transgression, is unmoved by the enchantments of the tempter, finds no sweetness in its besetting sins, but turns with detestation and abhorrence from the very thought of iniquity? Not less is it for these, and these alone, to feel that *self-sickness* whereby the heart revolts from all creature-confidence and strength, having been made sick of self, self-seeking, self-exalting, self-reliance, and self of every sort. The Lord afflicts us more and more with such self-sickness till we are dead to self, its puny conceits, its lofty aims, and its unsanctified desires.

Then there is a *twofold love-sickness*. Of the one kind is that love-sickness which comes upon the Christian when he is transported with the full enjoyment of Jesus, even as the bride elated by the favor, melted by the tenderness of her Lord, says in the fifth verse of the second chapter of the Song, "Stay me with flagons, comfort me with apples: for I am sick of love." The soul overjoyed with the divine communications of happiness and bliss which came from Christ, the body scarcely able to bear the excessive delirium of delight which the soul possessed, she was

427

so glad to be in the embraces of her Lord, that she needed to be stayed under her overpowering weight of joy. Another kind of love-sickness widely different from the first, is that in which the soul is sick, not because it has too much of Christ's love, but because it has not enough present consciousness of it; sick, not of the enjoyment, but of the longing for it; sick, not because of excess of delight, but because of sorrow for an absent lover. It is to this sickness we call your attention.

First, then, let us consider our text as the language of a soul LONGING FOR THE VIEW OF JESUS CHRIST IN GRACE.

Do ye ask me concerning *the sickness itself*: What is it? It is the sickness of a soul panting after communion with Christ. The man is a believer; he is not longing after salvation as a penitent sinner under conviction, for he is saved. Moreover, he has love to Christ and he knows it; he does not doubt his evidence as to the reality of his affection for his Lord, for you see the word used is "*My* beloved," which would not be applicable if the person speaking had any doubt about her interest; nor did she doubt her love, for she calls the spouse, "My *beloved*." it is the longing of a soul, then, not for salvation, and not even for the certainty of salvation, but for the enjoyment of present fellowship with him who is her soul's life, her soul's all. The heart is panting to be brought once more under the apple tree; to feel once again his "left hand under her head, while his right hand doth embrace her." She has know, in days past, what it is to be brought into his banqueting house, and to see the manner of love waved over her, and she therefore crieth to have love visits renewed. It is a panting after communion. Gracious souls are never perfectly at ease except they are in a state of nearness to Christ; for mark you, when they are not near to Christ, they lose their *peace*. The nearer to Jesus, the nearer to the perfect calm of heaven; and the further from Jesus, the nearer to that troubled sea which images the continual unrest of the wicked. There is no peace to the man who doth not dwell constantly under the shadow of the cross; for Jesus is our peace, and if he be absent, our peace is absent too. I know that being justified, we have peace with God, but it is "through our Lord Jesus Christ." So that the justified man himself cannot reap the fruit of justification, except by abiding in Christ Jesus, who is the Lord and Giver of peace. The Christian without fellowship with Christ loses all his *life* and energy; he is like a dead thing. He is without vivacity, yea, more, he is without animation till Jesus comes; but when the Lord sensibly sheds abroad his love in our hearts, then *his* love kindles ours; then our blood leaps in our veins for joy, like the Baptist in the womb of Elizabeth. The heart when near to Jesus has strong pulsations, for since Jesus is in that heart, it is full of life, of vigor, and of strength. Peace, liveliness, vigor—all depend upon the constant enjoyment of communion with Christ Jesus.

Beloved, all the joys of life are nothing to us; we have melted them all down in our crucible, and found them to be dross. You and I have tried earth's vanities, and they cannot satisfy us; nay, they do not give a morsel of meat to satiate our hunger. Being in a state of dissatisfaction with all mortal things, we have learned through divine grace, that none but Jesus, none but Jesus can make our souls glad. "Philosophers are happy without music," said one of old. So Christians are happy without the world's good. Christians, with the world's good, are sure to bemoan themselves as naked, poor and miserable, unless their Savior be with them. You that have ever tasted communion with Christ, will soon know why it is that a soul longs after him. What the sun is to the day, what the moon is to the night, what the dew is to the flower, such is Jesus Christ to us. What bread is to the hungry, clothes to the naked, the shadow of a great rock to the traveler in a weary land, such is Jesus Christ to us. What the turtle is to her mate, what the husband is to his spouse, what the head is to the body, such is Jesus Christ to us; and therefore, if we have him not, nay if we are not conscious of having him; if we are not one with him, nay if we are not consciously one with him, little marvel if our spirit cries in the words of the Song, "I charge you, O ye daughters of Jerusalem, if ye find my beloved, tell him that I am sick of love." Such is the character of this love-sickness.

We may say of it, however, before we leave that pint, that it is *a sickness which has a blessing attending it*: "Blessed are they that do hunger and thirst after righteousness"; and therefore, supremely blessed are they who thirst after the Righteous One—after him, who in the highest perfection embodies pure, immaculate, spotless righteousness. Blessed is that hunger, for it comes from God. It bears a blessing within it; for if I may not have the blessedness in full bloom of being filled, the next best thing is the same blessedness in sweet bud of being empty till I am filled with Christ. If I may not feed on Jesus, it shall be next door to heaven to be allowed to hunger and thirst after him. There is a hallowedness about that hunger, since it sparkles among the beatitudes of our Lord.

Yet it is a sickness, dear friends, which, despite the blessing, *causes much pain*. The man who is sick after Jesus, will be dissatisfied with everything else; he will find that dainties have lost their sweetness, and music its melody, and light its brightness, and life itself will be darkened with the shadow of death to him, till he finds his Lord, and can rejoice in him. Beloved, ye shall find that this thirsting, this sickness, if it ever gets hold upon you is *attended with great vehemence*. The desire is vehement, as coals of juniper. Ye have heard of hunger that it breaks through stone walls: but stone walls are no prison to a soul that desires Christ. Stone walls, nay, the strongest natural barriers, cannot keep a love-sick heart from Jesus. I will venture to say that the temptation of heaven itself, if it could be offered to the believer without his Christ, would be as less than nothing; and the pains of hell, if they could be endured, would be gladly ventured upon by a love-sick soul, if he might but find Christ. As lovers sometimes talk of doing impossibilities for their fair ones, so certainly a spirit that is set on Christ will laugh at impossibility, and say, "It shall be done." It will venture upon the hardest task, go cheerfully to prison and joyfully to death, if it may but find its beloved, and have its love-sickness satisfied with his presence.

Ye may inquire concerning the cause of this love-sickness. What maketh a man's soul so sick after Christ? Understand that it is the *absence* of Christ which makes this sickness in a mind that really understands the preciousness of his presence. The spouse had been very willful and wayward; she had taken off her garments, had gone to her rest, her sluggish slothful rest, when her beloved knocked at the door. He said "Open to me, my beloved; for my head is filled with dew, and my locks with the drops of the night." She was too slothful to wake up to let him in. She urged excuses—"I have put off my coat; how shall I put it on? I have washed my feet: how shall I defile them?" The beloved stood waiting, but since she opened not, he put in his hand by the hole of the lock, and then her bowels were moved towards him. She went to the door to open it, and to her surprise, her hands dropped with myrrh, and her fingers with sweet-smelling myrrh upon the handles of the lock. There was the token that he had been there, but he was gone. Now she began to bestir herself, and seek after him. She sought him through the city, but she found him not. Her soul failed her; she called after him, but he gave her no answer, and the watchman, who ought to have helped her in the search, smote her, and took away her veil from her.

Therefore it is that now she is seeking, because she has lost her beloved. She should have held him fast, and not have permitted him to go. He is absent, and she is sick till she findeth him.

Mingled with the sense of absence is *a consciousness of wrongdoing*. Something in her seemed to say, "How couldst thou drive him away? That heavenly bridegroom who knocked and pleaded hard, how couldst thou keep him longer there amidst the cold dews of night? O unkind heart! what if thy feet had been made to bleed by thy rising? What if all thy body had been chilled by the cold wind, when thou wast treading the floor? What had it been compared with his love to thee?" And so she is sick to see him, that she may weep out her love and tell him how vexed she is with herself that she should have held to him so loosely, and permitted him so readily to depart.

So, too, mixed with this, was *great wretchedness* because he was gone. She had been for a little time easy in his absence. That downy bed, that warm coverlet, had given her a peace, a false, cruel and a wicked peace, but she has risen now, the watchmen have smitten her, her veil is gone, and, without a friend, the princess, deserted in the midst of Jerusalem's streets, has her soul melted for heaviness, and she pours out her heart within her as she pineth after her lord. "No love but my love, no lord buy my lord," saith she, with sobbing tongue and weeping eyes; for none else can gratify her heart or appease her anxiety.

Beloved, have you never been in such a state, when your faith has begun to droop, and your heart and spirits have fled from you? Even then it was your soul was sick for him. You could do without him when Mr. Carnal-security was in the house, and feasted you, but when he and his house have both been burned with fire, the old love-sickness came back, and you wanted Christ, nor could ye be satisfied till ye found him once again. There was *true love* in all this, and this is the very pith of all love-sickness. Had not she loved, absence would not have made her sick, nor would her repentance have made her grieve. Had she not loved, there would have been no pain because of absence, and no sinking of spirits, but she did love, thence all this sickness. It is a delightful thing to be able to know when we have lost Christ's company, that we do love him—" 'Yea, Lord, thou knowest all things; thou knowest that I love thee.' I did deny thee, yea, in the moment of thy sorrow, I said, 'I know not the man.' I did curse and swear that men might think I was no follower of thine, but still thou knowest all things; thou knowest that I love thee." When you can feel this, dear friends, the consciousness that you love will soon work in you a *heart-burning*, so that your soul will not be satisfied till you can tell out that love in the Master's presence, and he shall say unto you, as a token of forgiveness, "Feed my sheep."

I do not doubt that in this sickness there had been *some degree of fear.* Sorrowful woman! She was half afraid she might never find him again. She had been about the city—where could he be? She had sought him on the walls and on the ramparts, but he was not there. In every ordinance, in every means of grace, in secret and in public prayer, in the Lord's Supper, and in the reading of the Word, she had looked after him, but he was not there; and now she was half afraid that though he might give his presence to others, yet never to her, and when she speaks, you notice there is half a fear in it. She would not have asked others to tell him if she had any assuring hope that she should meet him herself— "If ye find him," she seems to say, "O ye true converts, you that are the real grace-born daughters of Jerusalem; if he reveals himself to you, though he never may to me, do me this kindness, tell him that I am sick of love." There is half a fear here, and yet there is *some hope.* He feels that he must love her still, or else why send a message at all? She would surely never send this sweet message to a flinty, adamantine heart, "Tell him I am sick of love"; but she remembered when the glancings of her eyes had ravished him; she remembered when a motion from her hand had made his heart melt, and when one tear of her eyes had opened all his wounds afresh. She thinks, "Perhaps, he loves me still as he loved me then, and my moanings will enchain him; my groans will constrain him and lead him to my help." So she sends the message to him—"Tell him, tell him I am sick of love."

To gather up the causes of this love-sickness in a few words, does not the whole matter spring from *relationship?* She is his spouse; can the spouse be happy without her beloved lord? It springs from union; she is part of himself. Can the hand be happy and healthy if the life-floods stream not from the heart and from the head? Fondly realizing her *dependence*, she feels that she owes all to him, and gets her all from him. If then the fountain be cut off, if the streams be fried, if the great source of all be taken from her, how can she but be sick? And there is besides this, *a life and a nature* in her which makes her sick. There is a life like the life of Christ, nay, her life is in Christ, it is hid with Christ in God; her nature is a part of the divine nature; she is a partaker of the divine nature. Moreover she is in *union* with Jesus, and this piece divided, as it were, from the body, wriggles, like a worm cut asunder, and pants to get back to where it came from. These are the causes of it. You will not understand my sermon this morning, but think me raving, unless you are spiritual men. "But the spiritual judgeth all things, yet he himself is judged of no man."

What endeavors such love-sick souls will put forth. Those who are sick for Christ will first send their *desires* to him. Men use pigeons sometimes to send their messages. Why, what sort of carrier pigeons do they use? The pigeon is of no use to send anywhere but to the place from which it came, and my desires after Christ came from him, and so they will always go back to the place from which they came; they know the way to their own dovecot, so I will send him my sighs and my groans, my tears and my moans. Go, go, sweet doves, with swift and clipping wings, and tell him I am sick of love. Then she would send her *prayers*. Ah! methinks she would say of her desires, "They will never reach him; they know the way but their wings are broken, and they will fall to the ground and never reach him." Yet she will send them whether they reach him or not. As for her prayers, they are like arrows.

Sometimes messages have been sent into besieged towns bound to an arrow, so she binds her desires upon the arrow of her prayers, and then shoots them forth from the bow of her faith. She is afraid they will never reach him, for her bow is slack, and she knoweth not how to draw it with her feeble hands which hang down.

So what does she? She has traversed the streets; she has used *the means*; she has done everything; she has sighed her heart out, and emptied her soul out in prayers. She is all wounds till he heals her; she is all a hungry mouth till he fills her; she is all an empty brook till he replenishes her once again, and so now she *goeth to her companions*, and she saith, "If ye find my beloved, tell him I am sick of love." This is using the intercession of the saints. It is unbelief that makes her use it, and yet there is a little faith mixed in her unbelief. It was an unbelief but not a mischief. There *is* efficacy in the intercession of saints. Not of dead saints—they have enough to do to be singing God's praises in heaven without praying for us—but saints on earth can take up our case. The king has his favorites; he has his cupbearers; he has some that are admitted into great familiarity with him: give me a share in a good man's prayers. I attribute under God the success the Lord has given me, to the number of souls in every quarter of the earth who pray for me—not you alone, but in every land there are some that forget me not when they draw near in their supplications. Oh! we are so rich when we have the prayers of saints. When it is well with thee, speak for me to the Captain of the host, and if he should say to thee, "What was his message?" I have no other message but that of the spouse, "Tell him I am sick of love." Any of you who have close familiarity with Jesus, be the messengers, be the heavenly tale-bearers between love-sick souls and their divine Lord. Tell him, tell him we are sick of love. And you that cannot thus go to him, do seek the help and aid of others.

But after all, as I have said, this is unbelief though it is not misbelief, for how much better it would have been for her to *tell him herself*. "But," you said, "she could not find him." Nay, but if she had had faith she would have known that her prayers could; for our prayers know where Christ is when we do not know, or rather, Christ knows where our prayers are, and when we cannot see him they reach him nevertheless. Be ye satisfied to go to Christ yourself. If your brethren will go, well and good, but methinks their proper answer to your question would be in the language of the women in the sixth chapter, the first verse, "Whither is thy beloved gone, O thou fairest among women? Whither is thy beloved turned aside? That we may seek him with thee." They will not seek him *for* us they say, but they can seek him *with* us. Sometimes when there are six pair of eyes, they will see better than one; and so, if five or six Christians seek the Lord in company, in the prayer meeting, or at his table, they are more likely to find him. "We will seek him with thee."

Blessed love-sickness! we have seen its character and its cause, and the endeavors of the soul under it; let us just notice *the comforts which belong to such a state as this*. Briefly they are these—*you shall be filled*. It is impossible for Christ to set you longing after him without intending to give himself to you. It is as when a great man doth make a feast. He first puts plates upon the table, and then afterwards there cometh the meat. Your longings and desirings are the empty plates to hold the meat. Is it likely that he means to mock you? Would he have put the dishes there if he did not intend to fill them with his oxen and with his fatlings? He makes you long: he will certainly satisfy your longings. Remember, again, that he will give you himself *all the sooner for the bitterness of your longings*. The more pained your heart is at his absence the shorter will the absence be. If you have a grain of contentment without Christ, that will keep you longer tarrying; but when your soul is sick till your heart is ready to break, till you cry, "Why tarrieth he? Why are his chariots so long in coming?" when your soul fainteth until your beloved speaks unto you, and you are ready to die from your youth up, then in no long space he will lift the veil from his dear face, and your sun shall rise with healing beneath his wings. Let that console you.

Then, again, when he does come, as come he will, *oh, how sweet it will be!* Methinks I have the flavor in my mouth now, and the fullness of the feast is yet to come. There is such a delight about the very thought that he will come, that the thought itself is the prelude, the foretaste of the happy greeting. What! Will he once again speak comfortably to me? Shall I again walk the bed of spices with him? Shall I ramble with him amongst the groves while the flowers give forth their sweet perfume? I shall! I shall! and even now my spirit feels his presence by anticipation: "Or ever I was aware, my soul made me like the chariots of Amminadib." You know how sweet it was in the past.

Beloved, what times we have had, some of us. Oh, whether in the body or out of the body, we cannot tell—God knoweth. What mountings! Take ye of eagles' wings—they are earthly pinions, and may not be compared with the wings with which he carried us up from earth. Speak of mounting beyond clouds and stars!—they were left far, far behind. We entered into the unseen, beheld the invisible, lived in the immortal, drank in the ineffable, and were blessed with the fullness of God in Christ Jesus, being made to sit together in heavenly places in him. Well, all this is to come again, "I will see you again, and your heart shall rejoice." "A little while, and ye shall not see me; and again, a little while, and ye shall see me." "In a little wrath I hid my face from thee for a moment; but with everlasting kindness will I have mercy on thee, saith the Lord thy Redeemer." Think of this. Why, we have comfort even in this sickness of love. Our heart, though sick, is still whole, while we are panting and pining after the Lord Jesus.

And now, secondly, with as great brevity as we can. This love-sickness may be seen in A SOUL-LONGING FOR A VIEW OF JESUS IN HIS GLORY.

And here we will consider *the complaint* itself for a moment. It is the enjoyment of Eshcol's first fruits which makes us desire to sit under our own vine and our own fig tree before the throne of God in the blessed land.

Beloved, this sickness is characterized by certain marked symptoms; I will tell you what they are. There is a loving and a longing, a loathing and a languishing. Happy soul that understands these things by experience. There is *a loving* in which the heart cleaves to Jesus. A sense of his beauty! An admiration of his charms! A consciousness of his infinite perfection! Yea; greatness, goodness, and loveliness, in one resplendent ray combine to enchant the soul till it is so ravished after him that it crieth with the spouse, "Yea, he is altogether lovely. This is my beloved, and this is my friend, O ye daughters of Jerusalem." Sweet loving this—a love which binds the heart with chains of more than silken softness, and yet than adamant more firm.

Then there is a *longing*. She loves him so that she cannot endure to be absent from him; she pants and pines. You know it has been so with saints in all ages; whenever they have begun to love they have always begun to long after Christ. John, the most loving of spirits, is the author of those words which he so frequently uses—"Come quickly, even so, come quickly." "Come quickly" is sure to be the fruit of earnest love.

Then comes a *loathing*. When a man is sick with the first love-sickness, then he does not loathe—it is, "Stay me with flagons, comfort me with apples." When a man has Christ, he can enjoy other things; but when a man is longing after Christ and seeking after Christ, he loathes everything else—he cannot bear anything besides. Here is my message to Jesus: "Tell him—" what? Do I want crowns and diadems? Crowns and diadems are naught to me. Do I want wealth, and health, and strength? They are all very well in their way. No—"Tell him, tell the Beloved of my soul that I grieve after himself—his gifts are good—I ought to be more grateful for them than I am, but let me see his face; let me hear his voice. I am sick of love, and nothing but that can satisfy me, everything else is distasteful to me."

And then there is *a languishing*. Since she cannot get the society of Christ, cannot as yet behold him on his throne nor worship him face to face, she is sick until she can. For a heart so set on Christ will walk about traversing highway and by-way, resting nowhere till it finds him.

As to its object—what is that? "Tell him that I am sick of love"; but what is the sickness for? Brethren, when you and I want to go to heaven I hope it is the true love-sickness. I catch myself sometimes wanting to die and be in heaven for the sake of rest; but is not that a lazy desire?

There is a sluggish wish that makes me long for rest. Perhaps, we long for the happiness of heaven—the harps and crowns. There is a little selfishness in that, is there not? Allowable, I grant you; but is not there a little like selfishness? Perhaps, we long to see dear children, beloved friends that have gone before; but there is a little of the earthy there. The soul may be sick as it will, without rebuke, when it is sick to be with Jesus. You may indulge this, carry it to its utmost extent without either sin or folly. What am I sick with love for? For the pearly gates?—No; but for the pearls that are in his wounds. What am I sick for? For the streets of gold?—No; but for himself, who is the meat and drink of his saints; himself, himself—my soul pines to see him. Oh, what a heaven to gaze upon! What bliss to talk with the man, the God, crucified for me; to weep my heart out before him; to tell him how I love him, for he loved me and gave himself for me; to read my name written on his hands and on his side—yea, to let him see that his name is written on my heart in indelible lines; to embrace him, oh! what an embrace when the creature shall embrace his God—to be forever so close to him, that not a doubt, nor a fear, nor a wandering thought can come between my soul and him forever.

Ask ye yet again what are *the excitements of this sickness?* What is it that makes the Christian long to be at home with Jesus? There are many things. There are sometimes some very little things that set a Christian longing to be at home. "Ye daughters of Jerusalem, if ye find my Beloved, tell him, that I am sick of love." It is the home-song that brings the home-sickness. When we remember what he used to be to us, what sweet visits we have had from him, then we get wick to be always with him, and, best of all, when we are in his presence, when our soul is overjoyed with his delights, when the great deep sea of his love has rolled over the masthead of our highest thoughts and the ship of our spirit has gone right down, foundering at sea in the midst of an ocean of delights, ah, then its highest, its deepest thought is, "O that I may always be with him, in him, where he is, that I might behold his glory—the glory which his Father gave him and which he has given me, that I may be one with him, world without end."

Well now, friends, *what is the cure of this love-sickness?* Is it a sickness for which there is any specific remedy? There is only one cure that I know of, but there are some palliatives. A man that is sick after Christ, longs to be with him, and pants for the better land, singing as we did just now—

Father, I long, I faint to see
The place of thine abode.

He must have the desire realized, before the thirst of his fever will be assuaged. There are some palliatives, and I will recommend them to you. Such for example is a strong faith that realizes the day of the Lord and the presence of Christ, as Moses beheld the promised land and the goodly heritage, when he stood on the top of Pisgah. If you do not get heaven when you want it, you may attain to that which is next door to heaven, and this may bear you up for a little season. If you cannot get to behold Christ face to face, it is a blessed makeshift for the time to see him in the Scriptures, and to look at him through the glass of the Word. These are palliatives, but I warn ye, I warn ye of them. I do not mean to keep you from them, use them as much as ever you can, but I warn you from expecting that it will cure that love-sickness. It will give you ease, but it will make you more sick still, for he that lives on Christ gets more hungry after Christ. As for a man being satisfied and wanting no more when he gets Christ—why he wants nothing but Christ, it is true, in that sense he will never thirst; but he wants more, and more, and more, and more of Christ. Oh, strange is this, but so it is; that which we would think would remove the love-sickness, and is the best stay to the soul under it, is just that which brings it on more and more. But there is a cure, there is a cure, and you shall have it soon—a black draft, and in it a pearl— a black draft called Death. Ye shall drink it, but ye shall not know it is bitter, for ye shall swallow it up in victory. There is a pearl, too, in it— melted in it. Jesus died as well as you, and as you drink it, that pearl shall take away all ill effect from the tremendous draft. You shall say, "O death, where is thy sting? O grave, where is thy victory?" When you have once drunk that black draft, you are secure against that love-sickness forever. For where are you? No pilgrimage, no weary flight through cold either, thou art with him in paradise. Dost thou hear that, soul? Thou art with him in paradise, never to be separated, not for an instant; never to have a wandering thought, not one; never to find thy love waning or growing cold again; never to doubt his love to thee any more; never more to be vexed and tempted by sighing after what thou canst not view.

Till then, beloved, let us strive to live near the cross. Those two mountains, Calvary and Zion, stand right opposite one another. The eye of faith can sometimes almost span the interval. And the loving heart, by some deep mystery of which we can offer you no solution, will often have its sweetest rapture of joy in the fellowship of his griefs. So have I found a satisfaction in the wounds of a crucified Jesus, which can only be excelled by the satisfaction I have yet to find in the sparkling eyes of the same Jesus glorified. Yes; the same Jesus! Well spake the angels on Mount Olivet—"*This same Jesus*, which is taken up from you into heaven, shall so come in like manner as ye have seen him go into heaven." This same Jesus! My soul dotes on the words; my lips are fond of repeating them. This same Jesus!

19

THE BRIDE AND BRIDEGROOM

Altogether Lovely

"Yea, He is altogether lovely" (Song 5:16).

WHEN the old Puritan minister had delivered his discourse, and dwelt upon firstly, and secondly, and thirdly, and perhaps upon twenty-fifthly, before he sat down he usually gave a comprehensive summary of all that he had spoken. Everyone who carefully noted the summary would carry away the essence of the sermon. The summary was always looked upon by the Puritan hearer as one of the most valuable helps to memory, and consequently a most important part of the discourse. In these five words, the spouse here gives you her summary. She had delivered a tenfold discourse concerning her Lord; she had described in detail all his various beauties, and when she had surveyed him from head to foot, she gathered up all her commendations in this sentence: "Yea, he is altogether lovely." Remember these words, and know their meaning, and you possess the quintessence of the spouse's portion of the Song of Song.

Now, as in this allegorical song the bride sums up her witness in these words, so may I say that all the patriarchs, all the prophets, all the apostles, all the confessors, yea, and the entire body of the Church have left us no other testimony. They all spoke of Christ, and they all commended him. Whatever the type, or symbol, or obscure oracle, or open word in which they bore witness, that witness all amounted to this: "Yea, he is altogether lovely." Yes, and I will add, that since the canon of inspiration has closed, the testimony of all saints, on earth and in heaven, has continued to confirm the declaration made of old. The verdict of each particular saint and of the whole elect host as a body, still is this, "Yea, he is altogether lovely." From the sighs and the songs which mingle on

441

the dying beds of saints, I hear this note supreme above all others, "He is altogether lovely"; and from the songs unmingled with groans, which perpetually peal forth from immortal tongues before the presence of the Most High, I hear this one master note, "Yea, he is altogether lovely." If the whole Church desired to say with the apostle, "Now of the things which we have spoken this is the sum," she need not wait for a brief and comprehensive summary, for it lies before her in this golden sentence, "Yea, he is altogether lovely."

Looking at my text in this light I felt much humbling of spirit, and I hesitated to preach upon it, for I said in my heart, "It is high, I cannot attain unto it." These deep texts show us the shortness of our plumbline; these ocean verses are so exceeding broad that our skiffs are apt to be driven far out of sight of land where our timid spirits tremble to spread the sail. Then I comforted myself by the thought that though I could not comprehend this text in a measure, nor weigh its mountains in scales, or its hills in a balance, yet it was all mine own, by the gift of divine grace, and therefore I need not fear to enter upon the meditation of it. If I cannot grasp the ocean in my span, yet may I bathe therein with sweet content; if I cannot describe the king in his beauty, yet may I gaze upon him, since the old proverb saith, "A beggar may look at a prince." Though I pretend not so to preach from such a heavenly word as that before us, as to spread before you all its marrow and fatness, yet may I gather up a few crumbs which fall from its table. Poor men are glad of crumbs, and crumbs from such a feast are better than loaves from the tables of the world. Better to have a glimpse of Jesus, than to see all the glory of the earth all the days of our life. If we fail on this subject we may be better than if we succeeded upon another; so we will pluck up courage, seek divine help, and draw near to this wondrous text, with our shoes from off our feet like Moses when he saw the bush aglow with God.

This verse has been translated in another way: "He is all desires"; and so indeed Jesus is. He was the desire of the ancients, he is the desire of all nations still. To his own people he is their all in all; they are complete in him; they are filled out of his fullness.

> All our capacious powers can wish,
> In him doth richly meet.

He is the delight of his servants, and fills their expectations to the full. But we will not dispute about translations, for, after all, with such a text, so full of unutterable spiritual sweetness every man must be his own trans-lator, and into his own soul must the power of the message come, by the enforcement of the Holy Ghost. Such a text as this is very like the manna which fell in the wilderness, of which the rabbis say it tasted after each man's liking. If the flavor in a man's mouth was very sweetness, the angel's food which fell around the camp was luscious as any dainty he had conceived; whatever he might be, the manna was to him as he was. So shall this text be. To you with low ideas of Christ the words shall but glide over your ears, and be meaningless; but if your spirit be ravished with the precious love of Jesus there shall be songs of angels, and more than that, the voice of God's own Spirit, to your soul in this short sen-tence, "Yea, he is altogether lovely."

I am an engraver and I seek somewhat whereon I may engrave this heavenly line. Shall I take unto me ivory or silver? Shall I borrow crys-tal or gold? These are too common to bear this unique inscription: I put them all aside. Shall I spell my text in gems, with an emerald, a sapphire, a ruby, a diamond, or a pearl for each single letter? Nay, these are poor perishable things: we put them all away. I want an immortal spirit to be the tablet for my writing; nay, I must lay aside my graving tool, and ask the Spirit of God to take it: I want a heart prepared of the Holy Ghost, upon whose fleshy tablets there shall be written this morning no other sentence than this, and this shall suffice for a right royal motto to adorn it well: "Yea, he is altogether lovely." Spirit of God, find out the prepared heart, and with thy sacred hand write in eternal characters the love of Christ, and all his inimitable perfections.

We shall consider THREE POINTS OF CHARACTER which are very no-ticeable in these words, and the first which suggests itself is this: the words are evidently uttered by one who is under the influence of *overwhelm-ing emotion*. The words are rather a veil to the heart than a glass through which we see its emotions. The sentence labors to express the inexpressible; it pants to utter the unutterable. The person writing these words evidently feels a great deal more than any language can possibly convey to us. The spouse begins somewhat calmly in her description: "My beloved is white and ruddy." She proceeds with due order, commencing at the head, and proceeding with the diverse parts of the person of the Beloved; but she warms, she glows, she flames, and at last the heart which had for awhile been repressed is like fire within her bones, and she bursts forth in flaming words. Here is the live coal from off the altar of her heart:

"Yea, he is altogether lovely." It is the utterance of a soul that is altogether overcome with admiration, and therefore feels that in attempting to describe the Well-beloved, it has undertaken a task beyond its power. Lost in adoring wonder, the gracious mind desists from description, and cries with rapture, "Yea, he is altogether lovely."

It has often been thus with true saints; they have felt the love of Jesus to be overpowering and inebriating. Believers are not always cool and calm in their thoughts towards their Lord: there are seasons with them when they pass into a state of rapture, their hearts burn within them, they are in ecstasy, they mount up with wings as eagles, their souls become like the chariots of Amminadib, they feel what they could not tell, they experience what they could not express though the tongues of men and of angels were perfectly at their command. Favored believers are altogether enraptured with the sight they have of their all-beauteous Lord. It is to be feared that such raptures are not frequent with all Christians, though I should gravely question his saintship, who has never experienced any degree of holy rapture: but there are some saints to whom a state of overwhelming adoration of their Lord has been by no means an unusual thing. Communion with Jesus has not only entranced them now and then, but it has perfumed all their life with holiness; and if it has not caused their faces literally to shine like the face of Moses, it has made the spiritual glory to flash from their countenances, and elevated them among their fellow Christians to be leaders of the host of God, whereat others have admired and wondered.

Peradventure, I speak to children of God who know very little of what I mean by the overwhelming emotions created by a sight of our Lord; they have not so seen the Lord as to have felt their souls melting within them while the Beloved spake with them: to such I shall speak with sorrowful sympathy, being, alas! too much like unto them, but my prayer shall go up all the while, "Lord, reveal thyself to us, that we also may be compelled to say, 'Yea, he is altogether lovely.' Show us thy hands and thy side till we exclaim with Thomas, 'My Lord, and my God.' "

Shall I tell you why it is, my brethren, that many of you but seldom enjoy the exceeding bliss of Jesus' presence? The cause may lie partly in what is, alas! too common among Christians, *a great degree of ignorance of the Person of the Lord Jesus*. Every soul that sees Jesus by faith is saved thereby. If I look to Christ with a bleared eye, that is ever so weak and clouded with tears, and if I only catch a glimpse of him through clouds and mists, yet the sight saves me. But who will remain content with such a poor gleam of his glory as that? Who wishes to see only "through a glass, darkly"? No, let my eyes be cleansed till they become as doves by the rivers of waters, and I can see my Lord as he is seen by his bosom friends, and can sing of those beauties which are the light and crown of heaven itself.

If you do but touch the hem of Jesus' garment, you shall be made whole; but will this always satisfy you? Will you not desire to get beyond the hem and beyond the garment, to himself, and to his heart, and there forever take up your abode? Who desires to be forever a babe in grace, with a half-awakened dreamy twilight consciousness of the Redeemer? Brethren, be diligent in the school of the cross, therein is enduring wisdom. Study your Savior much. The science of Christ crucified is the most excellent of sciences; and to know him and the power of his resurrection, is to know that which is best worth knowing. Ignorance of Jesus deprives many saints of those divine raptures which carry others out of themselves, therefore let us be among those children of Zion who are taught of the Lord.

Next to this you shall find *the want of meditation* to be a very serious robber of the wealth of renewed hearts. To believe a thing is, as it were, to see the cool crystal sparkling in the cup; but to meditate upon it is to drink thereof. Reading gathers the clusters, contemplation squeezes forth their generous juice. Meditation is of all things the most soul-fattening when combined with prayer. The spouse had meditated much in this chapter, for otherwise she had not been able to speak in detail concerning her Lord. O saintly hearts, imitate ye her example! Think, my brethren, of our Lord Jesus: he is God, the Eternal, the Infinite, the ever blessed; yet he became man for us—man of the substance of his mother, like ourselves. Meditate upon his spotless character; review the sufferings which he endured on Calvary; follow him into the grave, and from the grave to the resurrection, and from the resurrection up the starry way to his triumphant throne. Let your souls dwell upon each of his offices, as prophet, priest, and king; pore over each one of his characters, and every scriptural title; pause and consider every phase of him, and when you have done this, begin again and yet again.

It is good to chew the cud by meditation, then shall the sweetness and fatness of divine truth come to your soul, and you shall burst forth with such rapturous expressions as that of the text, "Yea, he is altogether lovely." The most of you are too busy, you have too much to do in the world; but what is it all about? Scraping together dust, loading yourselves with thick clay. O that you were busy after the true riches, and could step aside awhile to enrich yourselves in solitude, and make your hearts vigorous by feeding upon the person and work of your ever blessed Lord! You miss a heaven below by a too eager pursuit of earth. You cannot know these joyful raptures if meditation be pushed into a corner.

Another reason why little of the Lord's beauty is discerned, is *the low state of the spiritual life in many a Christian*. Many a believer is just alive and no more. Do you not know such starveling souls? May you not be one such yourself! His eyes are not delighted with the beauties of Christ, he is purblind, and cannot see afar off; he walks not with Jesus in the garden of pomegranates, he is too feeble to rise from the couch of weakness; he cannot feed upon Christ, his appetite is gone—sure sign of terrible decline. For him there are no climbings to the top of Amana, no leaping for joy in the temple, no dancing before the ark with David; no, if he be but carried to the feet of Jesus in an ambulance as a sick man borne of four, it is as much as he has yet received. To be strong in the Lord, and in the power of his might, to have the wings of eagles with which to mount above the clouds of earth, to this many are strangers. But, beloved, there are noble spirits and better taught, who know something of the life of heaven even while here below. The Lord strengthen us with grace in our inner man, and then shall we drink deeper drafts of the wines on the lees well refined, and then also our eyes being open, we shall see Jesus more clearly, and bear fuller witness that he is "fairer than the children of men."

I am afraid that *the visits of Christ to our souls have been disesteemed, and the loss of those visits has not caused us corresponding sorrow*. We did not sufficiently delight in the beauty of the Bridegroom when he did come to us; when our hearts were somewhat lifted up with his love we grew cold and idle, and then he withdrew his conscious presence; but, alas! we were not grieved, but we wickedly tried to live without him. It is wretched work for a believer to try and live without his Savior. Perhaps some of you have tried it until at last you have almost succeeded. You were wont to mourn like doves if you had no word from your Master in the morning, and without a love token before you went to rest, you tossed uneasily upon your bed; but now you are carnal and worldly, and careless, and quite content to have it so. Jesus hides his face, the sun is set, and yet it is not night with you. O may God be pleased to arouse you from this lethargy, and make you mourn your sad estate! Even if an affliction should be needful to bring you back from your backsliding it would be a cheap price to pay. Awake, O north wind, with all thy cutting force, if thy bleak breath may but stir the lethargic heart! May the Lord grant us grace so to love Christ that if we have not our fill of him, we may be ready to die with hungering and thirsting after him. May we never be able to find a place to build our nest upon while our wing wanders away from the tree of life. Like the dove of Noah, may we drop into the water and be drowned sooner than find rest for the sole of our foot except upon the ark, Christ Jesus, our Savior.

Beloved, if none of these suggestions would hit the mark, and reveal the cause why so little is known of rapturous love to Christ, let me suggest another. Very often *professors' hearts are vain and frivolous;* they are taken up during the week with their business. This might plead some excuse; but when they have little spaces and intervals these are filled up with very vanity. Now, if the soul has come to look at the mere trifles of this world as all-important, is it any marvel that it should be unable to perceive the exceeding preciousness of Christ Jesus? Who will care for the wheat when he dotes on the chaff? And with this it will often happen that the professor's mind has grown proud as well as vain; he does not remember his natural poverty and meanness, and consequently does not value the riches of Christ Jesus. He has come to think himself an established, experienced Christian; he fancies that he is not like those foolish beginners who are so volatile and so readily led astray; he as acquired the wisdom of years and the stability of experience. O soul, if thou art great, Christ will be little; thou canst never see him on the throne until thou hast been on the dunghill thyself. If thou be anything, so much the less is Christ; for if he be all in all, then there is no room for anything else; and if thou be something, thou hast stolen just so much from the glory of thy Lord Jesus. Lie low in the dust, it is the place for thee. The humbler I am in myself, the more shall I be capable of seeing the enchanting beauties of Christ.

Let me just say these two or three words. I believe those are the happiest saints who are most overwhelmed with a sense of the greatness, goodness, and preciousness of Christ. I believe these to be the most useful saints, also, and to be in the Christian Church as a tower of strength. I pray that you and I, walking with God by faith, may nevertheless often have our festival days, our notable seasons, when he shall specially kiss us with the kisses of his love, and we shall drink larger drafts of his love, which is beter than wine. Oh, to be carried right away with the divine manifestation of the chief among ten thousand, so that our souls shall cry out in rapture, "Yea, he is altogether lovely." This is one characteristic of the text: may it be transferred to us.

A second is this, and very manifest it is upon the surface of the verse — here is *undivided affection.* "He is altogether lovely." Note that these words have a world of meaning in them, but chiefly they tell us this, that Jesus is to the true saint the only lovely one in the world. "He is altogether lovely"; then there is no loveliness anywhere else. It is as though the spouse felt that Christ had engrossed all the beauty and all the love-worthiness in the entire universe. Who among us will say that she erred? Is not Jesus worthy of all the admiration and love of all intelligent beings? But may we not love our friends and kinsfolk? Aye, but in him, and in subservience to him; so and so only, is it safe to love them. Did not our Lord himself say, "If any man love father or mother more than me, he is not worthy of me"? Except these are put on a lower stage than Jesus is we cannot be his disciples.

Christ must be monarch in the breast; our dear ones may sit at his footstool, and we may love them for his sake, but he alone must fill the throne of our hearts. I may see excellences in my Christian brethren, but I must not forget that there would be none in them if they were not derived from him; that their loveliness is only a part of his loveliness, for he wrought it in them by his own Spirit. I am to acknowledge that Jesus is the monopolizer of all loveliness, the engrosser of all that is admirable in the entire universe; and I am, therefore, to give him all my love, for "he is altogether lovely."

Our text means, again, that in Jesus loveliness of all kinds is to be found. If there be anything that is worthy of the love of an immortal spirit, it is to be seen in abundance in the Lord Jesus. Whatsoever things are true, whatsoever things are honest, whatsoever things are just, whatsoever things are pure, whatsoever things are lovely, whatsoever things are of good report; if there be any virtue, and if there be any praise, all can be found without measure in Christ Jesus. As all the rivers meet in the sea, so all beauties unite in the Redeemer. Take the character of any gracious man, and you shall find a measure of loveliness, but it has its bounds and its mixtures. Peter has many virtues, but he has not a few failings. John, too, excels, but in certain points he is deficient; but herein our Lord transcends all his saints, for all human virtues, all divine, are harmoniously blended in him. He is not this flower or that, but he is the Paradise of perfection. He is not a star here or a constellation there, he is the whole heaven of stars, nay, he is the heaven of heavens; he is all that is fair and lovely condensed in One.

When the text says again that Jesus "is altogether lovely," it declares that he is lovely in all views of him. It generally happens that to the noblest building there is an unhappy point of view from which the architecture appears at a disadvantage; the choicest piece of workmanship may not be equally complete in all directions; the best human character is deformed by one flaw, if not with more; but with our Lord all is lovely, regard him as you will. You shall contemplate him from all pints, and only find new confirmation of the statement that "he is altogether lovely." As the everlasting God before the world was made, angels loved him and adored; as the babe at Bethlehem or as the man at Bethany; as walking the sea or as nailed to the cross; in his grave, dead, and buried, or on his throne triumphant; rising as a forerunner, or descending a second time to judge the world in righteousness; in his shame, despised and spit upon, or in his glory, adored and beloved; with the thorns about his brow and the nails piercing his hands, or with the keys of death and hell swinging at his girdle; view him as you will, and where you will, and when you will, "He is altogether lovely." Under all aspects, and in all offices and in relations, at all times and all seasons, under all circumstances and conditions, anywhere, everywhere, "He is altogether lovely."

Nor is he in any degree unlovely; the commendation forbids the idea; if he be "altogether lovely," where could you find room for deformity? When Apelles painted Alexander, he laid the monarch's finger on an unsightly scar; but there are no scars to conceal when you portray the countenance of Immanuel. We say of our country—and who among us will not say it?—"With all her faults we love her still"; but we love Jesus, and find no strain put upon our heart, for trace of fault he has none. There is no need of apologies for Jesus, no excuses are required for him. But what is that I see upon his shoulder? It is a hard rough cross; and if I follow him I must carry that cross for his sake. Is not that cross unsightly? Oh, no! He is altogether lovely, cross and all. Whatever it may involve to be a Christian, we count even the reproach of Christ to be greater riches than the treasures of Egypt.

The world will honor a half Christ, but a whole Christ it will not acknowledge. The bat's-eyed Socinian saith, "I admire the man Christ, but I will not adore Jesus the God." To him the eternal Word is but half lovely, if lovely at all. Some will have Christ the exemplar, but they will not accept him as the vicarious sacrifice for sin, the substitute for sinners. Many will have Christ in silver slippers—my lord archibishop's religion—but they would not listen to the Gospel from a poor gracious Methodist, or think it worth their while to join the unlettered throng whose devout songs rise from the village green. Alas! how much we see of crosses of gold and ivory, but how little do men love the lowly cross of Jesus! Brethren, we think Jesus "altogether lovely" even in poverty, or when hanging naked on the cross, deserted and condemned. We see unspeakable beauty in Jesus in the grave, all fair with the pallor of death. Jesus bruised as to his heel by the old serpent is yet comely. His love to us makes him evermore "white and ruddy" to our eye. We adore him anywhere and everywhere, and in any place, for we know that this same Christ whose heel is bruised breaks also the serpent's head, and he who was naked for our sakes, is not arrayed in glory. We know that the despised and rejected is also King of kings, and Lord of lords, the "Wonderful, Counselor, The Mighty God, The everlasting Father, The Prince of Peace." "Yea, he is altogether lovely." There are no flaws in him.

The text intends us to know that Jesus is lovely in the highest degree: not lovely positively and then failing comparatively, but lovely superlatively, in the highest possible sense. But I leave this for our hearts to enlarge upon. I will close this point by saying, every child of God acknowledges that Christ Jesus is lovely altogether to the whole of himself. He is lovely to my judgment; but many things are so, and yet are not lovely to my affections; I know them to be right, and yet they are not pleasant: but Jesus as lovely to my heart as to my head, as dear as he is good. He is lovely to my hopes: are they not all in him? Is not this my expectation—to see him as He is? But He is lovely to my memory too: did he not pluck me out of the net? Lovely to all my powers and all my passions, my faculties and feelings. As David puts it, "My heart and my flesh crieth out for the living God"—the whole of the man seeking after the whole of the Savior; the whole Savior sweet and inexpressibly precious to the man's entire being. May it be so with you and with me. But is it so? Do you not set up idols in your hearts? Men of God, do you not need to take this scourge of small cords, and purge the temple of your souls this morning? Are there not buyers and sellers where Christ alone ought to be? Oh, to love him wholly, and to love him only, so that we have no eyes for other beauty, no heart for other loveliness, since he fills our souls, and is to us "altogether lovely."

The third characteristic of the text is that to which I desire to draw the most attention, and that is *ardent devotion*. I called the text a live coal from off the altar, and surely it is so. If it should drop into our hearts to set them on a blaze, it would be an unspeakable mercy. Ardent devotion flames from this sentence. It is the language of one who feels that no emotion is too deep when Jesus moves the heart. Do any chide you and say you think too much of your religion? It cannot be, it cannot be. If the zeal of God's house should eat us up until we had no existence except for the Lord's glory, we should not have gone too far. If there be corresponding knowledge to balance it, there cannot be too much of zeal for God. The utterance is that of one whose heart is like a furnace, of which love is the fire. "He is altogether lovely" — it is the exclamation of one who feels that no language is too strong to commend the Lord.

The spouse looked through the Hebrew tongue to find an intense expression, and our translators ransacked the English language for a forcible word, and they have put it in the most weighty way — "He is altogether lovely." There is no fear of exaggeration when you speak of Christ; hyperboles are only sober truth when we depict his excellences. We have heard of a portrait painter, who owed his popularity to the fact that he never painted truthfully, but always gave a flattering touch or two; here is one who would defy his art, for it is impossible to flatter Jesus. Lay on, ye men of eloquence, spare no colors, ye shall never depict him too bravely. Bring forth your harps, ye seraphs; sing aloud, ye blood-washed ones; all your praises fall short of the glory which is due to him.

It is the language of one who feels that no service would be too great to render to the Lord. I wish we felt as the apostles and martyrs and holy men of old did, that Jesus Christ ought to be served at the highest and richest rate. We do little, very little: what if I had said we do next to nothing for our dear Lord and Master nowadays? The love of Christ doth not constrain us as it should. But those of old bore poverty and dared reproach, marched weary leagues, passed tempestuous seas, bore perils of robbers and of cruel men, to plant the cross in lands where as yet Jesus was not known; labors that nowadays could not be expected of men, were performed as daily matters of commonplace by the Christians of the earliest times. Is Christ less lovely, or is his Church less loyal? Would God she estimated him at his right rate, for then she would return to her former mode of service. Brethren, we want to feel, and we shall feel if this text is deeply engraven on our hearts, that no gift is too great for Christ, though we give him all we have, and consecrate to Him all our time and ability, and sacrifice our very lives to him. No suffering is too great to bear for the sake of the Crucified, and it is a great joy to be reproached for Christ's sake. "He is altogether lovely." Then, my soul, I charge thee think nothing hard to which he calls thee, nothing sharp which he bids thee endure. As the knight of the olden time consecrated himself to the Crusade, and wore the red cross on his arm, fearing not to meet death at the hands of the Infidel, if he might be thought a soldier of the Lord, so we too would face all foes for Jesus' sake. We want, only refined and purified, and delivered from its earthly grossness, we want the chivalrous spirit once again in the Church of God.

A new crusade fain would I preach: had I the tongue of such a one as the old hermit to move all Christendom, I would say, "This day Christ, the altogether lovely One, is dishonored: can ye endure it? This day idols stand where he should be and men adore them; lovers of Jesus, can ye brook it? This day Juggernaut rides through the streets on his bloody way, this day God's Christ is still unknown to millions, and the precious blood cleanses not the nations, how long will ye have it so?" We, in England, with ten thousand Christian hearts, and as many tongues endowed with eloquence, and purses weighted with gold, shall we refuse our gifts, withhold our witness, and suffer the Lord to be dishonored? The Church is doing next to nothing for her great Lord, she falls short both of her duty and of the grim need of a perishing world. O for a flash of the celestial fire! Oh, when shall the Spirit's energy visit us again? When shall men put down their selfishness and seek only Christ? When shall they leave their strifes about trifles to rally round his cross? When shall we end the glorification of ourselves, and begin to make him glorious, even to the world's end? God help us in this matter, and kindle in our hearts the old consuming, heart-inflaming fire, which shall make men see that Jesus is all in all to us.

Thus I have shown you the characteristics of the text, and now I desire to USE IT IN THREE WAYS FOR PRACTICAL PURPOSES.

The first word is to you, Christians. Here is very *sweet instruction*. The Lord Jesus "is altogether lovely." Then if I want to be lovely, I must be like Him, and the model for me as a Christian is Christ. Have you ever noticed how badly boys write at the bottom of the pages in their copybooks? There is the copy at the top; and in the first line they look at that; in the second line, they copy their own imitation; in the third line, they copy their imitation of their imitation, and so the writing grows worse and worse as it descends the page. Now, the apostles followed Christ; the first fathers imitated the apostles; the next fathers copied the first fathers, and so the standard of holiness fell dreadfully; and now we are too apt to follow the very lees and dregs of Christianity, and we think if we are about as good as our poor, imperfect ministers or leaders in the Church, that we shall do well and deserve praise. But now, my brethren, cover up the mere copies and imitations, and live by the first line. Copy Jesus; "He is altogether lovely"; and if you can write by the first line, you will write by the truest and best model in the world. We want to have Christ's zeal, but we must balance it with his prudence and discretion; we must seek to have Christ's love to God, and we must feel his love to men, his forgiveness of injury, his gentleness of speech, his incorruptible truthfulness, his meekness and lowliness, his utter unselfishness, his entire consecration to his Father's business.

O that we had all this, for depend upon it, whatever other pattern we select we have made a mistake; we are not following the true classic model of the Christian artist. Our master model is the "altogether lovely" one. How sweet it is to think of our Lord in the double aspect as our exemplar and our Savior! The laver which stood in the temple was made of brass: in this the priests washed their feet whenever they offered sacrifices; so does Christ purify us from sin; but the tradition is that this laver was made of very bright brass, and acted as a mirror, so that as often as the priest came to it they could see their own spots in it. Oh, when I come to my Lord Jesus, not only do I get rid of my sins as to their guilt, but I see my spots in the light of his perfect character, and I am humbled and taught to follow after holiness.

The second use to which we would put the verse is this, here is a very *gentle rebuke* to some of you. Though very gentle, I beseech you to let it sink deep into your hearts. You do not see the lowliness of Christ, yet "He is altogether lovely." Now, I will not say one hard word, but I will tell you sorrowfully what pitiable creatures you are. I hear enchanting music, which seems more a thing of heaven than of earth: it is one of Handel's half-inspired oratorios. Yonder sits a man, who says, "I hear nothing to commend." He has not the power to perceive the sweetnesses, the delicious harmonies of sounds. Do you blame him? No, but you who have an ear for music, say, "How I pity him: he misses half the joy of life!" Here, again, is a glorious landscape, hills and valleys, and flowing rivers, expansive lakes and undulating meadows. I bring to the point of view a friend, whom I would gratify, and I say to him, "Is not that a charming scene?" Turning his head to me, he says, "I see nothing." I perceive that he cannot enjoy what is so delightful to me; he has some little sight, but he sees only what is very near, and he is blind to all beyond. Now, do I blame him? Or if he proceed to argue with me, and say, "You are very foolish to be so enthusiastic about a non-existent landscape, it is merely your excitement," shall I argue with him? Shall I be angry with him? No, but I shed a tear, and whisper to myself, "Great are the losses of the blind."

Now, you who have never heard music in the name of Jesus, you are to be greatly pitied, for your loss is heavy. You who never saw beauty in Jesus, and who never will forever, you need all our tears. It is hell enough not to love Christ! It is the lowest abyss of Tartarus, and its fiercest flame, not to be enamored of the Christ of God. There is no heaven that is more heaven than to love Christ and to be like him, and there is no hell that is more hell than to be unlike Christ and not to want to be like him, but even to be averse to the infinite perfections of the "altogether lovely." The Lord open those blind eyes of yours, and unstop those deaf ears, and give you the new and spiritual life, and then will you join in saying, "Yea, he is altogether lovely."

The last use of the text is, that of *tender attractiveness.* "Yea, he is altogether lovely." Where are you this morning, you who are convinced of sin and want a Savior, where have you crept to? Are you hidden away where my eyes cannot reach you? At any rate, let this sweet thought reach you. You need not be afraid to come to Jesus, for "he is altogether lovely." It does not say he is altogether terrible—that is your misconception of him; it does not say he is somewhat lovely, and sometimes willing to receive a certain sort of sinner; but "he is altogether lovely," and therefore he is always ready to welcome to himself the vilest of the vile. Think of his name. It is Jesus, the Savior. Is not that lovely? Think of his work. He is come to seek and to save that which was lost. This is his occupation. Is not that lovely? Think of what he has done. He hath redeemed our souls with blood. Is not that lovely? Think of what he is doing. He is pleading before the throne of God for sinners. Think of what he is giving at this moment—he is exalted on high to give repentance and remission of sins. Is not this lovely? Under every aspect Christ Jesus is attractive to sinners who need him. Come, then, come and welcome, there is nothing to keep you away, there is everything to bid you come. May this very Sabbath-day in which I have preached Christ, and lifted him up, be the day in which you shall be drawn to him, never again to leave him, but to be his forever and forever.